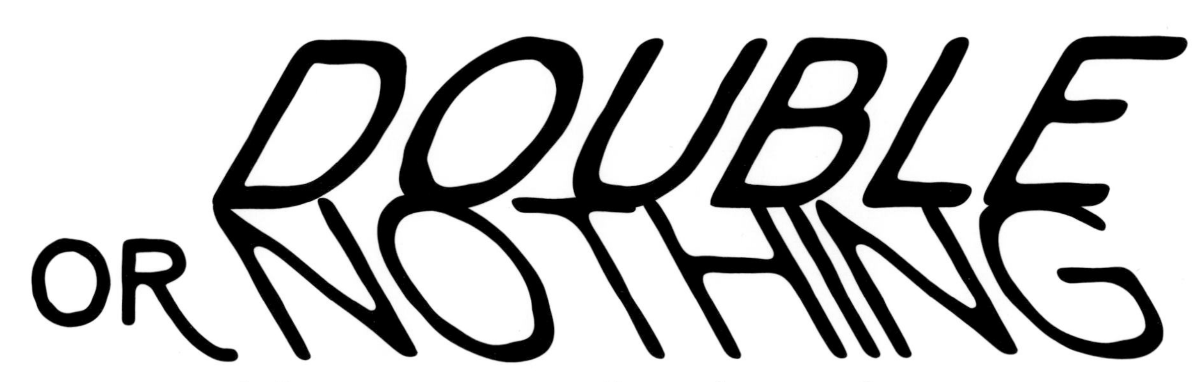

Reversible Knitting for the Adventurous

Reversible Knitting for the Adventurous

Alasdair Post-Quinn

Cambridge, MA
www.double-knitting.com

ISBN: 978-0-9982472-0-5
First Edition
Published by Fallingblox Designs, Cambridge, MA, USA
http://www.double-knitting.com

Models: Alison Warmuth, Patricia Grahmann, Grace Zimmerly & Stanislas Monfront

If you have questions or comments about this book, or need information about licensing, translating, custom editions, special sales, wholesale orders, or academic or corporate purchases, please contact Fallingblox Designs:
fallingblox@double-knitting.com.

This book conceived, designed, knitted, photographed, edited and printed in the United States of America.

This book is dedicated to my wife, Amanda, who still loves and supports me despite my infatuation with knitting;

to my boss, Anne, who allowed me to go part-time in order to pursue this part of my life's goals;

and to my cat, Embers, who would still rather sleep on a pile of yarn than play with it.

This book is also dedicated to the memory of Allison Warmuth, a skilled knitter and friend, who was killed in a traffic accident near her home in Boston a week after she spent a morning modeling for this book. The only payment she requested was a private lesson in double-knitting, which I will no longer be able to provide. I think she would be happy knowing that her photos will help to encourage more people to learn in her place. Thank you, Allison, for your warmth and kindness. Your fiber family at the Gather Here knitting group misses you.

TABLE OF CONTENTS

PATTERN BROWSER

Abaciscus

a large double-knit cowl with an unexpected twist

page 46

Hesperos

a double-knit scarf using off-the-grid colorwork

page 58

Hexworth

a double-knit textured scarf with slip-stitches

page 116

Eureka

a double-knit textured hat with a two-pattern option

page 122

Ferronnerie

a tam-o'shanter hat in double-knit entrelac

page 134

Atyria II

a double-knit hat combining off-the-grid colorwork and traveling stitches

page 154

Ranelva

a pair of double-knit mittens using the Eastern thumb

page 76

Waterford Crossing

a shawl in multicolor double-knitting

page 88

Kontinuum

a hat using double-knit intarsia in the round

page 104

Rustle of Leaves

a keyhole scarf with double-knitting and marled knitting

page 112

Twice as Sexy

an elegant necktie with double-knit traveling stitches

page 158

Heartbound Again

a double-knit cabled hat with an i-cord cast-on and a headband option

page 170

Spring Willow

a double-knit lace cowl

page 182

Adenydd

a double-knit lace shawl with modified Faroese construction

page 190

GLOBAL KEY

These symbols' definitions may be superseded by definitions in the pattern-specific keys. If there is confusion, assume the pattern's key is correct for following that pattern.

- Layer 1: AB pair
  Layer 2: BA pair
- Layer 1: BA pair
  Layer 2: AB pair
- No pair (page 26)
- Standard DK (KP) pair (in two-pattern chart, K only)
- Reverse DK (PK) pair (in two-pattern chart, P only)
- Cast-on pair (page 28)
- Bind-off pair (page 36)
- Pick Up pair (page 130)
- Linked pair (page 32)
- Slipped pair (page 33)
- Right-slanting decrease (page 50)
- Left-slanting decrease (page 50)
- Centered left-slanting double-decrease (page 52)
- Centered right-slanting double-decrease (page 52)
- Raised double-decrease (page 52)
- Left-slanting double-decrease (page 52)
- Right-slanting double-decrease (page 52)
- Linked right-slanting decrease (page 131)
- Linked left-slanting decrease (page 131)
- Linked right-slanting double-decrease (page 131)
- Linked left-slanting double-decrease (page 131)
- Right-lifted increase (page 53)
- Left-lifted increase (page 54)
- M1R increase (page 57)
- M1L increase (page 56)
- Yarnover pair (page 176)
- Quilted pair (page 120)
- Marled knit (purl on Layer 2) (page 110)
- Marled purl (knit on Layer 2) (page 110)
- RDK left-slanting decrease (page 120)
- RDK right-slanting decrease (page 120)
- RDK double-decrease (page 120)
- N (page 186)
- Reverse-N (page 188)
- Leave unused strands on front of work here (page 99)

See Chapter 8 (page 140) for cable techniques.

1 pair cabled 1 space to the right; work 2 BA pairs.

1 pair cabled 1 space to the left; work 2 BA pairs.

1 pair cabled 1 space to the right; work 1 BA pair & 1 AB pair.

1 pair cabled 1 space to the left; work 1 AB pair & 1 BA pair.

1 pair cabled 1 space to the right; work 2 AB pairs.

1 pair cabled 1 space to the left; work 2 AB pairs.

2 pairs cabled 1 space to the right; work 2 BA pairs & 1 AB pair.

2 pairs cabled 1 space to the left; work 1 AB pair & 2 BA pairs.

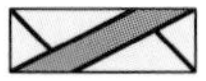

1 pair cabled 2 spaces to the right; work 1 BA pair & 2 AB pairs.

1 pair cabled 2 spaces to the left; work 2 AB pairs & 1 BA pair.

2 pairs cabled 2 spaces to the right; work 4 BA pairs.

2 pairs cabled 2 spaces to the left; work 4 BA pairs.

2 pairs cabled 2 spaces to the right; work 2 BA pairs & 2 AB pairs.

2 pairs cabled 2 spaces to the left; work 2 AB pairs & 2 BA pairs.

2 pairs cabled 1 space to the right; work 3 AB pairs.

2 pairs cabled 1 space to the left; work 3 AB pairs.

2 pairs cabled 1 space to the right; work 2 SDK AB pairs & 1 RDK AB pair.

2 pairs cabled 1 space to the left; work 1 RDK AB pair & 2 AB pairs.

2 pairs cabled 2 spaces to the right; work 2 SDK AB pairs & 2 RDK AB pairs.

2 pairs cabled 2 spaces to the left; work 2 RDK AB pairs & 2 SDK AB pairs.

2 pairs cabled 2 spaces to the right; work 2 SDK BA pairs & 2 RDK AB pairs.

2 pairs cabled 2 spaces to the left; work 2 RDK AB pairs & 2 SDK BA pairs.

2 pairs cabled 1 space to the right; work 2 SDK BA pairs & 1 RDK AB pair.

2 pairs cabled 1 space to the left; work 1 RDK AB pair & 2 SDK BA pairs.

1 pair cabled 1 space to the left; work 1 RDK AB pair & 1 SDK BA pair.

1 pair cabled 1 space to the right; work 1 SDK BA pair & 1 RDK AB pair.

1 pair cabled 1 space to the left; work 1 RDK AB pair & 1 SDK AB pair.

1 pair cabled 1 space to the right; work 1 SDK AB pair & 1 RDK AB pair.

GLOSSARY

This is not a glossary of all terms, but of the terms that are more likely to be unfamiliar to the average knitter or that I am using in a specific way that differs from the norm. For more detail on some of these, please visit the section on double-knitting vocabulary (page 18).

Pixel: a square on a chart, which may be populated with a color and/or a symbol

Pair: the basic element of double-knitting, consisting of two stitches in a row, the first from the front and the second from the back of the work (each pair will have a color order and a stitch order)

Color order: the order of colors in a pair, as read and worked from right to left (Ex: AB or BA)

Stitch order: the order of stitches in a pair, as read and worked from right to left (Ex: KP or PK)

Layer: one of the two outer pieces of fabric created by double-knitting

Layer 1: the layer typically depicted in the chart (Layer 1 rows are typically odd, when worked flat)

Layer 2: the layer not depicted in the chart; may be depicted in a reference chart in cases where it is not directly related to Layer 1 (Layer 2 rows are typically even when worked flat)

SDK: standard double-knitting, worked with KP pairs, so that both layers look like stockinette (also denoted by DK when not contrasted with RDK)

RDK: reverse double-knitting; worked with PK pairs, so that both layers look like reverse stockinette

Edge: for a flat piece, one of 4 borders around the piece (top, bottom, and sides); for a piece in the round, only the top and bottom are edges

Selvedge: a way of processing every other pair along a side edge to make the edge cleaner

Linked pair: a way of connecting the two layers, most often at the side edges, to keep the layers from coming apart at that point

Slipped pair: a way of processing a pair without working either stitch but still keeping the unused yarn hidden

Inside: the space between the two layers

Outside: the space not between the two layers, to the front or the back of the work

Front: the layer that faces you as you are working, distinct from Layer 1 or 2 as either layer can be either front or back

Back: the layer that faces away from you as you are working

Wyib: with (all) yarns in back

Wyif: with (all) yarns in front

Marling: the process of using two different yarns to create a blended color and texture effect

Reordering: the process of preparing a group of pairs for a technique, such as a decrease or cable, by separating them and reintegrating them in a different order

PSSO: pass single stitch over another (and off the needle)

P2SO: pass 2 stitches over another (and off the needle)

Eureka, page 122

Adenydd, page 190

NOTE FROM THE AUTHOR

When I began work on *Extreme Double-Knitting* (*EDK* for short) back in 2009, I was recently married, had just purchased a condo, and was the primary breadwinner in my newly-minted family. My wife Amanda had a massage business that was becoming more successful, but it wasn't yet able to provide for both of us. My job provided our healthcare, so I was nowhere near able to leave my job and work on knitting full-time.

This meant I had to balance the book project along with work, family, social life, and self-care. I was working with a relatively new indie publishing house. It was slow going, and I frequently stumbled along the way (add to this the fact that I learned to knit in 2003 — merely six years before I started working on *EDK*). I am a mostly self-taught knitter and have my own distinctive method, which I partially credit for the ease with which I can adapt to double-knitting techniques.

All my research indicated that much of the work I was doing had not been documented elsewhere; and even if some of it had been, there was no universal standard for double-knitting instructions. The big names of double-knitting past and present — Beverly Royce, Lucy Neatby, and M'Lou Baber — and the biggest name of knitting technique in general, June Hemmons Hiatt — each have their own way of describing what we do. Royce's book, first published in 1981, dealt exclusively in the antiquated "slip-stitch" method of double-knitting; most others use the modern method that has been in use since at least the late 1980s. Baber and Neatby each have their followings, but the ways they present their techniques do not necessarily agree (even if the result is largely the same).

I intended to add a new voice, rather than to throw my lot in with one camp or the other. After all, much of what I was doing was, by all accounts, new material. I had to make up some new terminology, and I had to make sure that the vocabulary I was using for the parts that had prior documentation agreed with the new stuff. I strove to keep my terminology as close to the existing vocabulary as possible, referring as much as I could to established techniques that should be familiar to many knitters. However, I made some mistakes, as can be expected; after all, I'm both human and relatively narrowly-focused in knitting. I used some terms that could have been more clear, and I devised new notation and terminology for things that didn't need it.

Knitting, like life, is a constant learning experience. My previous book was a snapshot of my knowledge and experience at the time it was written. I made some subtle changes when reprints allowed, but some would have required serious rewriting (and the accompanying layout modifications), so I decided to leave them be. Should I have the opportunity at some point in the future to release a true "second edition," rather than just a version with some errata fixed, I will happily make all the changes that reflect the knowledge I have gained since its inception.

The book you're reading now is likewise a snapshot of my knowledge and experience at the time it was printed. I expect I will continue to learn and discover new ways of doing and explaining things, and some years down the road, it's likely that I will look back and welcome the opportunity to rewrite parts of this manuscript as well. As an author (but more importantly as a human with a finite lifespan), I cannot constantly be rewriting old material to reflect newly gained knowledge. At some point, I have to say "this is good enough."

To me, at this point in time, this is more than good enough. At the end of *Extreme Double-Knitting,* I knew there was more to cover, but I could not possibly do it all in a single book; now that I'm done with this one, I have serious doubts as to whether I could possibly follow it up with another like it. However, I'm not one to be satisfied with the boundaries I'm currently operating under. It's going to be exciting to see where I go next; especially for me, since I'll be experiencing it before anyone else.

Alasdair Post-Quinn

INTRODUCTION

What is double-knitting?

Double-knitting is a method of making a fabric with no wrong side. In fact, double-knitting is a set of two layers, worked at the same time on the same set of needles, which may be separate or interlocked depending on the characteristics of the fabric. In general, I prefer to integrate colorwork into my double-knitting, which creates a more frequently interlocked (i.e., "stable") two-layered fabric.

Double-knitting, in its modern form, has only existed since the late 1980s. The first published pattern using the basic technique I explain here was printed in 1989 (and I would be thrilled if you found an earlier example — please let me know). Before that, double-knitting used the now-archaic "slip-stitch" method that was made famous by Beverly Royce. This method still has its uses, tubular double-knitting among them; but as a sole method of double-knitting, it is severely limited and limiting.

Why double-knit?

I can't tell you why <u>you</u> should double-knit, but I'll tell you why I do it. First of all, I was irked by the often-unattractive "wrong side" of most knitting, especially colorwork. Second, I didn't like the way the edges of pieces curled and distorted the fabric. Third, I live in a cold climate, so double-thick fabric is never wasted.

Double-knitting creates a supple reversible fabric; many (if not most) single-layer techniques can be adapted to use it. However, because the fabric is (at least) twice as thick as single-layer fabric in the same yarn, it's important to consider the weight of your yarn. Whereas more than half of the patterns in *Extreme Double-Knitting* were in worsted weight yarn, creating a fabric that would (in many cases) stand up on its own; the patterns in this book are skewed more toward finer weights, with an eye on making the resulting fabric more pleasant to wear in more moderate temperatures. Here, only 2 of the 14 patterns are in worsted weight, with all of the other patterns falling between lace weight and DK weight.

How is this book different from the previous book?

Double or Nothing is meant as a sort of sequel to *Extreme Double-Knitting*. This doesn't mean that you need to have worked through all of *EDK* to begin here, but it will help if you have some double-knitting experience. *EDK* was meant to start you off with the basics, assuming only that you know how to knit and purl. It went into significant depth when explaining the basic techniques, which spanned several chapters. In this book, I'm going to skim over many of the basic techniques. I'm going to cover most of what *EDK* covered, adding refinements and expansions here and there, in a relatively compact way. This way, a savvy knitter need not necessarily purchase the original book to work out of this one, and an experienced double-knitter will not find their time wasted by rehashing too much existing knowledge.

Once the foundations are covered, *Double or Nothing* jumps off the deep end and explores the depths of techniques that were either only introduced in the appendix of *EDK*, or not yet developed at its time of publication. As in *Extreme Double-Knitting*, I'll introduce a pattern once all the techniques needed to do it are covered. There are a few patterns in the chapters that address previously documented techniques, but each has a slight twist that wasn't covered or used in the same way in *EDK*.

On the importance of story

Extreme Double-Knitting sometimes reads like a technical manual, with even the fonts selected for their technical look. That was okay with me; the form of knitting I do is highly technical. I've been justifiably called an "engineer" of knitting more than once. However, I'm not an engineer by training. I was an art major, specializing in sculpture. My story is much deeper than can be contained in the format of a technical manual. I'm not a robot; I hope that, in some small way, my humanity is more prominent in this book.

In addition to my story, I want to tell the stories of the people whose journeys intersect with my own. I may never know their whole story, but for a small time we traveled together, and I can tell that part of it.

Another thing I'm doing differently from *Extreme Double-Knitting* is that I'm trying to use yarn I'm particularly excited about for some reason, not merely yarn that's easy to get. If I understand my audience as I think I do, you're not the type of people to be put off if you can't get the exact yarn in the exact same colors that I used. You're willing to go to some length to use awesome yarn, but you're also willing to substitute when necessary. So I'm going to talk up the yarns I chose, with the hopes that you'll also get excited about them, search them out, and use them (but I'll understand if you don't).

A Craftstory
or how I became a knitting designer of note

This story will continue throughout the book, adding a little color and flavor to the experience. Accordingly, each green box will have a snippet of my abridged life story in art and craft. Since the boxes are easy to see, it'll be easy for you to either seek them out or skip over them, as you prefer.

One of the most common questions I get asked is "How did you get into knitting?" There's almost always an undertone of "How did you (of all people) get into knitting?" or "How did (a guy like) you get into knitting?" – but most people are polite enough to leave the subtext where it lies. This is the story I tell:

I was at a craft-sharing event in college to teach origami, which is something I've been doing (and teaching) from an early age. My workshop was scheduled against a well-known visiting stencil artist, so nobody came to learn origami. Since I was not as interested in stencils, I decided to see what else was being offered and sat in on a knitting workshop. I got hooked, and the rest is history. The irony of this, of course, is that if a single person had shown up for my origami workshop, I wouldn't be writing this now.

continued on page 37

In pursuit of elegant solutions

I value process at least as much as product. Much of my work in double-knitting has involved a search for not only solutions, but elegant solutions to various problems. I could have released patterns earlier in a few cases, but if some element of the pattern struck me as inelegant, I shelved it and came back to it with a fresh mind. In almost every case, I have been rewarded with a much more satisfied mind — and hopefully more satisfied customers than I would have gotten had I released a pattern with an inelegant solution.

The most elegant solution will have all of the following properties:

Simplicity: Even a difficult technique can be broken down into easier pieces. An elegant solution can make a difficult technique seem simpler.

Efficiency: There may be multiple paths to the result you want, but there are long paths and short ones. An elegant solution will always use the path that minimizes unnecessary movement.

Economy: Yarn is a finite resource, and overuse of it is both wasteful and tends to create a lumpy fabric. An elegant solution will always use the smallest amount of yarn necessary.

Purity: Many problems can be solved by looking at them from a different angle. However, sometimes this will result in solutions that depart so radically from the original technique that the result can barely be considered the same. Process is as important as product here. An elegant solution minimizes departure from the base technique.

Universality: A solution is no good if it works in some circumstances but not others. An elegant solution works in all circumstances that are appropriate for it.

Repeatability: A solution is no good if it works once but never again. An elegant solution can be documented and repeated time and time again with the same result.

Attractiveness: If the product is lumpy or awkward looking, no matter how elegant the process was, the solution is not complete.

Like all rules, these can be bent a bit (not every solution is 100% elegant), and even if I believe I've found the most elegant solution now, it's possible that I will find an even more elegant one later.

CHAPTER 1

Foundations and Basic Techniques

Double-knitting Vocabulary

Before we begin, let's set some vocabulary to be used throughout this book. I don't necessarily expect everyone to adopt "my" language in their own work, but I can at least try to be consistent with my own terminology, as well as be clear about what I mean.

Let's start with the term "double-knitting" — the hyphen is important. The accepted term is "double knitting" without the hyphen, but as I wrote in *Extreme Double-Knitting*, that term is confusing because it can mean a number of things. Hyphenating it makes "double-knitting" an unambiguously whole term and separates it from other possible meanings of "double knitting." I will also sometimes refer to double-knitting as simply "DK" for short.

This brings us to another terminology distinction. DK-weight yarn, while often appropriate for double-knitting, doesn't have anything to do with the technique per se. It was so named because it is capable of "doubling" for either worsted or sport weight yarn (depending on size of needles used). The name was coined during WWII when materials were heavily rationed and a single yarn weight was created to do the work of two.

Now let's get into the structure of the fabric, beginning with the stitches. The smallest element of double-knitting is a pair of stitches — typically a knit and a purl, in that order. Other designers have attempted to distinguish this element from a pair of something else by calling the element a "DSP" or double-stitch pair. This feels cumbersome to me, so I just refer to the element as a pair. I won't use "pair" to refer to anything else in double-knitting.

While you may "knit" or "purl" a stitch (the smallest element of single-layer knitting), you "work" a pair. Because each pair consists of two stitches that are most often knitted and purled in turn, saying "knit a pair" is not wholly accurate.

Each pair has a "color order" and a "stitch order." The color order is simply a designation of which color is placed in which position in the pair (as read in the direction you are knitting). Assuming the colors are A and B, the most common color orders are AB and BA. The stitch order tells you which type of stitch goes in each position in the pair. The most common stitch orders are KP (knit/purl) and PK.

A pair (or stitch) can also be slipped for various reasons. It is assumed that all slips are done purlwise unless indicated otherwise. When a stitch must be slipped back in the other direction, it is always done so without imparting any twist. Since there is no standard vocabulary for working stitches backward, it is best to make sure any twisting or reseating of stitches happen during slips from left to right, and leave the slipping back untwisted. A slipped pair (see page 33) is notated with a ∇ in the chart.

A pair can also be linked for various reasons. The most common is on the edge of a flat piece, to keep the edge from separating and curling inside. A linked pair is notated with a + in the chart (see page 32).

The fabric itself also has some unique terminology: single-layer knitting has a "right" and "wrong" side, but double-knitting doesn't have either. The terminology of "facing side" versus "opposite side" I used in *Extreme Double-Knitting* is also inaccurate because, when working flat, you have the opposite side facing you half the time. "Even" and "odd" don't work in the round, and "front" and "back" likewise change with every row. I needed a way to designate a side of the work that would function throughout the pattern without conflicting with any directional terms — so I chose "Layer 1" and "Layer 2." Layer 1 is the layer that faces you in the chart, whereas Layer 2 is the uncharted layer that is created by following the double-knitting rules.

Similar but different: "front" (or "forward") and "back" mean the same as in single-layer knitting; they refer to the fabric as it is currently being worked (not necessarily as it's charted). This is not only useful for "wyif" and "wyib" but also for describing double-knit decreases, increases, and cables.

"Front" and "back" don't work as well in some instructions, especially for increases, where "inside" and "outside" are more universal. The outside can refer to either layer of the work; the inside is the space between the layers. Inserting a needle from front to back means different things when you're inserting it into the front layer or the back layer, but inserting a needle from inside to outside works for either one.

The most common fabric produced with double-knitting looks like stockinette on both layers (in most cases, with some kind of colorwork). This fabric is called "double-stockinette" and is often used for gauge swatches even when the final piece is done in some other surface design. The double-stockinette fabric (with or without colorwork) is called "standard double-knitting" or SDK for short.

Double-knit charting is essentially the same as single-layer knit charting; you just follow a different key and set of instructions. I refer to the individual squares in a chart as "pixels" (a computer term, short for "picture element"). Each pixel in the chart denotes one pair of stitches; the color and/or symbol in the pixel shows you how to process that pair.

A row or round (most often an even-numbered one) in which all pairs match the stitch order and color order in the row below is called a "matching row." This is similar to a "rest row" in single-layer knitting, but it's a bit more complex. Still, these rows are a blessing when they show up; they are most common in double-knit cables, lace, and off-the-grid colorwork.

Finally, I want to explain a little about the needles. As designers we often cater to the majority, but I feel that if it's easy to make a more inclusive transition without confusing people, I should do so. For this reason, I'm calling the two needles the "source" needle and the "working" needle. For right-handed knitters, the source needle (which contains the stitches from the CO or the previous row) is the left-hand needle, and the working needle (which contains the stitches from the row currently being worked) is the right-hand needle. However, these will be switched if you are a left-handed knitter. One caveat: as a left-handed knitter, you are probably used to mentally translating patterns as you go. This is no doubt frustrating. I hope my instructions can be followed in the left-hand direction as well, but it's likely that some other directional terms will be inaccurate, especially decreases, YOs, and cable twists. My apologies for that; in those cases I must cater to the majority in the interest of clarity.

Foundations of Double-knitting

Now that we've got the vocabulary out of the way, let's set up a platform for you to jump from. Without a firm foundation, much of what's in this book won't make a lot of sense. It's my hope that many people will be able to glean what knowledge they need from the basics covered here. But if you still find yourself confused, much of this is covered in considerably more depth in my first book, *Extreme Double-Knitting*. You can also get a good hands-on introduction from my Craftsy class, *Adventures in Double-Knitting*. If you find anything here that directly contradicts something in *EDK* or my Craftsy class, assume that this book is correct.

Speaking of firm foundations, I highly recommend that you familiarize yourself with a technique in single-layer knitting before attempting it in double-knitting. All skills are based on foundations; if you try to build the second story of a house without checking to see that the first floor is solidly built, you're going to have a disappointing and possibly painful experience.

For the same reason, I recommend that you familiarize yourself with standard double-knitting before attempting the more advanced patterns. I have traditionally designed my basic patterns as larger projects for a very good reason: a key to success in double-knitting is muscle memory. You won't get double-knitting muscle memory from a potholder. You will from a scarf or a cowl or a baby blanket. Once your mind and your hands are in agreement that you understand double-knitting, it will become far easier to add new techniques.

While it chafes at my sense of orderly presentation, I will cover cast-ons and bind-offs a little later. I will present the body of the work before the edges so that you know what you're aiming for before you start building.

There are multiple styles of double-knitting, but they all have this in common: All double-knitting is based on the idea that you're working two layers of fabric at once. Each stitch you make is part of one of the two layers. In most cases, you alternate layers with every stitch, which results in pairs of stitches which correspond to the same pixel in the chart, e.g., the first from Layer 1 and the second from Layer 2.

There are less-flexible styles of double-knitting in common use, but the most flexible style and the one that I (and most other double-knitting designers) prefer is graced with the simple name "modern double-knitting." This method, at its simplest, uses two ends of differing color that travel together and are used to achieve various patterns. The style is "modern" as compared to the somewhat archaic "slip-stitch" style, which borrows its techniques from tubular double-knitting and was the primary method of executing double-knit colorwork until the late 1980s when the "modern" style came into use.

A standard double-knit pair of any style follows a simple logic. Each pixel in a double-knit chart corresponds to one pair on the needle. Each pair consists of a knit and a purl, in that order. The knit and purl will always be worked in opposite colors from each other: either AB or BA (never AA or BB). In modern double-knitting, both ends will always travel together. This means that when knitting, both yarns will be at the back but only one color will be knitted; when purling, both yarns will be at the front and the other color will be purled.

In a Layer 1 row or in the round, the color of the pixel in the chart will correspond to the knit stitch and the purl stitch will be done in the opposite color afterward. On a Layer 2 row, the color of the pixel in the chart corresponds to the purl stitch in your pair, which means you must first knit with the opposite color from what is charted so that you may then purl in the charted color.

In quick and simple knitting terms, work a standard AB pair as follows: **K1A wyib, P1B wyif**; work a BA pair as follows: **K1B wyib, P1A wyif**.

As you can see, the only thing that changes is which color is worked in which position in the pair. When you change from an AB pair to a BA pair, the two layers will be linked together as the yarns switch sides. Because of this, the more color-changing that occurs in a pattern, the more stable the fabric is. Large swaths of a single color order remain easily separable layers, but smaller areas are harder to separate.

There is no "right" or "wrong" way to knit, and nobody should have to relearn knitting in order to double-knit. No matter your knitting method, it is possible to use it for double-knitting. Throughout the last decade, I've taught thousands of students and have seen countless solutions and adaptations as people figure out how best to double-knit in their preferred method. One of the most prevalent issues is the question of how to manage two yarns when you're used to working with one, or at least, working with two differently.

I am not an expert in each of these methods, and I'm not going to try to teach you how to do each one. But I'm going to give you some pointers on how to use each of these methods in double-knitting, as gleaned from thousands of students over the past decade of teaching. There are countless resources in other books, online, and likely at your local yarn shop if you want to learn a new knitting method.

English double-knitting

The English method of knitting usually involves using the right hand to "throw" a loop of yarn over the working needle. The yarn may have some tension but not as much as in Continental knitting — after all, you need to be able to loop it around the needle. Many people end up letting go of the working needle in order to manipulate the ends.

When you have two ends, you can choose to hold them together or on separate fingers, or not hold them at all, dropping and picking up the end you need for any given stitch. In the English method of double-knitting, it seems that the "ribbon" (see page 27) is more naturally positioned vertically than horizontally, with the ends more easily described as the top and bottom rather than the front and back ends. When the ends are at the back of the work, the topmost end is used to knit with; when the ends are at the front, the bottommost end is used to purl with.

Hold both ends to the back, so that the color being used on the front is uppermost and the color being used on the back is below it.

Insert the working needle into the next stitch knitwise; grab the end of the knit color . . .

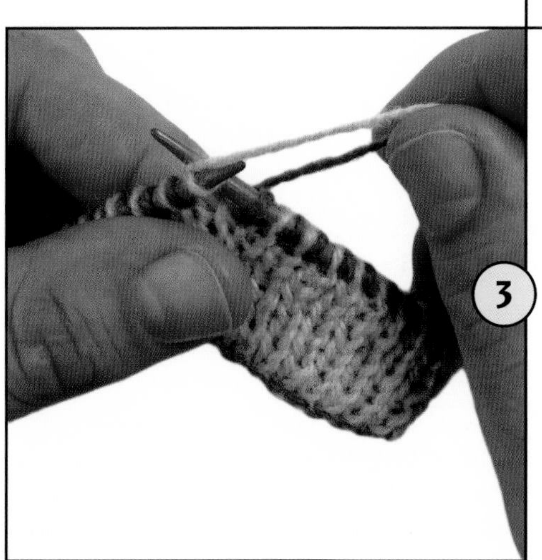

. . . and loop it around the tip of the working needle. Pull it through to finish the knit stitch. The other color may be dropped or simply held loosely, but should be out of the way of the knit stitch.

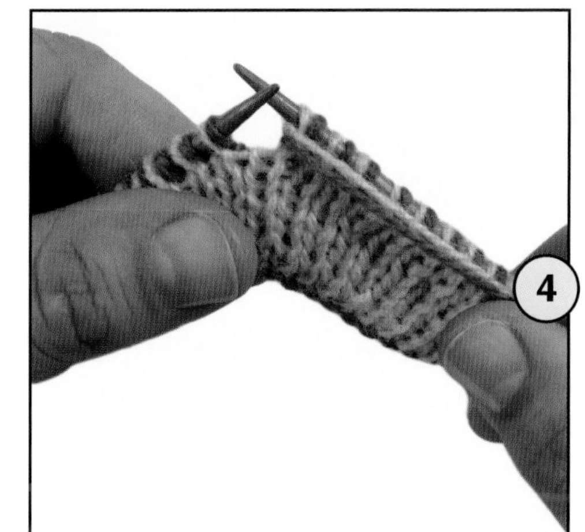

Bring both ends to the front; the positioning of the ends should stay the same (the color being used on the front is still uppermost, and the color about to be purled is below it).

Insert the working needle into the next stitch purlwise; grab the end of the purl color . . .

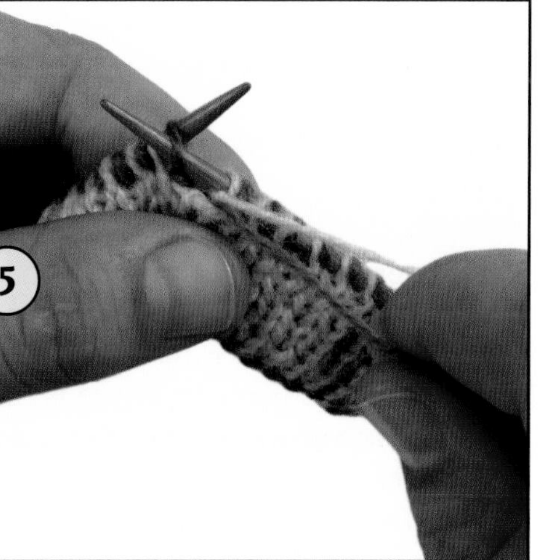

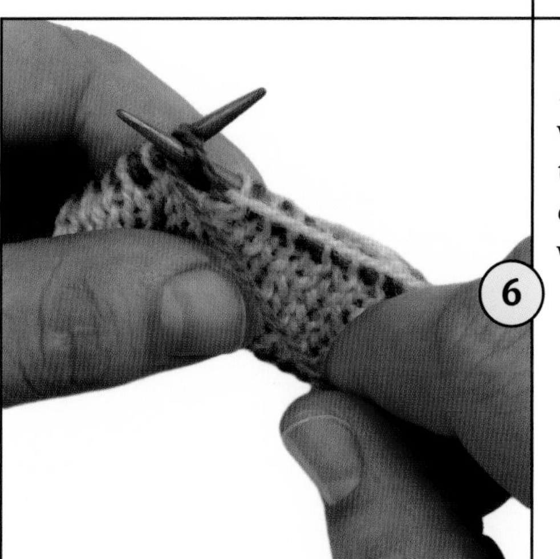

. . . and loop it around the tip of the working needle. Pull it through to finish the purl stitch. The other end should stay out of the way while doing this.

Continental double-knitting

Continental knitting involves using the working needle to "pick" stitches and pull them through loops. Generally, the yarn is tensioned on the left hand in some way, and this tension is leveraged to make it easier to pick up the strand with the working needle.

The main difficulty in double-knitting using this method is that, when holding two yarns together, most people's yarn-tensioning solution will backfire on them.

If you tension your yarn by gripping it with your lower fingers and wrapping it once or more around a finger to take up the slack, the two ends will twist around each other. The twisting is superficial, as it will go away as soon as you let go of the ends. But while you're knitting, it will make it difficult to separate the ends and keep them from twisting between pairs of the same color order. To fix this, I recommend you try wrapping the yarn around two different fingers, perhaps your index and middle fingers.

The other difficulty I've seen most often in the Continental method is the tendency to create bars (see page 40), not by forgetting to move both ends forward or back, but by splitting the ends apart when doing the purl stitch. The knit stitch is rarely an issue, but when bringing both ends forward and inserting the needle for the purl, make sure you put the needle behind both strands, into the next purl stitch, and then manipulate the purl color to finish the pair. If you put the needle in between the strands, it does the same thing as not bringing one end forward.

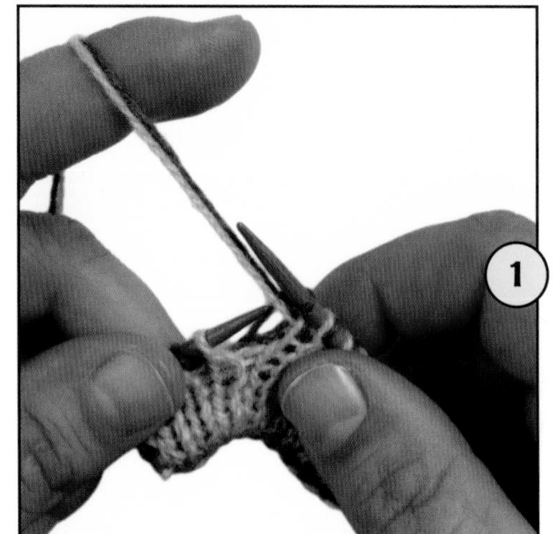

Begin with both ends in the hand holding your source needle and tensioned in whatever way is most comfortable for you (keeping the ends which approach the needles untwisted) with the color you intend to knit closest to the source needle. Bring both ends to the back of the work.

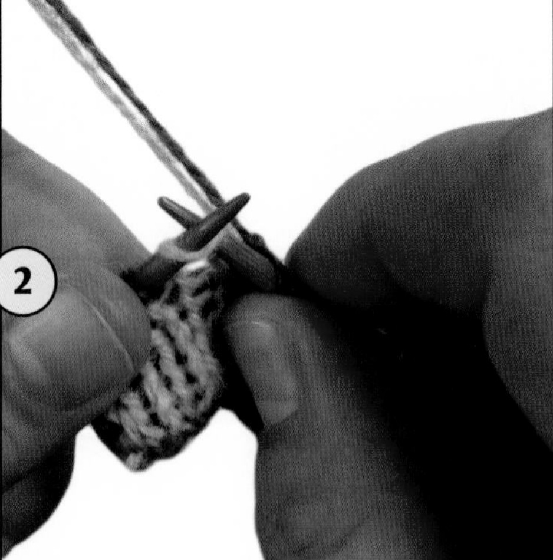

Keeping the ends' tension, insert your working needle into the next stitch knitwise . . .

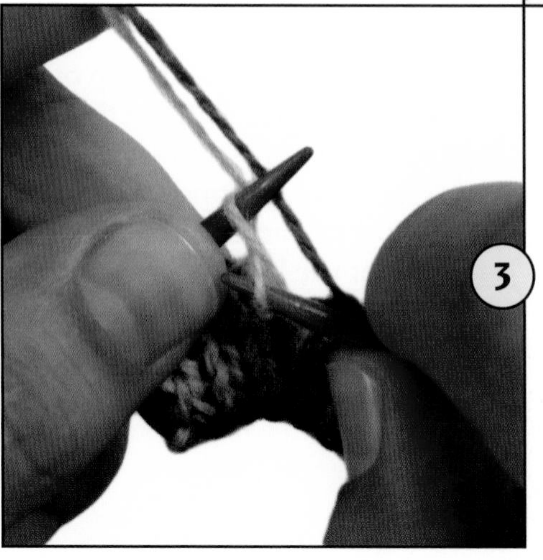

. . . then pick the color you need and pull it through.

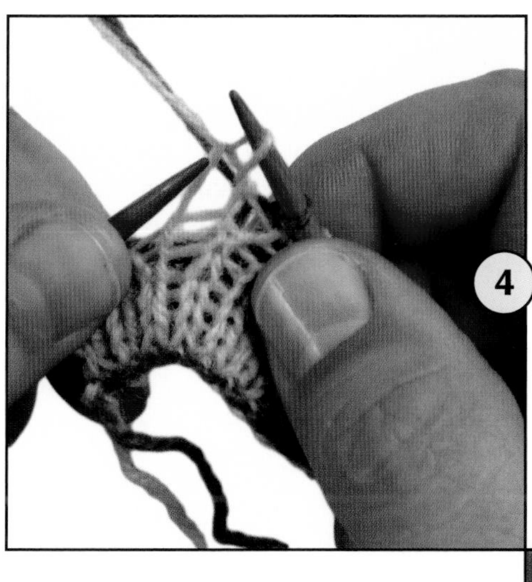

Here's the new stitch, in progress. Note that the tension is still held, which may momentarily distort the stitch, but it will even out as you proceed.

Bring both ends to the front, or simply bring the source needle behind the tensioned ends.

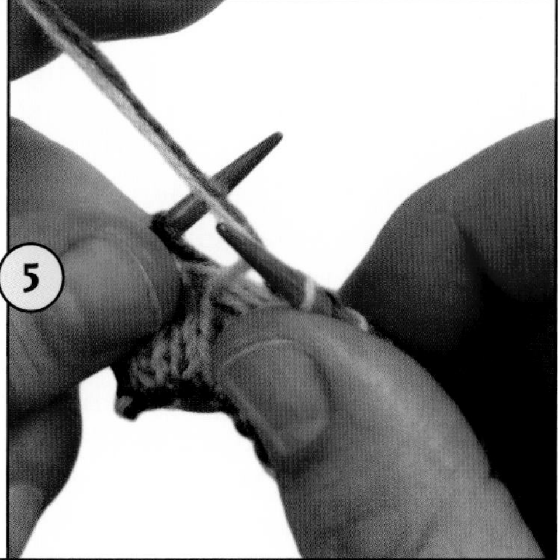

Bring the working needle behind both ends and into the next stitch purlwise.

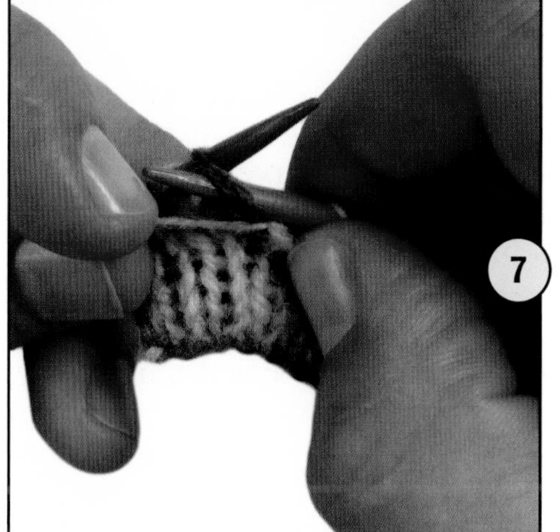

Use your finger to push the ends down to facilitate a small wrap around the needle tip to finish the purl stitch. You can use your thumb to hold the other color out of the way if necessary.

Pull the new loop through the stitch. While doing this, the tension between your finger(s) and the needles may slacken a bit, but you'll still be holding the tension elsewhere in your hand.

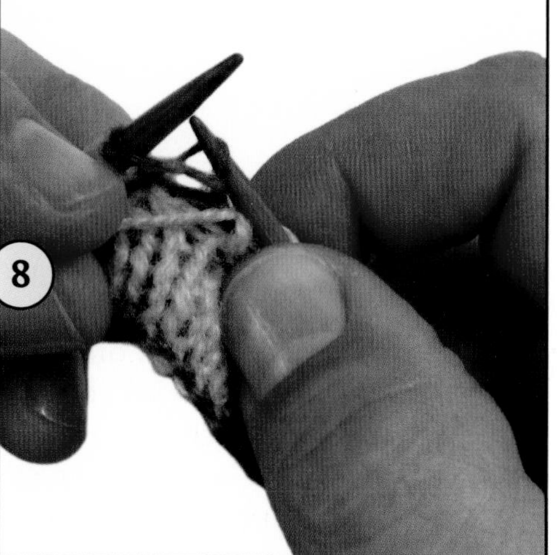

Position your finger(s) back in the original position. Here's the new purl stitch; the same caveat in Step 4 applies here too.

Norwegian purl

The Norwegian purl is a method of purling that doesn't require bringing the yarn forward. The yarn stays on the back of the work throughout the technique. It's a fairly complicated set of moves that serve to pull a loop of yarn forward and create a purl with it, never changing the position of the end. When I first encountered this method in one of my classes, I thought it was impossible to adapt to double-knitting since the whole point of the technique is <u>not</u> to move the yarn forward, and double-knitting requires you to move the yarn forward with every other stitch. Finally, I realized that there is a way. The important thing is not that the yarn you're working with is forward, but that the non-working yarn is out of the way at the front of the work. So if you're working with the Norwegian purl, you can reach behind the non-working yarn before beginning your purl move (similar to the move done in Continental style).

Portuguese knitting

Portuguese knitting is a method touted by Andrea Wong and others as an excellent, if unusual, way to tension your yarn using minimal hand motions. Instead of your ends traveling directly from your source yarn to your hands and then the needles, the yarn travels around the back of your neck. One color goes one way and the other color goes the other way so that you end up with an end coming from either side of your neck and joining at your needles. If this seems awkward, the more prevalent way is now to use a couple of special pins which you can put near your shoulders; these are much easier to remove when you need to put your knitting down, and would also make it easier to add more than two colors.

The general idea is that you use your body or the pins to tension the yarn and keep it more or less taut between your body and the needles. Then, a small motion of the thumb will position the yarn to be wrapped around the needle. Because the yarn stays at the front of the work throughout, similar to the Norwegian purl, the same caveats apply as to that method.

There are plenty of videos online about this method in general but few about double-knitting with it; however, I know that Andrea Wong teaches a workshop specifically about double-knitting using the Portuguese style and I recommend you seek her out if you can't adapt it on your own.

Combination knitting

Combination knitting is a method where you keep the yarns separated by holding one in the right hand (a la the English method) and the other in the left hand (a la Continental). True to form, when you work the color in your right hand, you throw it; when you work the color in your left hand, you pick it. The issue with this method in double-knitting is that the yarns must keep changing sides, and they don't naturally travel together unless you "force" them to do so. You just need to make sure you bring both yarns forward (independently) and both yarns back.

Alasdair's double-knitting method

This is the only method in which I can unequivocally claim to be an expert. I am a self-taught knitter, and I have honed my own style of knitting over many years. I'm going to attempt to explain it here, not necessarily to convert you but to help you understand what I do differently and why.

I do something I call a "left-hand wrap." Both English and Continental knitting are done largely with motions of the right hand, either to throw a loop around the working needle or to use the working needle to pick a stitch from a tensioned strand. In my method, my right hand moves very little except to guide the working needle into stitches. The actual stitch is created by a small movement of my left hand, often done with just a couple of fingers. I don't hold any tension in my ends, but I knit fairly close to my needle tips and give a little tug to my work after each stitch to further tighten up the stitches. Reading that, you'd probably assume I knit very tightly. To be fair, I knit tighter than most double-knitters, but since most double-knitters end up with a far looser gauge than they would in single-layer knitting, I like to think I just knit to gauge.

Since the ends are not tensioned, it doesn't really matter how many there are. I hold them loosely in my left hand and I use whichever is needed at any given time. I frequently re-evaluate the twist or braid of the ends, and I modify my technique to undo it as I go.

If I want my stitches twisted, as I frequently did in *Extreme Double-Knitting*, I can simply wrap both my knits and my purls toward me, seating them on the needles backwards. This is something I do less now that I'm designing for "the masses," who aren't likely to want to twist every stitch. But if I want to, it doesn't require any significant change to my techniques — just a slightly different rhythm to the stitches I'm making.

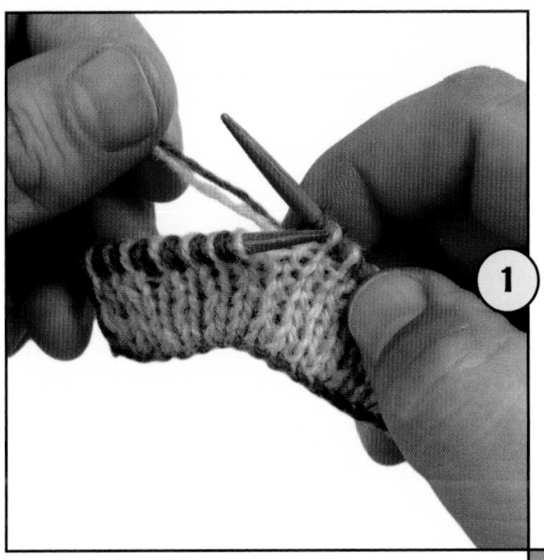

Bring both ends to the back; hold them loosely in the hand closest to the source needle (in this case, your left). The yarn you intend to knit with should be frontmost, and the other end should be behind it.

Insert the needle into the next stitch purlwise and make a small wrap with the knit color end. The other end should remain at the back and out of the way, but can be used to add a little tension to the move.

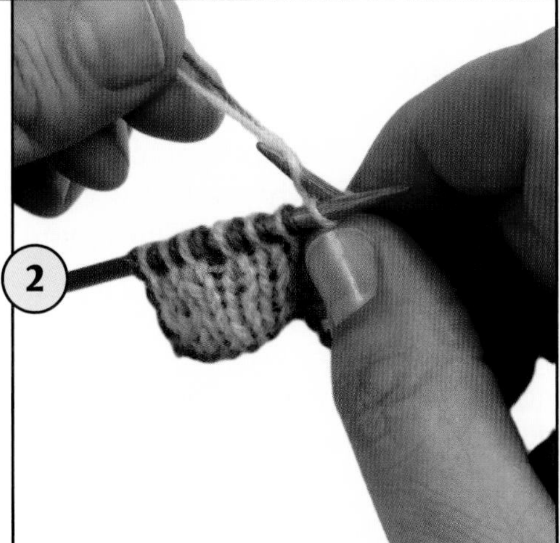

Pull the end through to complete the new stitch.

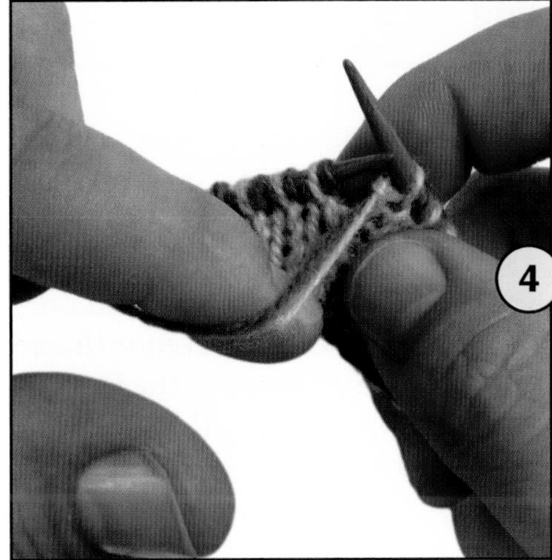

Bring both ends forward. Note that the knit color end is still frontmost, but the end you'll be purling with is now moved closer to the needles.

Insert the needle into the next stitch purlwise and make a small wrap with the purl color end. The other end should remain at the front and out of the way.

Pull the end through to complete the new stitch.

Reading Charts in Double-knitting

Most of the time, charts in double-knitting are the same as single-layer charts. I strive to use common symbols wherever possible, but there are reasons why I cannot always do so. The primary difference is in the way these symbols are followed: in a single-layer chart, every pixel is followed as a single stitch. In double-knitting, every pixel denotes a pair, but only the stitch from Layer 1 is notated. The stitch from Layer 2 is created based on the color order rules and any chart symbols, as laid out in the key and instructions. The exception to this rule is in two-pattern double-knitting, where both the knit and the purl from each pair are notated. You can read more about that technique on page 82.

There are two different types of moves in double-knitting: those that are adapted from single-layer knitting, and those that are unique to double-knitting. The ones which are adapted from single-layer knitting (e.g., knits, purls, increases, decreases, cables, yarn-overs) require only that you remember that you are double-knitting while you do them and replace them with their double-knit counterparts when you work them. Many of these use symbols which will already be familiar to you. The moves which are unique to double-knitting rely on there being two layers (linked and slipped pairs are good examples). These have new symbols that may be unfamiliar to you, but they will be described in the text and defined in the key of any pattern I write.

In general, as in single-layer knitting, a chart will be read differently flat versus in the round. In flat knitting, row numbers will appear along alternate edges of the chart. In the round, numbers will line up along the right edge of the chart, since you will always be beginning your round at the same edge of your work.

For flat double-knitting, a Layer 2 row (generally an even-numbered row) will require that you work the row from left to right, as well as reverse any colors you see charted (as mentioned on page 20). In addition, you will reverse the direction of any directional techniques such as increases, decreases, or cables. In most cases, as in single-layer knitting, these techniques are not worked on Layer 2 rows — but they can be.

Finally, there's the "no pair" symbol: in my notation, it's a black pixel with a white outline. This means the same as a "no-stitch" symbol in single-layer knitting. It's just a placeholder, and when you see it, skip over it to whatever's next in the chart.

Common Issues in Double-knitting

Gauge and tension

The most common issue in double-knitting is a difference in gauge between your single-layer knitting (assuming the same yarn and needles) and your double-knitting. In addition, you may find that your knit and purl gauges are subtly (or radically) different. This is especially noticeable when double-knitting in the round, at least when the piece has large fields of the same color order, since all of the stitches on one layer are worked as knits and all of the stitches on the other layer are worked as purls. When double-knitting flat, it's less of an issue since with each row, the roles of the layers are changed.

In double-knitting, your gauge will probably be different from your gauge in single-layer knitting, at least until you get more adept at it. I generally recommend you create a swatch using the same needles you'd normally use for the yarn you've chosen, then size up or down as needed. The more you do this, the more you'll see a pattern — and know whether you will usually need to go up a needle size, or down two needle sizes. The most common situation is for your double-knitting to be looser than your single-layer knitting, which will mean you'll want to go one or two needle sizes down. Case in point: I had a sample knitter who had to go down to US3 needles to match the gauge I had called for on US6 in one pattern. When she was unable to finish the project, I took it back and put it on the needles I had called for, matched her gauge and finished the piece.

If you're finding that your gauge is different on one layer of your work than on the other in the round, or if you're experiencing "rowing out" in flat double-knitting, work on tightening up the loose stitches (or, I suppose, loosening the tight stitches) once you've identified whether it's the knit or the purl that's looser (hint: it's usually the purls). This may require a modification to your knitting style, which may be a struggle for a little while, but hopefully the more even gauge will make it worth the work.

Adding more yarn

If you run out of yarn and need to add another ball to continue, you have a number of options. Of course, any of the normal methods of joining apply here (Russian join, spit-splice, or others). But I prefer to use the following method: If you're working flat, you can just leave the tail hanging out after the last edge stitch, and add the new yarn before working the linked pair. You should have two tails hanging out of the same place along the edge after doing this. Later, these two tails can be woven in.

If you're working in the round or can't make it to the edge, you can add yarn in the middle of the work, ideally in the middle of a long expanse of pairs in a single color order. Let an end hang out of the opposite-color layer of the work (e.g. if you're running out of Color A, let the tail hang on the Color B layer). Match up that tail with the new yarn and continue working. Once you've done a few rows or rounds with the new yarn, you can tie a loose overhand knot and weave the ends in opposite directions.

Weaving in ends

Double-knitting is hollow! Well, mostly. But it's a great fabric for hiding ends inside of. If you thread an end into a tapestry needle, you can run it inside the work. Check carefully on both layers to make sure you didn't push the needle outside the work on either layer before pulling through. If you run it around some of the internal links that happen when a color change is made, you can change directions to better anchor the end. When you come to the end, pull it through to the outside, cut it near the base, then tug on the fabric to suck it inside. You can also do an occasional duplicate stitch to really anchor in the yarn. This is also a great way to fix a color mistake if you happen to have one near the origin of the end(s) you're weaving in.

Blocking

Wet-blocking is best for double-knitting because the fabric is at least twice as stubborn as single-layer knitting. Steam-blocking isn't forceful enough to get the fabric to behave the way you want. That said, the process is largely the same as blocking any other knit fabric, with one exception: you need to flip the piece over (and/or inside-out) halfway through the process to make sure the whole thing dries. This will mean unpinning and re-pinning the work.

Two-color End Management in Double-knitting

One of the hassles in double-knitting, as in any colorwork where you have multiple strands running together, is the twisting up of the ends. This is something that inevitably happens, no matter how careful you are, but it's also something that you can control and fix (to some degree).

In two-color double-knitting, there are a number of reasons why your ends will twist up; the first two are inevitable.

- When working in flat double-knitting, the linked pair at the beginning of each row will cause a twist in the ends; there is no avoiding that.
- Every time you change color orders, the yarn from the back comes to the front and vice versa. This results in a 180-degree twist of your ends in one direction or the other.
- One of the more common mistakes is to twist the yarn in between stitches or pairs. This effectively creates a linked pair in the middle of a row, and also can create a little "blip" of color in between pairs where there shouldn't be any. This will happen less with practice.

You can, of course, let your work dangle out to untwist the ends, or play leapfrog with your yarn balls, but I would suggest a different solution: using the color changes. Where you change color orders, your yarn can make that 180-degree twist in either direction — clockwise or counterclockwise. Those terms mean little in knitting since you're not looking at the rotation of the yarns around each other head-on, as you would look at a clock. But they're useful to consider, because the yarns do rotate around each other.

At a color change, if you pick up the knit from underneath the other color strand, you're initiating a counterclockwise twist of the two yarns (for you spinners, a Z-twist). If you pick it up from over the top of the other color, you're initiating a clockwise twist (an S-twist). The linked pair, if followed as described on page 32, will create a counterclockwise twist. If you make your next color change clockwise, that will undo the twist made in the linked pair (while keeping the link intact).

This can be further applied to all other color changes. If you consistently make color changes in one direction, you're going to end up with your ends twisted around each other in that direction. However, if you can keep the presence of mind to do a clockwise twist for one color change and then a counterclockwise twist for the next one, you'll end up untwisting as you go. Personally, I don't always have such presence of mind, so I prefer to just keep an eye on my ends; every now and then I'll check to see if they're twisted up and in which direction. If they're twisted counterclockwise, I'll make my next several color changes clockwise to undo the end twists on the fly. If they're twisted clockwise, I'll make the next several color changes counterclockwise..

The ribbon analogy

To help my students visualize their ends' movement better, a common analogy I use in my workshops is that of the "ribbon." If you hold two yarns together, they can be imagined to be a ribbon with edges of two different colors. This may or may not directly apply to the way you hold your yarn (see methods, page 20), but I've found it helps many people to envision what's going on. If it doesn't help you, just skip over this and move on; you'll find your own visualization with practice.

Let's assume the ribbon has edges of Color A and Color B, and that it's held flat so that A is in the front and B is in the back. The ribbon can be moved from the front to the back of the work, but it doesn't actually change except in its relationship to the needle.

When the ribbon is at the back, the front edge (Color A, in this case) is presented to the needle for knitting, and Color B is further back and out of the way. When the ribbon is moved to the front, the back edge (Color B) is presented to the needle for purling, and Color A is further forward and out of the way. With the ribbon in this orientation, you are set up to make AB pairs (which, not coincidentally, have Color A on the front of the work and Color B on the back). As long as the ribbon stays in this orientation and doesn't twist, your layers will stay separate. If you twist the ribbon between two pairs of the same color order, you will end up with a link between the two layers and (in most cases) a visible bit of the other layer's color visible in the gap between the stitches (see twists, page 40).

Now, in order to make a color change to a BA pair, the ribbon does need to be twisted. You need B at the front and A at the back to create a BA pair, and you can twist the ribbon clockwise (by picking up the new knit color from underneath the new purl color) or counterclockwise (by picking up the new knit color from over the top of the new purl color). The direction doesn't matter; the resulting crossover of yarns will be inside the work. Once you've done the color change, the ribbon will be stable again in its new orientation.

Double-knitting Cast-ons

There are a lot of ways to cast-on for double-knitting; I daresay there are more ways to cast on for double-knitting than there are for single-layer knitting. This is because the simplest way to get the colors on the needle is to hold both ends together and cast on the way you normally prefer. With care, you can get a clean set of alternating-color pairs that can be worked from in double-knitting. However, the edge you will get with most of these methods will not be terribly attractive. I recommend you try a cast-on specifically made for double-knitting.

When I first encountered double-knitting back in the early 2000s, the methods for casting on left quite a bit to be desired. It became clear that most of the cast-on methods for double-knitting involved two to four "setup rows" before actually beginning the fun part. This created a single-color bottom edge of questionable quality and unnecessary length — far from the elegant solution I sought. After much experimentation and some help from a more experienced knitter, I adapted an existing single-color cast-on into a two-color technique, then honed and refined it over time.

For any cast-on, the notation in the pattern will be something to the effect of "CO 80 AB pairs." In a chart, if the cast-on is notated at all, it will use a Ջ symbol. The specific cast-on to use here is up to you.

The standard double-knit cast-on

This is what I consider to be the most elegant solution. The edge is clean, stable, nicely stretchy (but not overly so), and has a nice rhythm to the movements once you understand them. It's based on the "long-tail" cast-on. In standard knitting, you have the active end of the yarn over your index finger and the long tail over your thumb (or vice versa) — but here, we're using two active ends, one over the thumb and one over the finger.

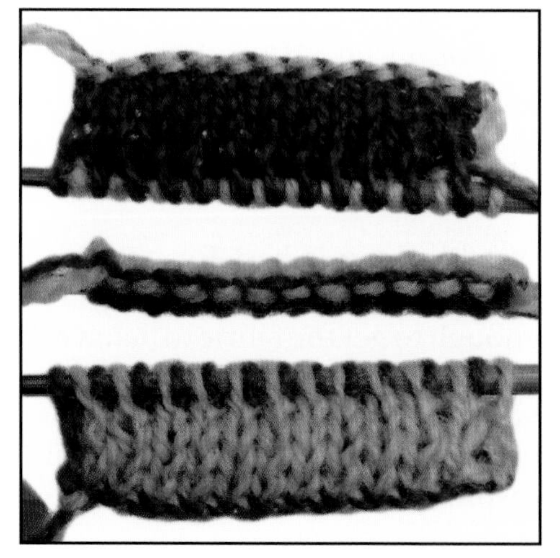

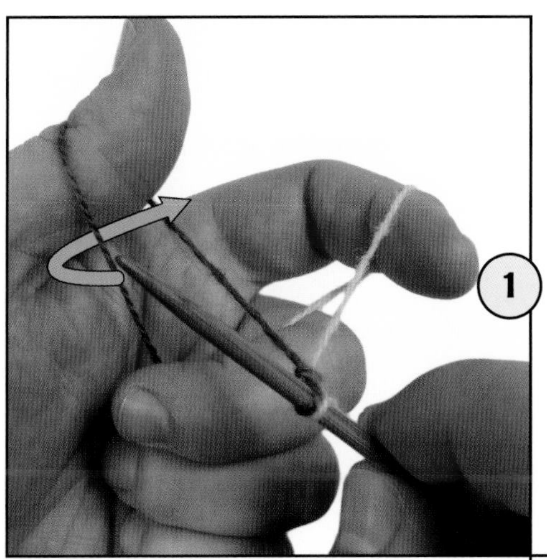

Make a slip knot with both ends held together. Put the slip knot on the needle and position your hands as for the long-tail cast-on, but with one active end over each finger and the tails out of the way. The first move is the same as the standard long-tail move: bring your needle in front of all strands, then insert it underneath the frontmost strand and in front of the next strand.

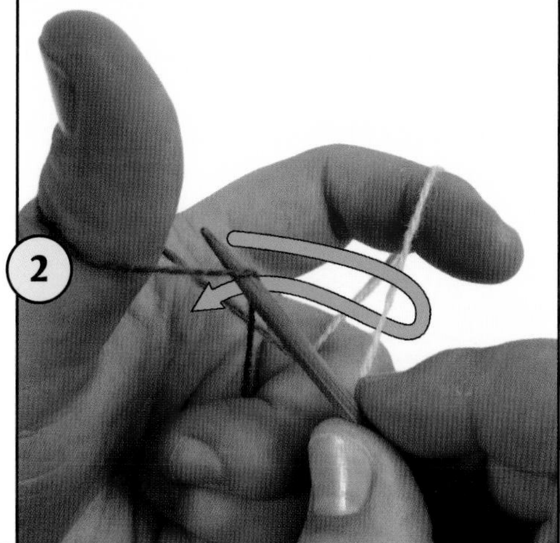

Continue the move by bringing the needle over the top of the second and third strands (as counted from the front), then catching the third strand on the needle and returning back through the space the needle originally entered through. Note that you are going through a loop of one color in order to pick up a stitch of the other color.

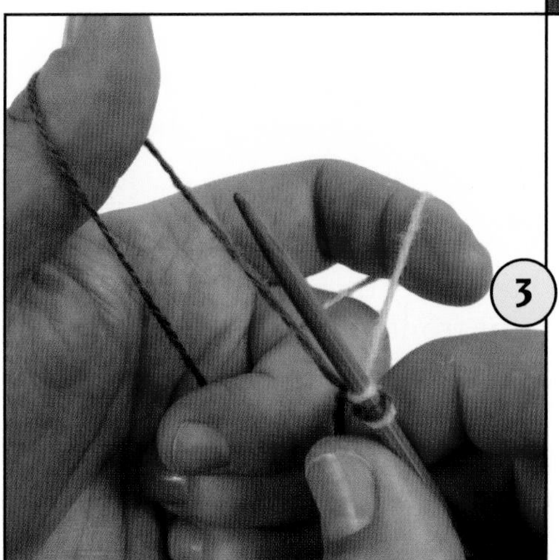

With the new stitch on your needle, drop the thumb loop and tighten. Reposition your hands; you should now have a new stitch on your needle in the color that is held on your finger.

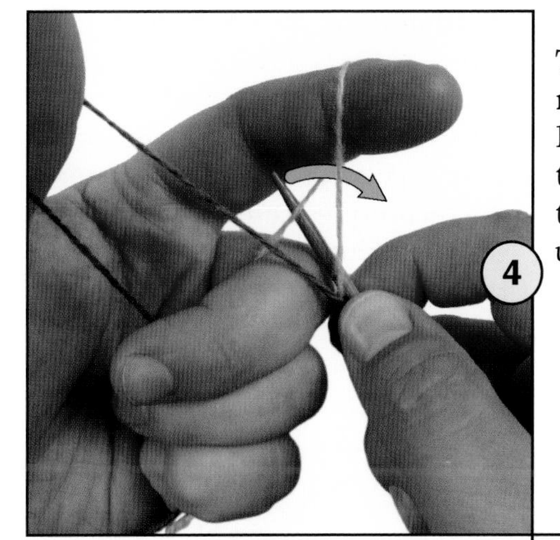

The second move is a reverse modification of the first move. Bring your needle behind all of the strands, then insert it between the rearmost two strands from underneath.

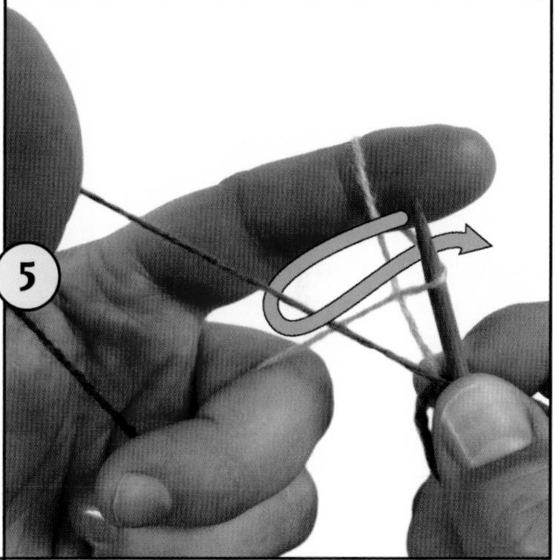

Continue the move by bringing the needle over the top of the second strand (as counted from the back) and underneath the third strand. Catch the third strand on the needle and return back through the space that the needle originally entered through.

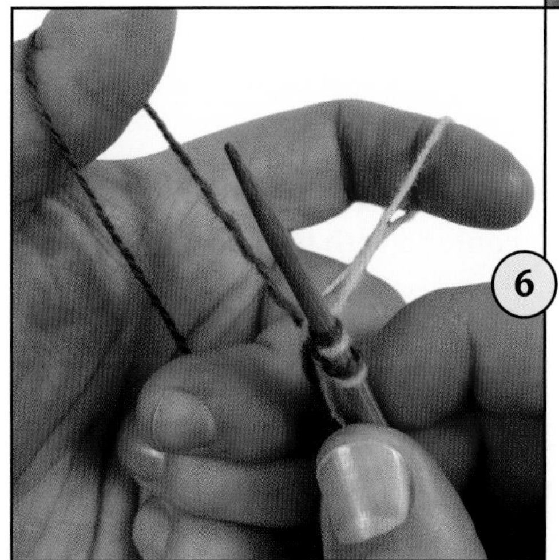

The new stitch should be the opposite color from the one created in the first move. With it on your needle, drop the finger loop and tighten. Reposition your hands to prepare for the next move. Continue alternating the first and second moves as dictated by the pattern.

An invisible double-knit cast-on alternative

This cast-on is called the Italian two-color cast-on. It's "invisible" in the sense that the edge looks like a Kitchener stitch, as if the two layers of the fabric were seamed together. The edge is very stretchy, and also much harder to make look perfectly clean. The technique is elegant in its way, but it doesn't fit my definition of an "elegant solution" as it fails in both simplicity and repeatability. Still, if the invisible edge is important to you, practice this well and you will get better at it, just like anything else. There is a corresponding bind-off on page 38.

The setup is the same as for the standard double-knit cast-on on page 28, but when you spread your fingers apart, instead of pulling the yarn into a Y shape, let the Y open into a diamond shape. You don't need to drop your finger or thumb loop at any point. The hand is mostly there to create tension on the two strands.

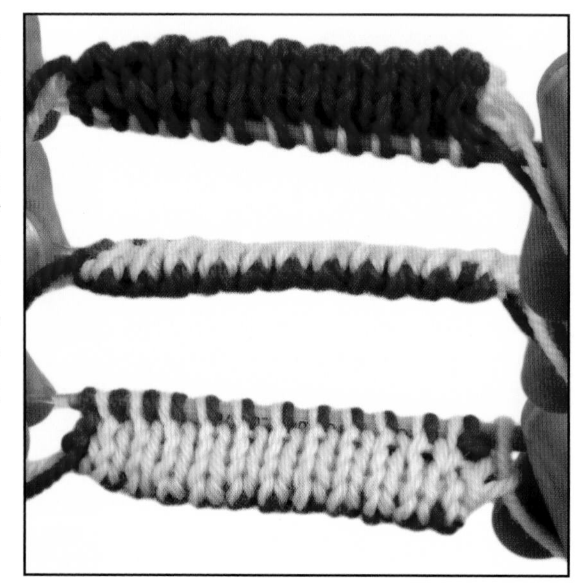

Like the previous cast-on, this one consists of two moves that are alternated. Unlike that cast-on, you have only two strands to contend with instead of four.

Start with your needle at the front and bring it underneath the front strand, then over the top of the rear strand.

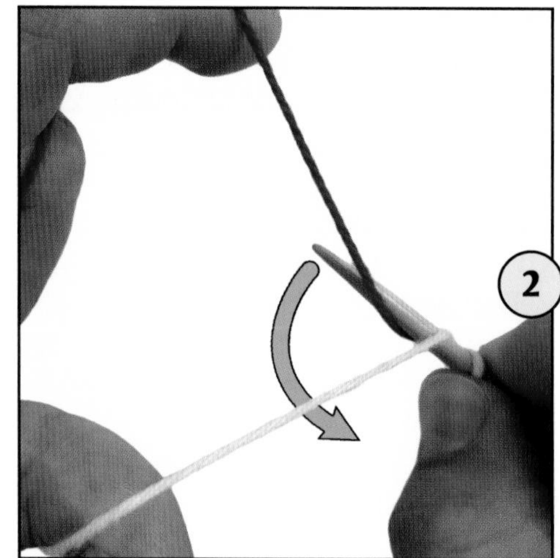

Catching the rear strand, bring your needle under the front strand again and to the front of the work.

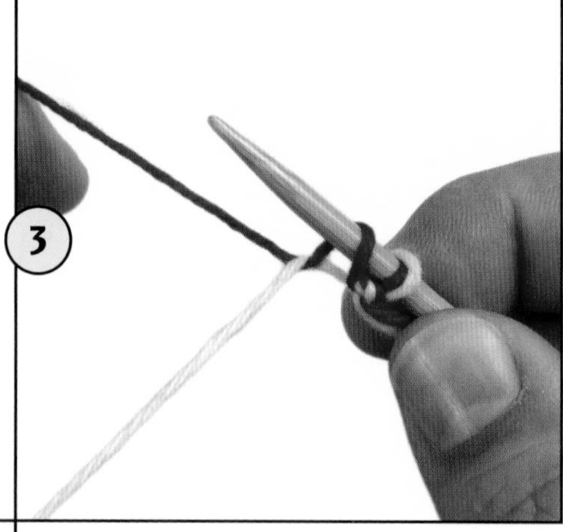

You've created a stitch in the color of your rear strand. As you can see, it's not very stable, so tighten it to snug it up against the rest of the cast-on and proceed to the next move.

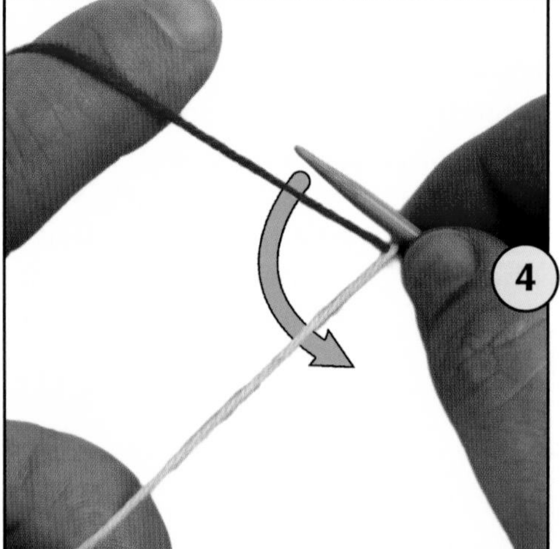

Hold the previous stitch in place until the next one is done.

For the second move, bring your needle behind both strands, then underneath both to come out at the front.

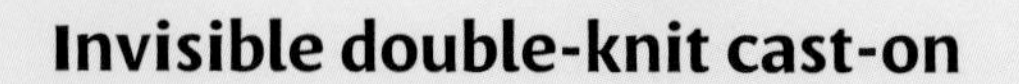

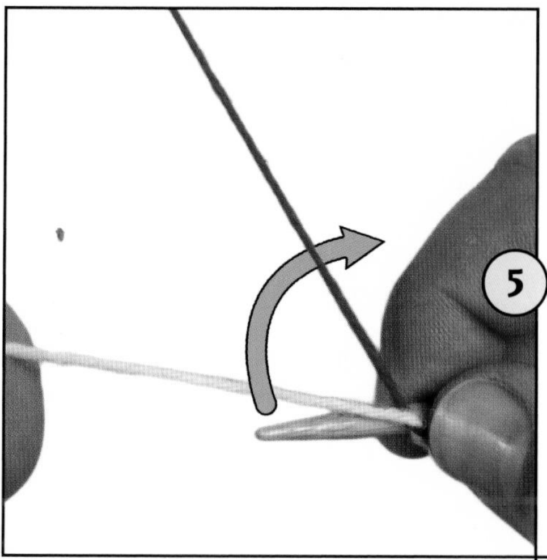

Bring the needle over the top of the front strand (catching the front strand on the needle) and underneath the rear strand, ending at the back of the work.

You've created a stitch in the color of your front strand. Tighten this up as well; hold this stitch in place until the next stitch is done.

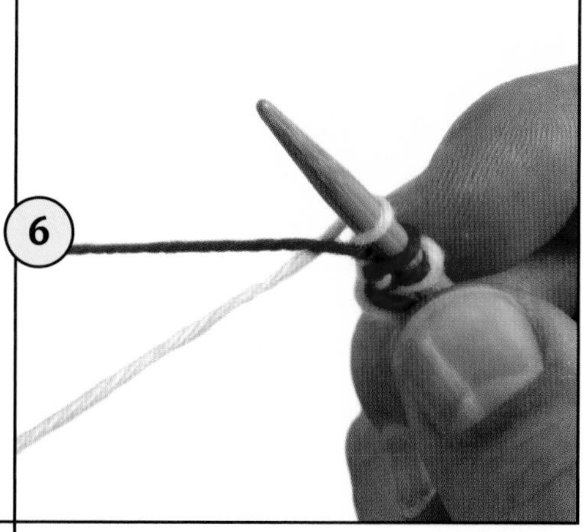

If you continue alternating the moves, you'll get a cast-on with alternating colors.

Because this cast-on is not as stable, you will need to be careful, especially at the beginning and end of the first row. At the beginning, make sure you twist the two ends together to make sure that they are linked together before you do the knit stitch. This is similar to a linked pair but it's not as much about making sure the layers don't separate as it is about keeping the first loose stitches secure. At the end of the first row, work the last pair rather than slipping it. Rows beyond the first row can be treated as normal.

An invisible double-knit cast-on variation

One of the perks of the Italian two-color cast-on is that it can be worked in pattern with very little consequence in flexibility or fluidity. If you're casting on for a flat piece, you're going to be casting on the pairs as if from Layer 2 — opposite color order and opposite direction. Keeping that in mind, begin casting on the same way you would for a normal invisible double-knit cast-on. When you want to make a color change, untwist your ends (clockwise) and switch fingers. This will cause the previous stitch to come loose on the working needle; just hold it in place until you've done the next stitch. You can make the color change counterclockwise instead, but this tends to make a lump in the edge at every color change, whereas my suggested method is totally smooth.

Unfortunately, there is currently no corresponding in-pattern bind-off, since the invisible bind-off uses only one strand (and thus one color).

When I call for a cast-on, I'll specify the number and color order of the pairs you'll need. For example, if the cast-on calls for BA pairs, follow either cast-on with Color B over your finger and Color A over your thumb. When the work is turned to begin the first row, they become AB pairs. If the project was worked in the round using the same chart, the pattern would instead call for AB pairs.

Double-knitting Side Edges

Now that you've finished your cast-on, you're almost ready to start double-knitting. But if you're working flat, you're also going to need to consider your side edges. These edges can perform a few functions but the most common in double-knitting is to keep the layers of your work linked together. If you leave the sides open, the edges may curl inside and, depending on the pattern you're working, the edge will remain open until the first color change.

A clean, finished-looking side edge is a real delight, and it is one of the things that gets commented on time and time again when I show my finished work. There are a multitude of edge solutions available for double-knitting — perhaps not as many as there are cast-ons, but if you've spent time looking at double-knit scarves, hot pads, etc., you may have seen some. One of the more common ones is a marled edge, created by simply working the last (and/or first) pair with both yarns held together. While this will lock the edge together, it's not an elegant solution because it lacks attractiveness. I'd like to present a few edges here that I think come closer to the requisite elegance, along with their uses, pros and cons.

These edges work by judicious application of two non-standard ways of processing a pair: a linked pair and a slipped pair, charted with a + and a ∇, respectively. In *Extreme Double-Knitting*, I used some more questionable notation and also had a third non-standard pair which was an "open pair." However, all pairs are open by default, so this proves unnecessary with my current notation.

A **linked pair** can be worked in a number of ways, but I find the one that is most elegant is to maintain the process for working any other pair but to twist the ends together between the stitches. Technically, this twist can be done while working either the knit or the purl with identical results, so I think it's easier to do it on the purl since your ends are on the front of the work and more easily seen. While it doesn't really matter in which direction you twist (the function of the twist is all that really matters) the most elegant solution has the efficiency of using the smallest effective amount of twist. Any more is both inelegant and unnecessary, not to mention prone to creating a lumpy edge.

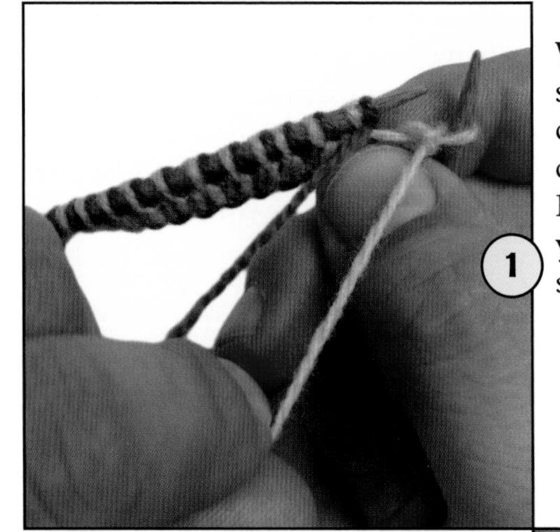

With yarns in back, knit the first stitch in the color indicated by the chart (most often it will match the color into which you are knitting). Bring the yarns to the front. Here you can see that the two ends are still separate.

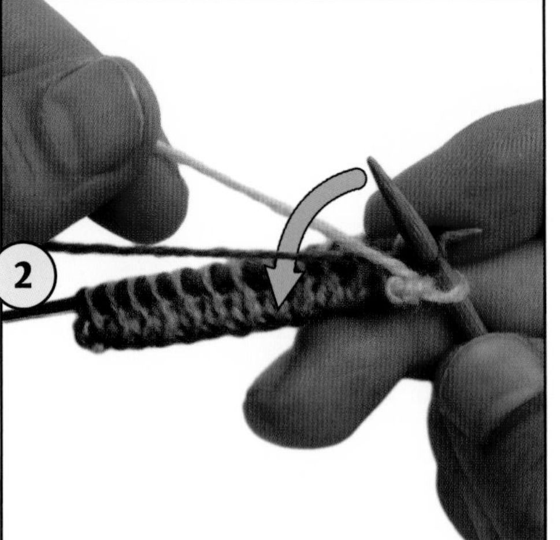

Insert your needle purlwise into the next stitch and finish the purl with the opposite color from the one you knit with, being careful to take the end from over the top of the other end. Note the crossing of the ends near the base of the needle.

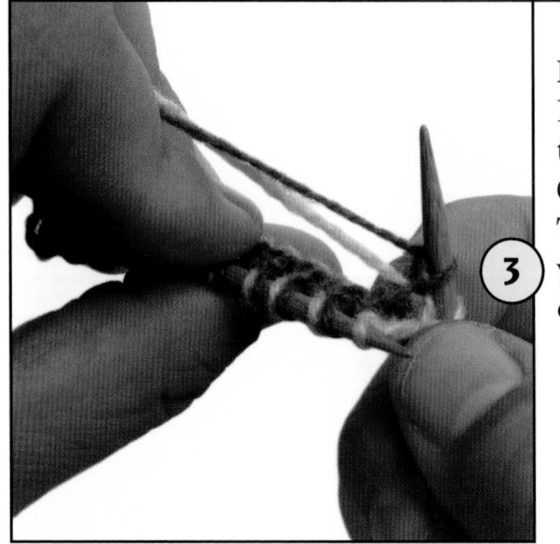

Here's the completed linked pair. I've stretched it out a bit; note how the Color A end crosses underneath Color B just below the purl stitch. This is the link; if this is present, you've succeeded in linking your edges together.

Linked pair

When worked as part of an edge, this creates a link between the "wrong sides" that face each other inside the work, but which is not otherwise visible. If too much twist is incorporated, the link will bulge and may create an unattractive protrusion either from your edge or between your pairs. When worked in the middle of a fabric, this is generally considered an error, since the result is that you'll end up seeing a "blip" of incorrect color in between stitches in an otherwise clear field. However, even in the middle of the fabric it will link the two layers together without a color change, so that could be useful if the side effects are less important to you.

A **slipped pair** is much simpler, and it works in more or less the way you'd imagine. Slipped pairs appear longer because they extend a pair from the row below into the next row. However, much like slipped stitches in single-layer knitting, they must be used with care. It's usually best not to slip the same pair in multiple rows because there's only so far you can stretch a loop that was not originally prepared for such use. For this reason, you'll normally see slipped pairs alternating either with standard pairs or linked pairs.

As you can see, all you're doing here is moving the yarn back and forth in the same way you would if you were working the pair normally, but instead of knitting and purling, you're slipping both stitches. The result is that the yarn travels unused between the layers. The most common use for this type of pair is as part of the selvedge in a flat double-knitted piece, but as you'll see later there are some other interesting uses for it.

At the end of your row (or wherever this move is called for), bring both yarns to the back and slip the first stitch purlwise.

Bring both yarns forward and slip the other stitch purlwise.

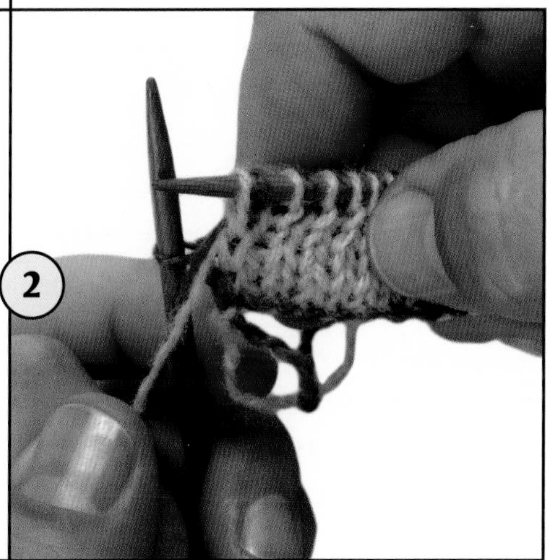

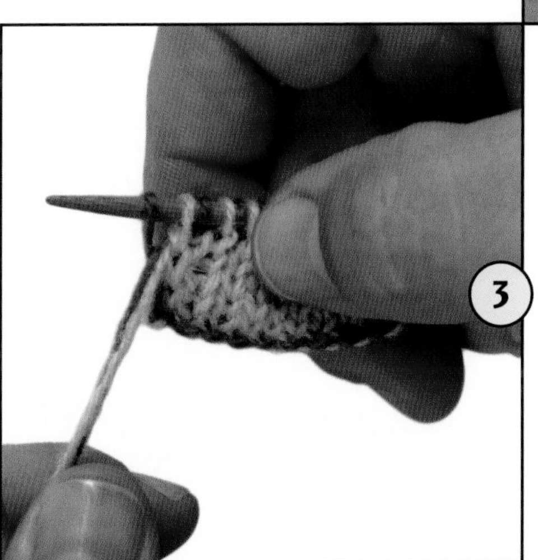

When the slipped pair is done, you'll notice that the ends appear to come out between the two stitches of the pair that was slipped.

Rustle of Leaves, page 112

These side edge solutions use existing techniques, including the linked and slipped pairs from the previous page, in various combinations to achieve particular goals. Depending on what you're aiming for, you can use the edge called for in the pattern, or substitute your own.

Linked double-knit edge

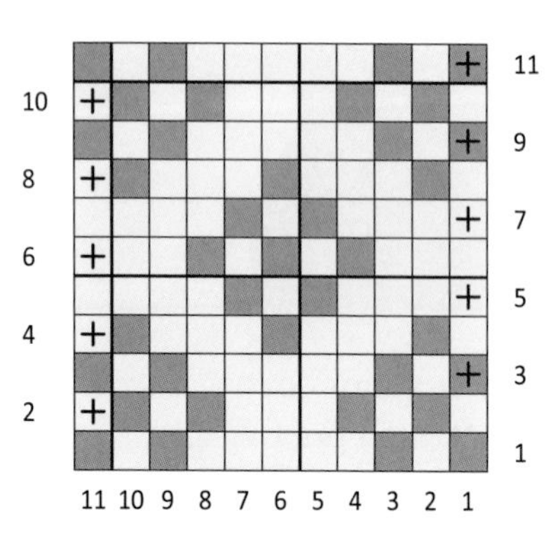

With this edge, it's possible to work your pattern all the way to the edge. However, the side effect is that the edge is much more difficult to keep clean; little issues with tension can become much more visible as the stitches are pulled in "unnatural" directions. But if it's important that your pattern has no visible side edge column, this is the edge to use. It will take longer to make it look clean, but as with anything else, practice makes perfect.

A linked edge is very easy to work. Simply work the first pair in every row as a linked pair, and work the rest of the pairs as charted. The linked pair can even be color-changed if the chart indicates that. While working this, periodically tug the two sides of the fabric near the edge to make sure that the links are working. If they're regularly not working and you can't figure out why, perhaps try the color-changed double-knit selvedge below. If there are periodic missing links (ha ha), you can seam up the holes after the fact.

If there is a color change at the edge of the work, a linked pair is not usually needed; the color change itself performs a similar function. However, for ease of illustration, the example above has linked pairs in all the possible locations.

Linked double-knit selvedge

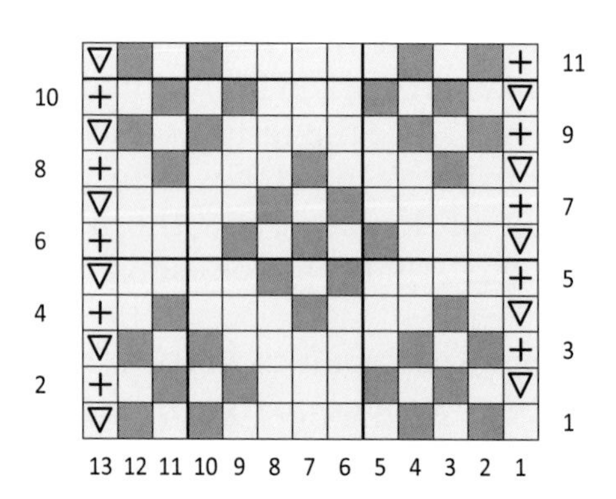

This is the edge I use most commonly in my flat double-knit projects. The combination of linked pairs and slipped pairs makes the edge very clean, tends to alleviate some tension issues, and the small bump created by the link is pulled one pair further inside, minimizing the possibility that it will be visible (as can more easily happen with the previous edge). Because this uses slipped pairs, the edge is not usually color-changed and it's usually best to add two extra pairs to your cast-on so the edges can be worked without interfering with your colorwork.

A linked selvedge is also easy to work, but requires a bit more attention to detail. The second row (and all subsequent rows) are worked slightly differently from the first:

1. Work the first pair as a normal (unlinked) pair. Continue your chart until you have one pair left on the needle.
2. Work the last pair in the row as a slipped pair. Turn the work.
3. Work the first pair as a linked pair with the knit through the back of the loop. Continue your chart until you have one pair left on the needle; slip as in Step 2 and turn.
4. Repeat Step 3 until you reach the end of the pattern.

The linked pair is processed differently when done in conjunction with a slipped pair so as to preserve the natural seating of the selvedge stitches. If you work the linked pairs all normally, one layer of each of your linked selvedges will be made up entirely of twisted stitches. This is not necessarily a major problem, but it can be fixed in the interest of an elegant solution.

As with the other linked edge, test periodically to make sure that all links are intact. The more you do this, the easier it will be for you to tell when a link is properly formed as you form it, and less error-checking will be necessary.

One thing you might notice is the predilection for double-knit selvedges to show a little bit of the other layer's edge color along the left edge of the work. This isn't exactly "by design," but it is an artifact of the structure of double-knitting. Since the two layers are not precisely lined up one on top of the other, but are offset by a half-stitch from each other (in the same direction as the loops on your needle, as a matter of fact), the back layer of the work will always be offset by half a stitch from the front, regardless of which layer is facing you. There will always be a little bit of the other color peeking around the corner. This is most pronounced in the linked and open selvedges but will happen on any edge.

The last two side edges can be worked either as standard edges or selvedges, but I recommend and prefer selvedges when practical.

Color-changed double-knit selvedge

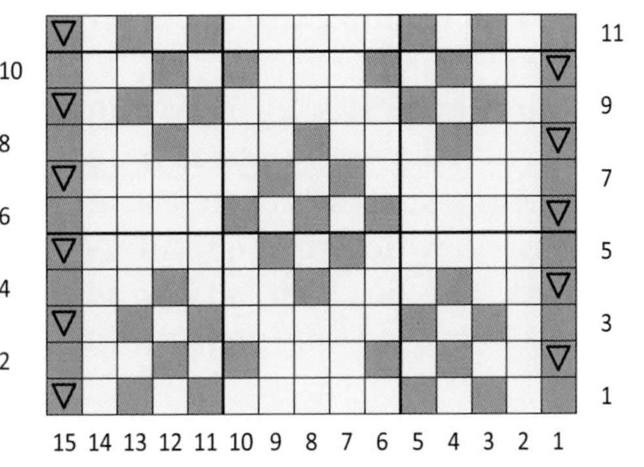

If the linked pairs are proving difficult for any reason, you can consider this selvedge, which uses the natural linking mechanism of color changes. In this method, you could set up the cast-on the same way as with your linked double-knit selvedge (with two extra pairs) and then change the colors of the first and last pairs in the row. However, because you can only change the edge pairs' color order when working the first pair (the last slipped pair can't be color changed since it's not worked), I recommend a more elegant solution that involves a little more preparation:

1. Cast on the appropriate number plus four more pairs, all in the opposite color from what the pattern calls for.
2. Work your first pair as normal, then begin following your pattern.
3. Work a slipped pair at the end. It should be the same color order as the first pair.
4. As you work your edges, remember to always match the color order from the row below before beginning your pattern.

This will create an opposite-color border around three edges of your work. With some judicious color-changing in the bind-off, you can complete the border on the fourth edge.

Open double-knit selvedge

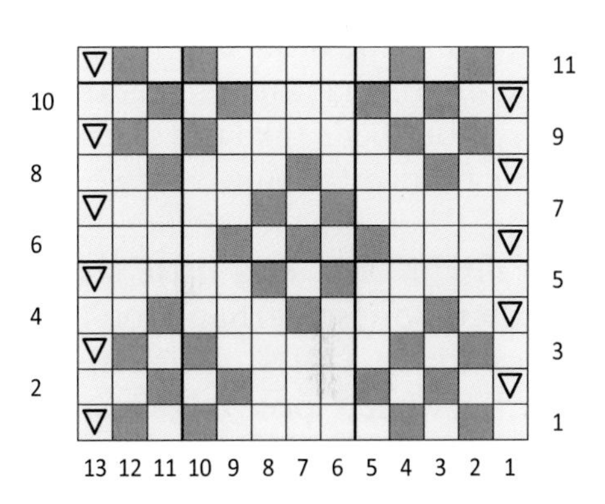

This is generally to be avoided, but there are reasons why you might want access to the inside of your work after you're done. Generally, once you've done whatever you're planning to do with it, you'll have to seam up the edge as well — but we'll cover that later (see page 73).

To keep your edge open, all you have to do is not work linked pairs. Instead of working the first pair with a twist, simply work it as a normal pair. At the end of each row, I recommend you slip the last pair for the sake of cleanliness. If it's important that the whole edge remains open, this is also a place where you should periodically check the edge to make sure no links show up. While you can cut them, it's not a good idea for the same reason it's not a good idea to steek without seaming first. Unfortunately, there is no easy solution to a link in the middle of an open edge; you'll just need to undo your work back to that point and make sure the edge is not linked when you do it a second time.

Double-knitting Bind-offs

There are three bind-offs I typically use in double-knitting, each with its pros and cons. If a bind-off appears in a chart (generally only for a bind-off within a row), it'll use a ✕ symbol.

Standard double-knit bind-off

The first is the most common, the easiest to do, and it (somewhat) resembles the standard double-knit cast-on. This bind-off also causes real excitement in my classes because of its implications for single-layer bind-offs.

The issue with bind-offs in general (and double-knitting bind-offs in particular) is that there's a tendency toward over- or under-compensating for tension. Let's take the simplest bind-off you know as a case example. In this bind-off, you work two stitches, then pull one over and off your needle. Then you K1, PSSO, K1, PSSO, etc. Every time you PSSO, that loop might take up a little slack from the next stitch and can tend to lengthen a bit, so perhaps you'll need to pull the yarn to tighten it before you continue. Unless your tension is 100% perfect, you're likely to end up with either a loose edge from undercompensating or a too-tight edge from overcompensating for the looser PSSO loops.

Unlike single-layer knitting where the PSSO loop is somewhat locked in place by the stitch worked directly after it, in double-knitting the two stitches are actually both live stitches, with nothing but the active yarn coming off them. The lengthening and tightening are more prevalent, but there is an elegant solution. This method is actually split into two distinct parts that are most often worked together (but not always).

The first part is a **prep row or round**.

1. Work one more row or round entirely in the same color order as the first pair in that row/round, or as the pattern indicates. If working flat with a selvedge, work the last pair instead of slipping.
2. If you're working flat on circular needles or DPNs, slide your work to the other end of the needle and then turn. If you're working on straight needles, turn and slip all stitches (purlwise) to another needle. If you're working in the round, just continue.

You should now have the working needle pointing out of the "wrong" edge of the work (unless you're working in the round). The second part is a **slipped bind-off**.

1. Slip 1 stitch knitwise. Slip 1 stitch purlwise, then PSSO.
2. Slip 1 stitch knitwise, PSSO; slip 1 stitch purlwise, PSSO.
3. Repeat Steps 1 and 2 until one pair is left on the needle. Break both ends; pass them together through both loops and tighten.

Here, instead of binding off as you work the row, work the whole row first. Then go back to the beginning and bind off, making sure to slip your knits knitwise and your purls purlwise. Because each stitch is already anchored in place by the stitches on either side of it and set at a specific gauge by the needle it was worked on, the loops don't change shape and the resulting bind-off is clean — not to mention about the same flexibility as the cast-on. By the way, this will also work with single-layer knitting!

If you find that this bind-off is still too loose, take it out and work the last row again with a smaller needle. If it's too tight, try a larger needle.

Kihnu Troi double-knit bind-off

This bind-off was used in a couple of places in *Extreme Double-Knitting*, and while I haven't used it here and don't use it frequently, it's worth mentioning since it's quite attractive. There is something called a Kihnu Troi cast on which gives a similar edge and alternating color stitches when finished. The bind-off version is a simple modification of the standard double-knit bind-off (see a photo of it, borrowed from *EDK*, on the next page).

1. Work the prep row/round from the standard double-knit bind-off.
2. Slip 3 stitches knitwise, purlwise, and knitwise respectively. Pass the first stitch over the next two and off the needle.
3. Slip 1 stitch purlwise; pass the first stitch over the next two and off.
4. Slip 1 stitch knitwise; pass the first stitch over the next two and off.
5. Continue alternating Steps 3 and 4 until you have two stitches left on the needle. Break both ends, pass together through both loops and tighten.

This bind-off is much less flexible than the previous one, so if you want more flexibility, I recommend you work it with a slightly larger needle.

The “row-below” phenomenon

All techniques, whether in single-layer or double-knitting, fall into one of two categories: techniques that operate on the current row or on the row below. The category into which a technique falls has some profound and unexpected effects on the reading of charts and the appearance of colorwork.

The basic knit and purl stitches are current-row techniques, as are yarn-overs and M1 increases. These stitches are worked directly from the source needle to the working needle, without any prior preparation.

Lifted increases, decreases, and cables are all row-below techniques. Most of these require some reordering of stitches on the source needle before a new set of stitches or pairs can be worked on top of them. Lifted increases are a little more directly row-below techniques, as evidenced by the fact that you specifically work into a stitch from one or more rows below the one on your source needle.

The important thing to remember about row-below techniques is that they don’t actually appear in the knitting in the same place they appear in the chart. The most pronounced example is cabled knitting. When you encounter a cable technique in a chart, you do some moves to reorder the stitches on the source needle so that they cross over each other, then you work a regular set of stitches across that set of reordered stitches in order to lock it in place. The result of this is that the actual cable twist shows up one row below the place where it shows up in the chart. The same is true for decreases (which also require a reordering of stitches on the source needle), and lifted increases, which don’t need reordering, but do require counting one stitch down from the source needle.

Kihnu Troi double-knit bind-off, page 36

Craftstory, continued from page 17

That’s about as far as I go with my story for most people. But for those who persevere, I’ll elaborate. Let’s start at the beginning.

My parents met in India. My father was a Near-East language scholar, traveling around the subcontinent, learning languages and taking photographs. My mother was (and still is) an ethnomusicologist, and was in India to do research for her dissertation on the music of the Indian courtesans. I was almost but not quite born in India, due to my mother’s mistrust of the hospital system there at the time. Instead, I was born in Western Massachusetts, but my parents moved to Vermont (where I acquired my earliest memories) shortly after that. My sister was born a year and a half later; a year and a half after that, my parents split up (which is, incidentally, where I got this hyphenated last name).

My father is now one of the world’s most sought-after makers of the uilleann bagpipes, and he began his infatuation with that pursuit in the same year I was born. There is probably a set of his pipes somewhere that is the same age as I am. It probably doesn’t work as well as I do. Like me, he was not trained to do what he ended up doing, but through a combination of innate woodworking skill and sheer obsessiveness, he developed his own style, built his own tools, and continued to refine his craft until he became one of the best in the world at what he does. His waiting list is years long.

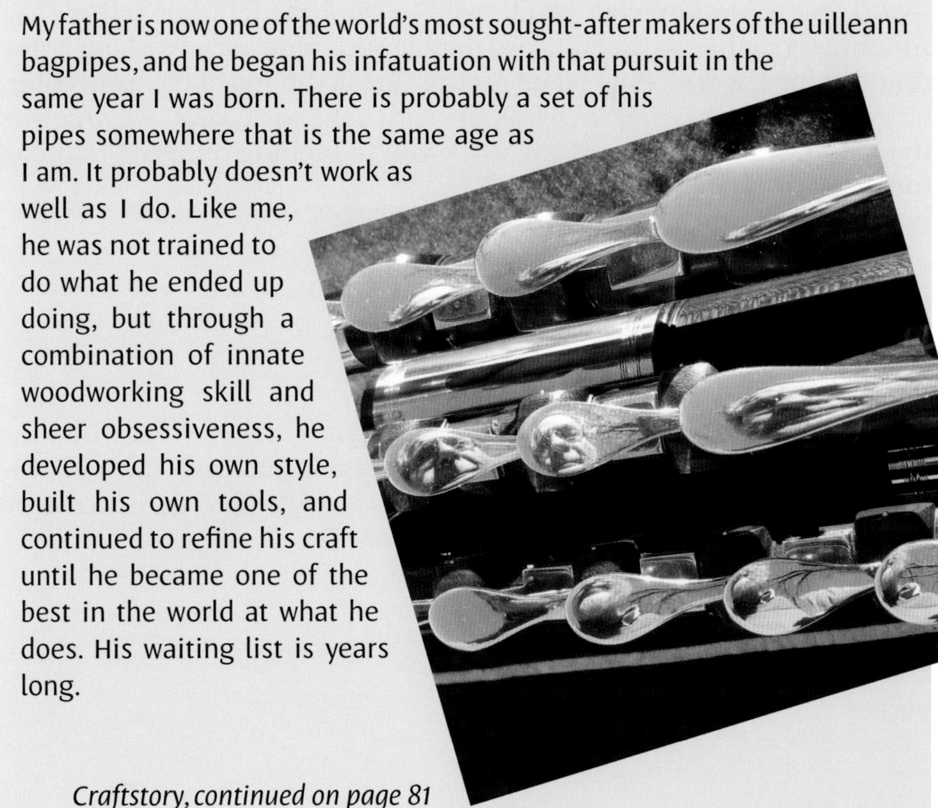

Craftstory, continued on page 81

Invisible double-knit bind-off

For those who prefer the invisible double-knit cast-on, you're probably hoping for a suitable bind-off. There is one, but it's not the easiest to achieve. You may already be aware of the Kitchener stitch; that's the cleanest way to get an invisible bind-off. However, there is no shortcut to perfect tension in Kitchener like there is for the previous bind-off.

Fortunately, even if the invisible bind-off is lacking repeatability (i.e., without practice it won't look clean) I have a way to give it simplicity and purity, at least. Normally, Kitchener stitching is done between two pieces of knitting on separate needles. When done, the two pieces are nicely attached in a near-seamless appearance. In double-knitting, Kitchener stitch can be done directly off the needle without separating the layers onto two needles, and the resulting edge (if done well) is quite attractive.

Begin with a row that's made up entirely of active loops. This means that if you're working flat, you'll need to work the last pair rather than slipping it (similar to the standard double-knit bind-off). Working in the round, your row is already set up for this. Break the end of the front color, leaving enough to weave in. Break the end of the back color, leaving 3-4x the width/circumference of the work you're binding off. Feed that end into a tapestry needle, then:

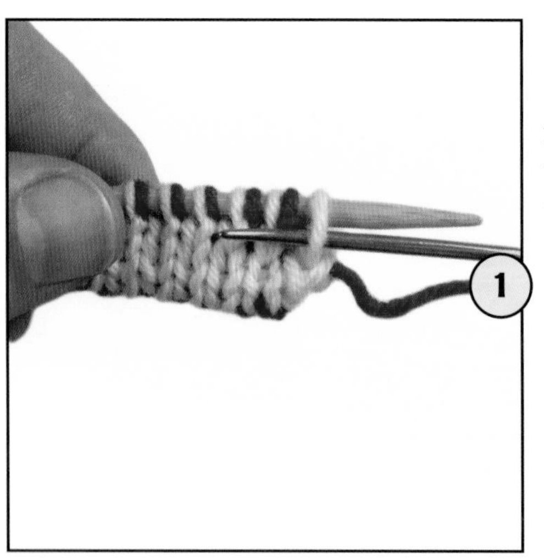

Insert the tapestry needle into the first stitch purlwise and pull the yarn through, leaving the stitch on the needle.

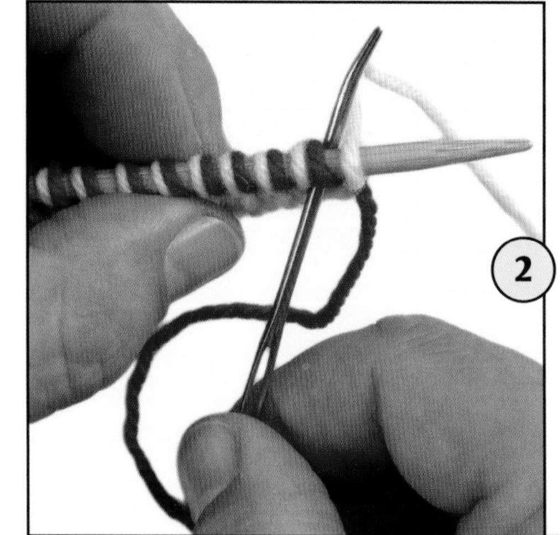

Insert the tapestry needle into the second stitch knitwise, letting the needle tip pass from front to back. Pull the yarn through, leaving the stitch on the needle.

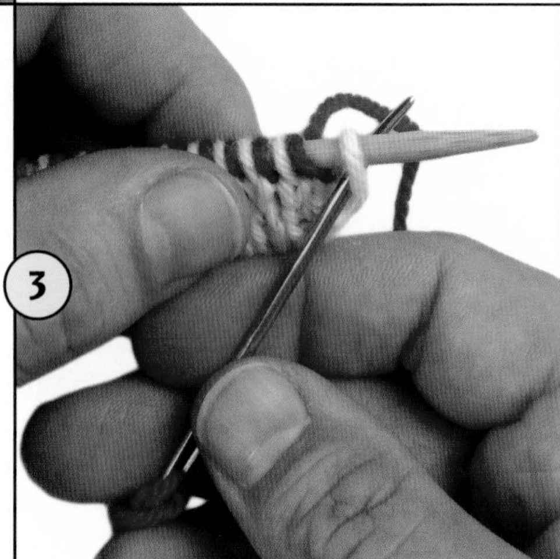

Insert the needle into the first stitch knitwise; pull it through, and let the stitch drop from the needle.

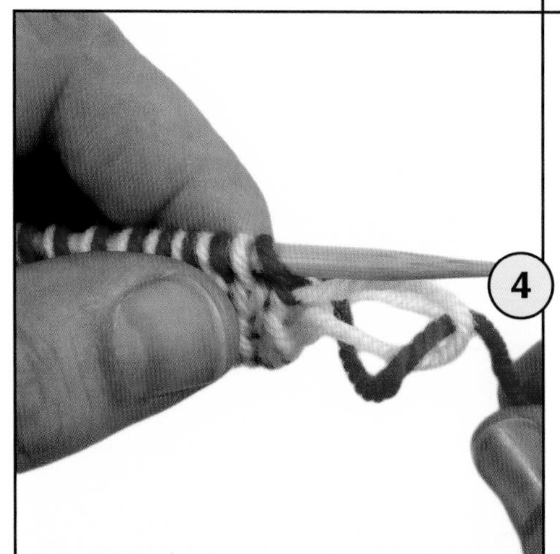

This first stitch that's dropped from the needle is a live stitch and will probably elongate somewhat when you let it drop. Carefully pull on the end to tighten it up, but not too much.

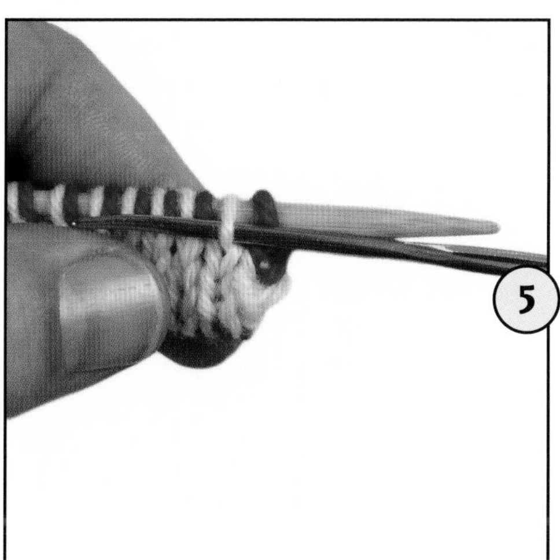

Insert the needle into the second stitch purlwise; pull it through, leaving the stitch on the needle.

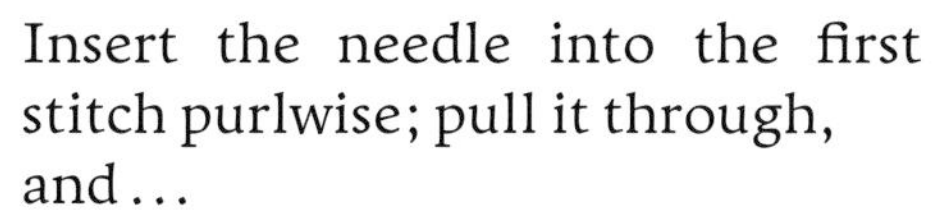

Insert the needle into the first stitch purlwise; pull it through, and . . .

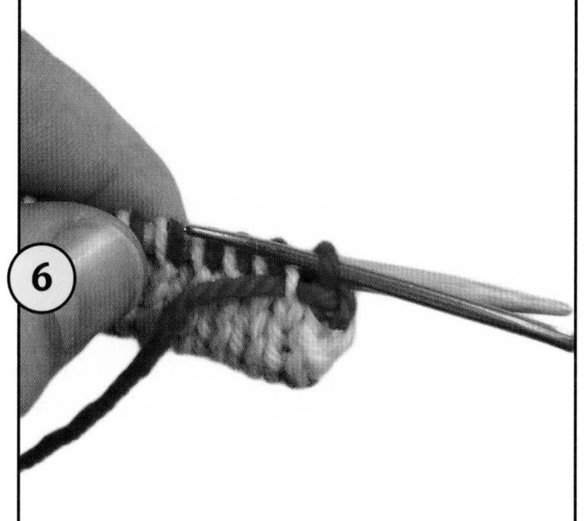

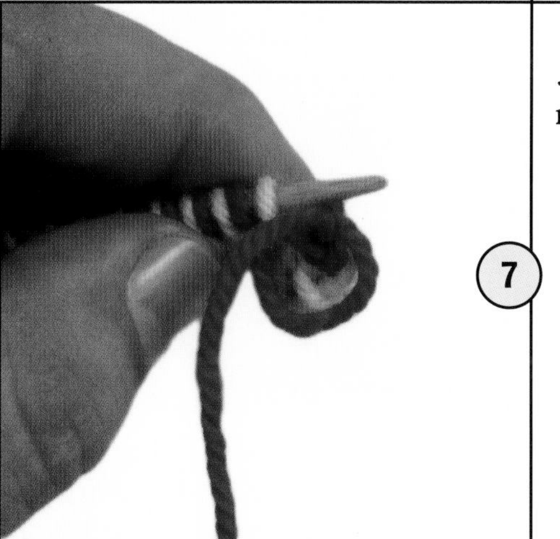

. . . let the stitch drop from the needle.

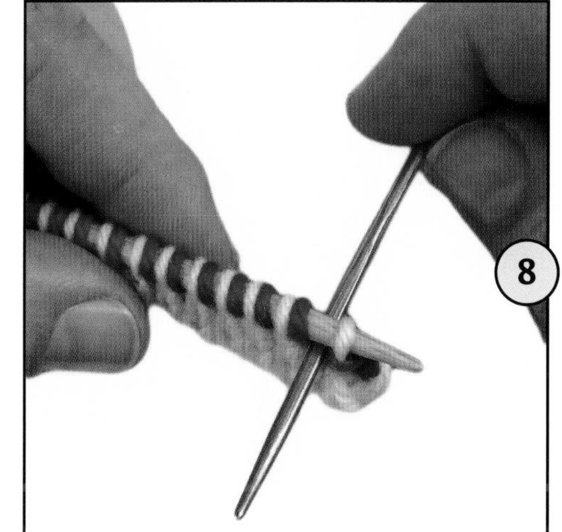

From the back, insert the needle between the first and second stitches and pull through to the front.

Insert the tapestry needle into the second stitch knitwise, letting the needle tip pass from front to back. Pull the yarn through, leaving the stitch on the needle.

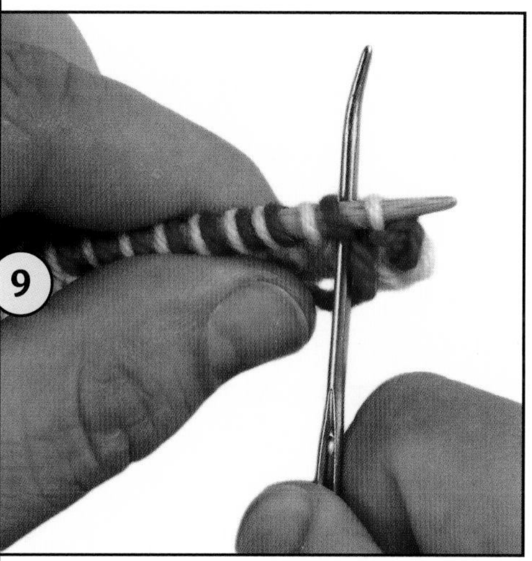

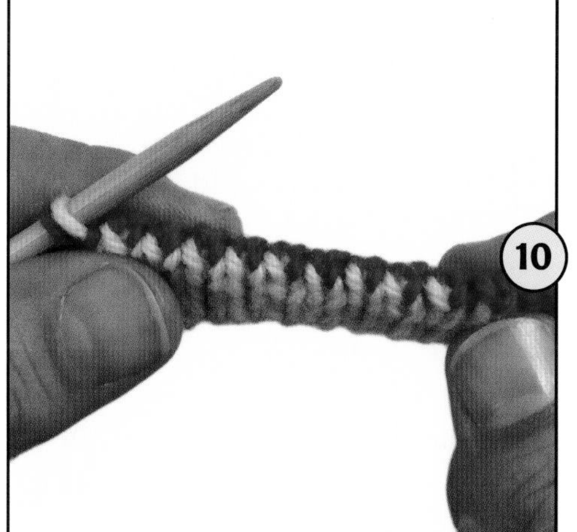

Repeat steps 3-9 until there are 2 stitches left on the needle.

To complete the bind-off, work the first of these stitches as in Step 3, and the final stitch as in Step 6.

EXERCISE: Flat Double-knitting

This book assumes some prior knowledge of double-knitting, and seeks to firm up and expand your existing knowledge. But if you're a little rusty and need a bit of practice before jumping into the larger projects, here's a little exercise similar to the one I use in my introductory classes.

Chart

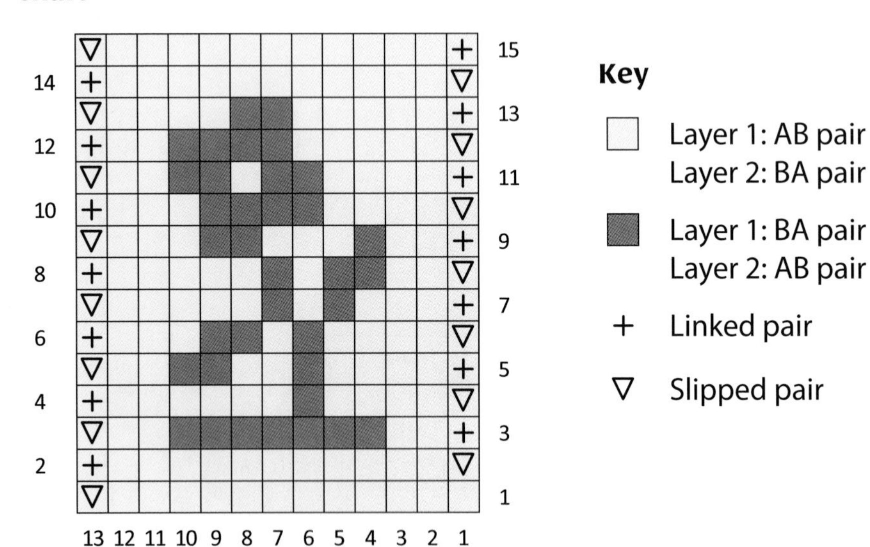

Instructions

With 2 well-contrasting colors designated Color A and Color B, cast on 13 BA pairs using the cast-on method on page 28.

Turn and follow the chart and key above, working linked and slipped pairs where charted. Linked and slipped pairs are explained in detail on pages 32-33.

When done with row 15, turn and work the bind-off as described on page 36. Weave in your ends (see page 27) and enjoy!

If you want to use one of the other cast-ons, side edge solutions, or bind-offs here instead, feel free to experiment.

Troubleshooting your Double-knitting

Bars

A bar across one face of your work means that you didn't move both yarns forward or back. The bar is actually the normal one that travels between two stitches, except that instead of traveling cleanly from one stitch to the next, it's now wrapped around to the other layer of the work. If you are a continental knitter or use the Norwegian purl, there are simple ways to keep this from happening (see pages 22 & 24). If not, you'll just need to be careful that when you bring one yarn forward or back, the other one comes with it.

If you find a bar in your work that's only one row below your current row, you can probably fix it on the fly by simply pulling it over its corresponding stitch to the other side of the work. If it's several rows down, you can do the same thing but it will require laddering down.

Twists

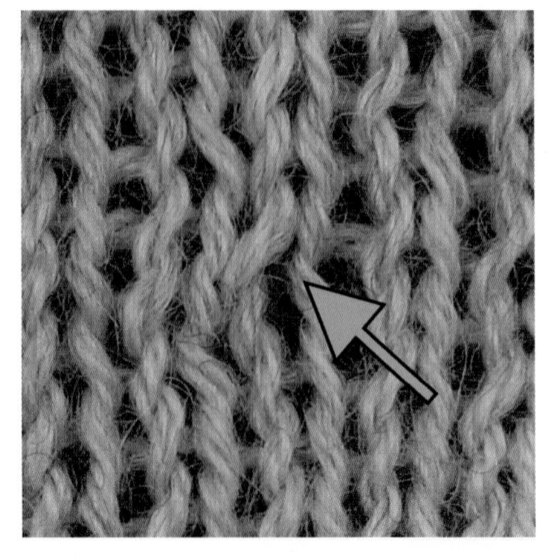

A twist occurs when the yarn ends rotate a full 360 degrees (or more) around each other between two stitches, either within a pair or between two pairs. It's visible due to a little "blip" of the opposite color between two stitches of the same color and may or may not be visible in the same location on the other layer. A twist of 540 degrees (360 + 180) at a color change will cause a similar issue. And a twist of 720 degrees or more between two pairs of the same color order will not only be very visible, it will cause a lump in your work. If your yarn ends are twisted around each other, make sure the twist is pushed well away from the needles. To get rid of the twist and/or keep it from happening, see the section on End Management (page 28).

Wrong colors in a row below

If you notice a color change was missed or incorrectly placed in a row below, you have a few options.

If it's in the row directly below and you've noticed it before putting a new pair on top of it, check to see if the pair is still in AB or BA color order. If an incorrect knit color was used and followed up with the opposite purl color, there is a quick way to switch the color order of that pair; see **Fixing a mistake in the row below** on page 42.

If you see an incorrect color further down in your work, you can rip back to that point. However, if it's a long way back, or you're not confident enough to rip back in double-knitting, you can consider duplicate stitching as an alternative. If this still doesn't float your boat, you can ladder down (again, this only applies if the pair needing to be changed is incorrect on both layers).

Laddering in double-knitting requires a technique called the **vertical lifeline**. To do it, you're going to need a piece of waste yarn at least twice as long as the vertical distance you need to travel, a tapestry needle, and a crochet hook. See page 44 for step-by-step instructions.

This technique was coined by Nathan Taylor, aka Sockmatician, who once found a mistake some 300+ rows down in a scarf and ran a vertical lifeline to keep from messing up the column above it. I personally probably would have just used a duplicate stitch, but this is worth knowing about even if you don't go to quite the same extreme as Nathan.

In either of these cases, if the pair consists of two of one color (color order AA or BB, for example), you will not be able to fix this. There's not enough slack on the unused color and too much slack on the color used twice. You'll need to undo your work back to that point and fix the pair.

Undoing your work

Eventually you will find that there is a mistake somewhere in your work that is too far back to fix on the fly and/or too egregious to ignore. There are two main methods of undoing your double-knitting: un-knitting (commonly called "tinking") and ripping back (commonly called "frogging"). I have a couple of tips on both.

If the mistake is relatively recent, or the fabric is too complex for ripping back, you can un-knit your work stitch by stitch. Using your source needle, you can hold the stitch one below the previous stitch on your working needle as you pull the stitch out. However, you will need to make sure to move your ends backward and forward as you go to keep them from getting trapped. For standard double-knitting, you'll keep your ends in the front when you undo a purl and in the back when you undo a knit (the same way they're positioned when you make the stitches to begin with).

If the mistake is far back in your work, you can remove the needle and pull out the yarns. Since you'll have at least two ends to manage, try to keep one end from racing ahead of the other. If one goes further ahead, pull the other one for a bit until they match up. As you approach the row in which you plan to reinsert the needle, slow down. Rip back to one row/round before the row you need, then as you undo the last row, insert the needle into the newly-freed stitches a few at a time. This minimizes the chance that you will lose stitches. Also, don't worry about how the stitches are seated on the needle. It's more important that they get on the needle at all; seating can be fixed on the fly as you work the next row or round.

Lifelines are also possible in double-knitting, if a little finicky. This will make the process of ripping back much more pleasant and manageable, since you can just rip back to the lifeline, and then reinsert your needle along the line. I usually use dental floss for this. If you are working in a pattern that uses increases and decreases, make sure you run your lifeline on an increase/decrease row. The row after it will be a little annoying to work as you finagle the lifeline around the stitches and the needles, but not nearly as annoying as attempting to do increases and decreases around a lifeline in the previous row.

In this sample from the exercise on page 40, in the just-completed row, you've forgotten to make the color-changed dot at the center of the flower. For the sake of argument, let's say you don't want to undo the last few pairs.

Instead, start the next row. When you encounter the pair that needs its color order switched, stop . . .

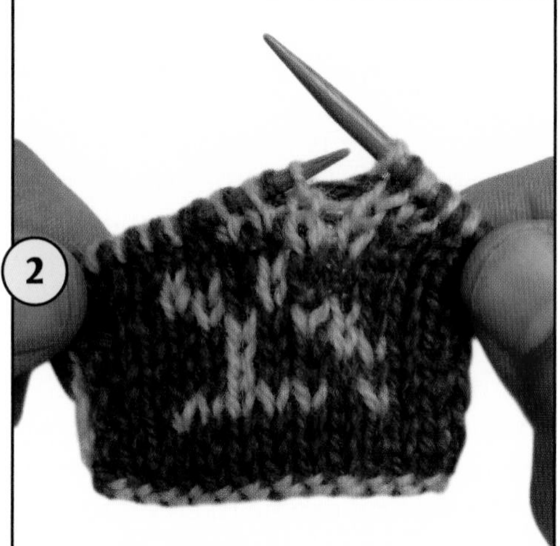

. . . and slip the first stitch onto the working needle.

Insert your source needle into the stitch below the stitch on your working needle from inside to outside . . .

. . . and drop the stitch off the working needle. Pass the held stitch from your source needle back to your working needle.

Now do the same thing for the other stitch in the pair: insert your working needle in the stitch below the next stitch on your source needle, from inside to outside . . .

… and drop the stitch off the source needle. Pass the held stitch from your working needle back to your source needle.

You now have two loose loops; the frontmost one was originally on the front of your work and the rearmost one was on the back. Now reach your working needle under the frontmost loop and over the top of the rearmost loop.

With a kind of scooping motion, pull the rearmost loop back through the other loop. To make sure this is done right, look at the way the resulting stitch is seated on the needle. If it's seated forward (right leg at the front), you did it right. If not, just fix the seating on the fly.

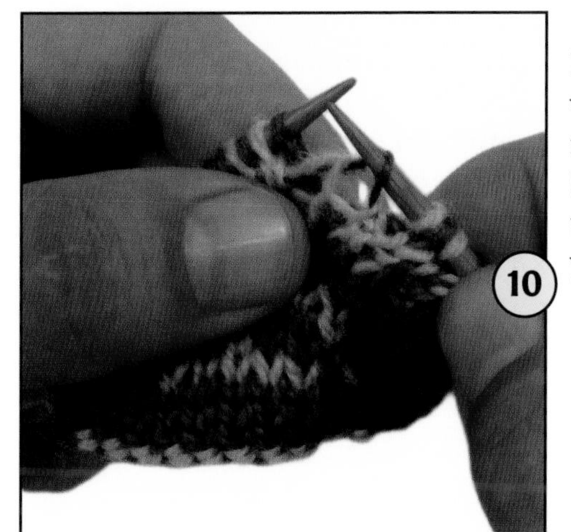

PSSO with the two stitches on the working needle, then use the source needle to pick up the remaining loop from inside to outside (check the seating as before to make sure you've done it right …

… and PSSO again with the two stitches on the source needle.

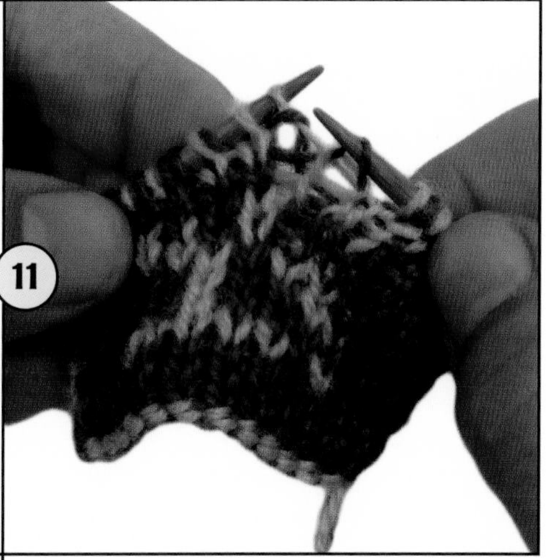

Slip the stitch back from the working needle to the source needle; your color change is now fixed. This photo shows the color change as viewed from Layer 1. In reality, you'll want to continue on with Layer 2 as you were working.

To fix a mistake that has gone unnoticed for several rows, you can ladder down before switching color orders. Here you can see a pair of the wrong color order in row 3, while we've just finished row 12.

Work or slip up to the column directly above the pair in need of fixing.

Drop the knit stitch of that pair only, leaving the purl on the needle. Begin laddering down (undoing each stitch) with a needle or crochet hook.

Continue undoing this column until you've undone the stitch on the front layer of the incorrect pair. The last loose loop at the bottom should be the knit stitch of the pair below the one that needs to be fixed.

Thread some waste yarn (somewhat longer than the vertical distance it has to travel, just to be safe) into a tapestry needle and insert the tapestry needle behind all of the loose loops. When you get to the loop that's going to be changed, skip over it and finish by inserting the needle into the last loose stitch at the bottom.

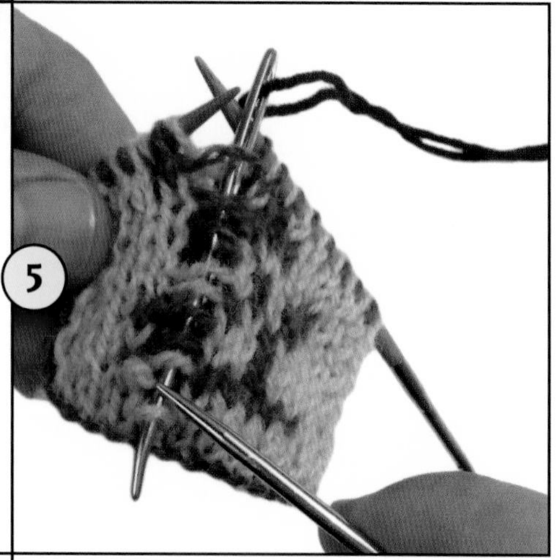

Pull the needle through and leave the waste yarn in its place, traveling vertically inside the work, behind all of the stitches except the one to be changed and through the last stitch. This is the vertical lifeline.

Now flip the work over. Drop the corresponding purl, and ladder that down as well. At the bottom, catch the last stitch on your crochet hook.

With your hook, reach inside and find the loop that you skipped over in Step 5, and pull that through the first loop.

9

Continue rebuilding the column using only loops on this side of the vertical lifeline. When you reach the top, put the last stitch back on the needle.

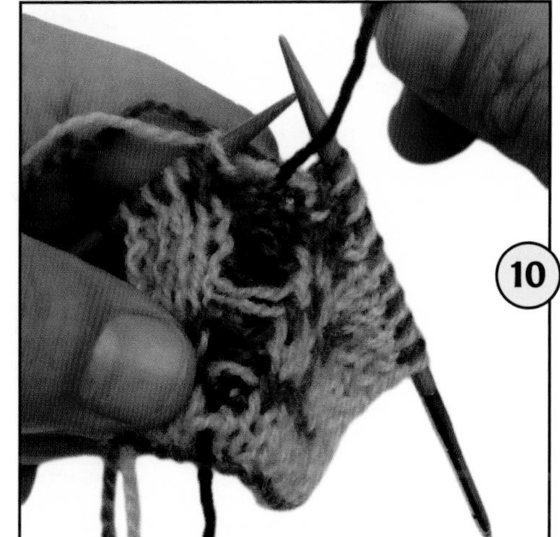

Turn the work over and remove the lifeline. Insert your crochet hook into the bottom stitch, finding the other loose loop from the other layer of the work and pulling that through to complete the color order repair.

Continue rebuilding this column using the remaining loose loops, and place the final stitch back on the needle.

Here's the work all done, as contrasted with Step 1. The mistake has now been fixed!

ABACISCUS

(ab-a-SIS-cus)

a large double-knit cowl with an unexpected twist

4 MEDIUM

Finished size & weight

As charted, this cowl is 42" around and 8-12" tall. At the largest size, the finished piece uses about 10.5 oz (658 yds) of yarn in total, so you'll have plenty of yarn left over — or you could make it bigger, I guess.

Theoretically, 3 repeats around would use 15.75 oz (986 yds) of yarn, which you'd still have enough to do. However, this would make the piece 63" around. If you want it smaller, one repeat would be 21" around but the repeat doesn't allow for more granular sizing so if you need it between sizes you'll need to change your needle size or yarn choice.

Materials & tools

[Color A]: Dirty Water Dyeworks Clara (100% Blue Faced Leicester wool; 550 yd/8.8 oz skein); Bluestone 238; 1 skein (or 2 skeins of Petite Clara).

[Color B]: Dirty Water Dyeworks Clara (100% Blue Faced Leicester wool; 550 yd/8.8 oz skein); Mauve 232; 1 skein (or 2 skeins of Petite Clara).

US 6/4.0 mm 40" circular needle or size required to achieve gauge.

Gauge in pattern

20 sts/25 rows = 4" in double-stockinette.

Sample knitted by Annie Webber

In *Extreme Double-Knitting*, I started off with two fairly large flat double-knit pieces — Corvus (a scarf made popular by its clean, elegant look) and Sierpinski (a baby blanket with a simple fractal pattern). The reason for such large pieces (rather than, say, a potholder) was to establish muscle memory through repetition so that future pieces would be easier. The more repetition, the stronger the memory. A scarf and a baby blanket in worsted-weight yarn require manageable but significant amounts of double-knitting. Most of the subsequent projects in that book are much smaller, but more technique-heavy. However, with a good base to work from, they're much easier to do.

A cowl is often a great beginner project. Since it's done in the round, you don't have to deal with edges or the mental gymnastics associated with facing Layer 2 every other row. You just have to follow the chart and not forget to read the instructions — there's a twist thrown in between charts.

One of my tenets is "buy local" whenever possible. This also means that if I know someone who, like me, is trying to keep a small craft-based business afloat, I keep them in mind when I'm deciding on those sorts of materials or products.

Dirty Water Dyeworks is one such company. Stephanie has been an active member of the Common Cod Fiber Guild (which I cofounded with a couple of friends back in 2008) for quite some time, and it's been great to watch her build her business from a small Boston-area brand to a yarn line popular all over New England (and beyond). Unlike many up-and-coming indie dyers, Dirty Water branches off from the solely superwash merino blends and takes risks with breed-specific wools as well. Granted, it's not much of a risk because people are getting more and more into yarns from breeds like Cormo, Polwarth, Targhee, and Blue Faced Leicester (BFL for short). The yarn I chose for this pattern is one such 100% BFL base, and the lovely hand and slight shimmer are more than enough reason to search out this yarn.

When I'm working on a new idea, sometimes I'll open a file in Illustrator and just start playing with shapes, seeing how they interrelate. In this case, I was playing with a hollow rectangle, and how it could be made to look like it was linking up with others like it. As the tiling progressed, I was reminded of a carved Chinese wooden screen.

My father lived in Taiwan for about a decade when I was in my adolescence, and when he finally came back, he was fluent in several Chinese dialects, and had amassed a large collection of Chinese art, including a number of wooden screens which he mounted in his windows. So when I cast about for a name for the new cowl pattern, I was mentally locked into a Chinese word. The working title was "Yingzao," which refers to a sort of ancient building-standards manual. But here's the thing about Chinese: a word's meaning can change depending on inflection. I didn't know the correct inflection, and I didn't want to be caught saying something rude or nonsensical due to the wrong inflection — so I put out a call for alternative name suggestions. The winner was Nathan Taylor (aka Sockmatician) with "Abaciscus."

Key

☐ AB pair

■ BA pair

Pattern

CO 208 AB pairs. Place marker(s) at beginning/end and (optionally) at halfway point (104 pairs in).

1. Follow Charts 1a+1b twice around, slipping markers if present.
2. Remove marker, **work 9 slipped pairs**, replace marker.
3. Follow Charts 2a+2b twice around, slipping markers if present.
4. Remove marker, **work 7 slipped pairs**, replace marker.
5. Repeat steps 1-4 once (twice) more for a total height of ~8 (12)".

BO with AB pairs, weave in ends, block if necessary and enjoy!

Chart 1a

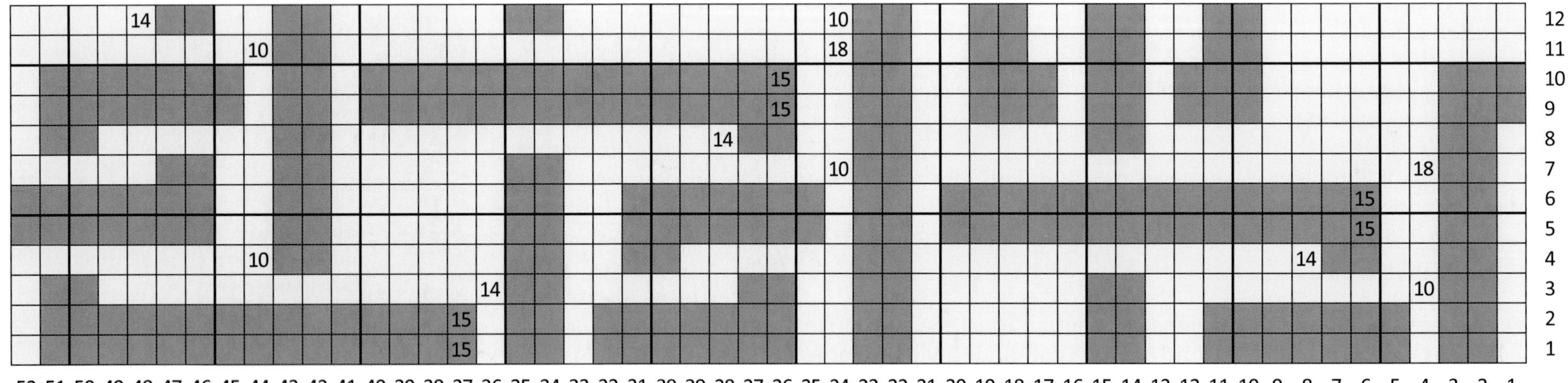

Chart 1b

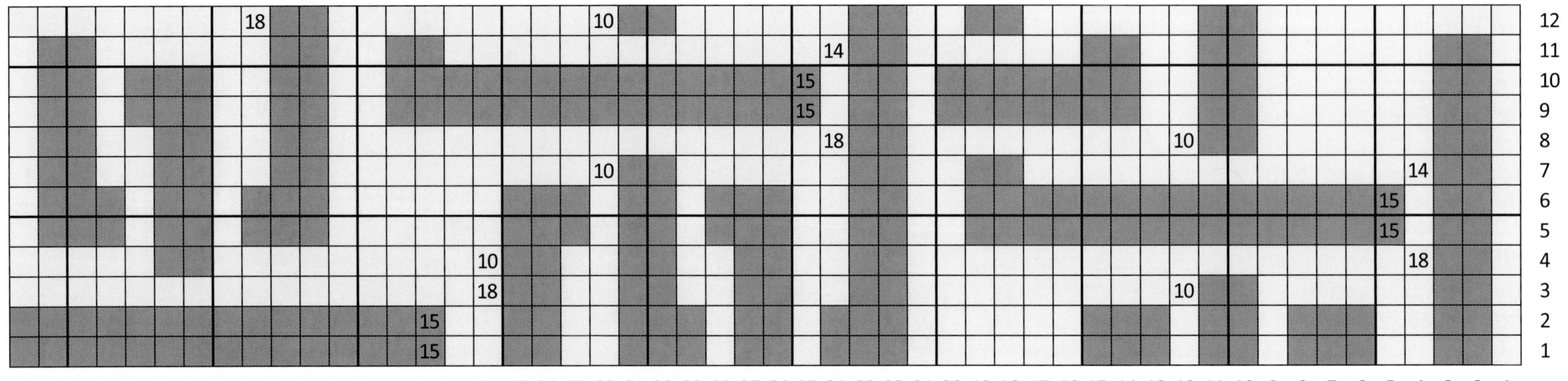

Pattern Notes

Pay special attention to steps 2 and 4. In these steps, the pattern is recentered by slipping pairs. Without recentering, this chart would be immense and would not fit on the pages of this book (and still be readable). If you are using a halfway marker, you will also want to move that 9 pairs or 7 pairs forward, respectively.

I've done something unusual in this chart that I think you'll appreciate it. Any time when there's a span of one color order that's longer than 7 pairs, I've included a number in the first pixel in the group. That number corresponds to the number of pairs before the next color change. Note that Charts 1a and 1b are simply a single chart broken in half to fit on the page, so the numbers will reflect that; the same is true for 2a and 2b.

Chart 2a

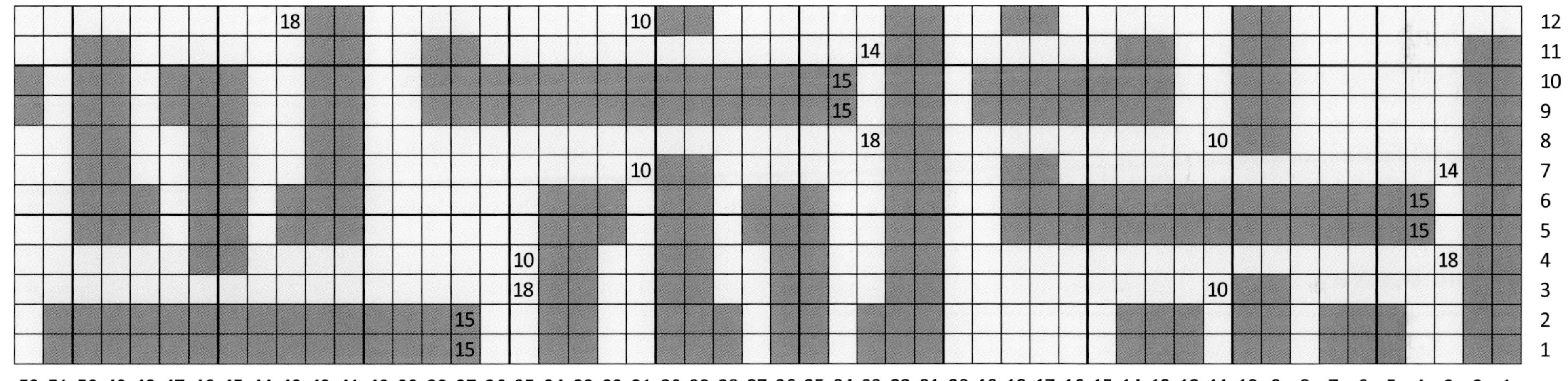

Chart 2b

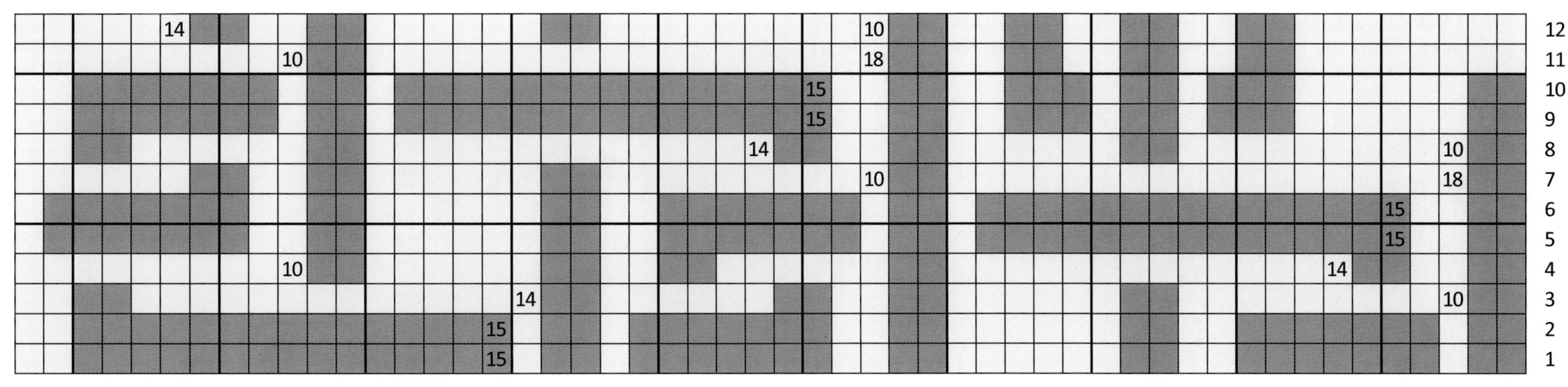

CHAPTER 2

Double-knitting Off The Grid

So now you've got the basics. You can cast on, work a piece of standard double-knitting in the flat or the round, and bind off. You can make a scarf or a cowl, a headband, wristlets, a hot pad, a dishcloth, or a blanket — but there's more, so let's jump off the grid! Increases and decreases can be used for shaping, but I like to use them decoratively, creating columns or sections of work that appear to move diagonally. The grid-based notation system we're all familiar with is sometimes a little inadequate here, but if you follow the chart row by row, you'll find things fall together as they should.

Double-knit Decreases

Decreases in double-knitting (making one pair out of two or more) are a little fiddly, but they have a rhythm and logic to them that is quite satisfying. All decreases require some reordering of stitches; since the two layers of knitting are interlaced on the needle, you need to free the stitches of the interference of the other layer before working the decreases. Both layers are interfering equally with one another, so separate them before working a decrease on the front followed by a corresponding decrease on the back.

Single decreases

There are two types of single-decreases, most often described as right-slanting and left-slanting. The right-slanting one has the leftmost pair on the outside of the work; the left-slanting one has the rightmost pair on the outside of the work. Regardless of which you are about to do, the stitch reordering is the same:

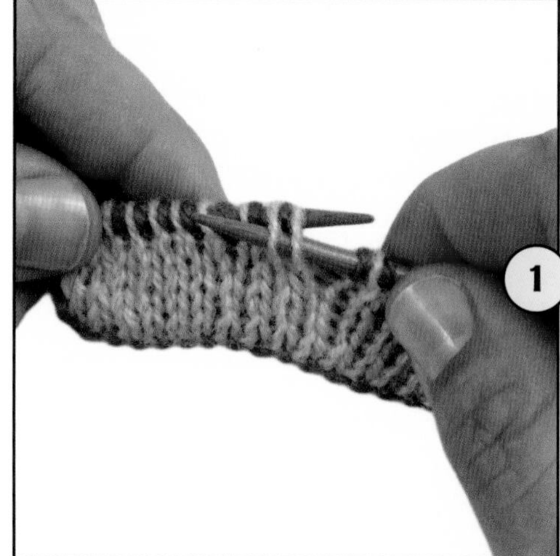

1

Insert the working needle into the first and third stitches on the source needle from the front.

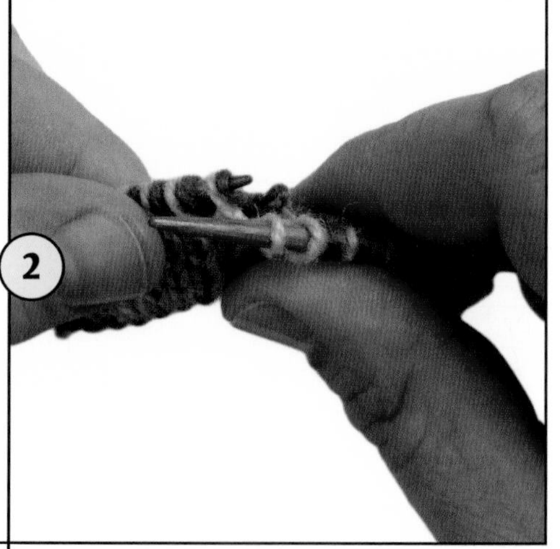

2

Hold the base of the first pair and pull the source needle out of 2 stitches. One is held by the working needle.

3

Insert the source needle into the newly-free stitch at the back and pass 2 stitches back to the source needle.

Reordering 2 pairs for a single decrease

You have now reordered 2 pairs from KPKP to KKPP and can begin a decrease. There are other ways to reorder the pairs, but this is my preferred method. There is a slightly more labor-intensive (but equally effective) method described in *Extreme Double-Knitting*. If you find that another way works better for you and achieves the same result, by all means use it.

To work a **left-slanting decrease (⟍)**:

1. Wyib, SSK in the color indicated by the chart.
2. Wyif, P2tog in the opposite color.

To work a **right-slanting decrease (⟋)**:

1. Wyib, K2tog in the color indicated by the chart.
2. Wyif, SSP in the opposite color.

For those not familiar with SSP, it's worked as follows: Slip 2 stitches separately knitwise; pass both back to the source needle; P2togTBL.

Note that these decreases, being directional, are worked in such a way that the two layers mirror each other. The effect is that the "slant" is in the same direction on both layers. An easy way to remember which purl-side decrease corresponds with the knit-side one you just did is to keep in mind that each decrease pair contains one decrease which uses a standard needle insertion (K2tog, P2tog) and one which uses a needle insertion "through the back of the loop" (SSK, SSP). If you work K2tog with P2tog, you haven't used one of each and have paired the decrease incorrectly; the same goes for SSK and SSP. Since you have to work the knit-side decrease first in most cases, it's easy to remember: if you worked the standard decrease (e.g., K2tog), then when you work the corresponding purl-side decrease, it must be the one with the back-of-the-loop insertion (SSP) and vice versa.

Double-decreases

For double-decreases, there are more options. The most commonly used are centered double-decreases, in which the first and third stitches fold over or under the center stitch in some way — but there are also directional variants as well. In all cases, the stitch reordering is the same:

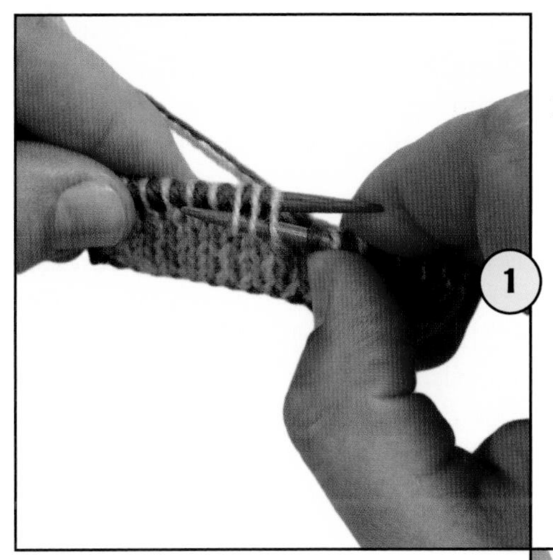

Insert the working needle into the first, third, and fifth stitches on the source needle from the front.

Hold the base of the first and second pairs and pull the source needle out of 4 stitches. Two of these are held by the working needle.

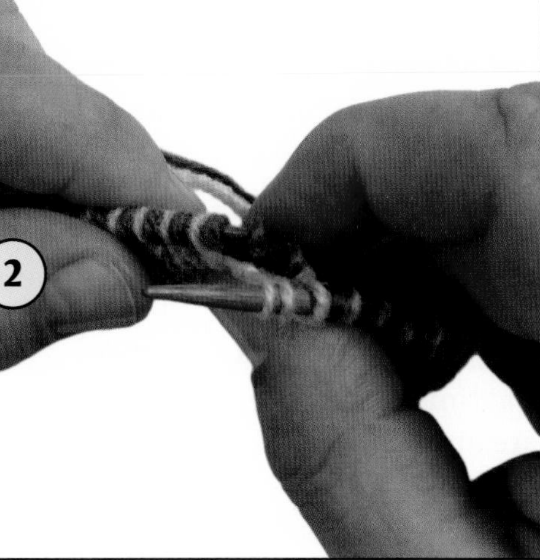

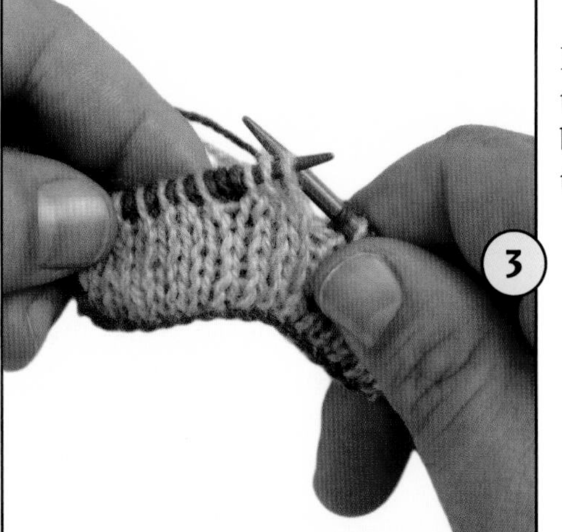

Insert the source needle into the two newly-free stitches at the back, and then pass 3 stitches back to the source needle.

Reordering 3 pairs for a double-decrease

You have now reordered three pairs from KPKPKP to KKKPPP and can begin a double-decrease. As with the single decreases, there is a slightly more labor-intensive method described in my previous book. If you find that another way works better for you and achieves the same result, by all means use it.

The only truly centered double-decrease is the raised double-decrease. This involves having the two outer stitches fold underneath the center stitch, which is thereby "raised" above them. These decreases, if lined up vertically, will create a kind of "ridge," which is why I used to call them "ridged" double-decreases. However, if they're not lined up, the ridge doesn't occur, and the traditional name is "raised." To work a **raised double-decrease** (⅄) in double-knitting, first reorder the pairs, then:

1. Slip 2 stitches together knitwise, K1 in color indicated by the chart, P2SO.
2. Slip 2 stitches separately knitwise, pass 2 back, slip 2 together as if to PTBL, P1 in the opposite color, P2SO.

There are two centered double-decreases that have a subtle directional element to them. It's not that there's a significant slant, but rather that either the right or left stitch will lie on top. In both cases, the center pair is furthest inside, and the first and third stitches fold over the top. Most of the time it's not structurally important which of these you use, but there are applications when it's visually important. If it doesn't matter, use the left-slanting one — it's easier.

To work a **centered left-slanting double-decrease** (⋋):

1. Slip 1 knitwise, K2tog in the color indicated by chart, PSSO.
2. Slip 1 purlwise, SSP in the opposite color, PSSO.

To work a **centered right-slanting double-decrease** (⋌):

1. SSK in color indicated by the chart, pass 1 stitch back to the source needle. Pass next stitch on source needle over and off. Slip 1 pwise.
2. P2tog in the opposite color, slip 1 stitch knitwise, pass 2 stitches back to the source needle. Pass the next stitch on the source needle over and off. Slip 1 purlwise.

Of course, there are two truly directional double-decreases as well. I haven't used these much in my current patterns, but it's good to know how to do them in case you ever need them:

To work a **left-slanting double-decrease** (⟍):

1. SSSK in the color indicated by the chart.
2. P3tog in the opposite color.

To work a **right-slanting double-decrease** (⟋):

1. K3tog in the color indicated by the chart.
2. SSSP in the opposite color.

SSSP works the same way as SSP, but with three stitches instead of two. Be especially careful with the P3togTBL!

Double-knit Increases

Unlike decreases, most double-knit increases (and certainly the ones that show up in the patterns in this book) can be done without any reordering of stitches. The key is to always complete a pair before going on to work the next one — which seems like a given, but it's surprisingly hard to remember.

There are increases that can't be efficiently done in double-knitting — KFB, for example, can be done but requires reordering stitches after the fact. I use two main types of increase which don't require reordering or preparation; work them on the fly as you would with any single-layer increase.

Lifted increases

For directional increases, I use pairs of lifted increases. These are increases worked off the side of a particular column of stitches, so that they "grow" in one direction or the other. They are worked into the pair two rows below the charted location. For this reason, they require a little bit of setup before they can be worked. You can't work them directly off a cast-on edge, and when working them in colorwork, you need to make sure to set up the colors below so that the increase will look natural.

For a **right-lifted increase (V)**:

With yarns in back, insert your working needle into the right leg of the stitch below the next front-layer stitch on your source needle, from inside to outside.

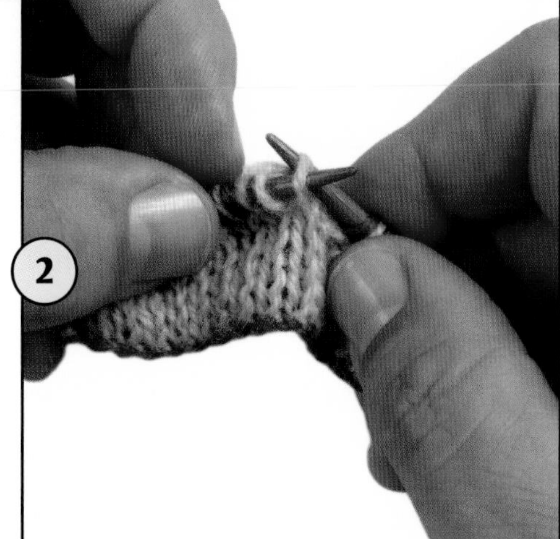

Insert your source needle into the front of the loop on your working needle. Finish the knit stitch with the color indicated by the chart. This is a KTBL.

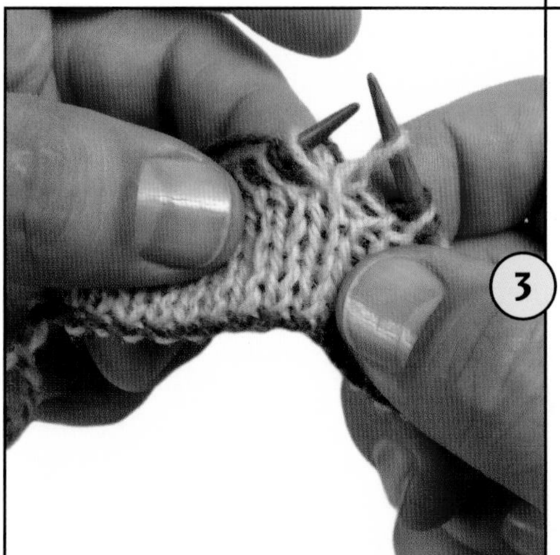

Here's the finished front-layer right-lifted increase. Note that the "stitch" in the row below the new stitch is twisted. If this is not the case, go back and try again, making sure you're inserting your needle the right way in Step 1 and knitting through the back of the loop in Step 2.

Bring both yarns forward. Flip your work up a bit so you can see the other layer. Insert your working needle into the right leg of the stitch below the next back-layer stitch on your source needle, from inside to outside.

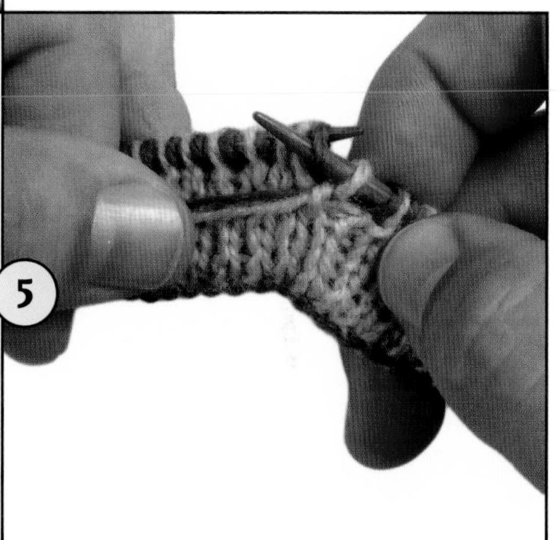

Insert your source needle into the back of the loop on your working needle. Finish the purl stitch with the opposite color from that used for the knit stitch. This is a normal purl.

Here's the finished back-layer right-lifted increase. Like the front-layer one, the "stitch" in the row below should be twisted.

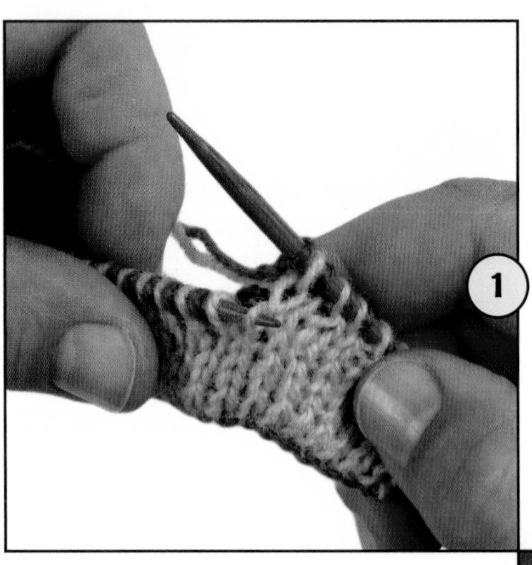

For a **left-lifted increase (\)**:

With yarns in back, insert your source needle into the left leg of the stitch two below the previous front-layer stitch on your working needle, from inside to outside.

Knit with the color indicated by the chart. Because the stitch into which you are knitting is seated backward on the needle, this may be difficult. Persevere!

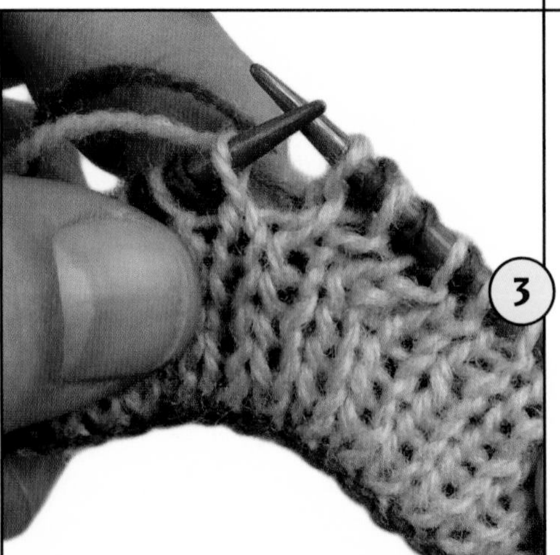

Here's the finished front-layer left-lifted increase. If you have done the two previous steps correctly, the resulting "stitch" in the row below will be twisted closed. If it's not, undo it and try again.

Bring both yarns forward. Flip the work up a bit so you can see the back. Insert your source needle into the left leg of the stitch two below the previous back-layer stitch on your working needle, from inside to outside.

Return your work to a more natural position and PTBL with the opposite color from that used for the knit stitch. Like the knit stitch, this will be twisted and may be more difficult, but it's necessary to keep a hole from forming.

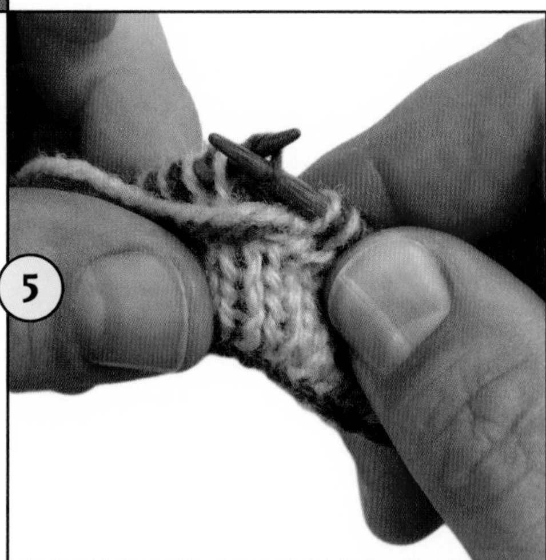

Here's the finished back-layer left-lifted increase. Like the front-layer version, this should be twisted closed.

For a **double-lifted increase** (there is no chart symbol for this; it's just two increases on either side of a central pair):

1. Work a right-side increase as described on page 53, in the color order indicated by the chart.
2. Work the center pair normally, in the color order indicated by the chart.
3. Work a left-side increase as described on page 54, in the color order indicated by the chart. This will be tight since you've already worked into the right legs of the same pair, but persevere.

M1 increases

A "make one" increase (or M1 for short) uses the bar in between two stitches to create an increase. I consider this to be a non-directional increase, although there is a very subtle directionality which mostly manifests by the increased pair hugging one side of the gap a little tighter than the other. However, it's sometimes necessary, especially in lace, to specify M1L (which hugs the right side) or M1R (which hugs the left side). If only "M1" is mentioned, use whichever you find easier. While normally I would use "inside" and "outside" in the instructions, I'm using "front" and "back" here because there will be cases where you need to do M1 increases into a set of bars that were a color change in the row below. Because the bars are crossed, it's hard to tell which is the inside and which is the outside, but front and back are easier to understand.

Following increase symbols in charts

My increase notation has changed more frequently than much of my other notation over the years, because I have been trying to find the clearest way to express what I'm doing. In doing so, I've had to depart somewhat from standard notation. This is not because there's really anything different about following double-knit vs. single-layer increases. But when you're using them decoratively with colorwork, you need to specify a color order for each pair you make, whether it's a standard pair or one generated by an increase. The important thing to remember is that whenever you make an increase, you're placing a new pair in between two existing pairs. That new pair can be created in a number of ways, depending on the effect you're going for. The way that pair is created is dictated by the chart, as is the color order in which it's created.

M1 increases are simple to read, because the increase occurs in between the two pairs, in the same place as shown in the chart. Lifted increases are also simple, as long as you remember that in my notation, a lifted increase symbol denotes only one pair. The shape of the symbol shows you whether it's a left- or right-lifted increase. Often in single-layer knitting, when there is no colorwork involved, a similar symbol will denote two pairs — one new pair and one pair that continues a column from the row below. Here, since the two pairs may be the same or different color orders, I have chosen a notation that makes that possible and easy to follow.

A side effect of this is that the technique that used to be charted as a double-increase no longer exists. A double-increase is simply two lifted increases on either side of a center pair, and it is now charted that way. The way the symbols sit on the chart makes it clear that you must increase into the right leg of one stitch and later increase into the left leg of the very same stitch.

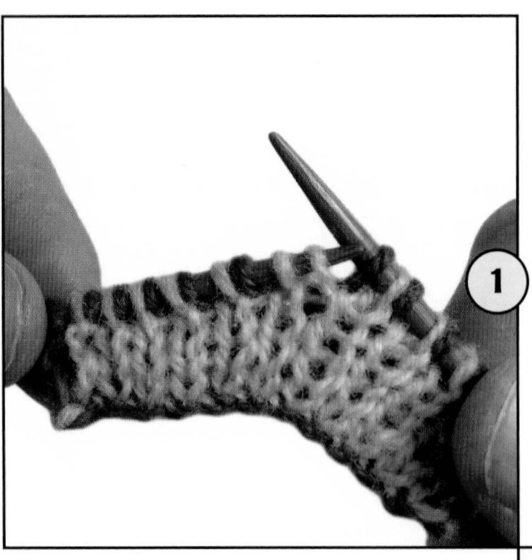

To work an **M1L increase (M)** in double-knitting:

Move both yarns to the back. With your source needle, pick up the bar matching the color of the knit stitch as indicated in the chart, from front to back.

KTBL in the color indicated by the chart.

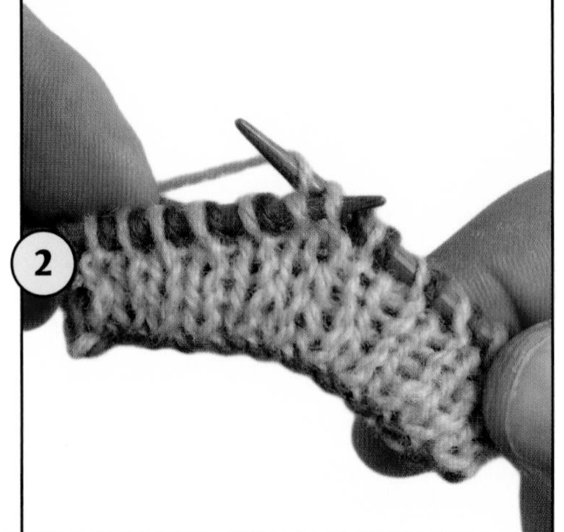

Here's the front-layer M1L increase completed. Note that the bar is twisted to create as unnoticeable of a hole as possible, and that it matches the color of the new stitch. As you can see, it hugs the pair to the right more closely.

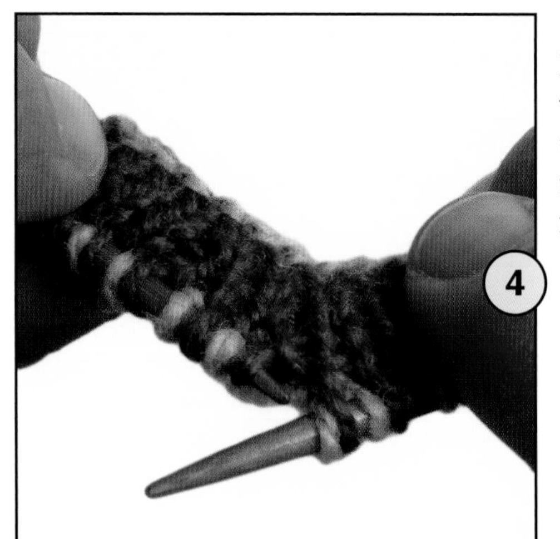

Bring both yarns forward and flip your work up a bit so you can see the back layer. With your source needle, pick up the unused bar from back to front.

Return your work to a more comfortable position and purl in the opposite color from the previous knit.

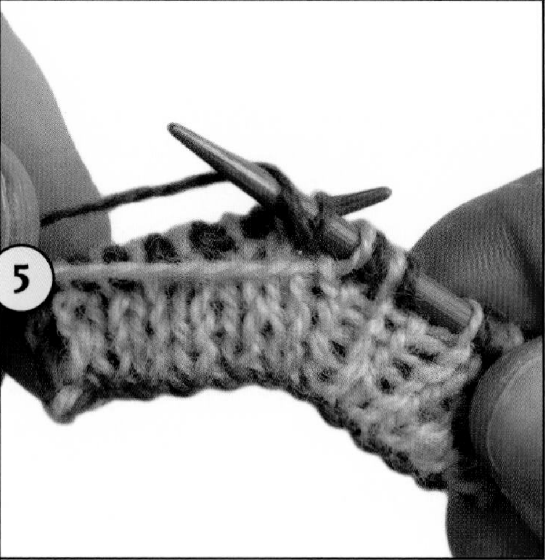

Here's the back-layer M1L increase completed.

To work an **M1R increase** (Ϻ) in double-knitting:

Move both yarns to the back. With your source needle, pick up the bar matching the color of the knit stitch as indicated in the chart, from back to front.

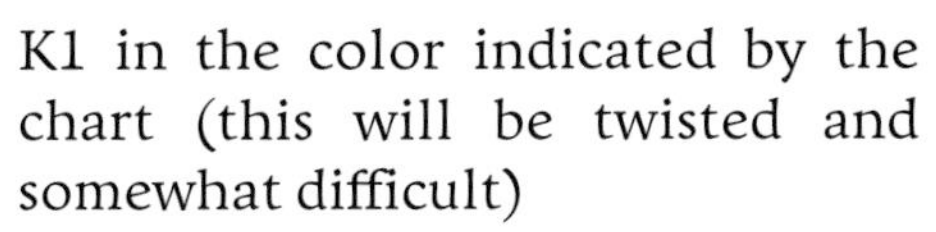

K1 in the color indicated by the chart (this will be twisted and somewhat difficult)

Here's the front-layer M1R increase completed. It should hug the pair to the left more closely.

Bring both yarns forward and flip your work up a bit so you can see the back layer. With your source needle, pick up the unused bar from front to back.

PTBL in the opposite color from the previous knit.

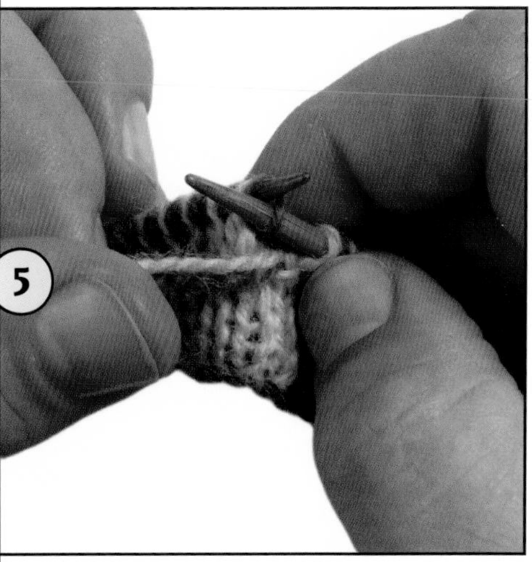

Here's the back-layer M1R increase completed.

HESPEROS

a double-knit scarf using off-the-grid colorwork

Finished size & weight

The finished piece is approximately 77" long by 6" wide and uses about 340 g (935 yds) of yarn in total. Since you'll have 400 g, you'll be all set.

Materials & tools

[Color A]: Plucky Knitter Primo Sport (75% superwash merino, 20% cashmere, 5% nylon; 275 yd/100 g skein); Shimmy (tan); 2 skeins.
[Color B]: Plucky Knitter Primo Sport (75% superwash merino, 20% cashmere, 5% nylon; 275 yd/100 g skein); Lady Violet (purple); 2 skeins.

US 4/3.5 mm straight or circular needles.

Gauge in pattern

23 sts/28 rows = 4" in double-stockinette.
27 sts/26 rows = 4" in pattern.

Years ago, while working on *Extreme Double-Knitting*, I was using a pattern by Kieran Foley to hone my skills in double-knit increases and decreases. I could not publish that pattern to illustrate these techniques at that point, so I instead took what I learned and applied it to a pattern of my own — the enigmatic Silk Road tie, published in *Extreme Double-Knitting*. This tie was the result of a bunch of sketches I had made, in which I played with the different ways two horizontally-mirrored sets of chevrons could interact. The first was the spiral I used in the tie, but there were plenty of other options. I wanted to show them all off, but I didn't want to make a huge number of patterns to do it. Instead, I opted to show them all in one scarf, and the pattern Hesperos was born. In this scarf, the underlying chevrons show in the middle, but they begin to shift around as the next set of chevrons is worked slightly offset from the previous one. Using only the clearest and cleanest of my experimental results, I generated mazes, Greek keys, diamonds, and, yes, more spirals. To further show off the reversible nature of the fabric, the increases and decreases are worked into a more widely-spaced pattern, unlike the dense 1x1 patterning in the tie.

One of the first patterns I discovered after the spirals was a sort of Greek key pattern, also known as a "meander," referring to the way that the path wanders but ultimately ends up going in some particular direction.

"Hesperos" is ancient Greek, both the name of a god and of one of the "wandering stars" that were eventually determined to be planets (Venus, in this case). Venus is also the name of the Roman goddess of beauty. So, for this pattern, the name "Hesperos" is meant to express the beauty of wandering, getting lost, finding your way, and getting to your destination in the end.

Plucky Knitter is another yarn company I stumbled across while at one of my teaching gigs. I was lucky enough to be teaching at Stitches South, the only such event at which Plucky Knitter vends. Their booth was mobbed (and rightly so!). A fellow designer introduced me to the owners, who told me what makes their yarn special: unlike many independent dyers, they don't use bases that are commercially available — all of their bases are exclusive to them, so their yarns are unique. In addition, they have a stunning range of colors, and most of their bases can be dyed in any of these. Spoiled for choice, I picked an unconventional combination, and have never regretted it. The one thing I do regret is that I have not managed to attend another show where they were vending, but I'm sure our paths will cross again and more amazing things will come of it.

Key

☐	Layer 1: AB pair Layer 2: BA pair
■	Layer 1: BA pair Layer 2: AB pair
+	Linked Pair
▽	Slipped Pair
/	Right-slanting decrease
\	Left-slanting decrease
⋏	Centered left-slanting double-decrease
⋏	Centered right-slanting double-decrease
⋏	Raised double-decrease
V	Right-lifted increase
V	Left-lifted increase
M	M1R Increase
M	M1L Increase

Pattern

CO 43 BA pairs.

Work 10 repeats of Chart 1.

Follow Charts 2-12 in sequence.

Work 10 more repeats of Chart 1.

BO, weave in ends, block if necessary and enjoy!

Pattern Note

The selvedge in this pattern is sort of a hybrid of the linked double-knit selvedge and the color-changed double-knit selvedge. Most of the edge relies on color changes to link together, so there's no need to make linked pairs there, but in places where the next pair is not a different color order, a linked pair is the most prudent choice. If you prefer to make linked pairs in all eligible locations along the edge, feel free; it's not necessary but there's something to be said for getting into a predictable rhythm.

Chart 1

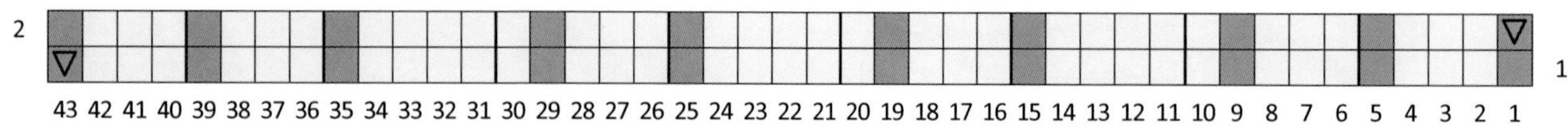

Chart 2

Chart 3

Chart 4

40
39
38
37
36
35
34
33
32
31
30
29
28
27
26
25
24
23
22
21
20
19
18
17
16
15
14
13
12
11
10
9
8
7
6
5
4
3
2
1
43 42 41 40 39 38 37 36 35 34 33 32 31 30 29 28 27 26 25 24 23 22 21 20 19 18 17 16 15 14 13 12 11 10 9 8 7 6 5 4 3 2 1

Chart 5

Chart 6

Chart 7

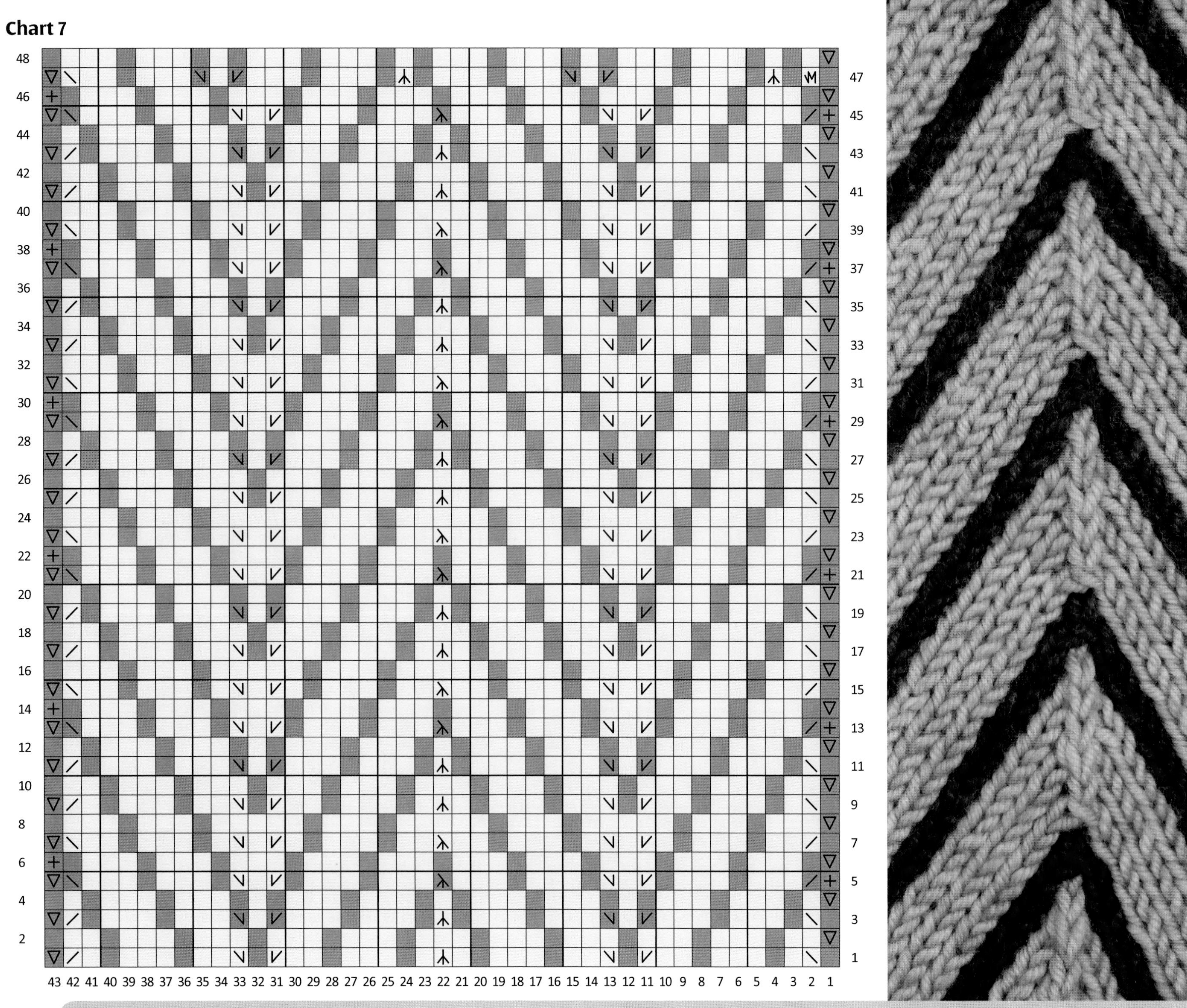

Chart 8

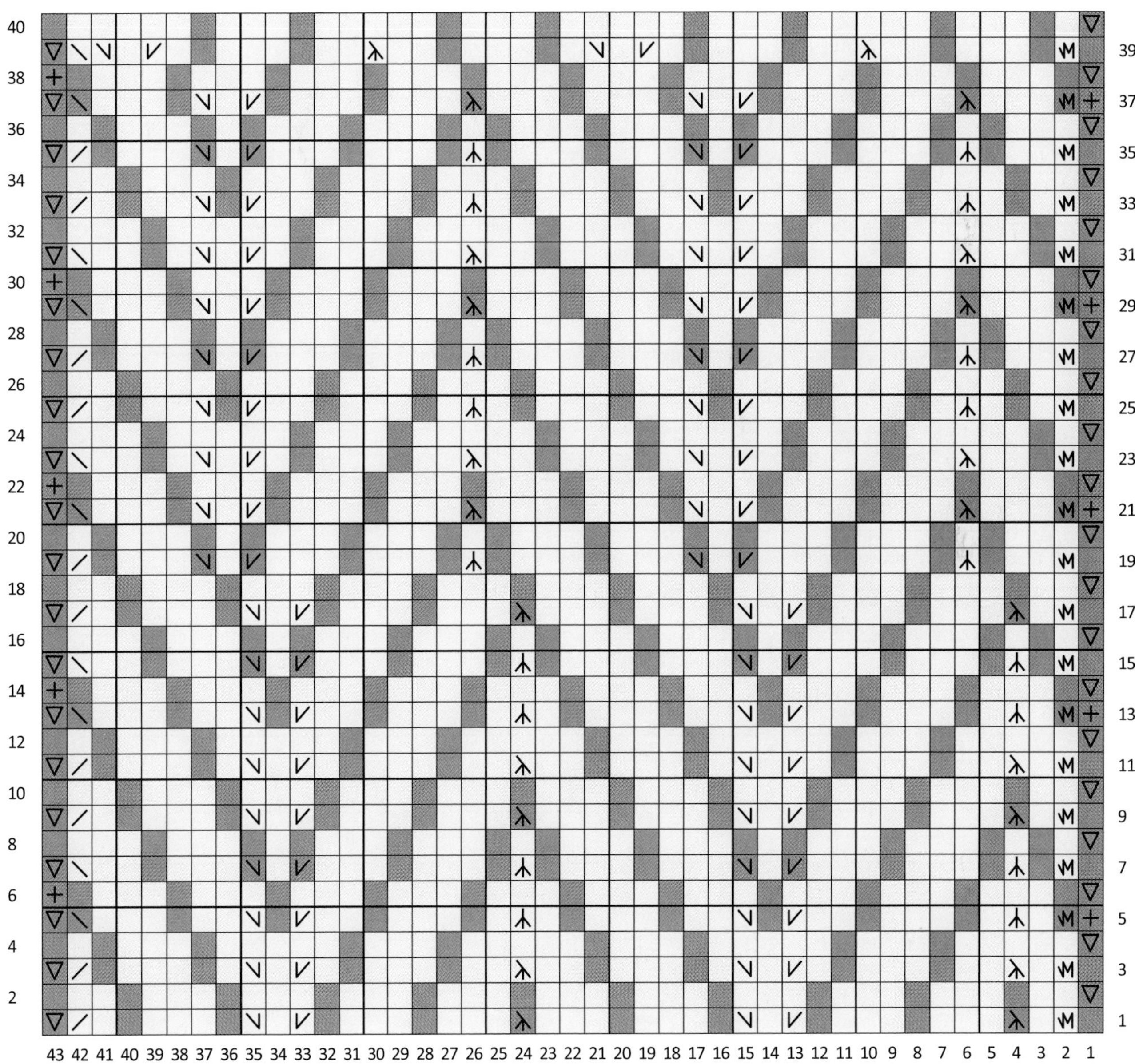

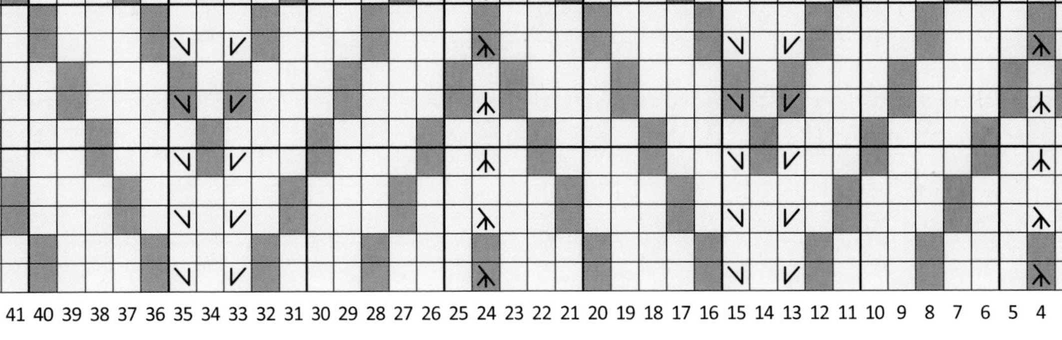

Chart 9

Chart 10

40 39 38 37 36 35 34 33 32 31 30 29 28 27 26 25 24 23 22 21 20 19 18 17 16 15 14 13 12 11 10 9 8 7 6 5 4 3 2 1
43 42 41 40 39 38 37 36 35 34 33 32 31 30 29 28 27 26 25 24 23 22 21 20 19 18 17 16 15 14 13 12 11 10 9 8 7 6 5 4 3 2 1

Chart 11

Chart 12

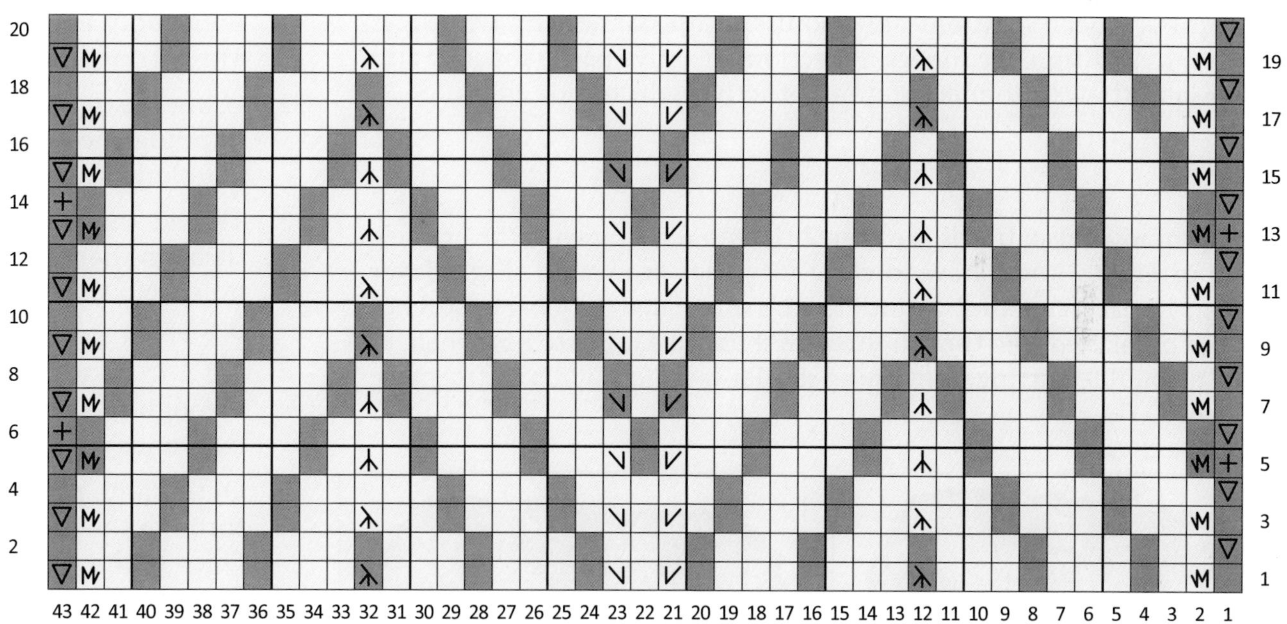

CHAPTER 3

Closures and Seams

As long as you're working flat or minimally-shaped circular double-knitting, you may have to work with top, bottom, and side edges. But if you're working a garment that ends in a different way, a bind-off isn't going to help you. Instead, you might want to connect your active pairs together in some way. A radial solution may be needed for the crown of a hat, but linear solutions are also useful for connecting two edges together. In addition to connecting sections of active pairs, you may also want to know how to connect sections of active pairs to side edges.

Cinching

Since all of my hat patterns are done brim-up (ending with the crown), it's important to know how to close off a hat crown. In single-layer knitting, you decrease the hat until there's some small number of stitches left, then break and feed the tail through the active loops to hold them in place. In double-knitting, something similar is done, but it's a little more involved.

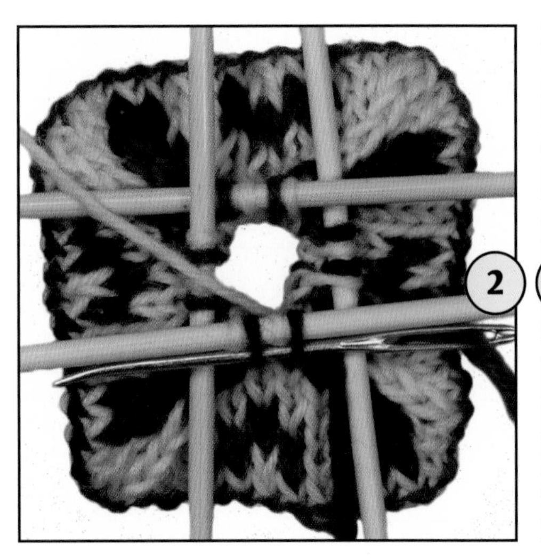

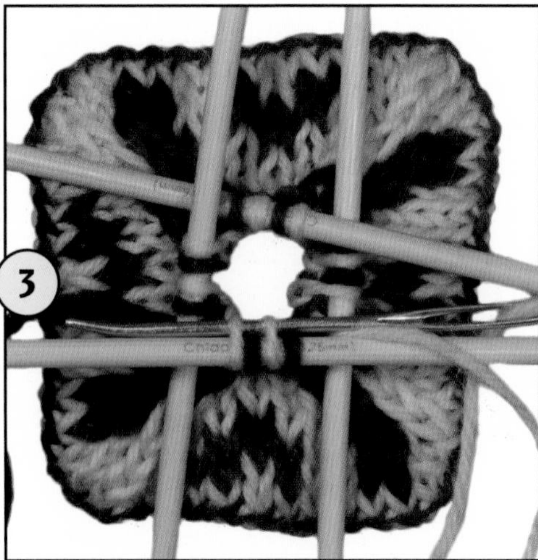

First of all, each layers must be cinched individually. To ensure they remain connected as much as possible, I prefer to use the yarn from Layer 2 to cinch Layer 1, and vice versa. Since you can't usually see much of the yarn used to work this technique, it doesn't really matter what color it is.

1. Break both ends with somewhat more than enough to weave in. Thread one end into a tapestry needle.
2. Using the tapestry needle, thread through the knit stitches only, skipping the purls, along the outside of Layer 1, Don't remove your knitting needles!
3. Thread the other end onto the tapestry needle and thread it through the purl stitches along the outside of Layer 2 (inside the hole). Now you can remove the knitting needles. Don't tighten just yet!
4. Tie a loose overhand knot between the two ends; pass one end through the hole to the other layer of the work. Carefully pull both ends until both the knot and the hole have tightened.
5. Optionally, put one of the ends on a tapestry needle and pass it through the (now much tighter) hole in the center of the crown. Once both ends are on the same layer of the work, tie another loose overhand knot, and pass the end through the hole back to the other layer. Make sure the cinch from Step 5 is tight, then pull the two ends tight. This will create a secure knot inside the work and the cinch is now permanent.

At this point, you can weave in the ends as usual.

Shown here are Steps 2 and 3 from this section in *Extreme Double-Knitting*; the rest can be found in that book if it's still unclear.

Seaming in Double-knitting

While I opt for seamless construction whenever I can, seaming is sometimes an unavoidable process. It will require some experimentation to get seams as clean as possible, but I can provide some suggestions, depending on what you need.

Side-to-side seaming

If you are seaming together the edges of two flat double-knit pieces, you'll need to plan ahead a little bit. You can use mattress stitching on both layers, but since that method pushes a couple of columns of stitches on each edge inside the work, you'll need to make sure you have somewhere to put those edges (or the seam will end up lumpy and untidy). The best way to achieve this is to work your edges with the open double-knit selvedge (see page 35). Since both edges will be open, you can push the seam inside the work more readily. Alternatively, you can work a linked double-knit selvedge and sew the links themselves together. Unlike the mattress-stitch method, this only needs to be done once.

Top-to-bottom seaming (No-brain Kitchener)

To connect a cast-on to a bind-off edge (or a CO to a CO, or a BO to a BO), there's a method I like to call "No-brain Kitchener," as coined by my friend Alphonse Poulin. What he taught me was based on a regular Kitchener stitch in single-layer knitting, but in double-knitting, you don't need to do anything even resembling Kitchener stitch to do this — it's much more in keeping with duplicate stitch. There are no loose loops at any point. Just take two non-side edges (COs or BOs or one of each) and line them up facing each other, edge to edge. Then take some extra yarn (or, if you have the length, one of your tails), and begin stitching one edge to the other. This is done on one layer at a time; when you're done with the first layer, flip it over and use the other tail or another length of extra yarn in another color to stitch the other layer closed. When you're done, the two edges will be hidden completely inside the work.

While this resembles duplicate stitching, you can't really call it by that name since you're creating new stitches rather than tracing over old ones.

To see this in progress, check out the step-by-step guide on pages 74-75.

Top or bottom to side seaming

This is a fusion of No-brain Kitchener and side-to-side seaming. You can't get a completely invisible seam this way since the direction of the fabric is changing, but you can get a clean transition. You will want a linked double-knit selvedge for this; an open one won't work cleanly. Once you've aligned the two edges you want to connect, begin stitching similar to the No-brain Kitchener above, but rather than connecting to a second CO or BO edge, loop through the links inside the double-knit selvedge. Each of those links is made up of two loops: one from the front layer and one from the back layer. If you can, when seaming on one layer, use the loops that are closest to you. Then, when you turn it over and repeat with the other yarn, you can go through the other set of loops.

Keep in mind that there are half as many links as there are rows, so if you need to seam more stitches across the top edge than there are links inside the side edge, you're going to have to get a little creative.

Seaming between layers

In order to do this, you need to be able to get between the layers, and it's not easy to seam two layers together when you can only see their outer faces. The only reason I can currently think of to do this is if you have an open selvedge (see page 35), and you want to close it. Generally, if you simply wanted a closed selvedge, you would have just worked a linked double-knit selvedge. But if you needed to insert something into the inside of your work and then close up the edge, this would be the best way to do it.

Depending on the rest of the piece (specifically, depending on what happens at the top and bottom corners) you have a couple of options. Probably the cleanest one would be to use a mattress stitch between the two layers, but that will pull two columns of stitches inside the work, and the top and bottom corners may get kind of messy. Instead, you may want to simply sew your facing purl bumps together just inside the edge. If you don't pull too tight, this should be more or less invisible and will look very much like a regular double-knit selvedge.

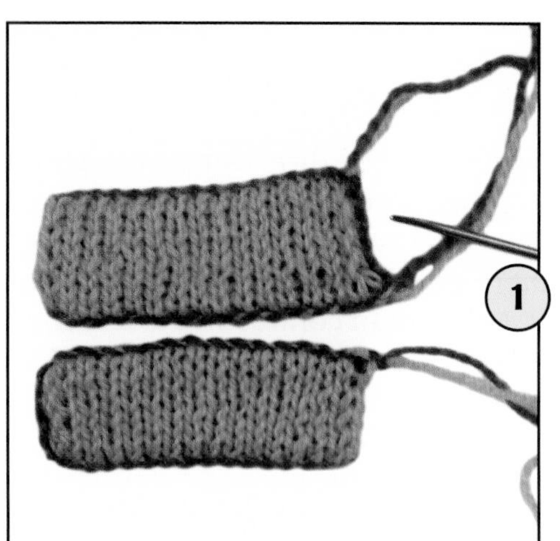

Begin with two pieces of double-knitting, fully bound off. Set them down with their bind-off edges facing each other. Thread one end from the upper right corner of the lower piece into the tapestry needle. Here, it's Color A.

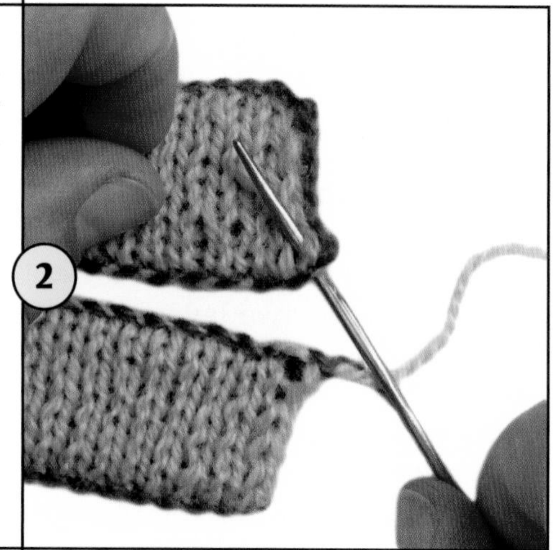

Insert the needle in between the layers at the lower right corner of the upper piece and out to the front in between the legs of the first visible stitch.

Thread the needle behind the left leg of the first stitch and the right leg of the second on the lower piece, and pull the end through.

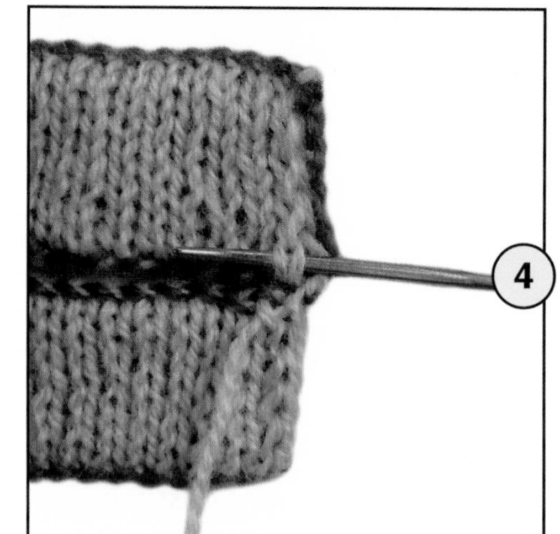

Thread the needle behind the left leg of the first stitch and the right leg of the second on the upper piece, and pull the end through.

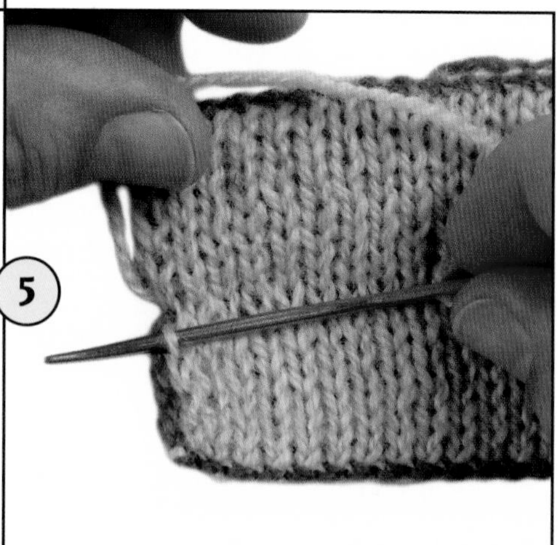

Continue as illustrated in Steps 3 and 4. At the end, run the needle through the last leg on the lower piece, and pull the end through.

Here's the work seamed all the way across (with the end woven in).

Flip the work over; you can clearly see the bind-off edges now held together by the stitching on the other layer. Thread the other color from the lower piece into the tapestry needle and insert the needle in between the layers at the lower left corner of the upper piece and out between the legs of the first visible stitch (this is a mirror image of Step 2).

This is a mirror image of Step 3 . . .

. . . and this, predictably, is a mirror image of Step 4.

Continue as illustrated in Steps 8 and 9. At the end, run the needle through the last leg on the lower piece, and pull the end through.

Weave in any remaining ends, and you're all set.

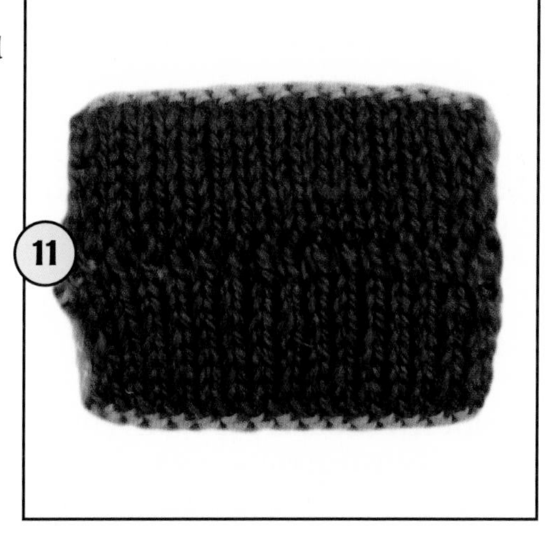

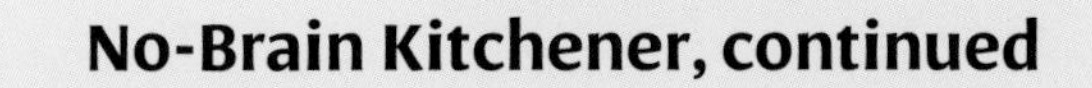
Closeup of Ranelva, page 76

RANELVA

a pair of double-knit mittens using the Eastern thumb

Finished size & weight

For Medium (Large) size:

Cuff: ~7" circumference, 2.5" tall from CO to first increase

Body: ~8.5" circumference, 4.5 (5)" tall from thumb gusset to closure.

Thumb: ~3" circumference, 2 (2.5)" tall from thumb gusset to closure.

Each medium-sized mitten takes about 20 g of each yarn or 40 g (140 m) total, so 1 pair is 80 g (280 m). A large mitten is less than 20% larger so it should be possible to get 2 large mittens out of 100 g of yarn. However, better safe than sorry: buy 2 balls of each just in case.

Materials & tools

[Color A]: Rauma Finullgarn (100% wool; 175 m/50 g ball); 4186 Bright Teal (blue-green); 1 ball.

[Color B]: Rauma Finullgarn (100% wool; 175 m/50 g ball); 488 Eggplant (deep purple); 1 ball.

US2/2.75 mm needles in your choice of small-diameter solution (DPNs, magic loop, or 2 circulars) or needle size required to achieve gauge.

Gauge

24 sts/34 rows = 4" in double-stockinette.

I haven't made, let alone designed, very many mittens. However, I've worn a fair few while growing up in Vermont. I feel like I've got a pretty good handle (pun intended) on how they're normally constructed. I do like to add my own style to things, and in my (one) previous mitten design as well as this one, I've done things a little differently from your average mitten.

One of these things will be immediately obvious: the fingertips are not centered on the body of the mitten. Instead, they're centered roughly on the middle finger, which is most people's tallest finger. In other words, the decreases for the body of the mitten begin sooner on the outside edge than on the edge closest to the thumb. Speaking of which, the other major difference is the thumb style. The Eastern Thumb is quite underutilized in mittens, but I like the elegant lines of it, the way the increases follow the muscles of the hand, and the way the thumb feels like it's part of the mitten, rather than an afterthought. Also, although it's not alone in this, the Eastern Thumb is worked symmetrically, so there's no need for a left and right mitten — they'll both work for either hand.

When I first started teaching at the big knitting shows (Stitches, Interweave, and Vogue), I found myself face-to-face with one of my own patterns in a booth I didn't know at the time. It was my "Open for Business" sign, which had been done in the booth's yarn. Called "Wall of Yarn," they were very enthusiastic about my designs, and it turned out that they have a very interesting story.

Wall of Yarn is the primary US importer of a line of yarns from Norway called Rauma. Rauma has an amazing variety of colors, and, as it turns out, their Finullgarn matches up nicely with Kauni Effektgarn, another favorite of mine which has been heavily used in my standalone patterns.

One of the shop's proprietors, Jeffrey Wall, has been translating Rauma's patterns from Norwegian to English and boosting their yarn sales with unique colorwork patterns. They were happy to have me design something in their yarn, and I have plans to continue using their yarns in the future. They have begun to help me by selling my books and patterns at many of these shows, and have even begun to stock Kauni Effektgarn in part to support my Parallax patterns.

As I began designing these mittens, I first settled on the all-over colorwork pattern they were going to use. Like many of my other charts, the noodling and doodling in Illustrator generated a fascinating but very simple pattern that reminded me of rivers or rippling water. Since the yarn is Norwegian, I looked up rivers in Norway to find a good name — and what a surprise! It turns out that Rauma, the name of the yarn, is also the name of a river in Norway. Clearly it was meant to be. I chose Ranelva, another river's name, for the mittens.

Chart 1

Chart 4a

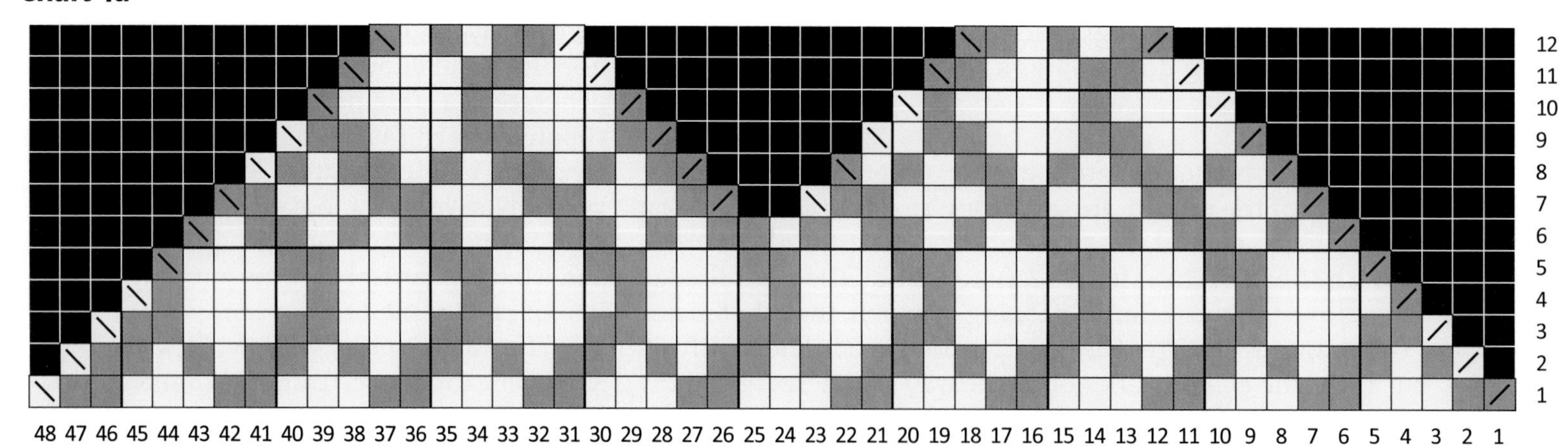

Chart 5a

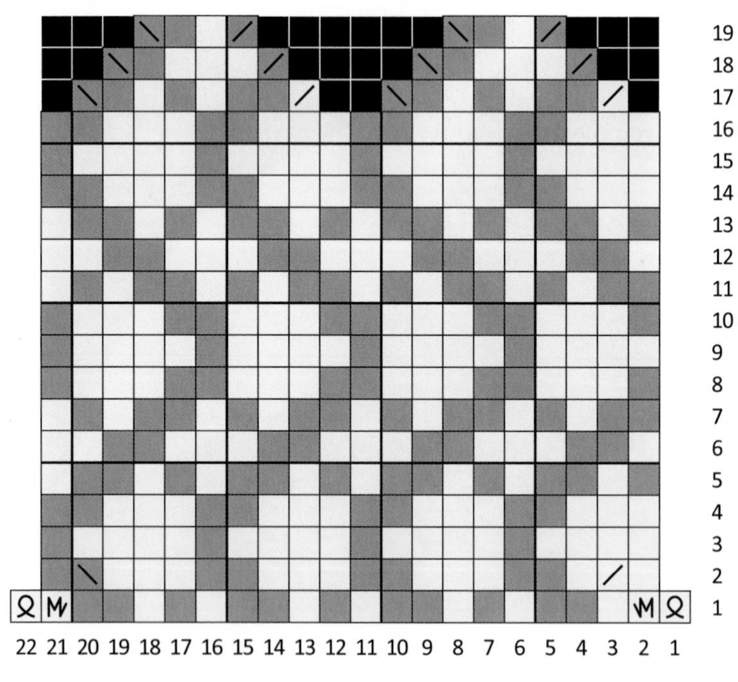

Chart 2b

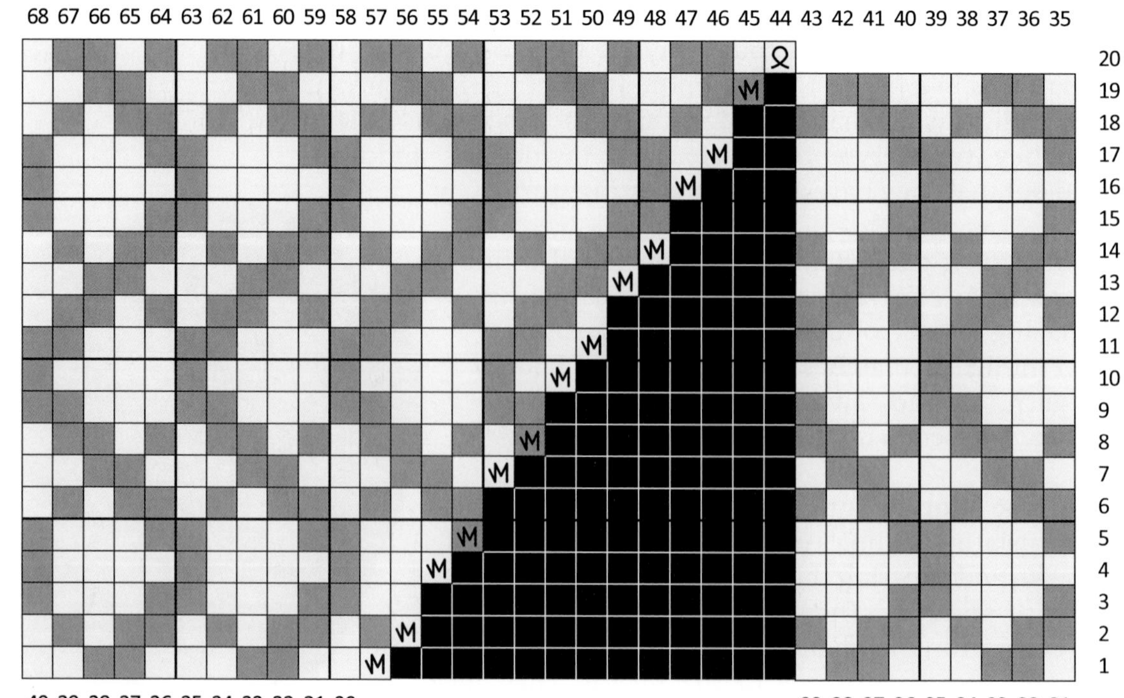

Chart 3

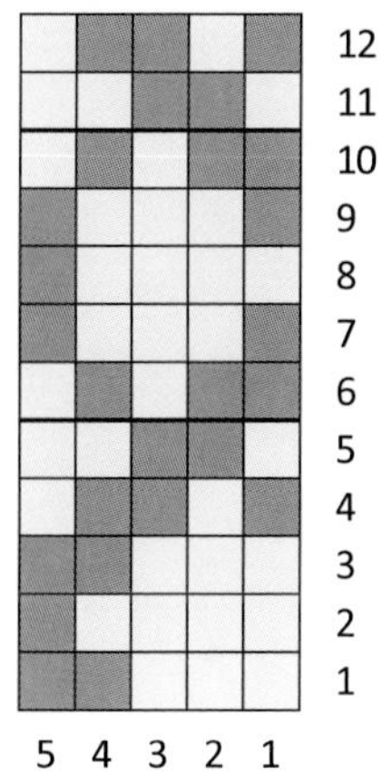

Pattern

Key may be found on page 80.

Medium and Large sizes both start the same way; sizing is done only in the body and thumb. The cuff is elastic enough to allow either sized hand through. There is no Small size, sorry.

Cuff

With magic loop or two circular needles, CO 40 AB pairs (20 pairs on each needle). If using DPNs, CO 10 AB pairs on each of 4 needles. Join, being careful not to twist, PM at beginning/end.

Work 8 repeats around of Chart 1 twice (total of 24 rounds). If you want to fold up the bottom for contrast and extra warmth, work 8 repeats around of Chart 1 four times. This will probably require you to break into another pair of skeins. On final round of Chart 1, work 11 pairs, PM, work 18 pairs, PM, work 11 pairs.

Body

Follow Charts 2a+2b. Work increases after first marker and before second marker in each increase round. In Round 20, work 24 pairs as charted, RM, CO 2 AB pairs, put next 18 pairs on a holder for thumb, RM, work last 24 pairs. Total number of stitches is now 68; 50 of these are the body pairs currently on the needle; 18 are thumb pairs currently on a holder.

Work 10 repeats around of Chart 3 twice. Work the first 4 (8) rounds again for medium (large) size.

Follow Chart 4a (b) to decrease down to 14 pairs (7 on each needle). BO and break off yarn with about a foot of each tail left.

Chart 2a

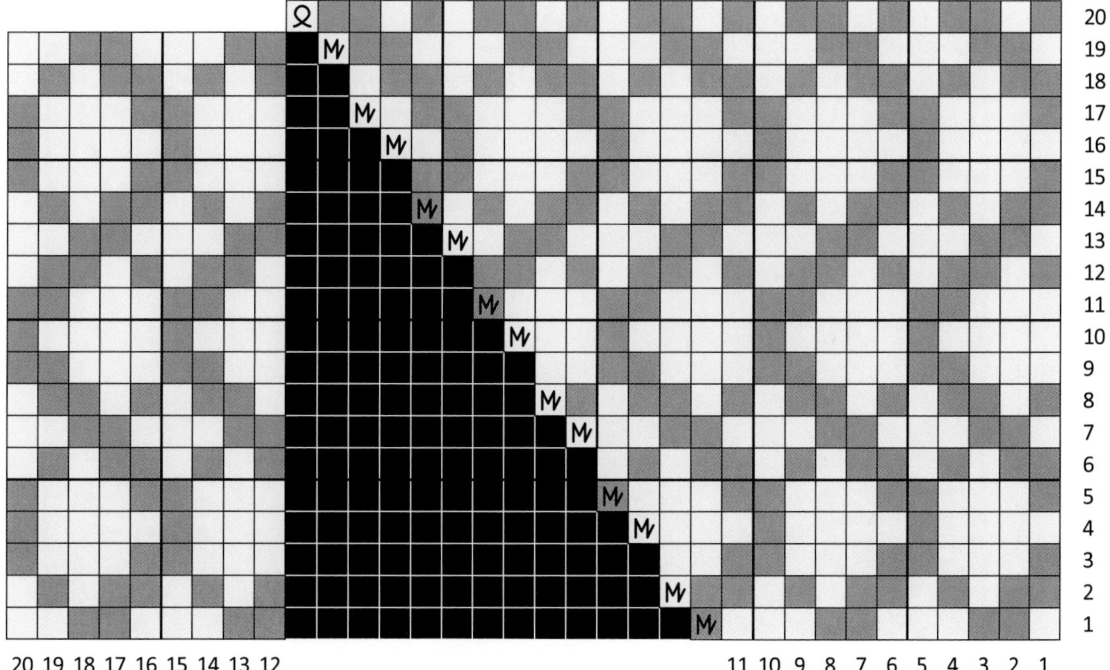

Thumb

Put 18 held thumb pairs onto the needle again, splitting them into 9 and 9. Make slipknot, CO 1 AB pair, M1L pair from gusset, work pixels 3-20 of Round 1 of Chart 5a (b), M1R pair from other side of gusset, CO 1 AB pair. Remove slipknot before proceeding with Round 2. Total number of stitches is now 20. Complete chart for your size to decrease down to 8 pairs (4 on each needle). BO and break off yarn with about a foot of each tail left.

You now have 3 holes to close off — one at the tip of the thumb, one at the tip of the fingers, and one in the thumb gusset. Take the Color B end nearest each and push it through the hole to the inside of the mitten. Using each Color A end and a tapestry needle, No-brain Kitchener the holes together. Turn mitten inside out and repeat with each Color B end.

Weave in all ends, repeat all steps for a second mitten, block if necessary and enjoy!

Key

☐	AB pair
■	BA pair
M	M1L Increase
M	M1R Increase
Ω	Cast-on Pair
\	Left-slanting decrease
/	Right-slanting decrease

Chart 4b

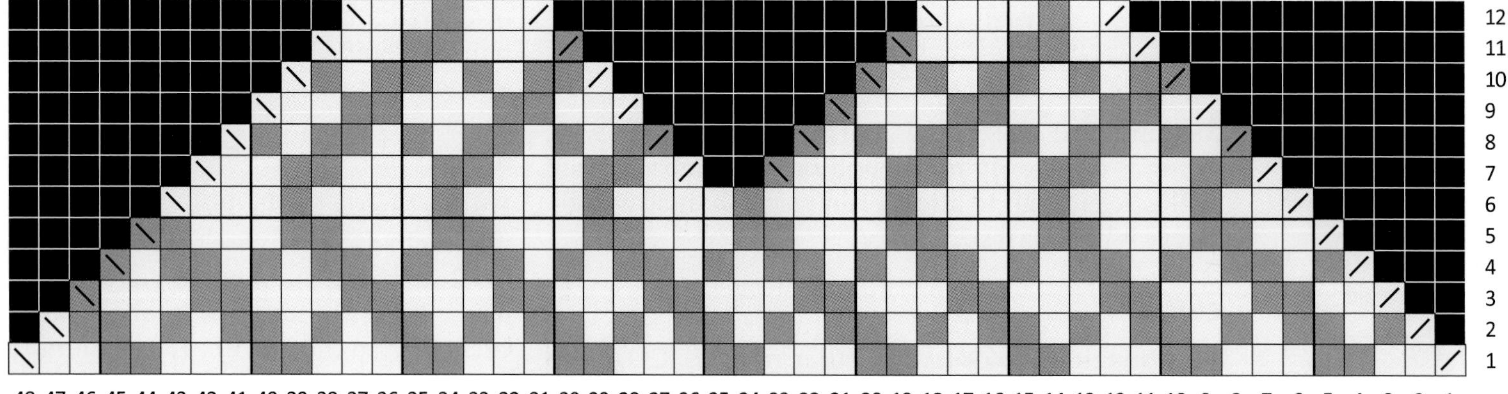

Chart 5b

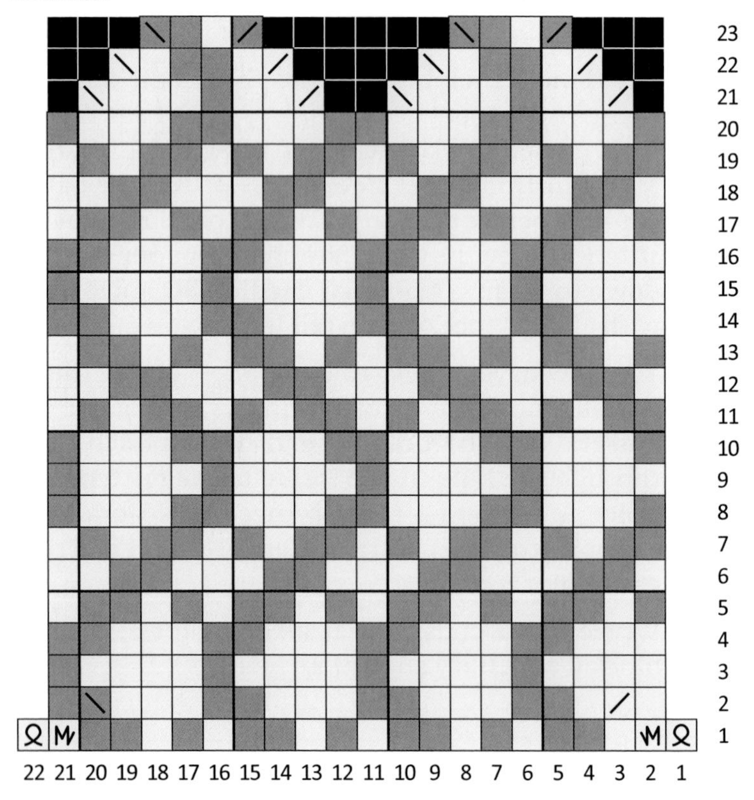

Craftstory, continued from page 37

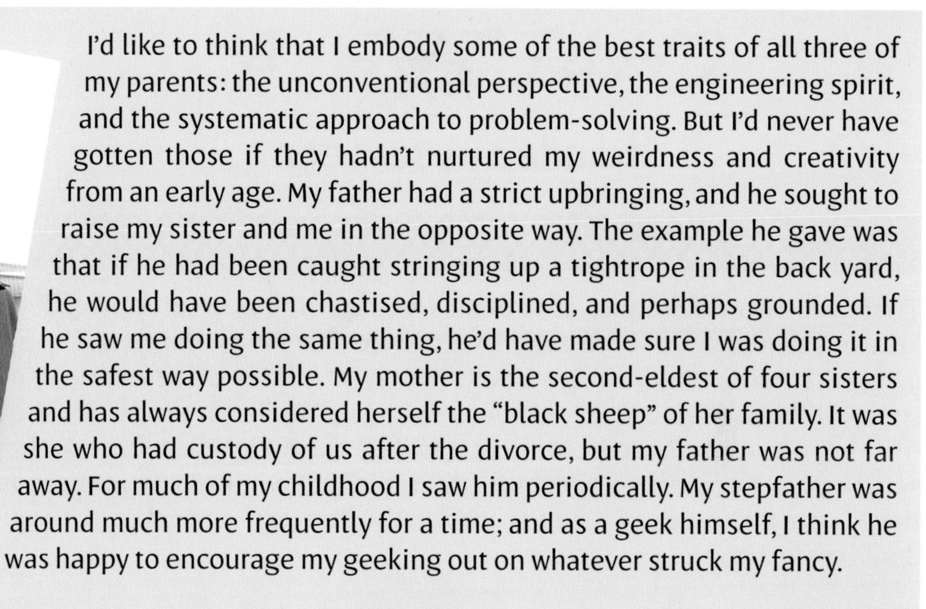

My mother travels all over the world, but lately has been spending most of her research time with the nomadic herders in Mongolia. She's a professor of ethnomusicology, but her focus is unconventional, even by the standards of her unconventional field. She's received international recognition, but has also butted heads with several administrators who just didn't "get" the importance of her work. Nevertheless, she's unwilling to back down or change who she is or what she does for the comfort of others, and this is one of the things that gives her work so much impact.

My stepfather, who joined our family when I was in elementary school and split with my mother shortly after I turned 18, had been a family friend for some time and has also been a father figure. He was a choir director and a technical services librarian for the college in the town where I grew up. It was due to his influence that we had computers around and that I got comfortable using and tinkering with them from an early age.

I'd like to think that I embody some of the best traits of all three of my parents: the unconventional perspective, the engineering spirit, and the systematic approach to problem-solving. But I'd never have gotten those if they hadn't nurtured my weirdness and creativity from an early age. My father had a strict upbringing, and he sought to raise my sister and me in the opposite way. The example he gave was that if he had been caught stringing up a tightrope in the back yard, he would have been chastised, disciplined, and perhaps grounded. If he saw me doing the same thing, he'd have made sure I was doing it in the safest way possible. My mother is the second-eldest of four sisters and has always considered herself the "black sheep" of her family. It was she who had custody of us after the divorce, but my father was not far away. For much of my childhood I saw him periodically. My stepfather was around much more frequently for a time; and as a geek himself, I think he was happy to encourage my geeking out on whatever struck my fancy.

When I was growing up in Vermont, art, music, and (of course) knitting were all around me. Both my mother and my grandmother knitted. The smell of rustic yarn (Bartlett was a favorite) still brings me back to childhood memories. However, I was never taught to knit. Frankly, I think they just didn't trust me with pointy sticks. And lest you jump to the conclusion that my gender had anything to do with it, I did counted cross-stitch and Chinese knotwork (similar to macramé), as well as other crafty pursuits. I spent a lot of time as a kid in the local pottery studio, making weird creatures and both useful and useless items.

Craftstory, continued on page 101

CHAPTER 4

Stranded in Between

There are two techniques that bend some of the basic rules of double-knitting that were covered extensively in *Extreme Double-Knitting*. I'm not using them as heavily in this book, but they deserve a little time since they will be used in one or two patterns here. While they may not seem like they have anything in common (aside from their reversibility), they actually have one very important (but invisible) common denominator: they both make use of strands hidden in between the layers of your double-knitting.

Two-Pattern Double-knitting

So far, the double-knitting we've been talking about has consisted of pairs of just two different color orders. With that limitation, the result is always the same: one layer of the work is always a mirror-image of the other layer in reversed colors.

However, with a subtle change in the rules, some good planning, and rigorous adherence to the resulting chart, you can work a double-knit fabric with a completely different pattern on each layer.

The most common use of two-pattern double-knitting is for making letters. In standard double-knitting, a letter that shows up correctly on one layer will be a mirror-image letter on the other. With two-pattern double-knitting, a letter or even a whole word can be worked so that it's readable on both layers.

When working words, the entire word is flipped so that one letter may not have the same letter on the opposite layer — and from that you can extrapolate that any two motifs (or even all-over patterns) can be worked on opposite layers. There are practical limitations, of course, which I will cover later.

In standard double-knitting, a pair must have color order AB or BA. However, in two-pattern double-knitting, a pair can also be AA or BB, leaving the unused yarn as a strand running inside the work (this happens naturally as you move the yarns together from front to back and vice versa).

If you can choose where to deposit colors on the fly, any chart can be worked on the front and any other chart can be worked on the back. The key is figuring out how to know where to deposit your colors, and for that you need to understand how to read and follow a two-pattern chart.

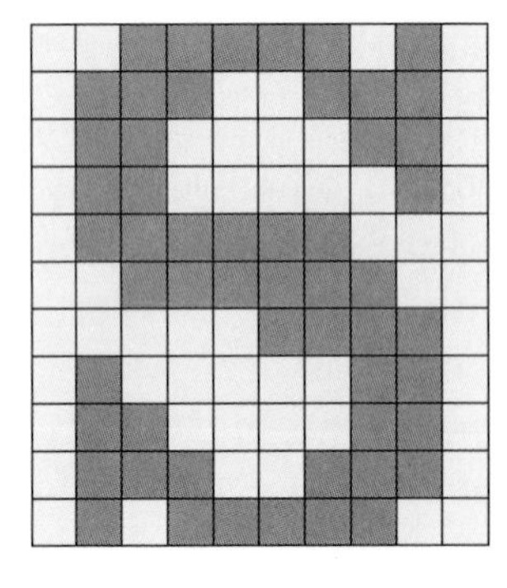

A two-pattern chart consists of two individual charts that have been interlaced to become a single chart. Let's take this letter S as an example. In standard double-knitting, Layer 2 would show you a mirror-image S. With two-pattern double-knitting, the letter is readable on both layers.

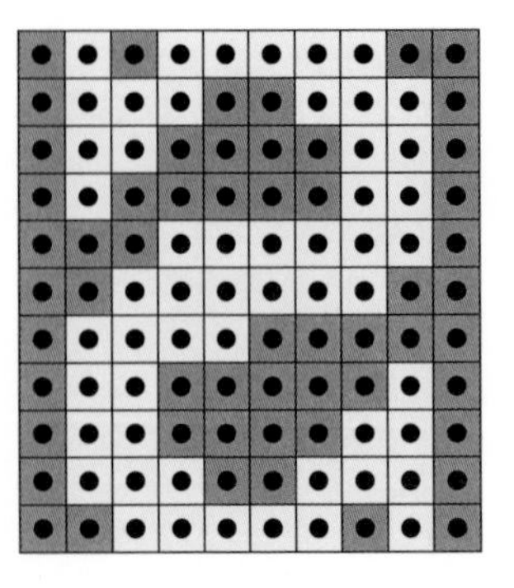

This is achieved by making a second chart that is reversed in color, orientation, and stitch type. As viewed from one side, Layer 1 is made entirely of knits, and Layer 2 is made entirely of purls. When the work is flipped over, the purls that made up Layer 2 now appear as knits on the outside of the work. You can think of the second chart as a view of Layer 2 if Layer 1 was somehow missing.

In order to knit one layer from one chart and the other layer from the other chart, you could work Row 1, Pixel 1 from one chart, then Row 1, Pixel 1 from the other chart. However, that gets tedious and you will easily get lost. Instead, I prefer to interlace the two charts so that it's easy to see every stitch you'll be making. You sacrifice legibility; the resulting chart does not look like what you will get when you knit it, but as long as you follow it without question, it'll work.

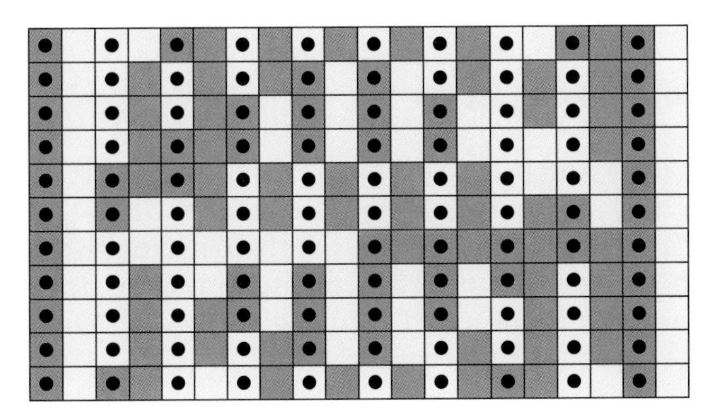

As you can see, each pair is now stretched apart in the chart, so you can see both the knit and the purl. Since there's no logical connection between the colors of each stitch in a pair here, it's best that you can see it all.

To increase clarity, I will often accompany a chart such as the one above with a pair of "reference charts" that show the correct outcome of both layers, as viewed from the outside of the work.

Unlike in standard double-knitting charts, every pixel in a two-pattern chart indicates a single stitch, not a pair. And, just to keep it easier to follow, the second stitch in every pair is notated with a purl dot. In addition, the columns of pairs are most often separated by thicker lines to further reduce the confusion. On Layer 1 rows, you keep the KP stitch order but you follow the chart to determine the color order of each pair. On Layer 2 rows, you do the same thing — but on the chart, the pixels with purl symbols are worked as knits, and the empty pixels are worked as purls. This is consistent with many people's experience working wrong-side rows: in order to show a knit stitch on the right side, you purl when working on the wrong side (and vice versa). Also, note that you do not reverse colors from what's charted, as you would with a standard double-knit chart. In this way, you can see that working two-pattern charts is more literal than following many other double-knit charts, if not necessarily as intuitive.

There is one caveat when working in two-pattern double-knitting: it is possible to have large numbers of single-color pairs in a row. In that case, you will be stranding the other color inside the work. Keep in mind that the length of this strand is only half of what it appears to be (what appears as 8 stitches in a two-pattern chart is actually only 4 pairs), but it can still cause tension issues with your finished work. For this reason, if a strand is running for longer than 3 or 4 single-color pairs (6 or 8 two-pattern stitches of the same color), make sure to give the fabric on your working needle a tug before using that color again. This will give the strand a little slack and minimize the chance of it distorting your fabric.

The other effect of this strand is the likelihood of it showing up in between your stitches when the fabric is stretched. This is not usually an issue if the single-color expanse is surrounded above and below with other colors, but if there's a section of a single color that extends vertically, it's more likely that the various strands will show up there. There's no way around this — it's just an occurrence I try to avoid while planning.

Two-pattern work can also be (and most often is) worked within an area of standard double-knitting. You can switch from one style to the other whenever you need to. Two-pattern charts take up more space (because more information needs to be imparted), so there's no reason to waste space expressing entire rows or columns of standard double-knit pairs.

For this reason, I have a notation I like to use when working two-pattern double-knitting within a field of standard double-knitting: a solid contrasting color or bold-dashed border and sometimes a bit of text that says "Follow Chart X here." This could outline a small box for a single letter, or it could surround an entire chart minus the edge/selvedge symbols (which must be worked as standard pairs, and therefore can't be included). The exception is when working an all-over pattern in the round: not only are there no edges, there's also no surrounding area of standard double-knitting, so it is possible to do the entire thing as a two-pattern chart.

Multicolor Double-knitting

Once you've realized that one rule can be changed, you may begin to imagine other ways to bend the rules of double-knitting. Using some of the skills you learned in two-pattern double-knitting, it becomes possible to add a third color as well. However, adding a strand of Color C to the mix means that it's no longer possible to simply "reverse" the colors (AB to BA), and instead it becomes necessary to rotate the colors (e.g., AB, BC, CA). Each pair becomes a group with yarns in three positions: one for the knit stitch, one for the purl, and one running as a strand between them. Unlike two-pattern double-knitting where strands occur only when working AA or BB pairs, there are strands throughout a three-color piece. It is nearly impossible to keep these strands from affecting your fabric's flexibility and gauge, so my best advice is simply to try to knit a little looser and don't pull too hard on any given end as you work.

As in two-pattern double-knitting, a multicolor chart will have a reference chart, but usually just one. The color rotation will be set up in the pattern's key, and Layer 1 will be charted as usual. A smaller Layer 2 reference chart will be provided so you can check your work.

When working in flat multicolor double-knitting, Layer 2 rows will have you following the color order of each pair in reverse, as set out in the key. For example, if the key sets up an AB, BC, CA rotation, those are the three color orders you'll see (and make) in pairs on Layer 1 rows. On Layer 2 rows, the pairs will present reversed — as AC, CB and BA. Of course, when working in the round, you never have Layer 2 facing you so you'll only see the AB, BC, and CA pairs.

Following that logic will tell you how to follow the chart: For example, assuming the same color order rotation as mentioned above, if you are working on a Layer 1 row and there is a pixel on the chart in Color A, you will knit in A and purl in B; a pixel in Color B will be knit in B and purled in C; and a pixel in Color C will be knit in C and purled in A. As you see, the knits are worked as the chart indicates, and the purls are worked as the key indicates. On a Layer 2 row, the charted color indicates the purl (which is, of course, a knit on Layer 1). Since the purl is worked second, you'll need to consult the key to see which color to knit. As you proceed in the pattern, you'll notice that pixels of each color order are always worked in a particular way on whichever layer is facing you, and you can use the same color order that appeared last time you worked that type of pair, reducing the need for constant references to the key.

Multicolor Double-knitting Edges

Edges in multicolor double-knitting are a special concern as well. Since the edge only consists of two colors, something must be done with the third. This applies to the side edges of each flat row, but it also applies to the bottom (cast-on) and top (bind-off) edges whether working flat or in the round.

Multicolor double-knit cast-on

This sounds scary! And frankly, it looks terrible. I have tried three-color cast-ons and they are not worth the trouble for the less-than-clean look you get. The most elegant solution is simply to make a two-color cast-on (generally choosing the color order corresponding to the background of both layers, if there is one), and then begin carrying a new color when you start a row or round that requires one.

Multicolor double-knit bind-off

This works on the same principle as the cast-on: work the last row that requires the third color, and break its end with enough length to weave in. Then work the bind-off of your choice.

Multicolor double-knit selvedge (multicolor linked pair)

In general, a selvedge keeps the same color order all the way up the sides of your flat piece. In multicolor double-knitting, this means that there is consistently a third color to be wrangled with in that selvedge. The twist that links the side edges together is an ideal place to link in that third strand. If you don't link it in at the edge, you run the risk of having the strand carried with you from the last time you used it, then carried back to the next time in the next row without any connection to the rest of the fabric. This is likely to create a hole in your work. There are a few ways to avoid this, but the one I suggest requires at least two pairs at the border (the selvedge and one more pair of the same color order) for the cleanest edge.

See page 86 for the step-by-step instructions.

Color Orders Illustrated

To show the multicolor options visually, I've borrowed part of a chart from *Extreme Double-Knitting* because it has a nice small repeat. As you can see, there are three colors used in most rows; if properly rotated, the rows which have only two colors showing will use the third color somewhere on Layer 2.

Here are the 6 possible color arrangements for this chart:

As you can see, each of the columns shares a color in one role; the other two colors simply change places. Since it is important that each color on Layer 1 has a different color on Layer 2 and no one color is used in the same role twice, it's possible to match up each of these arrangements with two others from elsewhere in the array. Removing the duplicates, we're left with 6 possible color order rotations:

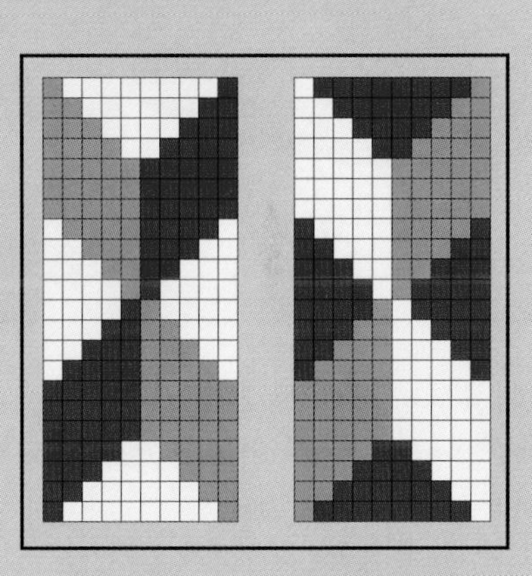

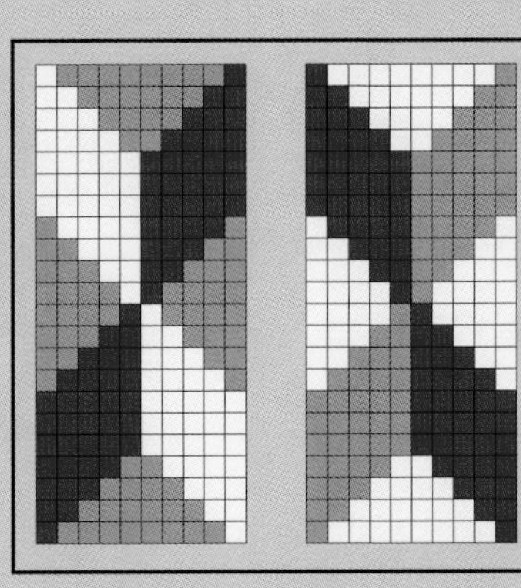

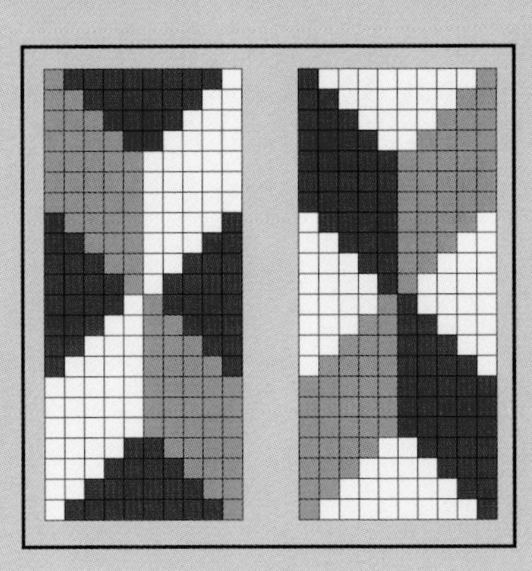

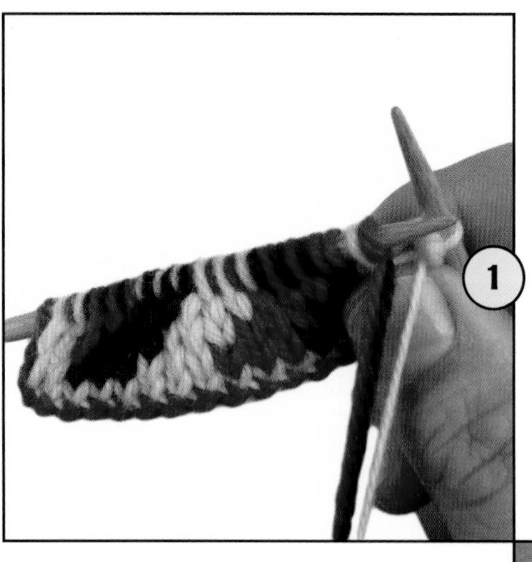

With all yarns in back, KTBL in the color indicated by the chart.

Bring yarns to the front. Twist the ends so that the color you need to purl passes underneath the other two strands from back to front. Complete the purl.

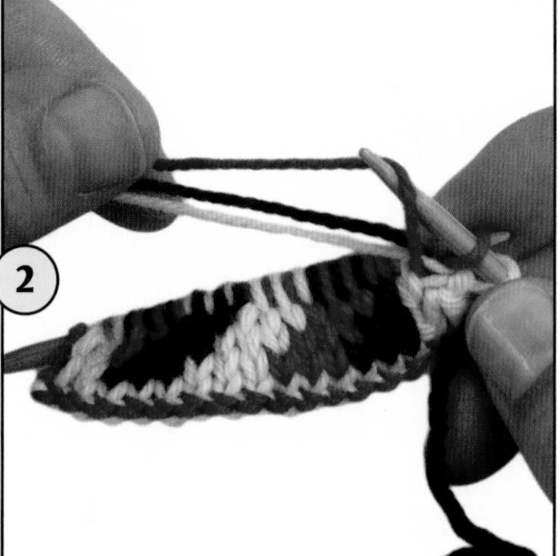

3

Here you can see the first completed link. This is the same as the standard linked pair back on page 32. However, you can also see that the third color is not yet incorporated into the link.

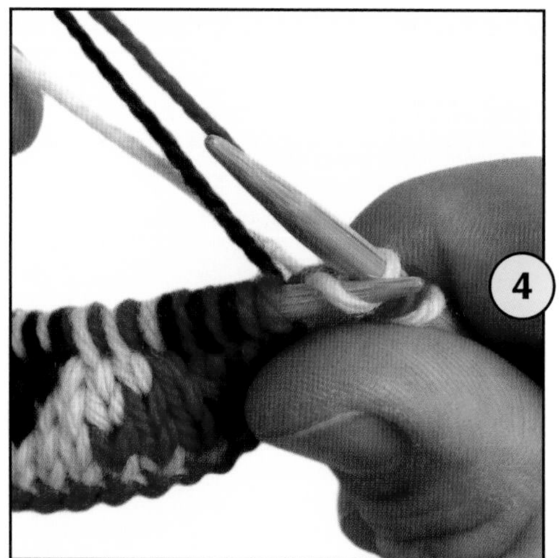

Bring yarns to the back. Twist the ends so that the color you need to knit passes underneath the other two strands from back to front.

Complete the knit. Note that the third color is crossing over down at the base of this stitch.

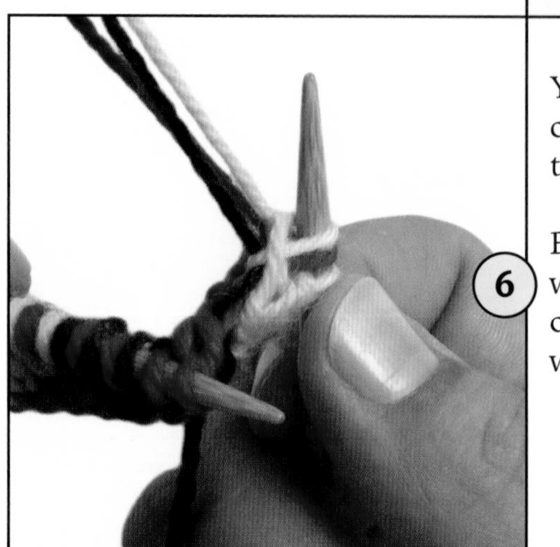

You can now see that the third color is linked into the bottom of the third stitch.

Bring yarns to the front. Purl with the same color as in Step 2 to complete the second pair; continue with your chart.

As you can see, the multicolor linked pair uses a pair of twists, one done on the second stitch (between the front and back colors) and one on the third (between the front color and the third strand) of a two-pair group. This is a substitute for the normal linked pair used in standard double-knitting. The slipped pair at the other end of the row is still worked in the same way. There is no separate multicolor linked pair symbol in the chart, but if you are working with three colors and you encounter a linked pair symbol in the chart, you will need to make sure all three colors are included so you'll need to do the multicolor link. This will, by the way, also work with 4 or more colors — the second link will take care of any and all strands traveling inside the work. There is no need to do a separate link for each color after the first two have been done.

Multicolor end management

In two-color double-knitting, your yarns tend to twist around each other (see two-color end management, page 28). In the worst case scenario, you can just let the work dangle and untwist its ends. In three-color double-knitting, you run the risk of braiding — which, needless to say, doesn't just dangle out. You can do some complicated yarn-ball leapfrog, but you can also learn to manage your ends and do some untwisting on the fly.

Let me begin by explaining how to keep the braid from occurring. With two colors, you can hold the two yarns together as if they were a ribbon (see page 27). If you hold the three yarns in a fixed shape, it has to be a triangle, or a kind of flexible triangular prism. Each face of the prism represents a particular color order, while the opposite point represents the yarn that will be hiding inside when a pair of that color order is worked. As you rotate the prism, the roles of the three yarns change. The prism, like the ribbon, can be rotated in either direction. However, it can also be turned inside out by pulling the point through the opposite face. This is to be avoided since this is how braids begin. But, as with two-color end management, the presence of mind to avoid the braid is not always present — so I will show you how to undo it as you go.

At some point, while working in three-color double-knitting, you'll notice that your yarn is all tangled up. The first thing you should do is to let it dangle out — either let the whole piece dangle, or if it's too big, lash the three balls of yarn together with a rubber band and let them dangle instead. This "simplifies" the situation by getting rid of any plain twist. You may find that the worst tangles are not that bad after getting rid of the twist this way. Once this is done, you can deal with any remaining braiding.

If you've ever made a braid, you know that if you break it down to its simplest components, it's just a series of two-strand crossings — but not always the same two strands. This means that in order to untwist a braid, you don't need to worry about all three strands, only the next two at any given time. As in two-color double-knitting, you may have an opportunity to undo part of the twist at each color change. If you can't, no big deal — just try not to add more twist and wait for the next color change. Soon enough you'll be able to undo the next twist (and the next, etc.) until all three yarns are again separate. This is a bit of an art form. The important thing is not to force an untwist; it may create more problems than it solves. The more you do it, the more it will become second nature.

Multicolor two-pattern double-knitting

Using the method of creating a two-pattern chart on page 82 and the multicolor methods described here, it is possible to take two unrelated three-color charts and interlace them so that each shows up on one layer of the final piece. In *Extreme Double-Knitting*, I used this technique to great effect in the Falling Blocks hat, and I later used it to its logical extremes in the 52 Pickup patterns.

When working three-color two-pattern double-knitting, you will end up with 9 possible color orders: AB, BC, CA, AC, CB, BA, AA, BB, and CC. The first six color orders are the same as the ones you'd have in regular three-color double-knitting, with the strand of the unused color running in between. The last three color orders use the same color for the knit and the purl, which means that the two unused strands will run between them. When coming to the end of a run of these pairs, it's doubly necessary to keep an eye on your tension, because two over-tightened strands will distort the fabric more strongly than one.

Incidentally, when working two-pattern double-knitting in four colors, you have 16 possible color orders; five colors will have 25 possible color orders, etc. The rule goes that any number of colors will have the square of that number of possible color orders.

WATERFORD CROSSING

a shawl in multicolor double-knitting

Finished size & weight

The blocked size is approximately 63" wide and 21" deep, as worn (as knitted, reverse those numbers). According to my best calculations, this piece uses 120 g (516 yds) each of Colors A and B, and 134 g (577 yds) of Color C. Even if it's a little more than that, you should be fine with 200 g of each color.

Materials & tools

[Color A]: Plucky Knitter Oxford (75% merino wool, 25% cashmere; 430 yd/100 g skein); Princess Phone (green); 2 skeins.

[Color B]: Plucky Knitter Oxford (75% merino wool, 25% cashmere; 430 yd/100g skein); Miss Manners (magenta); 2 skeins.

[Color C]: Plucky Knitter Oxford (75% merino wool, 25% cashmere; 430 yd/100 g skein); Skies Of November (blue); 2 skeins.

US4/3.5 mm 24" or longer circular needles, or needle size required to achieve gauge.

Gauge in pattern

25 sts/29 rows = 4" unblocked in double-stockinette.

24 sts/26 rows = 4" blocked in double-stockinette.

Sample knitted by Charles Parker

I'm a big fan of cables and cable-like motifs. I also love working in multiple colors, as you may have noticed in my previous book and in many of my standalone patterns. While I have not done many designs in multicolor double-knitting for this book, I thought it would be a good idea to cover one or two things I hadn't done in *Extreme Double-Knitting*. The multicolor patterns in that book are mostly in the round; I have since honed my techniques for working flat multicolor double-knitting. The body of the work remains much the same as, say, the Struktur hat; but because you are working flat, you're going to be seeing both layers as you work (which requires a slightly different way of following the chart).

I told my Plucky Knitter story in a previous pattern, and this is done in another of their yarns.

Instead, let me explain about the colors. These three colors are not, at first glance, particularly compatible. Perhaps they're even a little jarring. I wasn't sure when I picked them up why I thought they worked so well together — but every time I looked at them I thought about Kristin Nicholas, who taught me that "chartreuse goes with everything!" So this piece became an homage to Kristin Nicholas, and that's all the justification these colors need.

This pattern was originally called "Knots & Crossings," but that didn't make much sense since there isn't a "noughts & crosses" pattern involved. There are Celtic-style knots and colorwork crossovers, but the wordplay just wasn't as deep as I prefer. So I cast about for a new name.

I thought about the pattern and the knots and realized what was unique about them. Celtic cables in knitting don't often change direction in the middle of a row, but the adapted Viking patterns do (as evidenced by the designs of Elsebeth Lavold). Since part of the pattern's name was already "Crossing" I started thinking about Viking crossings and found out that Vikings founded the first city in Ireland, named Waterford. It's a fact that Scandinavian crafts influenced Irish folk art. However, I am not a historian, and I can't be sure that the cable motifs that were so prevalent in Irish illustration were an evolution of this early infusion of Viking aesthetics. But I'll take some poetic license and acknowledge the similarity between some of the two cultures' artistic sensibilities with this pattern's new name, "Waterford Crossing."

Chart Guide B

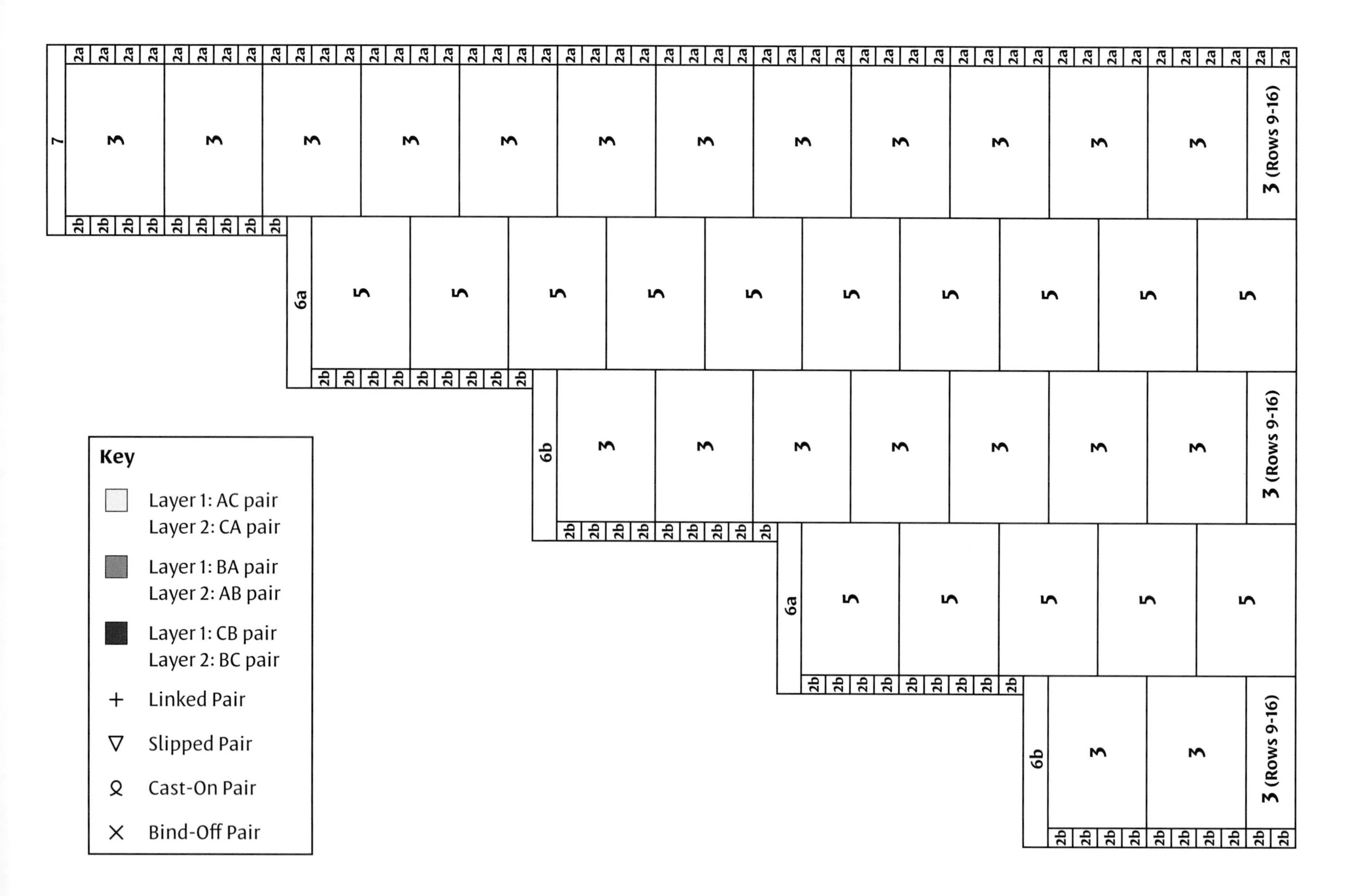

Chart Guide A

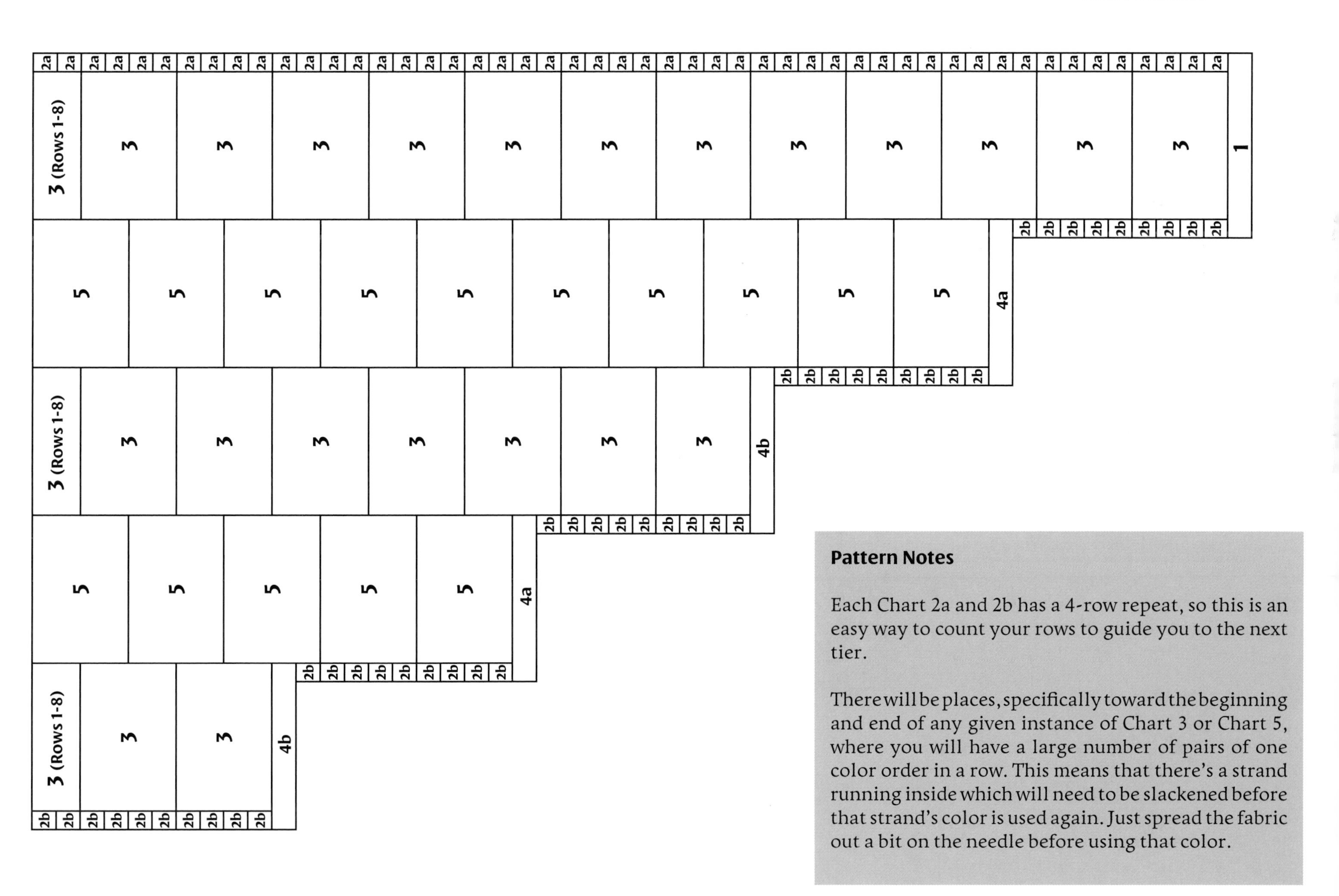

Pattern Notes

Each Chart 2a and 2b has a 4-row repeat, so this is an easy way to count your rows to guide you to the next tier.

There will be places, specifically toward the beginning and end of any given instance of Chart 3 or Chart 5, where you will have a large number of pairs of one color order in a row. This means that there's a strand running inside which will need to be slackened before that strand's color is used again. Just spread the fabric out a bit on the needle before using that color.

Pattern Reference

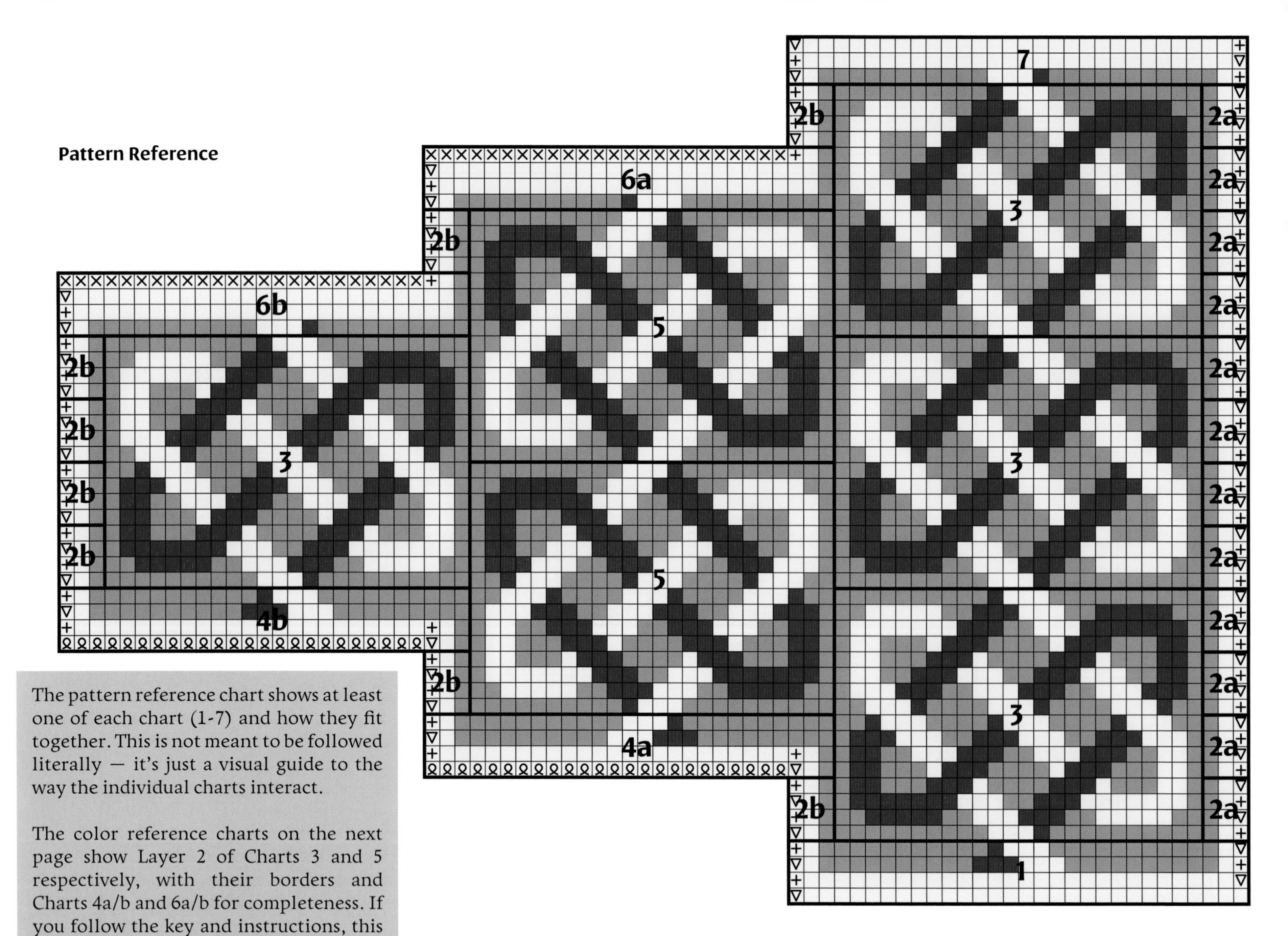

The pattern reference chart shows at least one of each chart (1-7) and how they fit together. This is not meant to be followed literally — it's just a visual guide to the way the individual charts interact.

The color reference charts on the next page show Layer 2 of Charts 3 and 5 respectively, with their borders and Charts 4a/b and 6a/b for completeness. If you follow the key and instructions, this is what the other layer should look like.

hart 3+ Color Reference

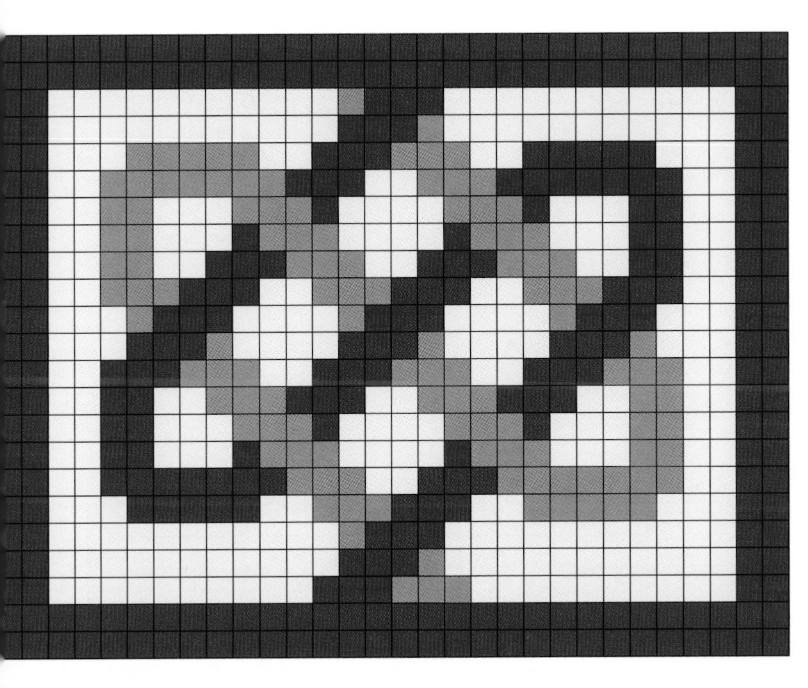

hart 5+ Color Reference

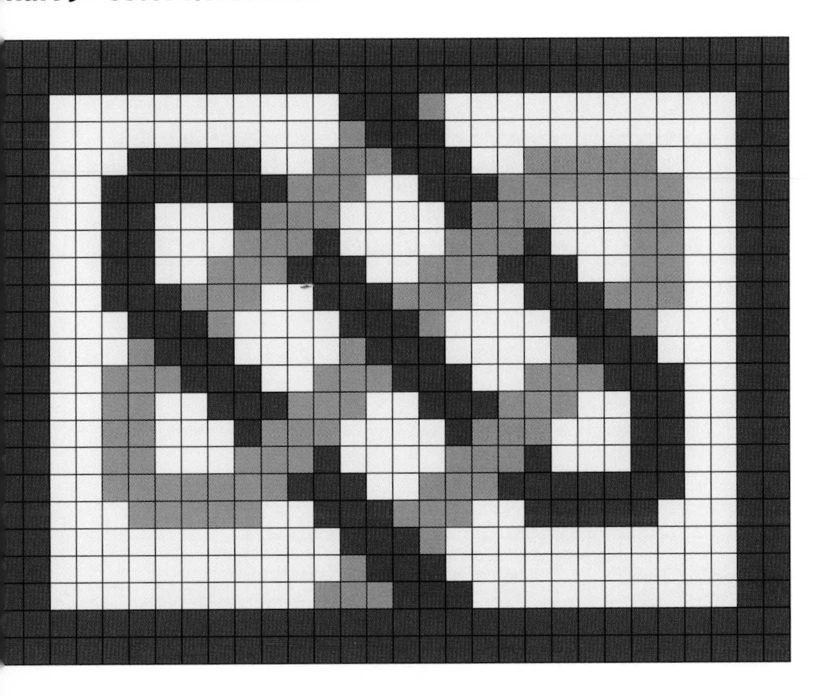

Pattern

Key and Chart Guides A and B are on pages 90-91. All other Charts are on pages 94-95.

CO 30 AC pairs.

First half:

Work as indicated in Chart Guide A.

Begin by following Chart 1. Add in Color B as you begin Row 3.

After 9 repeats of Charts 2a and 2b (2.25 repeats of Chart 3), follow Chart 4a instead of 2b (as shown). 4a begins like 2b, but when finished with the final slipped pair, take Color B and bring it between A and C, draping it over your working needle to keep it out of the way. Position the remaining ends as in the original CO and cast on 24 AC pairs.

Turn, work as charted, and when you reach your hanging end of Color B, let it rejoin the other 2 colors and work a three-color linked pair as you normally would at the beginning of a row.

Follow Chart Guide A through all 5 tiers to the end. Charts 4a and 4b start the same way, the only difference is how the colors are positioned in Rows 3 and 4.

Second half:

Work as indicated in Chart Guide B; join new skeins when necessary.

When you reach the first instance of Chart 6b, work the first row and then break Color B with enough length to weave in. Work Chart 6b Row 2, adding in Color B again toward the end of the row. (The alternative is leaving Color B attached and running a 24-pair strand between the layers which will play merry hell with the blocking later.) On Row 3, hold Color B with other 2 colors for first 3 pairs of chart (first 2 pairs form new left border), then leave Color B behind (same method as for Charts 4a and b above). Continue with rest of row. Turn, first work indicated BO stitches as a normal row in indicated colors, picking up Color B where it was left and working it into a 3-color linked pair. Finish row. Slide needle to opposite end, work slipped BO on indicated pairs, leaving 2 pairs of border at end. Slide needle back to end where active yarns are and continue the pattern. Follow these instructions for all instances of Charts 6a and 6b in the pattern.

Continue following Chart Guide B until you've completed the last Chart 3. Work Chart 7, breaking off Color B before Row 2, then work another CA row to BO after chart is complete. Block if necessary, weave in ends and enjoy!

Chart 1

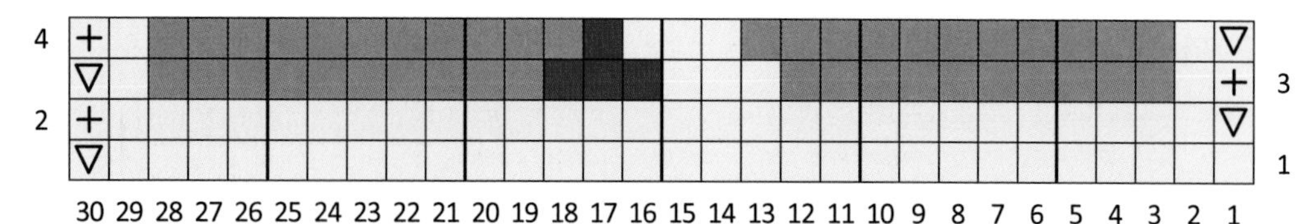

Chart 2b

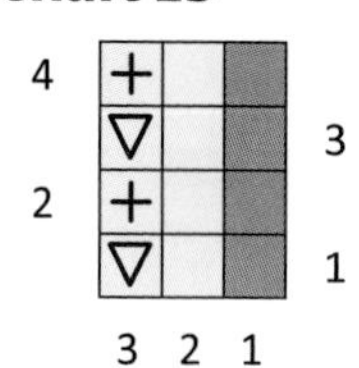

Chart 2a

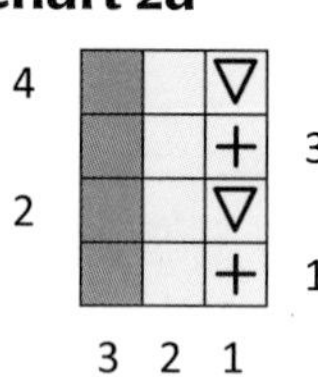

Chart 3

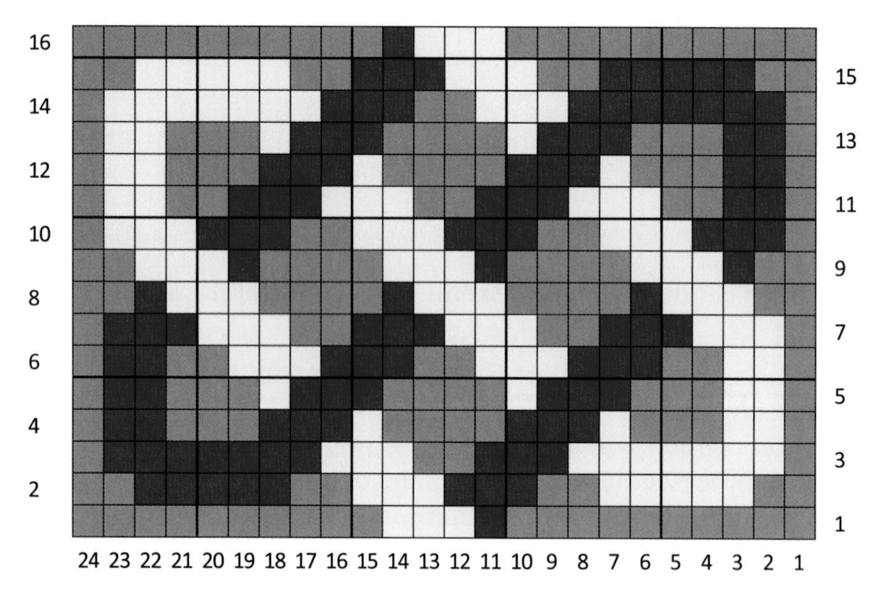

Chart 6b

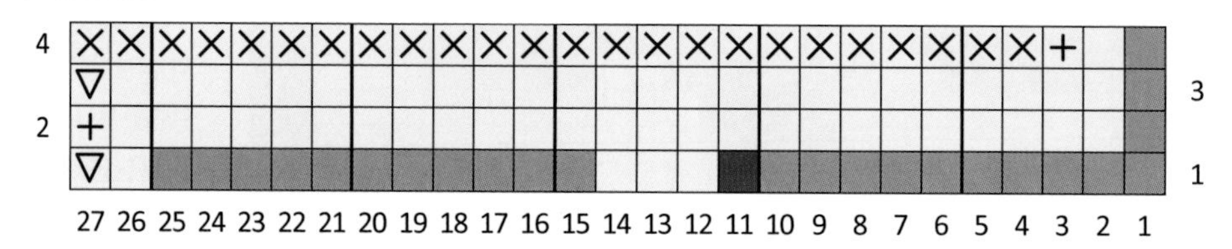

Chart 4b

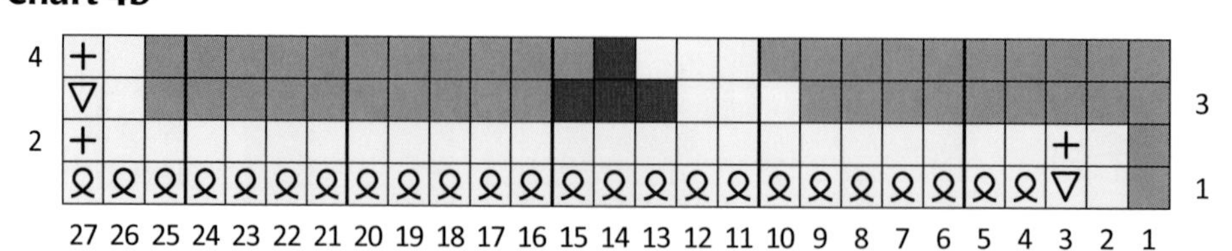

Chart 7

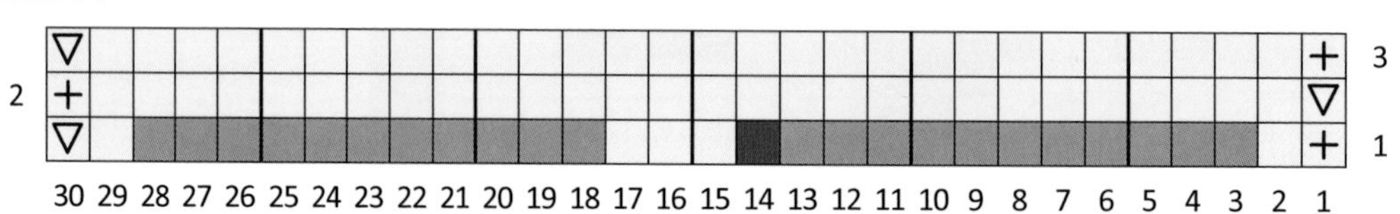

Chart 5

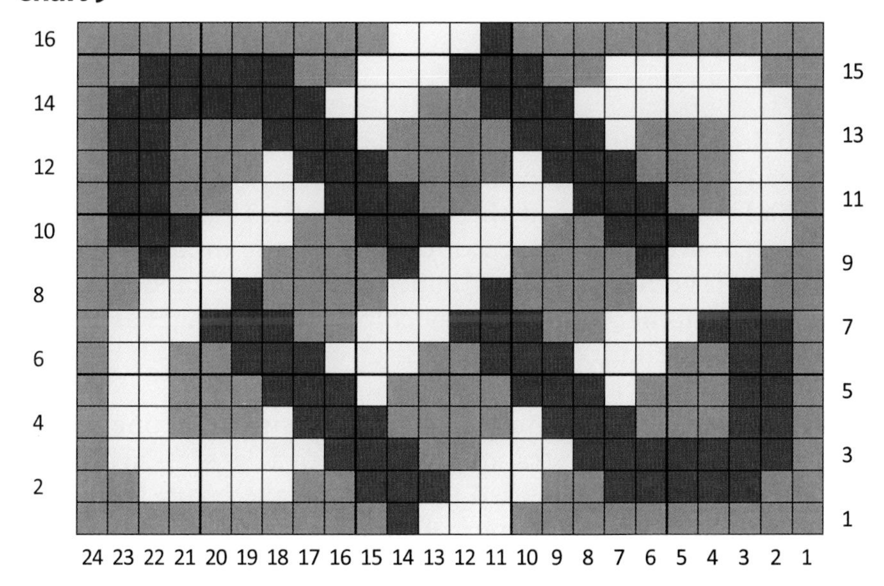

Chart 6a

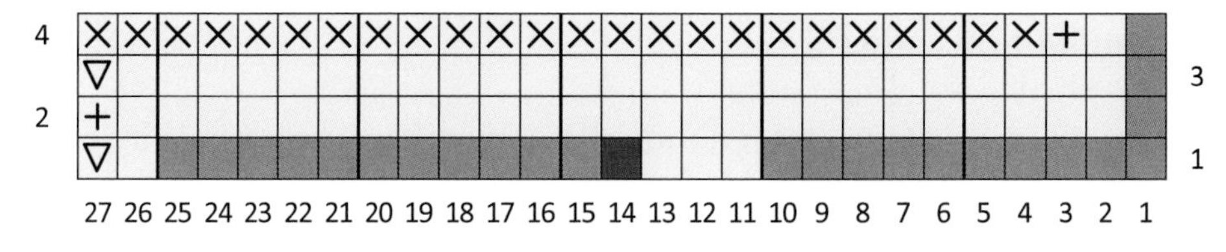

Chart 4a

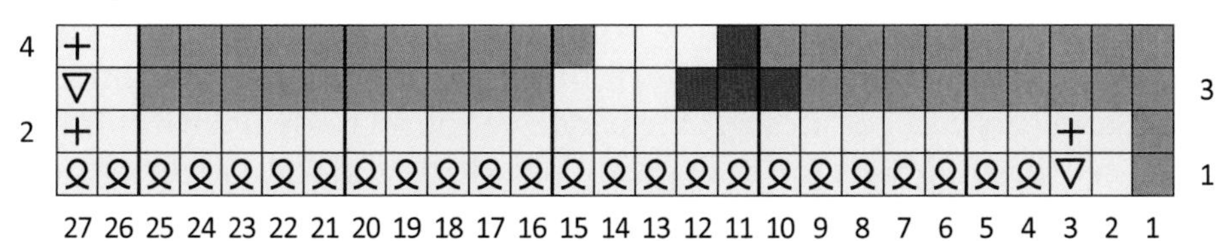

CHAPTER 5

Double-knitting Intarsia

Everything up until this point had been covered in *Extreme Double-Knitting*, with some added refinements. The patterns you've seen have used techniques that have been documented for a while now, but each one has added a little tweak or two to keep things interesting. However, I'm never content to merely change things incrementally. If you've worked through some of my existing patterns (from this book or previously published work), you've probably got a good background in double-knitting. Now it's time to take that foundation and put it to good use.

Double-knitting Intarsia

This is one of those techniques that I put off developing for a while, but the time it's spent stewing on the back burner has seasoned it nicely. In single-layer knitting, intarsia is a colorwork method that involves using one color at a time, judiciously connecting a new color at the beginning of a section, and then dropping it to add another at the end of the section. It's best used for large motifs that would require floats of significant length in stranded knitting. The result is a fabric that uses less yarn and has a gauge far closer to standard knitting than stranded knitting does, due to diminished stress on the fabric. However, it is often difficult to achieve clean transitions between color sections, since intarsia's signature "twists" tend to pull rows in unusual directions. I'm not going to delve into single-layer intarsia techniques, but I highly recommend that before you attempt to do intarsia in double-knitting, you first try it in single-layer knitting.

During the search for an elegant solution to double-knit intarsia, I was derailed by my interest in technique purity; I wanted to make two layers that were each intarsia in their own right. In other words, I wanted to use four colors such that one layer was in two colors, and the other one was in two completely different colors. I had already played with doing this without intarsia, but the result was two separate layers of stranded knitting — interesting, but without any benefit over just making two layers of stranded knitting, and then sewing them together.

In order to do away with the strands, I played with ways to use intarsia twists instead. I never found an elegant solution until I gave up on trying to make the layers separate at the intarsia twists. I had thought that I would use regular double-knit color changes in the intarsia sections to keep the layers together, but this is limiting. It would be far better to have the fabric link together at the intarsia color group changes as well as at any standard double-knit color changes.

The solution ended up being simple: use the two strands as one and make an intarsia twist. These two strands at the edge of a flat section of double-knitting would ordinarily be used to create a linked pair. Instead, you can cross them with a second group of two strands, which both links the fabric together and makes a transition to a new pair of ends. The resulting intarsia twist actually hides inside the fabric, between the two side edges. And because the fabric is reversible, the same technique works on either layer — unlike single-layer intarsia where the twists are only done from the same perspective every other row.

Flat double-knit intarsia

The vast majority of intarsia is done in flat fabric. Because intarsia involves leaving a strand on the far side of each section, if you were to try the same technique in the round you'd quickly run out of strands to work with.

For a simple example, let's assume you have two plain rectangular sections to work. In single-layer intarsia you'd need two strands. In double-knitting, you're going to need four — because each color on Layer 1 will need a corresponding color on Layer 2. Even though you'll only be working with two at a time, four strands will be hanging off your project and this can get messy. One way I've found to deal with this is to make 2 center-pull balls for each group of colors, and then wrap a rubber band or "yarn bra" around each group to keep them connected. If you've got 4 colors, group them together as A/B for Group 1 and C/D for Group 2.

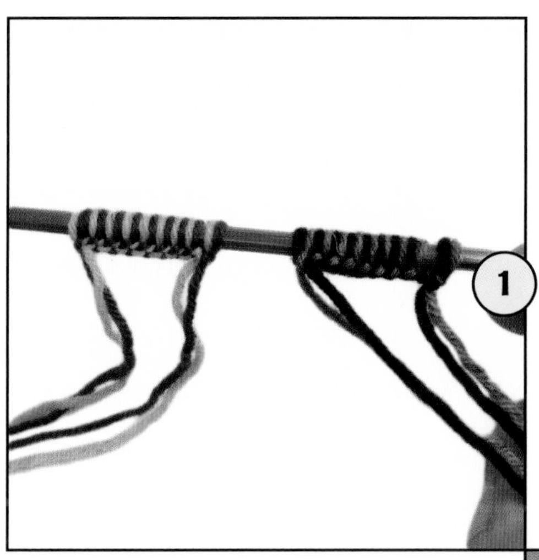

Begin by casting on with Group 2 in CD color order. If you're going to follow this as an exercise, choose a small but significant number of pairs (such as 8 or 10).

Cast on the same number with Group 1 in BA color order.

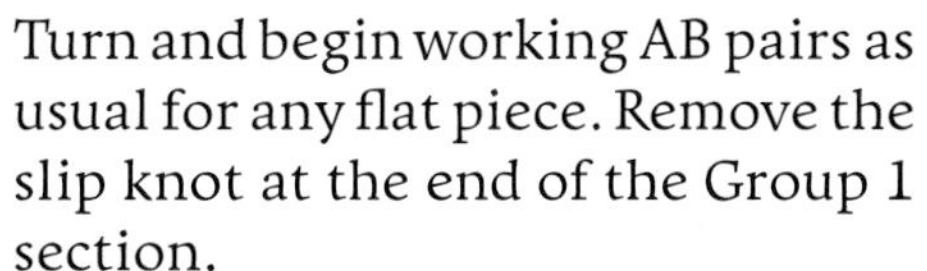

Turn and begin working AB pairs as usual for any flat piece. Remove the slip knot at the end of the Group 1 section.

You should now have the ends of Groups 1 and 2 together. Bring both sets of ends to the front; lay the Group 1 ends across Group 2; then bring the Group 2 ends over Group 1 and to the back.

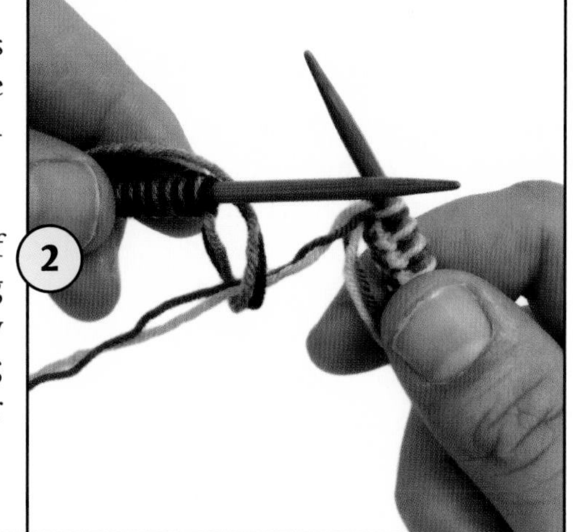

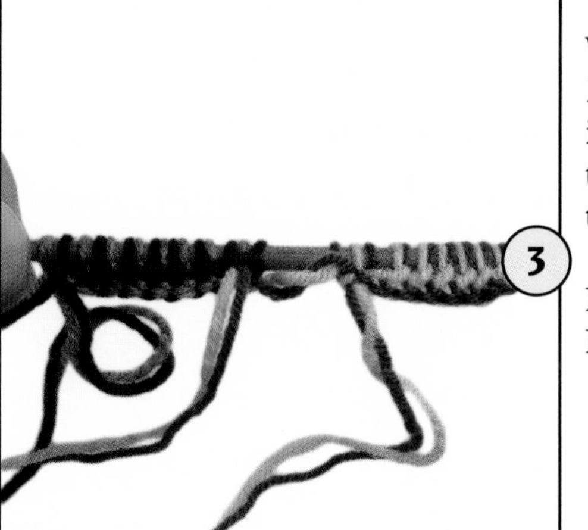

Work Group 2. Note that the Group 1 ends should now be trapped in a loop of Group 2. No need to tighten it, as that will be done on the way back.

Finish the section of Group 2 with DC pairs, and remove the slip knot.

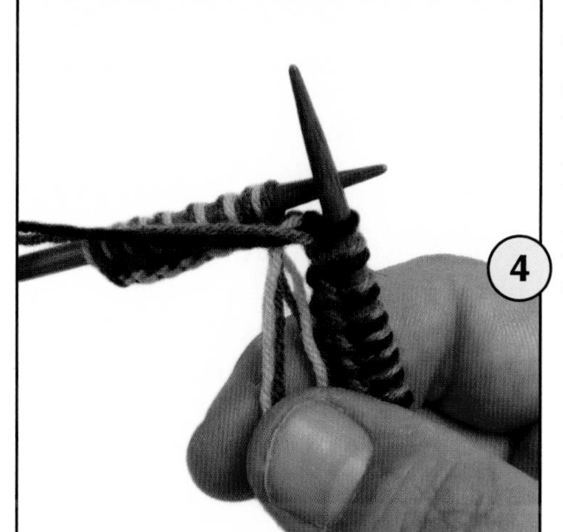

Turn and work the next section in CD pairs with a linked pair at the beginning of the row and a slipped pair at the end of the section.

Repeat Steps 2 and 3 with the ends of Groups 2 and 1.

Here's Step 4 in progress.

Work the next section in BA pairs with a slipped pair at the end of the section.

Repeat Steps 2-5 as needed, omitting the slipknot removal instructions.

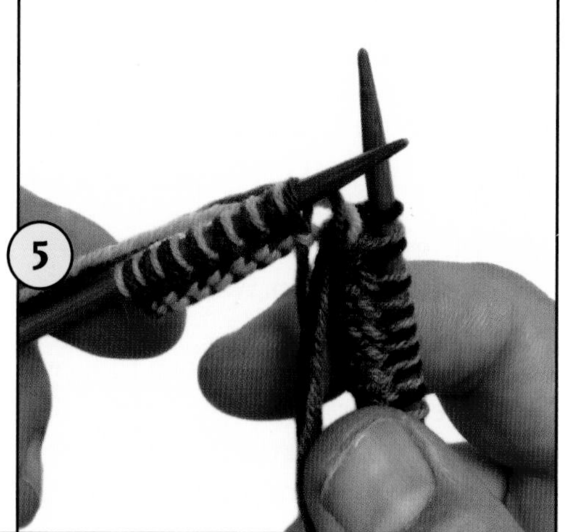

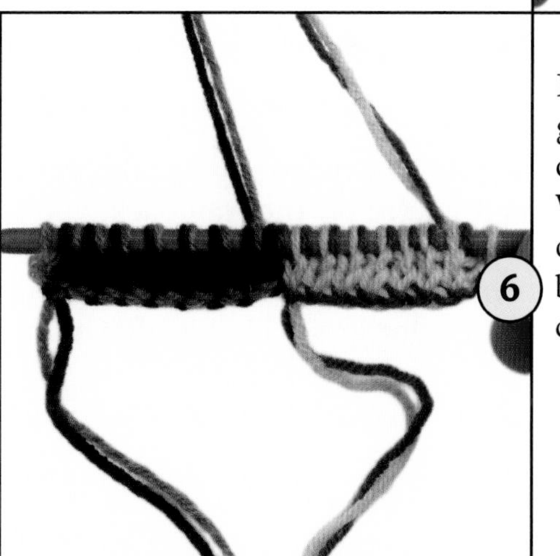

If you follow this for a while, you'll get a swatch with two differently-colored columns on each layer. Within each section, you can work double-knitting color changes, but you have the added intrigue of color group changes as well.

Moving color group changes

What if you want to work a double-knit intarsia motif where the color group changes aren't in the exact same place in every row? Here's where it gets interesting.

If you want to move a color group change left (in the same direction you're working), pick up the new group and let all 4 ends travel together as you work with the original group for however many pairs are needed. The unused ends will travel inside. There's no need for an actual intarsia twist here; just begin working with the new color group (which was traveling inside) and leave the previous group at the front. If you are careful to pick up the new group from behind, you won't even twist the groups' ends around each other when you do it.

If you want to move a color group change right (in the opposite direction), you've got a couple of options. The simpler (but slightly messier) one is to stop where you want the new color to come in, slip the rest of your stitches until you come to the next group's ends, and then slip back with the ends in hand, bringing them between the layers until you encounter the first group again. Then, make the intarsia twist, and work with the new group going forward.

There is a more elegant way to move the color group change to the right, but it requires some planning. Say your pattern has the color group change moving 2 stitches to the left in each row. On your Layer 1 rows, these will be moving to the left, whereas looking at Layer 2, they'll appear to move to the right. You can move the color change left and prep for the next row in the same move. Let's assume you're working with Groups 1 and 2. When you reach the end of Group 1, pick up Group 2 and hold it along with Group 1 while you work 2 more pairs in Group 1. Then, still holding both groups, work 2 pairs in Group 2. Leave Group 1 at the front, and continue with Group 2. Now, when you're on the way back, you'll encounter the Group 1 ends at the place you need them, and you can simply work a normal double-knit intarsia row. This can be a bit confusing, but it's not difficult if you simply break each color group change down into 3 steps:

1. Pick up the new color group where it lies.
2. Work the color group change where it's charted.
3. Leave the previous color group at the front where indicated.

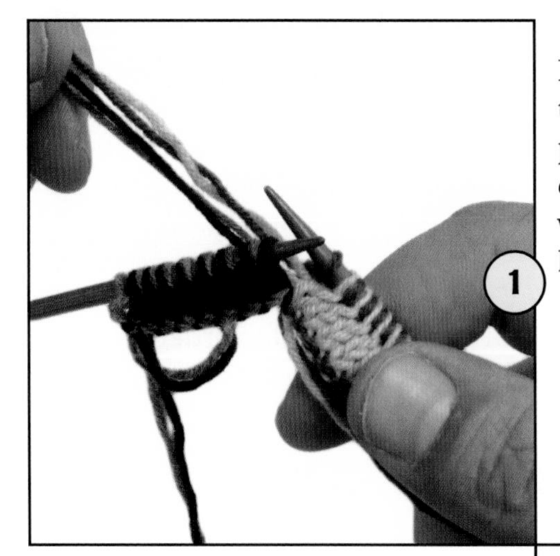

Here we are at the location above the color group change in the previous row. The ends of the new color group are on the back of the work. When you encounter them, hold them with your other ends.

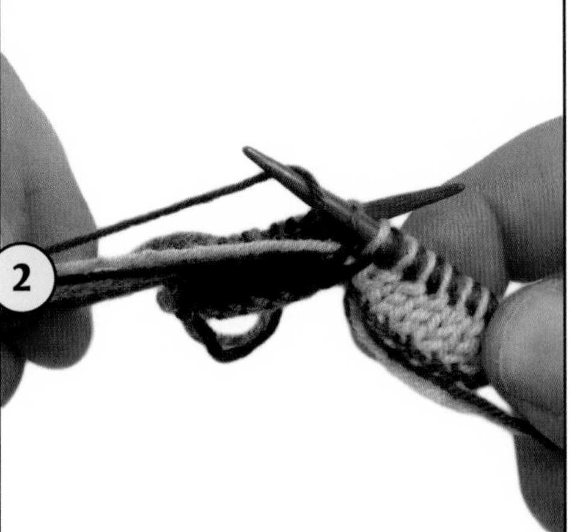

Knit and purl as normal, but let the new color group travel along with the ends you're currently using. This is the same process used in multicolor double-knitting.

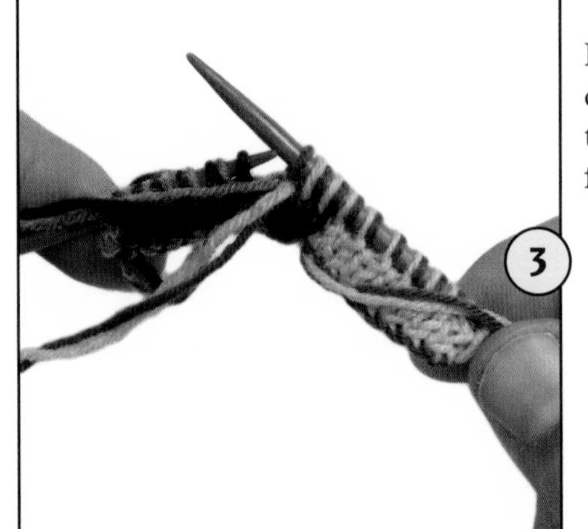

Here are 2 pairs done in the original color group. Notice that the new color group is exiting the fabric in the same location.

Moving a color group change right

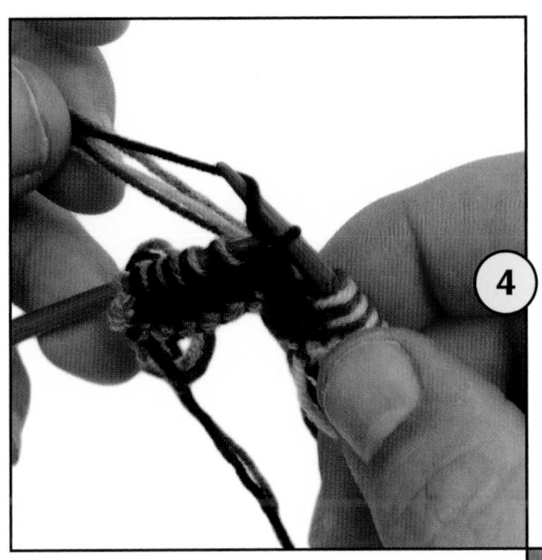

When you begin the pairs of the new color group, take the knit from over the top of the previous color group. This will ensure that the previous color group will be most easily able to be left at the front in the next step.

When you have finished 2 pairs (in this example) in the new color group, bring the ends of the previous color group to the front of the work, and leave them there as you finish your row.

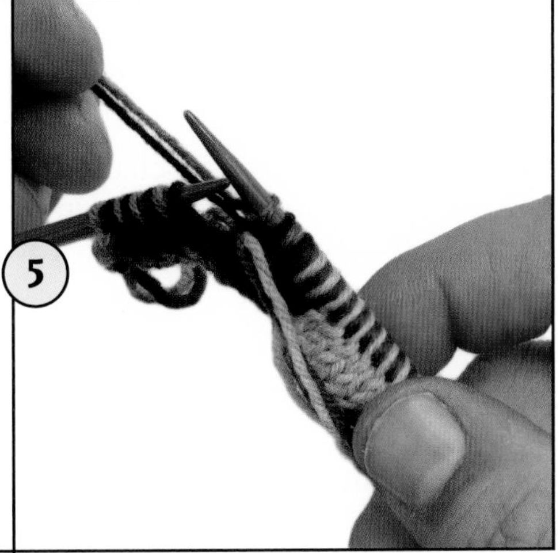

Here is the completed row. Note that the first color group is worked on top of two pairs of the second color group in the row below, and that the first color group's ends are left at the front 2 pairs beyond the color group change.

Moving a color group change right, continued

To help you visualize this a little better, I've created a chart symbol () that lies on the line between two pairs. This is the place in Step 3 where the ends would be left at the front of the work. The first step doesn't need to be charted, because the work itself will tell you to pick up the new group where it lies. Then, in the second step, make the color group change where the chart indicates. But unless you're paying attention to the next row, you won't know where to leave the previous group's ends so that they'll be in the proper place when you come back. Hence the new symbol, which is meant to look a little like an opening between two pairs.

Closeup from Kontinuum, page 104

EXERCISE: Flat double-knit intarsia

This little swatch will walk you through the basics of double-knit intarsia. Like any other flat double-knitting, the first pair in the row will be linked and the last pair will be slipped. However, at some point between those edges, there will be a color group change. That change will move around, which will necessitate some extra preparation in some rows.

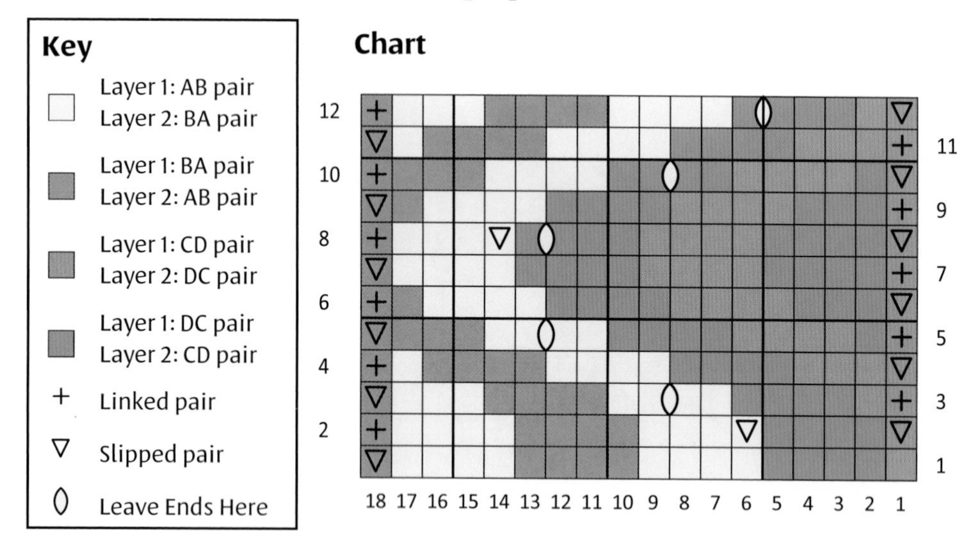

Colors A and B will be assigned as Group 1 and Colors C and D will be assigned as Group 2.

Cast on 13 AB pairs with Group 1, then cast on 5 DC pairs with Group 2. Turn your work; you should see a CD pair first on your needle.

Layer 1

Layer 2

Row 1: Work 5 pairs as charted in Group 2; remove the slip knot. Bring both groups to the front, make an intarsia twist, and then continue following the row with Group 1. Remove the slip knot and turn.

Row 2: Work 13 pairs as charted in Group 1 (don't forget the slipped pair at the end of this group). Make an intarsia twist, and finish this row with Group 2. Turn.

Row 3: Work 5 pairs as charted in Group 2, then hold all 4 ends together and work the last pair in this section with Group 2. Continue holding all 4 ends and work 2 pairs with Group 1 as charted. Leave Group 2 ends at the front and finish the row with Group 1. Turn.

Rows 4, 6, 9, and 11: Work all pairs as charted, making the intarsia twist and the group change in the indicated location. Turn.

Row 5: Work 8 pairs as charted in Group 2, then hold all 4 ends together and work 2 more pairs in this section with Group 2, and then work the first 2 pairs in the next section in Group 1. Leave Group 2 ends at the front and finish the row with Group 1. Turn.

Row 7: Work 12 pairs as charted in Group 2, and then hold all 4 ends together and work 1 more pair in this section with Group 2. Leave Group 2 ends at the front and finish the row with Group 1. Turn.

Row 8: Work 5 pairs as charted in Group 1, and then hold all 4 ends together and work 1 pair in Group 2. Leave Group 1 ends at the front and finish this row as charted in Group 2. Turn.

Row 10: Work 6 pairs as charted in Group 1, then hold all 4 ends together and work 2 more pairs in this section with Group 1, and then work the first 2 pairs of the next section in Group 2. Leave the Group 1 ends at the front and finish this row with Group 2. Turn.

Row 12: Work 10 pairs as charted in Group 1, then hold all 4 ends together and work 2 more pairs in this section with Group 1, and then work the first pair of the next section in Group 2. Leave the Group 1 ends at the front and finish this row with Group 2. Turn.

If you want to continue the pattern, repeat Rows 1-12 (omitting instructions about slip knots in Row 1).

Bind-off:

Work one more row with 5 CD pairs, an intarsia twist, and then 13 BA pairs (making sure to work the last pair rather than slipping it). Slide back to the beginning, and work the slipped bind-off as usual.

Double-knit Intarsia in the Round

Intarsia in the round is kind of a misnomer. Over the years, people have tried to find ways to work it, with varying degrees of success. It's accepted that it can't actually be done, but there are ways to make it look as if it had. These involve working flat, but connecting the two side edges together on the fly so that a tube is formed. You still need to turn at the edge and work back in the other direction, but the result at least appears to be done in the round. The predominant way of doing this up until recently was to use a short-row technique to "wrap and turn" as follows: connect one edge to the other at the wrap, then turn to go back around (repeating every time the edge is reached). The edge becomes a seam, and if you're lucky and/or skilled, it will be more or less invisible. If you want to try this, there's a section on double-knit short rows on page 126.

However, it is truly wonderful that we are living in an age of innovation, and I am fortunate that I have been allowed to adapt someone else's innovation in order to enhance my own. Anne Berk's "Annetarsia" method is a true stroke of genius in intarsia, and it's possible to adapt to double-knitting with little trouble. I will explain it as best I can here, but if you want to get deeper into the technique, Anne has instructions for it in her Craftsy class as well as in her book *Annetarsia Knits*.

Anne Berk's method involves making a preliminary twist between the first and last ends before you begin the round, and then working with the trapped loop in the last section. This invariably results in a situation where you need to pass a ball of yarn through a loop to make sure an end is not trapped — but that's a small price to pay for such a perfectly finished look in the end.

In double-knitting, the method works the same — except, as with flat double-knit intarsia, Layer 2 rows are identical in technique to Layer 1 rows (the color orders change accordingly, of course). The easiest way to explain it is with step-by-step instructions (see pages 102-103).

These are merely the fundamentals of double-knit intarsia; you now have the building blocks to achieve more complex results as well — adding a third or fourth group and beyond, creating double-knit motifs within the intarsia color blocks, etc.

Craftstory, continued from page 81

The one art form that my whole family had in common was music. Music was everywhere, and it's been a big part of my life from day one. As a young man, I was part of innumerable choirs and musicals in and out of school. I sang in a Russian children's choir, a church choir, and my school chorus. I sang (and even starred) in musicals. I took piano lessons, violin lessons, and saxophone lessons. I never really became adept at any instrument other than voice, which came naturally to me. I sang as a soprano when I was a child, then when my voice broke I sang as a tenor or a bass. I was terrible with languages (other than English), or perhaps I just didn't have the patience to learn them well. I also never learned to read music properly, so I never really enjoyed singing solo and stuck to groups when possible.

That issue sunk my future in singing when I got out of my hometown and into college. I auditioned for a chorus, but I never made it past the first round since I couldn't read music. The whole competitive nature of singing in the college acapella scene further traumatized me to the point where I am now so sensitive about my voice that I can't even handle situations where my singing voice is heard on its own without a panic attack. Due to similar circumstances, I became too self-conscious for dancing as well, even though I was good at it. With performance-based arts off the table, I sank my creative teeth into physical art forms – drawing, painting, sculpture, and all kinds of crafts as well.

Craftstory, continued on page 129

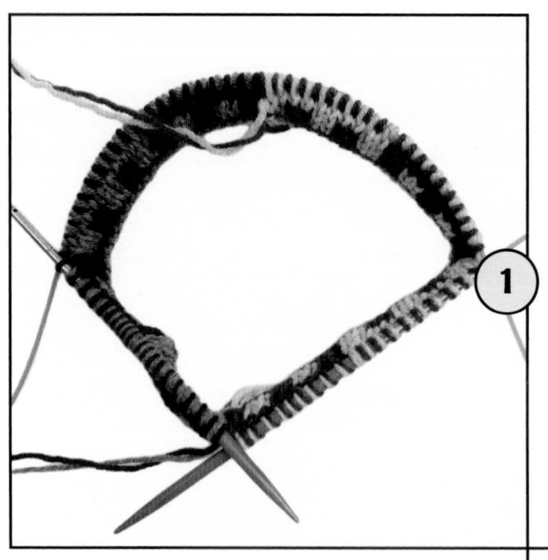

Here's a bit of double-knit intarsia already set up in the round. Note that there are two color group sections, (Group 2 and Group 1). The row we're about to begin starts with Group 2, and the active ends of Group 1 are on the other side of the circle.

Bring the Group 1 ends across the circle and in between your needles to join the Group 2 ends. If you are using more than two color groups, bring the ends of the last group forward. In other words, if you have three groups on the needle in numerical order and you're about to begin a row with Group 1, bring the ends of Group 3 across; this will be the last group you work with in that row.

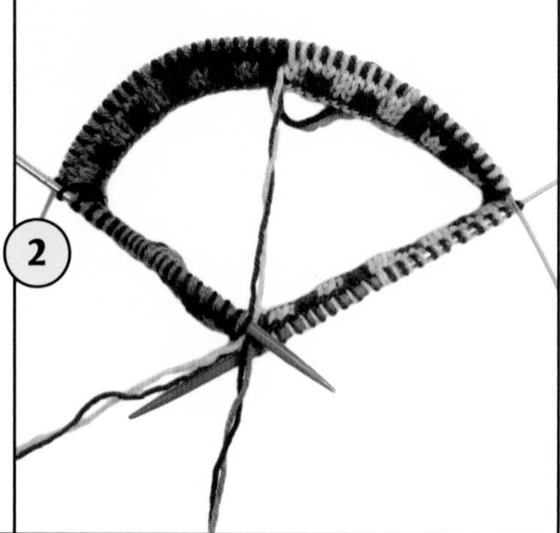

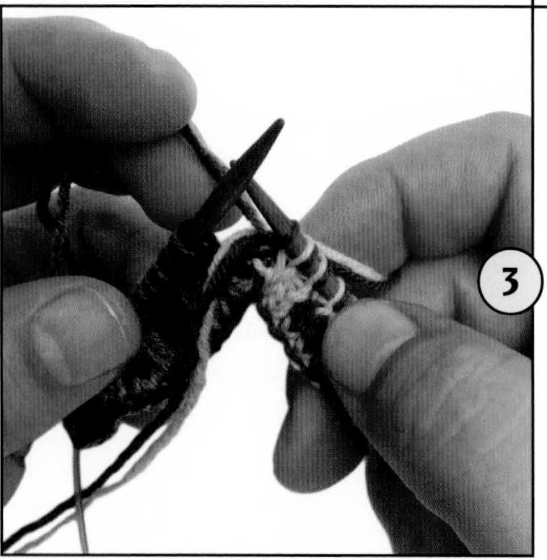

Make sure the ends of Group 1 pass in between the source needle and the ends of Group 2. Leaving the ends of Group 1 at the front, begin working with Group 2.

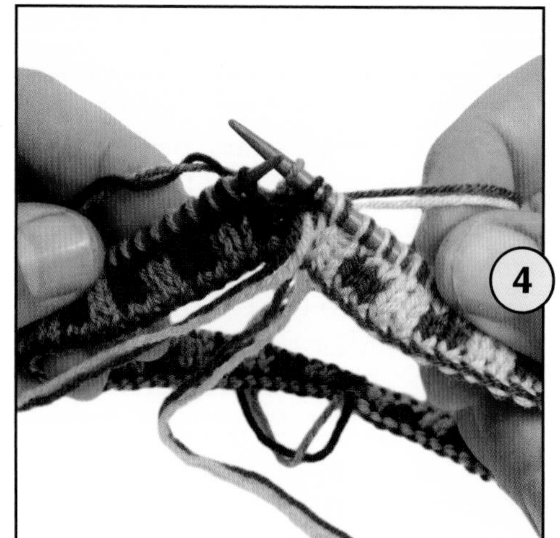

This should trap the ends of Group 1 in the edge of the Group 2 section. You can pull on the Group 1 ends to ensure they can slide freely back and forth but will remain trapped unless you undo the pairs in Group 2 back to the color group change.

Work the rest of the Group 2 section. You are now at the beginning of the Group 1 section. This is where the ends that were brought across the circle in Step 2 began. You'll notice that the ends are still trapped at the far side of the circle.

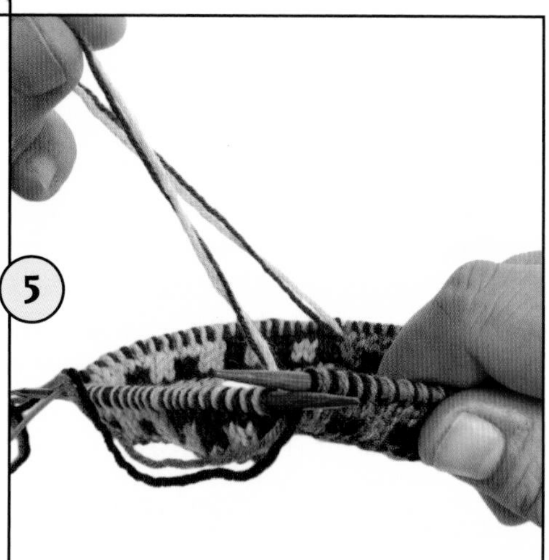

When working with the trapped loop, when you need more yarn just pull on the loop. It'll feed more yarn from your source balls, but the ends will be passing through the body of your work on the other side of the circle. Bring the trapped loop to the front along with the Group 2 ends . . .

... and work an intarsia twist as usual.

You can now see that the ends of Group 2 are twisted into the edge of the Group 1 section. Leave them alone, and begin working the Group 1 section.

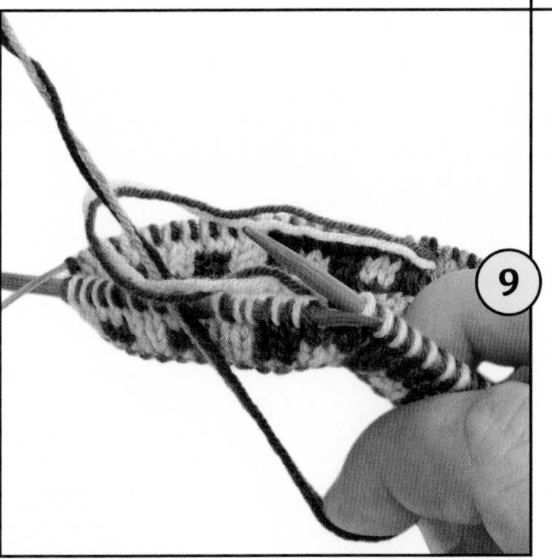

At some point before you reach the end of the Group 1 section, pay attention to the fact that the intarsia twist has trapped your Group 2 ends. You need to free them, and the only way is to pass the source balls of Group 2 through the loop of Group 1. Feel free to lengthen the Group 1 loop as much as you need to; you can always shorten it later.

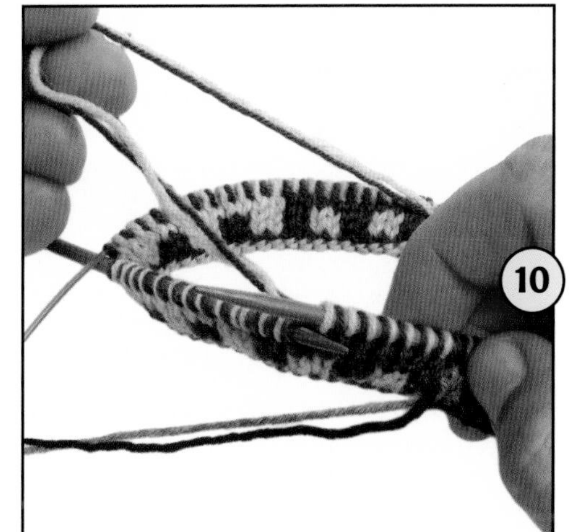

With Group 2 fully freed from the Group 1 loop, finish working the section of Group 1 with the trapped loop.

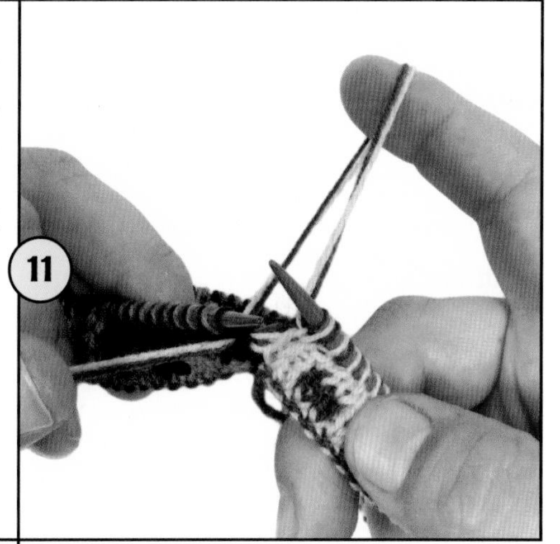

When you reach the end of Group 1, your trapped loop will begin and end in almost the same place. Simply pull the active ends through the edge of Group 2, and the trapped loop will come with them and disappear.

Here's the completed color group change. To proceed with the next row, turn the work inside out, and then follow the same instructions, while changing only the color group numbers. Always turn inside out by pulling the cast-on edges through the middle; if you wrap them around the outside, you'll tangle up your ends.

KONTINUUM

a hat using double-knit intarsia in the round

Finished size & weight

This hat is about 8.5" from brim to crown and 18" in circumference. Don't worry; it's super stretchy and fits my 23" head as well as my models' smaller heads. As worked for the sample, this pattern uses less than half of each 25 g mini-skein, so you will have enough yarn to make it taller or possibly knit a second one.

Materials & tools

[Color A]: Yarn Carnival Goat Roper (80% superwash merino, 10% cashmere, 10% nylon; 100 yd/25 g mini-skein); Medium Gray; 1 skein.

[Color B]: Yarn Carnival Goat Roper (80% superwash merino, 10% cashmere, 10% nylon; 100 yd/25 g mini-skein); Purple; 1 skein.

[Color C]: Yarn Carnival Goat Roper (80% superwash merino, 10% cashmere, 10% nylon; 100 yd/25 g mini-skein); Charcoal; 1 skein.

[Color D]: Yarn Carnival Goat Roper (80% superwash merino, 10% cashmere, 10% nylon; 100 yd/25 g mini-skein); Magenta; 1 skein.

[Color E]: Yarn Carnival Goat Roper (80% superwash merino, 10% cashmere, 10% nylon; 100 yd/25 g mini-skein); Pale Gray; 1 skein.

[Color F]: Yarn Carnival Goat Roper (80% superwash merino, 10% cashmere, 10% nylon; 100 yd/25 g mini-skein); Blue; 1 skein.

US 2/2.75 mm 16" circular needle or needle size required to achieve gauge.

Preferred small-diameter solution in US 2/2.75 mm

Gauge in pattern

27 sts/40 rows = 4" in pattern.

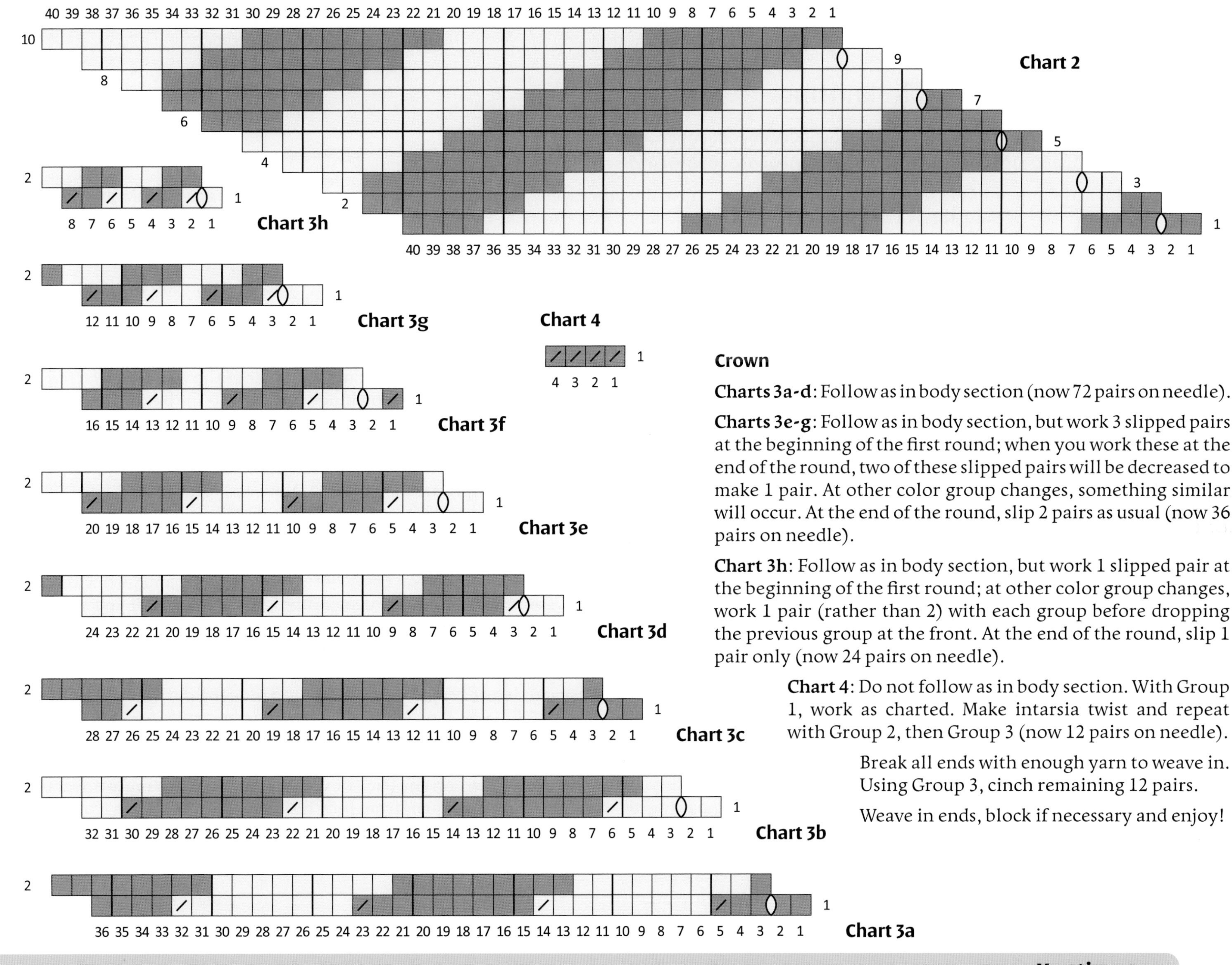

Crown

Charts 3a-d: Follow as in body section (now 72 pairs on needle).

Charts 3e-g: Follow as in body section, but work 3 slipped pairs at the beginning of the first round; when you work these at the end of the round, two of these slipped pairs will be decreased to make 1 pair. At other color group changes, something similar will occur. At the end of the round, slip 2 pairs as usual (now 36 pairs on needle).

Chart 3h: Follow as in body section, but work 1 slipped pair at the beginning of the first round; at other color group changes, work 1 pair (rather than 2) with each group before dropping the previous group at the front. At the end of the round, slip 1 pair only (now 24 pairs on needle).

Chart 4: Do not follow as in body section. With Group 1, work as charted. Make intarsia twist and repeat with Group 2, then Group 3 (now 12 pairs on needle).

Break all ends with enough yarn to weave in. Using Group 3, cinch remaining 12 pairs.

Weave in ends, block if necessary and enjoy!

CHAPTER 6

Textured Double-knitting

I touched on this in the appendix of *Extreme Double-Knitting* but didn't really go very far with it, partly because this is a style of double-knitting already well covered by Lucy Neatby. However, it's well worth understanding, and it's a foundation you're going to need for some later patterns — so I'm going to take you through it here. Most textured double-knitting is a combination of two different techniques. Like knit and purl in textured single-layer knitting, in double-knitting we have SDK (standard double-knitting, with knit sides out) and RDK (reverse double-knitting, with purl sides out).

When working textures into standard knitting, the only vocabulary you need for the body of the work are "knit" and "purl." By combining these, you can create a nearly endless array of textures, raised motifs, and bases on which to build other knitting techniques. In double-knitting, you're normally working only in knits on the front layer; the purls on the back layer are just reversed knits — you never see the purl side in the finished object. However, if you remember from the section on double-knitting vocabulary (see page 18), I mentioned that every pair has both a color order and a stitch order. Regardless of the color order, the stitch order is typically a knit stitch followed by a purl stitch (KP). But it's possible to use PK pairs instead, creating reverse double-knitting or RDK for short. The first stitch is still part of the front, and the second is still part of the back, so when you purl the first and knit the second, you'll end up with a purl bump on the outside of your work on both sides. But don't just jump in there — it's not quite that simple.

If you work PK pairs but you keep all other double-knitting rules intact (specifically the one about moving the yarn forward and backward together), you're still going to end up with double-stockinette. The only difference will be that the first stitch in your pair will be on the back of the work, and the second stitch will be on the front. If you worked an entire project like this, it'd end up looking very nearly the same as any other double-knit piece (the edges would be the only place where a careful observer would see a difference). If you mixed up KP and PK pairs in a single piece — say you did one row in KP, then the next in PK — you'd end up with something I call Japanese double-knitting. You can read more about that in the appendix. But if what you want is simply to have reverse double-stockinette (purls on the outside of your work), you need to maintain the front/back relationship of the stitches in the pair, while changing both stitch types. How do you do that?

Before I answer that, you need to understand a little bit of the structure of knitting in general. When you knit or purl, the layer of the work against which you hold your yarn dictates the layer of the work that the purl will be formed on. This is why you hold your yarn to the back in order to knit — so that the purl will form on the back of the work, showing a knit on the front. Accordingly, if you hold your yarn to the front, the purl will be formed on the front (the exception being the Norwegian purl, which uses a more complicated maneuver). Now, let's add double-knitting into the mix. When you knit, you hold both ends to the back and knit with one of them. This creates a purl inside your work (and by extension a knit outside) and leaves the other strand out of the way. The same happens on the other layer when you bring both yarns forward and purl with one of them. The movement of the two yarns together is key — if you move only one, the purl is created on the outside of the whole fabric, not just the back of one layer.

However, this only applies if you want to hide the purls. If you want them out in public, you'll need to break that cardinal rule in which both ends always travel together. Remember, if you want a purl on the front of your work, the yarn you want to use to make that purl must travel to the front. If you want a purl on the back of your work, that yarn must travel to the back. To keep both yarns from interfering with one another, you must do both simultaneously.

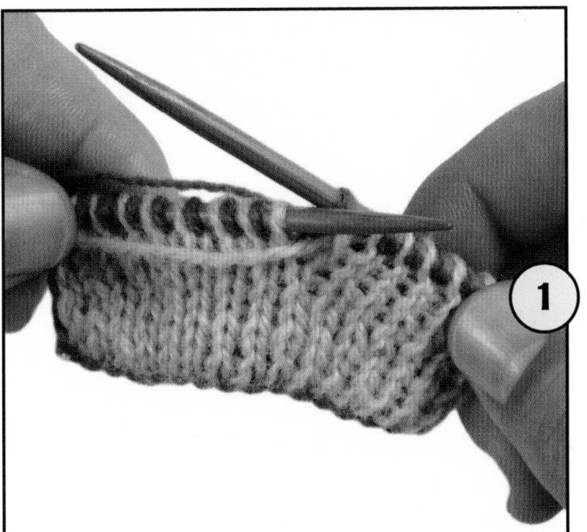

Here's how you work a **PK pair**:

Position your yarns so that the color that is first in the color order (the front color) is at the front, and the other color is at the back of the work.

P1 with the color at the front . . .

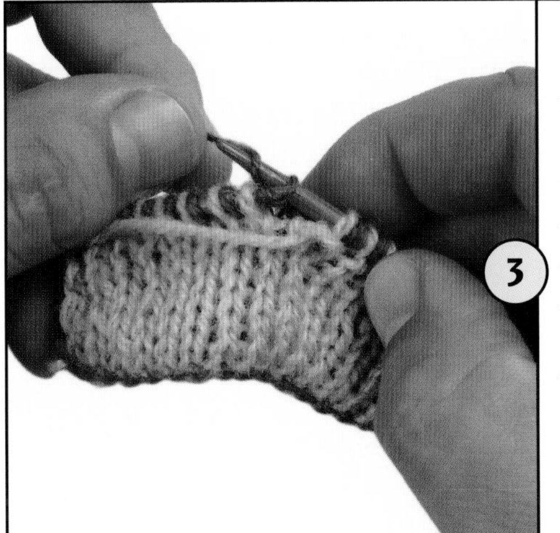

. . . and K1 with the color at the back.

It's really quite simple — and quick to do, since you don't have to move the yarns backward and forward unless you need to do some kind of transition (in color or stitch or both).

Transitions in textured double-knitting

In standard double-knitting, all the ugly stuff is hidden. When you make a transition, it's generally a color change, and knit stitches transition smoothly into other knit stitches both vertically and horizontally regardless of color. On the back, however, neither one looks very good. Horizontal color order transitions (color changes within a row) in RDK merely lack cleanliness: the edges are sort of blurry. Vertical color order transitions (color changes from row to row) look terrible, with little blips of color above and below the solid color areas.

So let's break this down directionally. Horizontal transitions are simple: avoid changing color order without stitch order in a row incorporating PK pairs. If you're working an RDK section, you will most often want to change color order as well as stitch order. In other words, if you're working in AB color order and PK stitch order, the cleanest transition is to BA color order and KP stitch order. The next best thing to do would be to change stitch order without color order; this would be a clean transition but it does not link the layers together.

Vertical transitions in RDK are more complex. The issue is not with the stitch order; if there is no color order change from row to row, there will be no awkward vertical "bleed" of colors as they change. This one fact is the key to keeping that effect from occurring: if you change the stitch order in one row and then the color order in the next, you will avoid those little blips of color (in the same way you avoid this issue when color-changing from row to row in single-layer ribbing). This does require two rows to complete a transition, but it's worth the planning.

For example, say you have a column of KP pairs in BA color order on a background of PK pairs in AB color order. The KP pairs stack up for a while, then end with a transition into the background stitch and color order. At the top of this column, there's a messy bit where the stitches change from knit to purl and from Color B to Color A at the same time. The messy bit can be avoided by doing a row of all AB color order, but at the column of KP pairs you work a section of KP pairs also in AB color order. This makes a clean transition in color. In the following row, you match your color order but you change the stitch order above that KP column to PK (now matching your background). The final look of this technique is much cleaner and any slight stitch inconsistencies will be far less likely to be noticed than the color inconsistencies resulting from not doing it.

See examples of this on the next page.

Edges in textured double-knitting

If you're working your textured double-knitting flat, you'll need to deal with your edges. PK pairs do not make clean edges. I recommend you work regular linked pairs in KP stitch order at the beginning of your row, then change to PK on the next pair. The slipped pair at the end of the row is worked the same as any other slipped pair. The examples above are also good illustrations of the look of edges in a primarily RDK sample.

Marled Knitting

This technique was actually used in my last book under a different name: lock-knitting (or lock-purling). It's been through a number of name changes, but the technique is the same. It isn't actually a double-knitting technique, but it can be used alongside double-knitting. In double-knitting (as with single-layer knitting), it's important to preserve the stitch/pair count from row to row unless you're doing some increase/ decrease techniques for shaping. Most of the time, we maintain the pair count by simply working another pair on top of the previous one. However, there are other moves one can do that preserve the pair count but create fabric that's not double-knitted. You may well have done this before in a different context. It's not uncommon to hold two yarns together and just work as if they were one. You can do it if you want to thicken a yarn that only comes in thin weights, or if you want to mix up two disparate fibers. Here, I do it to create a textured "third color" blend of the two colors I'm already working with — a marled effect.

The abbreviation for this type of stitch in patterns is MK (for marled knit) or MP (for marled purl). While I don't use them in charts in this book, it's possible to chart them with the symbols I used in *Extreme Double-Knitting*: Ꭓ for MK and **Ꭓ** for MP.

I always prefer to MK when doing this in flat knitting so that I get garter stitch, which is also reversible. But if you're doing it in the round (see the "Footsies" in *Extreme Double-Knitting*, for example), you'll need to alternate MK and MP rounds to get the same effect.

Now, because the yarns will tend to twist around each other while doing this, you probably won't have any consistency in the resulting pairs — some will end up as AB and some will be BA. As long as you're just doing more marled pairs in the next row, there's no issue with this; indeed, it's what you should strive for.

However, if you want to transition (vertically) into double-knitting again, you're going to want to clean up your row a bit as you do it. If, for example, you want a row in AB color order, some of your marled pairs will already be AB and you can work them as usual. You will need to switch the BA pairs; to do this, just reach through the first stitch and pull the second one out. This switches the color order, and you can continue. If the pair is twisted up such that it's easier to bring the far color over the top instead of through the middle of the near color, feel free. Just make sure that one stitch passes through the other for the cleanest transition.

With very little change in gauge, double-knitting and marled knitting can be combined within a row. There is no need for any special horizontal transition, since the marled pairs are all linked together by default. However, you should always transition back to double-knitting for the edges if there are any. Marled edges look awful, but double-knit selvedges look clean and elegant. Likewise, your cast-on and bind-off should also use the standard double-knitted versions for the most presentable look.

See the step-by-step instructions on the next page.

To use marled knitting, just process your pairs differently: rather than knitting and purling each stitch with a single yarn, hold both yarns together and knit the pair together (same as a K2tog) with both yarns. The pair is replaced with a new pair, so your pair count is maintained.

This is abbreviated as MK (marled knit). You can also MP (marled purl) for a similar effect. Here's a completed MK...

...and here it is again (viewed from the other layer) masquerading as a completed MP.

End Management in Textured Double-knitting

While working in textured double-knitting, you're constantly splitting your ends and recombining them. When working in PK pairs, your ends are on either side of your work, and when working in KP pairs they're together again. The way you achieve this is up to you and your own style of knitting, but I'll explain my recommended method. If you're working a section of RDK in AB color order, then changing to a section of SDK in BA color order, and then back again, you'll begin with Color A on the front and Color B on the back. When you reach the color/stitch change, you'll bring Color A to the back to join Color B. Since they're now together and on the back of the work, they're ready for the KP section. When you finish that section, your yarns will be at the front. Move only Color B to the back, and you're ready for the PK section again.

If by some chance you have to make a color change in RDK without a stitch order change, things get a little weird. Because the colors are on the opposite layers of the work from where you want them and there's a needle in between them, you will have to manually switch the ends — bring A from back to front, and B from front to back. You will have a choice of which to do first, which will allow you the same choice of twist direction you normally have in standard double-knitting. This isn't difficult to do, but it does tend to break up the flow of your knitting. However, this is not a common thing to need to do, and I'm really only including it here for completeness' sake.

Marled knitting is also a blessing for end management issues; since the technique is meant to have a mottled look, blending the two colors it incorporates, it's totally fine to have stitches that "eat up" the twist. So if your ends are twisted up and you're in a marled section, push the twist gently toward the working needle and incorporate the twisted ends into the next several stitches until it's gone. I do not recommend doing this on the last marled row, since it will be harder to separate the twisted loops to make double-knitting again in the next row.

RUSTLE OF LEAVES

a keyhole scarf combining double-knitting and marled knitting

Finished size & weight

Dimensions as worked for the sample are about 7" wide by 40" long. At this length, the total weight is 10.3 oz (about 721 yds); since you'll have 16 oz it's absolutely possible to make it up to 54" long without the keyhole if you like.

Materials & tools

[Color A]: Miss Babs Yowza! (100% superwash merino; 560 yd/8 oz skein); Forever (blue); 1 skein.

[Color B]: Miss Babs Yowza! (100% superwash merino; 560 yd/8 oz skein); Wanna Go Crazy (red multi); 1 skein.

US 6/4.0 mm straight or circular needles, or needle size required to achieve desired gauge.

Gauge in pattern

20 sts/26 rows = 4" in double-stockinette.

This is a pattern that was bouncing around in my mind, looking for a way out, when Craftsy rang me up to see about doing a kit to support one of the new yarn lines they were beginning to stock. This was back in 2013, not too long after my first Craftsy class came out. The idea behind this scarf was to have a maple leaf motif that tumbles down the center column, and the outer edges rippling and ruffling around it, tracing the movement of a leaf on the wind. I chose colors that evoked “autumn maple leaf” and “clear blue sky,” knowing that the other layer would be somewhat surreal — blue leaves against a Martian sky, perhaps.

I made it a keyhole scarf because I was short on time, but also because it was an interesting twist — and because, if the hole was the same width as the center section, the ruffles would flip out on either side and lock the scarf in place. I finished it and sent it off to Craftsy, where they took a lovely set of photos . . . which only showed the Martian sky layer. Oh well. The piece is relatively simple but intriguing, and shows the beginnings of double-knit texture very well: the combination of double-knitting and marled knitting.

I was delighted to see that Miss Babs provided one of the yarn lines they wanted patterns for, since I’d been seeing them at Rhinebeck and other shows for some time but their booth was always so mobbed that I had barely been able to set foot inside (let alone become familiar with their yarns). One of the reasons, as it turns out, is that they don’t wholesale to shops. One of the few places you ever get to fondle the giant, luscious skeins is at big shows like Rhinebeck. Otherwise, you can order it online, but that really only works if you’re already familiar with it — or you’re willing to take a chance on reviews alone. Since it was offered, I took it, sight unseen (or unfelt, anyway); and, like many before me, I am a convert. Miss Babs, who I have had the pleasure of meeting in person since, has an incredible range of colors and fiber contents, not merely the standard stuff. I ended up working with a 100% superwash merino because it was what was offered, but I look forward to playing with more interesting fibers from them in the future.

The name of this pattern, “Rustle of Leaves” is straightforward. “Rustle” sounds like “ruffle” and the leaves are right out where you can see them. I like wordplay, but sometimes simple is best.

Key

- Layer 1: AB pair / Layer 2: BA pair (light square)
- Layer 1: BA pair / Layer 2: AB pair (dark square)

Chart 1

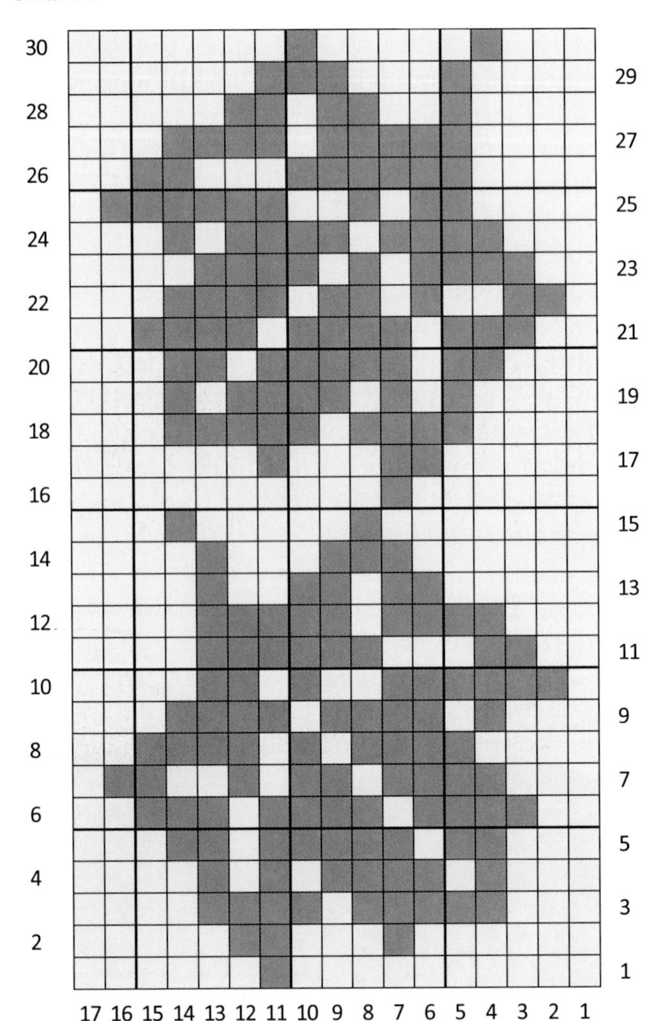

Pattern

CO 35 BA pairs.

1. Work 1 AB pair, MK 6 pairs, wrap & turn.
2. MK 6 pairs, work 1 slipped pair. Turn.
3. Work 1 AB pair, MK 3 pairs, wrap & turn.
4. MK 3 pairs, work 1 slipped pair. Turn.
5. Work 1 AB pair, MK 8 pairs, follow Chart 1 Row 1, MK 8 pairs, work 1 slipped pair. Turn.
6. Work 1 BA pair, MK 6 pairs, wrap & turn.
7. MK 6 pairs, work 1 slipped pair. Turn.
8. Work 1 BA pair, MK 3 pairs, wrap & turn.
9. MK 3 pairs, work 1 slipped pair. Turn.
10. Work 1 BA pair, MK 8 pairs, follow Chart 1 Row 2, MK 8 pairs, work 1 slipped pair. Turn.

Steps 1-5 complete a Layer 1 row; steps 6-10 complete a Layer 2 row. Continue repeating these 10 steps (working through the rows of Chart 1) until 6 full repeats of Chart 1 (12 leaf motifs) have been worked.

Pattern Notes

The short rows in this pattern are worked as in single-layer knitting, not double-knitting, so there are no explicit instructions for this technique. One note: in each short row, you'll be wrapping around a marled pair with both yarns held together — there is no need to separate the yarns in order to complete this technique. There is also no need to pick up your wraps on the way back to hide them; garter stitch hides wraps well enough.

If you want your ruffles less ruffly, omit steps 3+4, 8+9, and for the keyhole steps omit steps 13+14, and 20+21. If you want no ruffles at all, repeat steps 5 and 10, and for the keyhole, steps 15-17, 22 and 23.

If you don't want a keyhole, omit steps 11-23 and just keep working steps 1-10 until the scarf is as long as you want it. 14 repeats of Chart 1 will be approximately 5.5' long, for example.

Pattern, continued

Then work the following steps 11-23 to create a keyhole approximately ¾ of the way along the length of the scarf:

11. Work 1 AB pair, MK 6 pairs, wrap & turn.
12. MK 6 pairs, work 1 slipped pair. Turn.
13. Work 1 AB pair, MK 3 pairs, wrap & turn.
14. MK 3 pairs, work 1 slipped pair. Turn.
15. Work 1 AB pair, MK 8 pairs, work 17 AB pairs.
16. Slip 17 pairs back to source needle and BO across all pairs. When you have 1 stitch (not pair) left before the marled section, slip 3 stitches (1 purl and 1 marled purl), PSSO and return marled pair to source needle.
17. MK 8 pairs, work 1 slipped pair. Turn.
18. Work 1 BA pair, MK 6 pairs, wrap & turn.
19. MK 6 pairs, work 1 slipped pair. Turn.
20. Work 1 BA pair, MK 3 pairs, wrap & turn.
21. MK 3 pairs, work 1 slipped pair. Turn.
22. Work 1 BA pair, MK 8 pairs, CO 17 BA pairs.
23. MK 8 pairs, work 1 slipped pair. Turn.

Then repeat steps 1-10 for two more Chart 1 repeats (4 leaf motifs).

BO in AB pairs. Weave in ends, block if necessary and enjoy!

HEXWORTH

a double-knit textured scarf with slip-stitches

1 SUPER FINE

Finished size & weight

The finished and blocked piece is approximately 72" long by 7" wide and uses about 240 g (936 yds) of yarn or 120 g (468 yds) of each color. This means you will go a bit over into the second pair of skeins; if you'd rather, you can make the piece a bit shorter and save on yarn — but I don't think you'll regret having extra of this stuff.

Materials & tools

[Color A]: Bijou Basin Ranch Tibetan Dream (85% Tibetan yak down, 15% nylon; 440 yd/113 g skein); Lohengrin (blue multi); 2 skeins.

[Color B]: Bijou Basin Ranch Tibetan Dream (85% Tibetan yak down, 15% nylon; 440 yd/113 g skein); Natural Brown; 2 skeins.

US 5/3.75 mm circular or straight needles, or needle size required to achieve desired gauge.

Gauge in pattern

24 sts/35 rows = 4" in pattern, unblocked.

26 sts/32 rows = 4" in pattern, blocked.

Sample knitted by Mari Weideman

If the last pattern was a good example of the beginnings of double-knit texture, this pattern shows the next steps. The honeycomb pattern is adapted almost verbatim from a standard single-color or two-color stranded pattern. Because I wanted the two layers to remain linked together, I needed to adjust things a little bit: the slipped pairs are stacked in such a way that they pull as hard as possible on the sides of the hexagons to keep them uniformly sized. However, the rows where those slipped pairs are done are not linked together, since no actual color changing is occurring. The tension is relieved at the last possible moment, before moving into another set of unlinked rows. While working, the pattern looks like slightly distorted bricks; it's only when you block it that the hexagons take more definite shape.

When I work with a yarn vendor at one of the big shows, it means that they've agreed to sell my books and patterns for me so that I don't have to be there when I can't be (usually during my classes). It's also a benefit to them, as they get to show off some eye-catching pieces that will hopefully draw people into their booth.

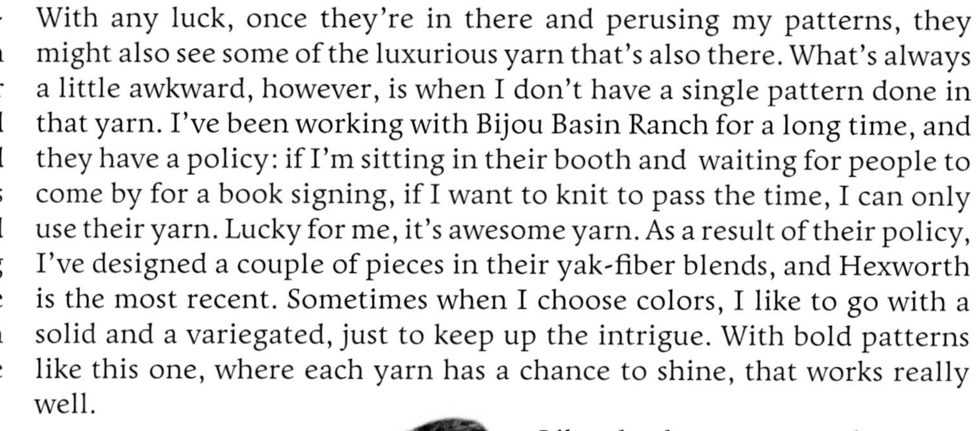

With any luck, once they're in there and perusing my patterns, they might also see some of the luxurious yarn that's also there. What's always a little awkward, however, is when I don't have a single pattern done in that yarn. I've been working with Bijou Basin Ranch for a long time, and they have a policy: if I'm sitting in their booth and waiting for people to come by for a book signing, if I want to knit to pass the time, I can only use their yarn. Lucky for me, it's awesome yarn. As a result of their policy, I've designed a couple of pieces in their yak-fiber blends, and Hexworth is the most recent. Sometimes when I choose colors, I like to go with a solid and a variegated, just to keep up the intrigue. With bold patterns like this one, where each yarn has a chance to shine, that works really well.

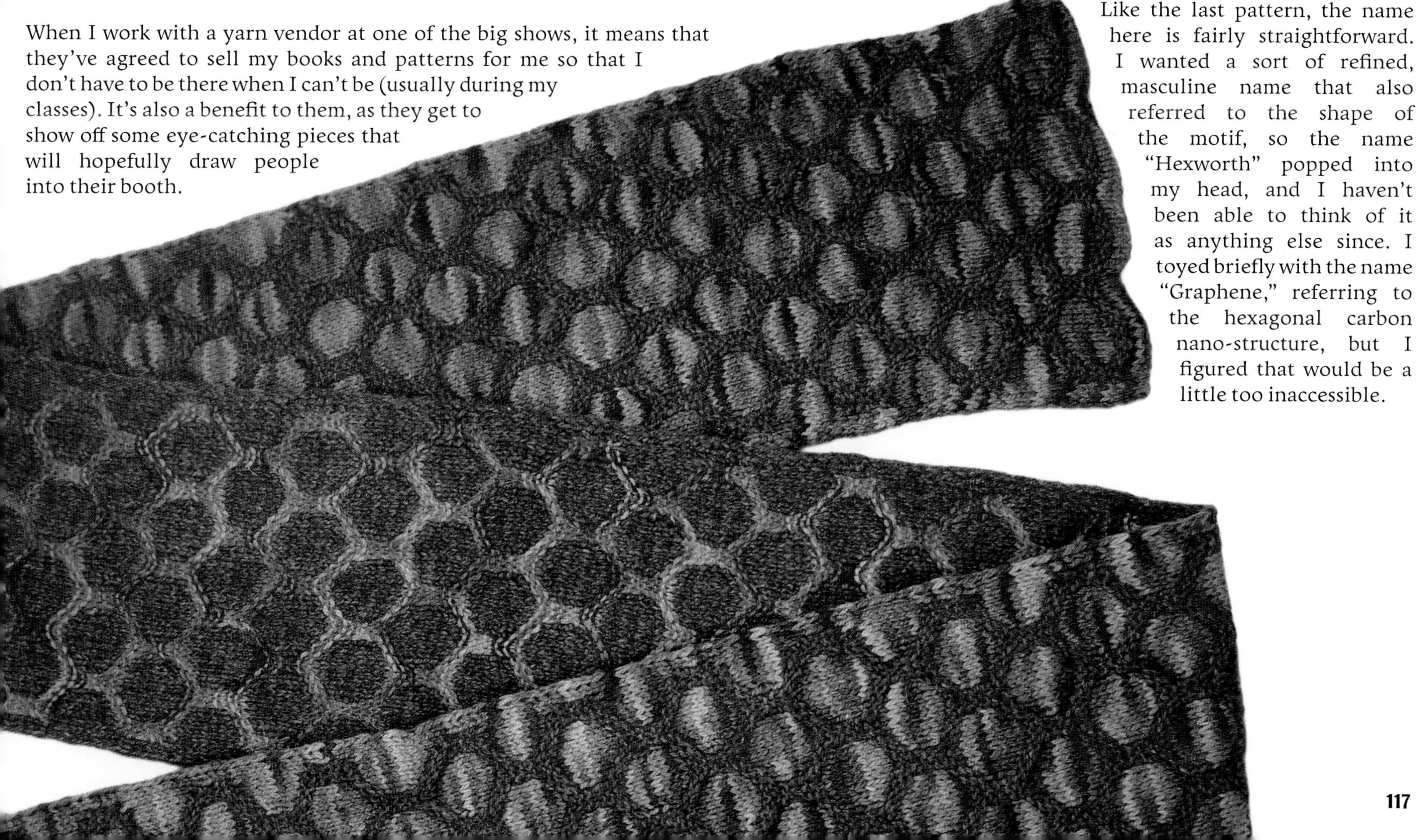

Like the last pattern, the name here is fairly straightforward. I wanted a sort of refined, masculine name that also referred to the shape of the motif, so the name "Hexworth" popped into my head, and I haven't been able to think of it as anything else since. I toyed briefly with the name "Graphene," referring to the hexagonal carbon nano-structure, but I figured that would be a little too inaccessible.

Chart 3

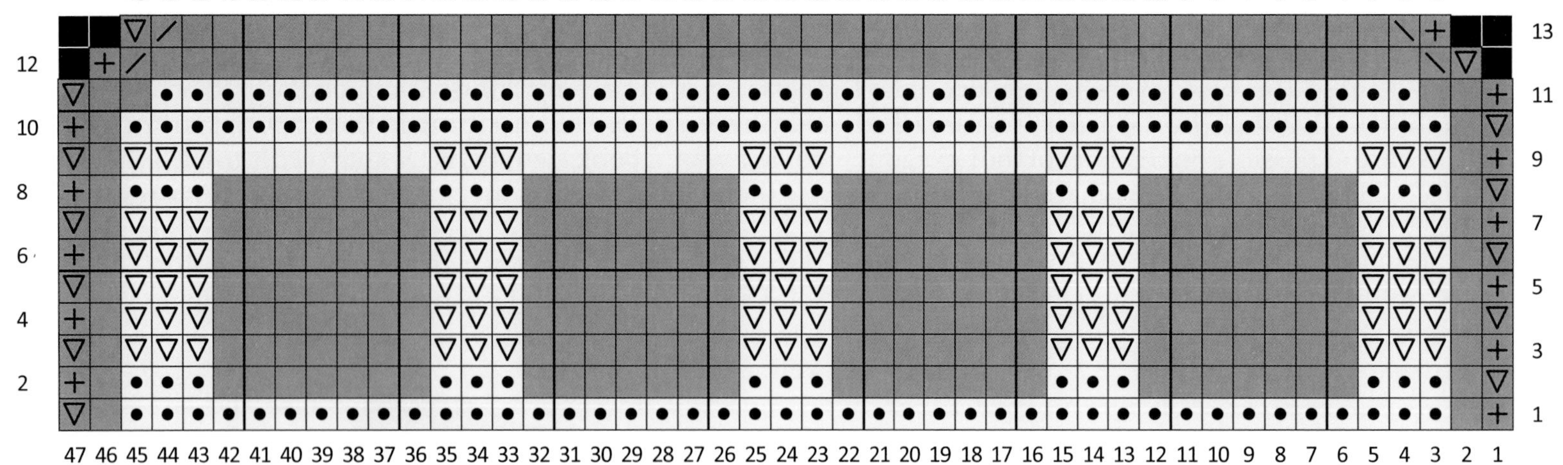

Chart 2

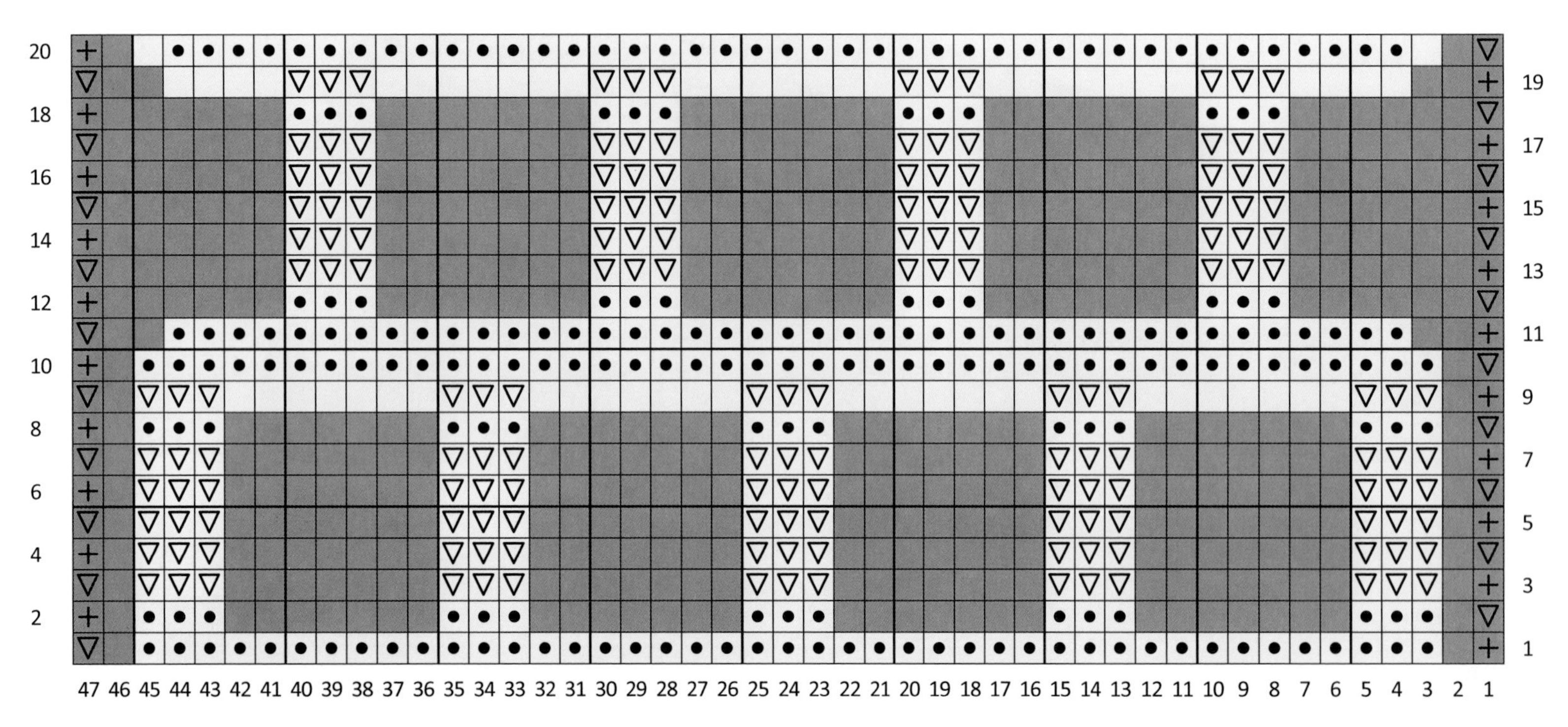

Chart 1

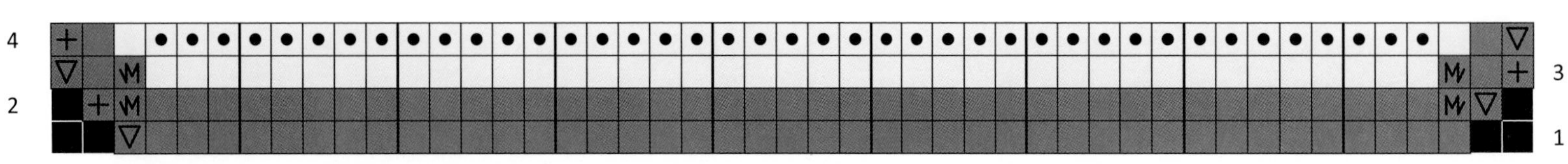

Pattern

CO 43 AB pairs.

Follow Chart 1, ending with 47 pairs.

Work 27 repeats of Chart 2 or until scarf is 5' long (unblocked).

Follow Chart 3, ending with 43 pairs.

BO, weave in ends, block and enjoy!

Key

☐ (white)	Layer 1: AB pair Layer 2: BA pair
■ (gray)	Layer 1: BA pair Layer 2: AB pair
■ (black)	No Pair
⊙	Reverse DK (PK) pair
+	Linked Pair
▽	Slipped Pair
M1L symbol	M1L Increase
M1R symbol	M1R Increase
/	Right-slanting decrease
\	Left-slanting decrease

Pattern Notes

Note the triple columns of slipped pairs in Chart 2, Rows 3-7 and 13-17 (as well as in Chart 3, Rows 3-7). The idea here is that you will keep slipping the same pairs you made back in Rows 2 and 12, until you finally work another set of pairs on top of them in Rows 8 and 18. You want these pairs to remain roughly the same height as any other pair, so as you're slipping, take care not to pull too hard. This is what creates the short vertical edge of the hexagons, so if you manage to elongate the stitches you're not going to end up with clean hexagons. Since it is a grouping of 3, it will be harder to elongate them but it's best not to try.

Also in Chart 2, Rows 2, 8, 12 and 18 are critical. The bulk of this pattern does not have any color changing throughout rows, except for the edges. This means that very little of the fabric is linked together, so you have to make sure to put in rows that include color changes. These rows are the only ones that hold the whole fabric together, so they're very important.

The two colors I've chosen for this pattern are usually very distinct in contrast, but there is a part between the purple and the green where Color A approaches Color B. When you have pairs of these two in RDK, there's no issue since the two yarns are held separately; in SDK, however, there can be confusion. Because the confusing area is generally only a few pairs long, if you are using the same colorways I've chosen, I recommend you just look forward on your strands and it will be easy to identify which is Color A and which is Color B that way.

Increases and decreases in textured double-knitting

One of the nice things about PK pairs is that they hide shaping so nicely. Nobody ever looks to see how purls line up, so increases and decreases can be hidden with much more ease than in standard double-knitting.

Decreases are set up in the same way — reordering from PKPK to PPKK this time since we're using a different stitch order. The important thing is that you have two stitches from the front, then two stitches from the back (or three from the front followed by three from the back for double-decreases). The actual decreases, once the pairs are set up, are worked in the reverse order but the same pairing — a right-slanting decrease is worked SSP, K2tog; and a left-slanting decrease is worked P2tog, SSK. To be honest, because everything is so well hidden, the directionality of the decreases is probably not a big concern (you can get away with P2tog, K2tog). A double-decrease is worked, again, in the reverse order from a standard double-knit double-decrease (with the purl technique first and the knit technique second).

Increases in RDK are worked as M1s (there's really no point in doing lifted increases when you can't see the knit layer of the work). Standard double-knit M1s are worked from inside to outside, but now the stitch order is changed so you're going to be working from outside to inside — but really, all that's happening here is that you're working a regular double-knit M1 in reverse order:

1. With source needle, pick up bar between stitches on front from inside to outside. P1 in yarn at the front.
2. With source needle, pick up bar between stitches on back from inside to outside. K1tbl in yarn at the back.

Quilted Double-knitting

This technique differs from the method I've been calling quilted double-knitting up until recently. Fortunately, this was something I had been playing with between books and never really did anything with, so there's no documented version of the previous experiment. Lucy Neatby and I independently developed this technique and consulted on a name. She hadn't decided but since we needed to choose to keep things consistent, she settled on "quilted," which fits the technique well.

Quilted double-knitting serves to link your fabric together vertically (from row to row), rather than horizontally (at color changes within a row). This is especially important when you consider the idea of rows or large sections where there is a vertical transition from one color/stitch order to the other. As in standard DK, when doing horizontal stripes, the only color changes occur at the edges and the entire body of the work is still hollow even though vertical color changes are being made. This is because color changes only link the fabric together horizontally (within a row), not vertically.

To make a **quilted KP pair**:

Slip the pair's first stitch knitwise, then pass it back to the source needle.

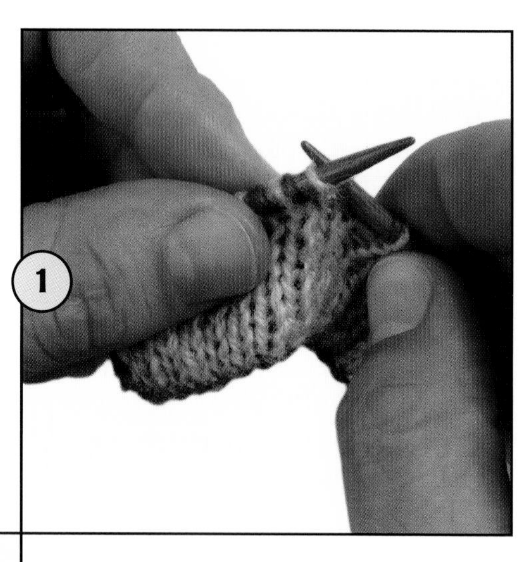

Insert the needle into the first stitch as if to purl...

Quilted double-knit pair

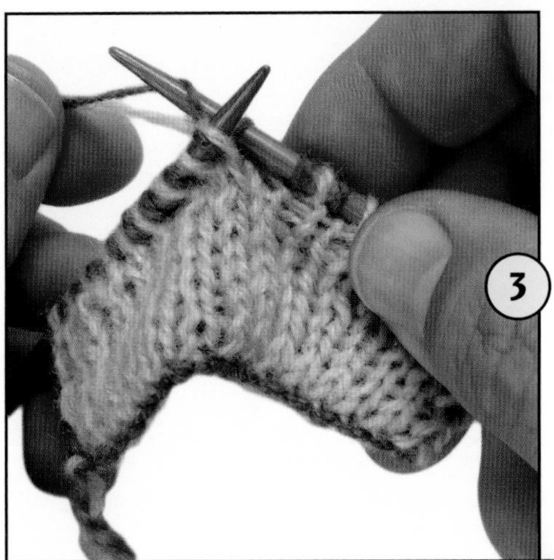

… then the second stitch as if to knit, pulling the second stitch through the first and knitting it. As you can see from the photo, you don't need to pull the stitch all the way through the loop before knitting it.

Here's the completed knit stitch. Note that it has now been fully pulled through the previous knit stitch.

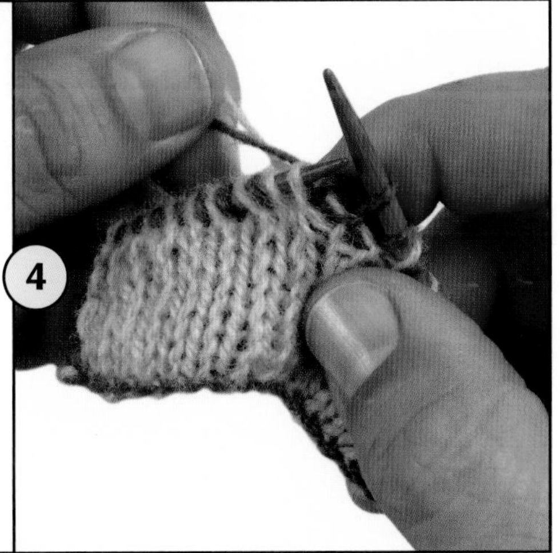

PTBL the new second stitch.

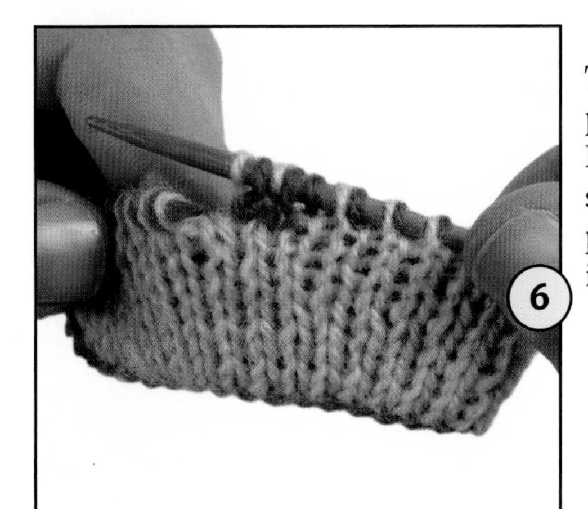

This works the same whether the pair in the previous row is PK or KP, but it will create a noticeable seam if it's KP. If the pair in the previous row is PK, it'll be next to invisible.

The back and front of this look subtly different. On the front, the legs of the stitches below will remain closed; on the back they'll be open. You cannot close the legs on the back, but you can twist the back stitch by purling normally (rather than through the back of the loop). Either way will cause the front and back to look different, but it's good to have options.

This move is notated with a ⌀ — which both reads as a backwards Q to remind you of the technique name and serves as a visual representation of the move itself, which involves pulling one stitch through the opening in the other.

One caveat: due to the "row-below" phenomenon, this technique will appear to "eat up" the previous row. If it's important that the row below be left intact, you'll want to work one more row before the quilted row.

A quilted PK pair is also possible, although I have not used it yet for anything. The technique is largely the same as above, but once the pair is reordered you work a PK pair rather than a KP one.

EUREKA

a double-knit textured hat with a two-pattern option

Finished size & weight

For the 20" size, the finished piece is 8.5" tall from brim to crown and uses 94 g (258 yds) of yarn, just under half of what you'll have, which means the larger (23") size is well within the reaches of the material. Or you could make a second one.

Materials & tools

[Color A]: A Hundred Ravens Aesir (100% superwash merino; 274 yd/100 g skein); Brass (gold); 1 skein.

[Color B]: A Hundred Ravens Aesir (100% superwash merino; 274 yd/100 g skein); Redwood (brown); 1 skein.

US 5/3.75 mm 16" circular needle, or size required to achieve gauge.

Preferred small-diameter circular solution in matching size.

Gauge in pattern

20 sts/30 rows = 4" in pattern.

To put a cap (pun intended) on the textured double-knitting in this book, I decided to cram all the techniques I still wanted to teach into one pattern.

I love hats, as they're a great way to try out and learn a technique (or techniques) without resigning yourself to a massive project. You don't need to knit a sweater in order to learn RDK decreases or quilted double-knitting. Sure, both techniques could come in handy in a sweater, but why not just do a hat? The sweater can come later.

This hat is mostly made up of triangles. All of the inverted triangles are done in purls, and all of the crown decreases are hidden in the purls. Two triangles placed base to base make a diamond, and even if the two triangles are different colors, the diamond will be hollow unless something is done to link the fabric together vertically. Enter the quilted pairs, keeping your fabric stable and saving the day.

I first encountered A Hundred Ravens at a local sheep & wool show. A good friend and sample knitter of mine was staffing the booth and lured me in with soft yarn and vibrant colorways (as you can probably understand). While I have lately been trying to avoid superwash merino, the base is so ubiquitous that it's hard to avoid it completely. And sometimes it's worth it.

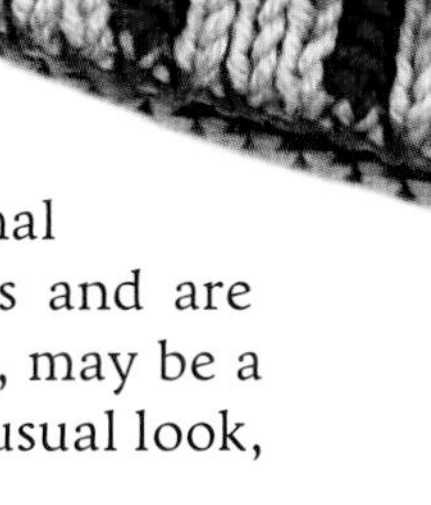

AHR is another local yarn company, like Dirty Water Dyeworks, that I've had the pleasure of watching grow from a local to a regional and, perhaps, even a national brand. They're still small, but they've got great colorways and are well worth checking out. The yarn I chose for this hat, Aesir, may be a superwash merino, but it's an 8-ply sport/DK which has an unusual look, springy texture, and great stitch definition.

The original name for this hat was going to be "Achtung," but when I showed it to my local guild (while Kate from AHR was presenting, no less!), someone noticed the exclamation point on the front and called it a "thinking cap" — so the name "Eureka" was born. There is a second version called "Eureka?" that has question marks instead of exclamation points (worked in two-pattern double-knitting, of course) for those who are less confident about their discoveries.

Pattern

Brim

For a 20 (23)" hat, CO 96 (112) BA pairs. Join, being careful not to twist.

Place marker. Work 24 (28) repeats of Chart 1 around.

Repeat Chart 2 until work is ~2" tall.

Body

In Charts 3 through 7, after every even-numbered round, remove marker, slip 1 pair, and replace marker. The next round will begin at the new marker.

Work 24 (28) repeats of Chart 3 around.

Follow Chart 4 (4+5) twice around. In Rounds 13-22, inside the red box, follow Chart 4a for an exclamation point or Chart 4b (in two-pattern DK — follow Chart 4b Key) for a question mark (see example below). If you like, you can follow 4a in one repeat and 4b in the other.

Crown:

Work 12 (14) repeats of Chart 6 around, changing to your small-diameter needle solution when necessary, ending with 48 (56) pairs.

Work 6 (7) repeats of Chart 7 around, ending with 12 (14) pairs.

Cinch crown, weave in ends, block if necessary and enjoy!

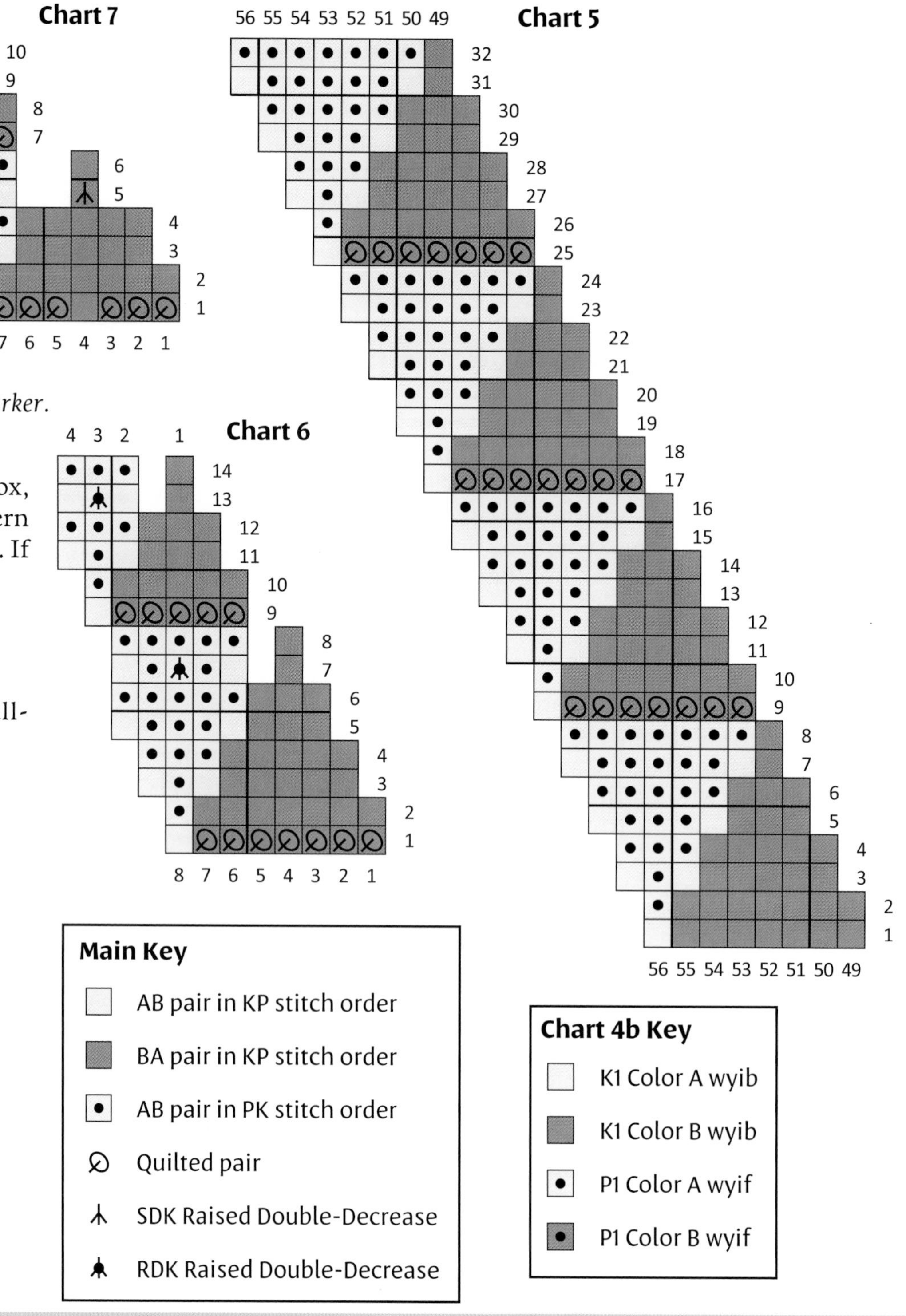

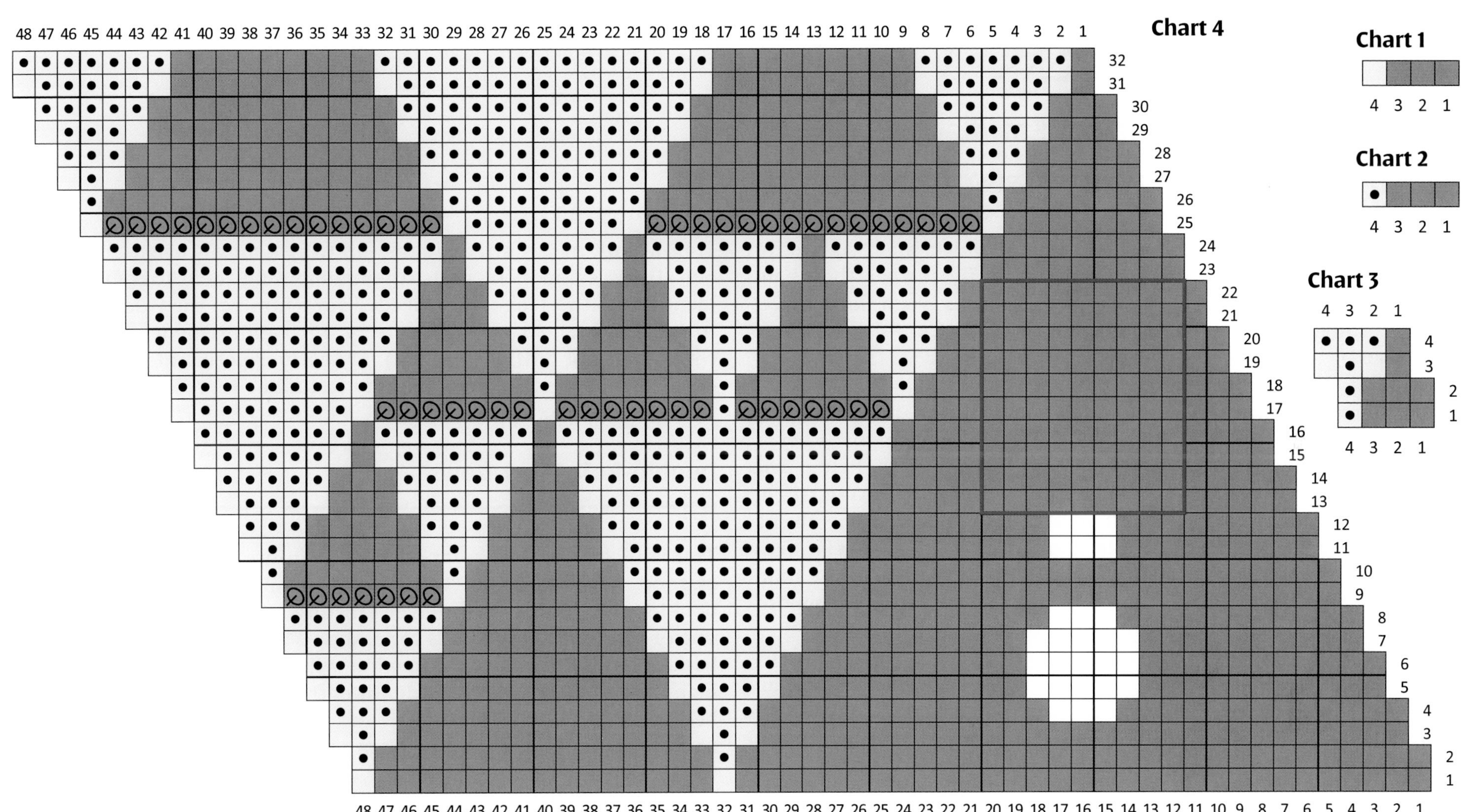

Chart 4b

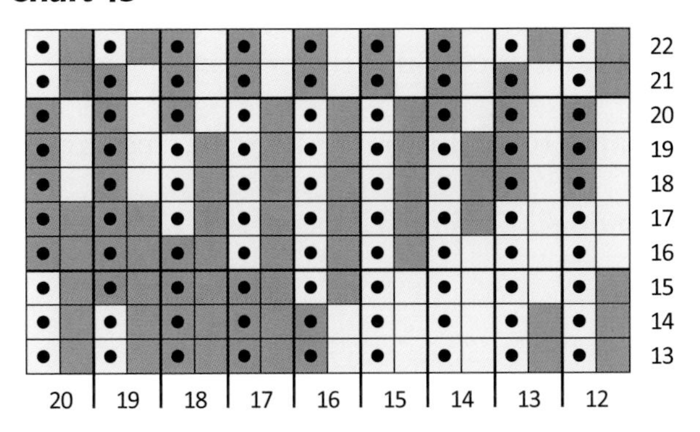

Chart 4b Reference Charts

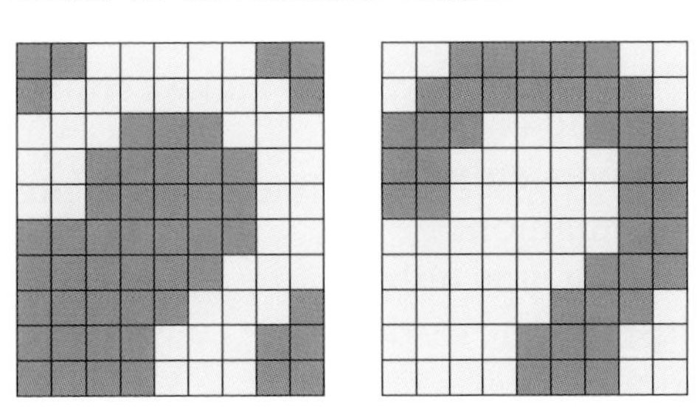

Chart 4a

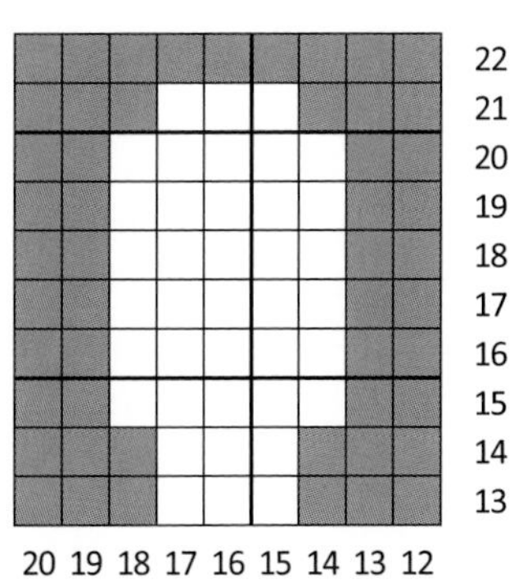

CHAPTER 7

Double-knitting Entrelac

Entrelac is a fascinatingly complex fabric in which small squares are knitted and attached to one another on the fly (rather than being stitched together later). The resulting fabric looks like a fluffy basket-woven cushion, which is fitting, since the word is from the French for "interlaced."

Each square is worked off the edge of a previous one, and all of them are turned 45 degrees from vertical in one direction or the other, so they appear as diamonds. They are actually rectangles, being twice as tall as they are long, but a combination of oblong knitting stitches and their tiled alignment causes them to appear square in the finished piece. Because they are small flat pieces of knitting, even entrelac in the round is technically worked flat. When you reach the end of the round of diamonds, you'll turn and do the next set of diamonds in the opposite direction.

Because of the place where the yarn finishes at the end of the round and where the next round has to start, the yarn must always be broken and begun again. This gives the opportunity for the next set of diamonds to be in a different color than the last, adding some intrigue.

The wrong side of single-layer entrelac has always irked me. It's a beautiful fabric on the right side, but the other side, even when done as cleanly as possible, is a seamed, cratered mess. You're free to disagree, but after my first foray into entrelac, I decided I'd figure out how to hide the wrong side by double-knitting it. After much experimentation, I found some surprising things that made me think that double-knitting and entrelac were truly made for each other. For example, in single-layer entrelac there are typically two different sets of instructions for the diamonds — one that leans left, and one that leans right. In double-knitting, you only need the one, because in the next row or round, you can just flip the work and follow the same instructions for the next set of diamonds.

Translating any pattern to double-knitting is mostly a matter of figuring out all the component parts, then combining them together. If I can identify all the techniques needed for entrelac, then determine how to work each one in double-knitting, I'm well on my way to a proof of concept (if not a whole pattern). My early experiments in double-knit entrelac indicated a few gaps in my technique repertoire, which I have since patched up.

Double-knit Short-Rows

This will come in handy for shaping in future patterns, but entrelac is as good an excuse as any to figure out how to translate short-rows to double-knitting. In single-layer knitting, a short-row is the result of one of a number of methods for ending a row early, turning and going back. It's most often used for shaping, with the most common application being the turning of sock heels. In entrelac, you use short-rows at the beginning to make the initial set of triangles that give your work that 45-degree angle. The phrase "wrap and turn" is associated with short-rows: the way you avoid a hole in your work is to wrap the yarn around the next stitch before turning to change direction. The wrapped stitch must, at some point, be processed a second time to hide the visible wrap from view. Therefore, short-rows are a combination of two techniques: one to make the short-row, and one to hide the evidence.

To make a **short-row "wrap & turn"** in double-knitting, see page 127.

To do a **wrap pickup** in double-knitting, see pages 128-129.

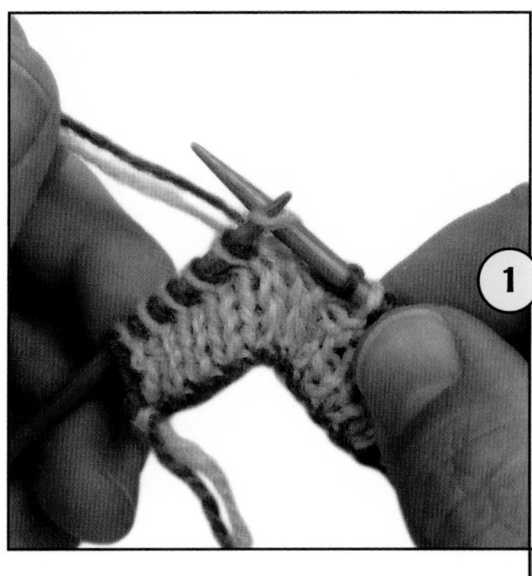

At the point where you want to turn, work a slipped pair but slip the first stitch knitwise.

Note that the knit stitch is now seated twisted on the needle. This will be important when you pick up the wraps to hide them later. Finish the slipped pair with a regular purl.

Separate the ends to the front and the back, matching the color order of the pair you just slipped.

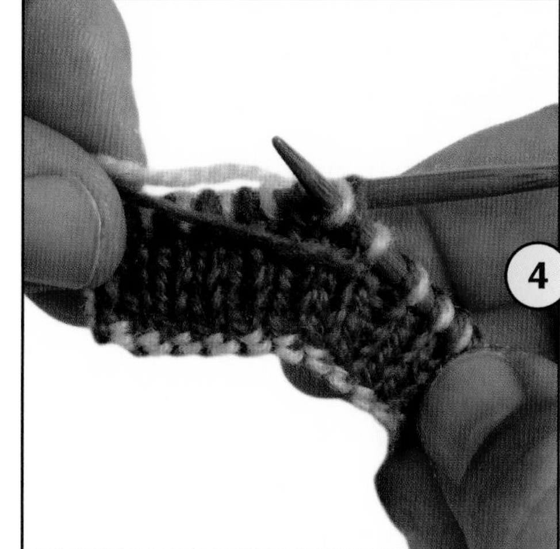

Leaving the ends where they are, slip the pair back to the source needle, and turn the work over.

Bring the end from the front to the back to join the other end. Then work the next row as dictated by the pattern.

Here's the piece from the original orientation, a couple of pairs after the wrap. You can see the wrap going around the base of one of the pairs.

When you need to work a new pair on top of the wrapped pair, hide the wraps by picking them up and working them with their corresponding pairs.

Work up to the wrapped pair.

Pull the wrap on the front up onto the source needle …

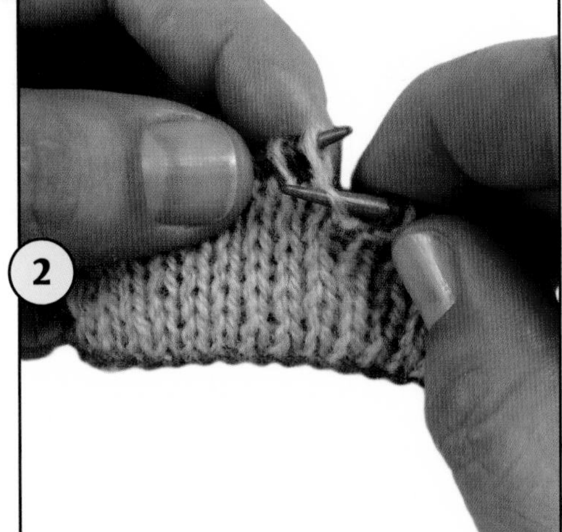

… to join the stitch it was wrapped around. It doesn't matter if it stays in front or jumps over to the back but both stitch and wrap should be on the source needle next to each other.

Wyib, knit both the wrap and the stitch through the back of the loop (K2togTBL) with one color (usually matching the color of both the stitch below and the wrap).

Here's the completed knit stitch with its wrap picked up and hidden inside the work.

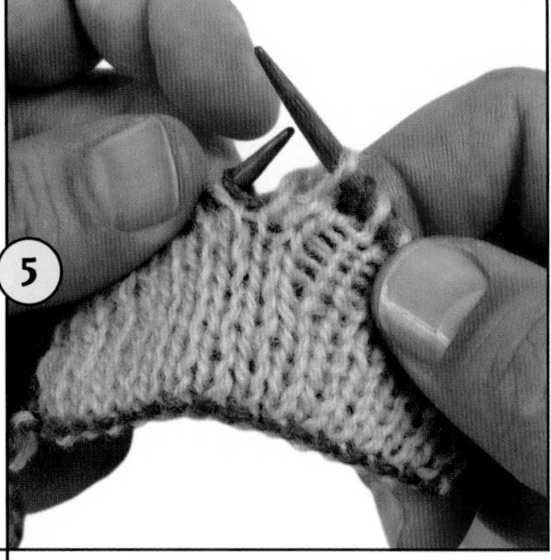

Flip the work up so you can see the other layer. Pull the wrap on the back up onto the source needle …

... to join the stitch it was wrapped around, as in Step 3. Bring the work back to a more natural orientation to continue.

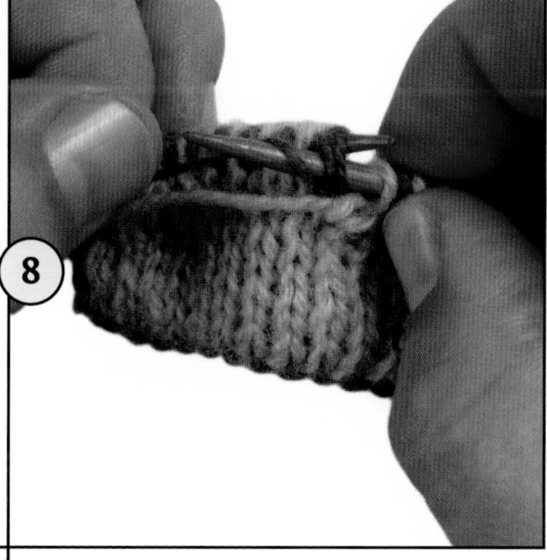

Wyif, purl both the wrap and the stitch (P2tog) with the opposite color from the previous knit.

Here's the completed purl stitch (as shown from Layer 2) with its wrap picked up and hidden inside the work.

Craftstory, continued from page 101

You may remember from early in this story that I got into knitting later in life, when nobody came to an origami class I was teaching. Origami (the Japanese art of paperfolding) had been a passion of mine for quite some time. I began it when I was 4, and I did it sporadically (especially around Christmas when we decorated our tree with all kinds of origami models). I didn't get really serious about it, however, until age 11 or 12. I became one of the youngest teachers at our local craft center and I taught origami to other kids and adults for many years. I sold origami models at local craft fairs, and I got heavily involved in the origami "scene," going to the yearly convention in New York almost every summer. I made lasting friendships and eventually became known as one of the higher-level folders (since I could do even the most complex moves with ease). I also designed a paper airplane which I entered in the time-in-air competition every year and I won handily every time.

But the origami scene, like any other scene, is different at the top. While I was creating strange experiments with geometry and color, as well as playing with freeform curved sculptural surfaces, the other designers at my level were working on making anatomically correct insects and getting deeper and deeper into the math and engineering where I, with my art and craft background, could not easily follow. There was a clique-ishness that I couldn't get past, and since folders who were technically capable of doing my designs weren't interested in them, I got discouraged and turned away from the whole scene. I still teach origami occasionally, but by and large, knitting has now fulfilled my need for a creative outlet – and now my strange experiments with geometry and color are actually of interest to people.

Craftstory, continued on page 132

Picking Up Pairs

This is one of those places where the solution I discovered really shows off the elegant combination of double-knitting and entrelac. I had struggled for quite some time to find a good way to pick up stitches along an open selvedge in such a way that the edge closes. I was envisioning a cast-on that somehow pulled stitches through the sides of other stitches — but in the end, the solution was staring me in the face the whole time. In entrelac, the things that look like diamonds are actually twice as tall as they are wide. It's just the way they interlock that makes them appear square. This means that you might be picking up, say, 3 stitches (or pairs, in double-knitting) along an edge that's 6 rows tall. Well, if you do a linked selvedge along a 6-row flat double-knit piece, you end up with 3 linked pairs.

The links, if you pull the edge gently apart, show up as a loop of one color interlinked with a loop of the other color. Since there are 3 of them, and 3 pairs to pick up, you simply use the links to create the pairs.

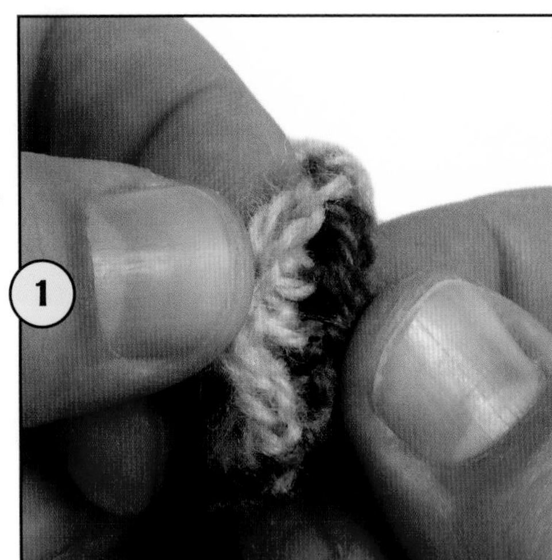

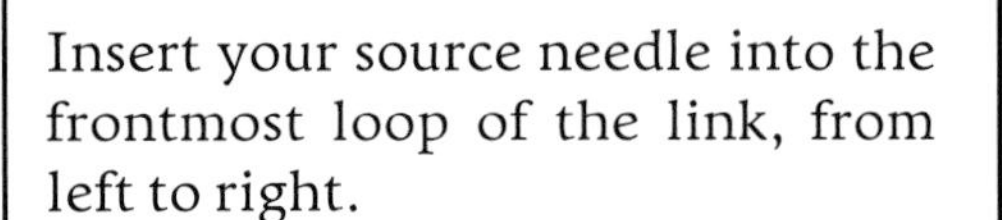
Insert your source needle into the frontmost loop of the link, from left to right.

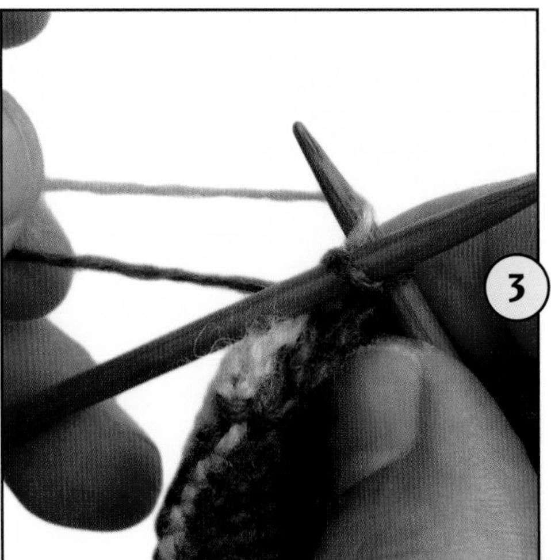

K1 with the color indicated by the chart or instructions.

Insert your source needle into the rearmost loop of the link, from left to right.

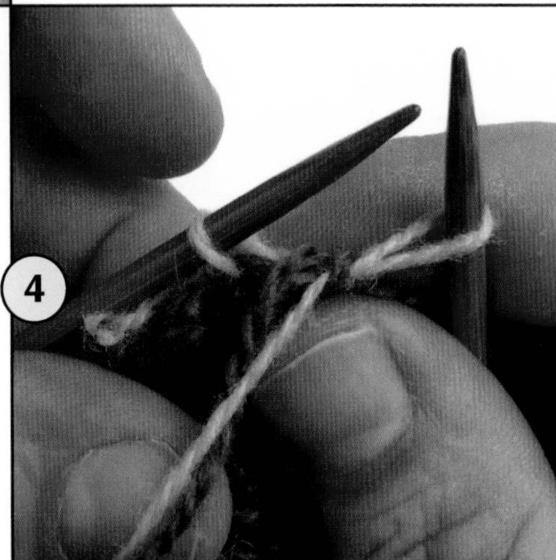

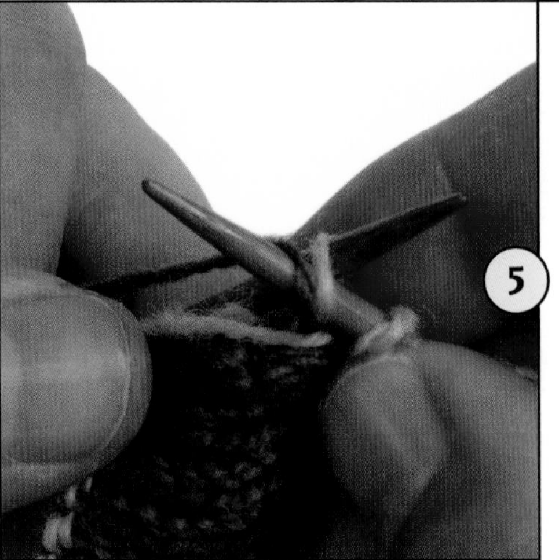

P1 with the opposite color from that used for the previous stitch.

Here are a few pairs picked up along the edge, as shown from Layer 2 . . .

. . . and the same pairs as viewed from Layer 1.

If you need to pick up fewer pairs than there are links, the pattern will guide you, but the general idea is that you can insert your needle into two links in a row and then K2tog and P2tog. You can use corresponding decreases (see page 50), but since the result is hidden from view, it's not important.

If you need to pick up more pairs than there are links, you can work a CO pair between two picked-up pairs. If this seems to be giving you a hole (it will depend on your tension), you can pick up twice into a single link. Try not to pick up more than two stitches out of each loop; if you do, you will stress the loop and end up with your stitches sort of bunched together as if from a double-increase.

Linked Decreases

There are cases where it's more practical to do two techniques at once than try to do them separately. While this seems counterintuitive, it is sometimes possible to do a "row-below" technique and a current-row technique in the same move. One obvious application of that would be a linked decrease, where a linked pair and a decrease are worked simultaneously. Since the decrease is done with the stitches in the row below, the new pair that is created can be linked or unlinked.

This is especially useful in double-knit entrelac. An entrelac "diamond" has 4 edges, each of which is processed in a different way. It was important to me that all 4 edges be linked together, which leaves the middle of the diamond free to be worked plain (and therefore with separate layers), with colorwork, or with some other double-knit technique. The beginning of the diamond is the picked-up edge and that's already closed. One side edge is a regular selvedge using linked and slipped pairs. But the opposite edge needs to be decreased with the active loops of the previous diamond. Linking the decreases solves the other two edges at the same time since the other side edge and the top edge of an adjacent diamond are decreased together and become, in a way, the same edge.

To work a **linked single decrease (⋇) or (⋇)**:

1. Reorder your pairs from KPKP to KKPP
2. Wyib, work your knit-side decrease in the direction and color indicated by the chart.
3. Wyif, insert your working needle as if to work the purl-side decrease in the corresponding direction.
4. Twist the two ends, and finish the purl in the opposite color from the knit.

This should come easily to you if you've done any reasonable number of linked pairs along the edges of any flat double-knit piece.

You can also work a linked double-decrease in much the same way, but with a reordering of 3 pairs from KPKPKP to KKKPPP. In the pattern accompanying this chapter, the double-decrease that is linked as part of the crown decreases is a left-slanting one (i.e., SSSK, P3tog). The symbol for this is a combination of the linked pair and left-slanting double-decrease symbols (⋇). The right-slanting one is ⋇.

What you may notice from this description, especially if you've ever worked single-layer entrelac before, is that the decrease involves the last pair in the row, and yet it is a linked pair. Normally the linked pair is first and the slipped pair is last, but because I could not both slip and decrease at the same time I opted to make the linked pair at the end of the row. However, there's also a linked pair at the beginning of the row. So in order to keep the selvedge look that I wanted on both edges, I opted to alternate the links and slips a little differently. On the Layer 1 rows, both edge pairs are linked, one normally and one as part of a linked decrease. On the Layer 2 rows, both edge pairs are slipped. The result is essentially indistinguishable from the standard double-knit selvedge.

Double-knitting Backward

This is a totally optional technique, but you may find it helpful as an alternative to constantly turning your work when you're only working a few pairs between edges.

It's not really possible for me to describe this in a way that will apply to everyone. Because everyone knits differently, everyone will end up knitting backward differently. The advice that's been given before is also good here: insert your needle into the stitch in the way you'd normally purl, then turn your work over. Look at how the same move looks from the other side. Then, turn it over again and begin the stitch, but before you actually pull it through, turn the work over and see how it looks and feels to do the same movement from the other side. Practice this for a while, knitting a row, then purling a row backward, etc.

Knitting backward in single-layer knitting is done partially to avoid turning the work, but often is only done in stockinette. In double-knitting, you have to be able to purl backwards as well, which means you're going to have to follow the instructions above with your knit stitches as well, and practice by doing a reverse-stockinette swatch — purling a row, then knitting a row backward, etc.

Once you have both of those techniques down, it's time to try them together in double-knitting. Don't forget that when you get to a row you'll be working backward, you're going to be starting with a (reverse) purl, not a knit. Also, you're going to need to repeat a bit of the process above with the linked pair — since this can't be translated to single-layer knitting, you'll need to try it in double-knitting, then see how it feels to make it from the other side of your work.

Craftstory, continued from page 129

In high school, I had always been infatuated with hands-on classes. My school had a vocational/technical school attached to it, but my parents, being academics themselves, steered me away from such pedestrian pursuits. The one class that spilled over into the regular curriculum was a drafting class, and since this was before the modern age of computers, we learned to use drafting boards, pencils, and rulers to make all kinds of things. We even went so far as to prototype papercraft objects we had to draft, then cut out, and finally assemble. This was heaven for me, but I wasn't allowed to go any further.

Fortunately, we also had an amazing art teacher who allowed me to exercise all kinds of creative urges. I spent a lot of extra time after school working on art projects there. But art, despite my love for it, was not the serious pursuit my mother and stepfather wanted for me, and I ended up looking at colleges with an eye on something in the computer science or engineering areas. I chose the university I eventually attended for the strength of its computer science program, but it quickly became apparent that the language-learning difficulties that caused me so much trouble with music would also keep me from doing well with computer languages as well — and I gave up that pursuit too. I struggled through the first three years of college, taking refuge in the art department (as I had in high school).

The art department at this university was not known for its open-mindedness. They had tracks for drawing, painting, printmaking, sculpture, and art history. The drawing and painting teachers were hopelessly literal; too much stress was placed on figure drawing and realism. I broke out of the boundaries wherever I could, and my grades suffered for it. However, I had prior experience with printmaking and sculpture in high school, and I took to those with gusto.

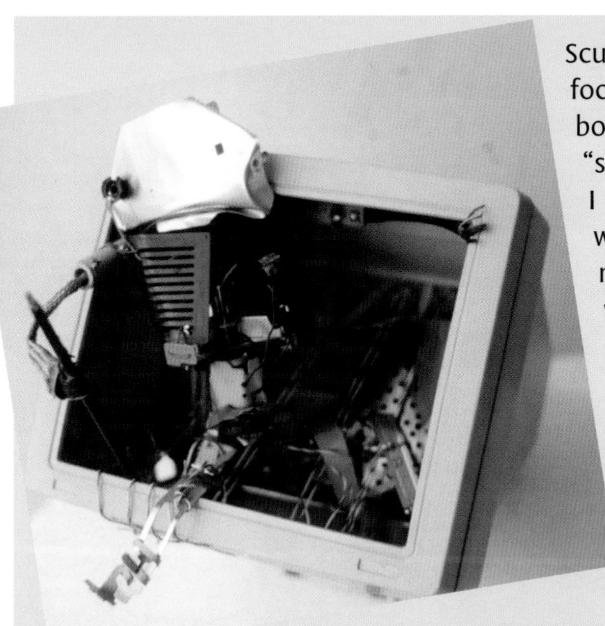

Sculpture, fittingly, became my focus, and I began creating a body of work which I called my "scrap metal culture." When I was a child, my stepfather would bring home broken machines for me to play with, and I got very adept at figuring out how things were built and taking them apart. The result of this was a lot of little mechanical parts. I revisited this in college as I scavenged the campus for broken computers, typewriters, or anything that had the promise of intriguing mechanical parts. I amassed several huge bins of parts, sorted roughly by size. I leafed through them until inspiration struck, then crafted parts into creatures. It was important to me, probably from my background in origami, that the reassembly be done by hand, without tools or adhesive.

In my junior year, I decided I wanted to take advantage of the much better art departments at other schools nearby. Credits could be transferred from school to school within certain networks, so it was just a matter of getting approval from the chair of the department. I decided I wanted to learn photography, something I'd been doing casually, often with my father, since I was young. But the chair of the department delivered this memorable line: "If I let you get course credit for photography, I'd have to let you get credit for basket weaving." Alfred Stieglitz turned over in his grave, and I dropped out at the end of the year. I had failed one class every semester, and even though I had made up my lost credits by taking summer classes, my girlfriend at the time was also planning on dropping out – so I decided to join her.

She and I had a choice: go and live with my family in Vermont or with hers in Maine while we figured out our next steps. I'd always liked Maine, so that's where we went. I had been doing computer helpdesk work at college, and I figured I could find a computer job of some kind – no such luck. We both ended up working in restaurants for several years. I gained a love of cooking (and no insignificant amount of weight) while at these jobs. The first one was a brick-oven bakery, and I added a whole bunch of items to the menu which they still use to this day. The second was a soul-food restaurant run by two African-American transplants from Mississippi. My fondest memory of this place was the night that I had made the jambalaya (as I did most weeks) and someone came up to our open kitchen and asked for the chef who'd made that dish. I volunteered hesitantly, and he shook my hand. He said he ran a cooking school in New Orleans and that mine was the best jambalaya he'd ever eaten in his life.

While in Maine, we also started and ran a cooperative art gallery in an old meatlocker; we called it "Art Carné." We had two rules: no lighthouses and no moose; we didn't want to be the same as every other art gallery in Maine. Among the artists we had connections with were Abbott Meader, Walter Easton, David McLaughlin and Abby Shahn. We had a membership of 30+ artists, and each month their work rotated through the gallery; they each paid a small monthly fee and together we paid the rent on the place; if something sold, the gallery would take small cut of the sale as well. We worked there in our off hours, but art is a tricky business, and we couldn't make it pay as well as we had hoped. We had fun, though, while it lasted.

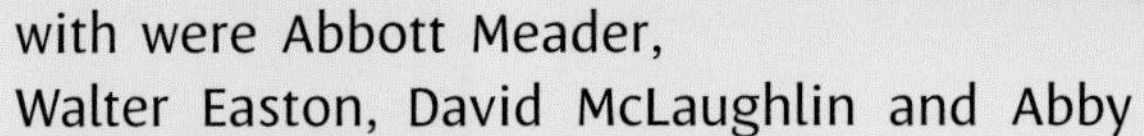

Craftstory, continued on page 147

FERRONNERIE

a tam-o'shanter hat in double-knit entrelac

Finished size & weight

For a small (medium, large) hat, the brim will be 17.5 (20, 22.5)" in circumference. The rest of the hat is meant to be slouchy so it's hard to measure brim-to-crown distance in any meaningful way. Approximately 34 (39, 44) g each of Colors A & B and 22 (26, 29) g each of Colors C & D will be needed — so no matter which size you want you should have no problem using only 1 skein of each color.

Materials & tools

[Color A]: Quince & Co Finch (100% wool; 221 yd/50 g skein); Audouin 157 (off-white); 1 skein.
[Color B]: Quince & Co Finch (100% wool; 221 yd/50 g skein); Lupine 116 (lavender); 1 skein.
[Color C]: Quince & Co Finch (100% wool; 221 yd/50 g skein); Caspian 155 (beige); 1 skein.
[Color D]: Quince & Co Finch (100% wool; 221 yd/50 g skein); Frank's Plum 114 (dark purple); 1 skein.

US 3/3.25 mm 16" circular needle, or size required to achieve gauge.
US 3/3.25 mm 32" or larger circular needle, or size to match first needle.

Gauge in pattern

25.5 sts/36 rows = 4" in double-stockinette.

Something that occurred to me while working on samples for this pattern: the two layers don't look appreciably different. A slight difference in the arrangement of colors, perhaps. So I set about trying to see how I could make it more distinctive. The result is a subtle but amazing illusion that will astound your fellow knitters (unless you give the trick away). Non-knitters will just see it as a striking pattern. So here's the setup: you know how in standard entrelac, you do rows of diamonds? Each of those rows (or rounds) is generally done with a single solid or variegated strand of yarn. When you do the next set of diamonds, you have the opportunity to change to another strand in a new color (you don't have to, but you can). The result is that a standard entrelac piece in the round can give you concentric rings of diamonds if you change colors with each new set. To avoid the checkerboard look, you'd use more than two colorways.

In double-knit entrelac, you can do the same thing but use two colors — one for the front and one for the back. The result could be the same, but it doesn't have to be. When you have two colors, either one of them can be the front or back stitch in any given pair. This means that you can use colorwork within the diamonds, but it also means that you can change the whole diamond's color on the fly. In other words, a single round of double-knit entrelac diamonds can consist of diamonds of two different color orders. At the point where you begin picking up stitches for the next diamond, just begin with a new color order. If you line up your diamonds properly, you'll get what appears to be radial color changes rather than concentric. This is not possible in standard entrelac unless you want to use a new strand for every diamond, which results in more ends than anyone should ever have to weave in.

In this hat, I've chosen to use the radial color order trick I just explained, but also add in colorwork that spirals in toward the center. If the colorwork makes the hat too busy for you, you can leave it out.

The yarn I'm using here is from Quince & Co., which is super popular lately. When I first stumbled across them at a shop in Maine, the patterns they had were, by and large, done in a single colorway. This seemed a shame to me since they had so many colors and good weights of yarn for colorwork. I love their yarn and, particularly, the stitch definition in Finch; I wanted to showcase it with something really stunning, so it was a shoo-in for double-knit entrelac.

The term "entrelac" is derived from a French word for "interlacing" which describes what the fabric looks like when finished, especially in single-layer versions. Double-knitting it sort of flattens the fabric out a bit, but the interlaced look is not diminished completely. Because the technique is French, I looked for a French word for the name. The chart I'd chosen for the colorwork parts is based on a common wrought-iron shape, so I found a term "ferronnerie d'art" which refers to wrought-ironwork. "Ferronnerie" evidently just means "ironwork," which, when worked in wool, calls to mind another play on words — irony.

Chart 1

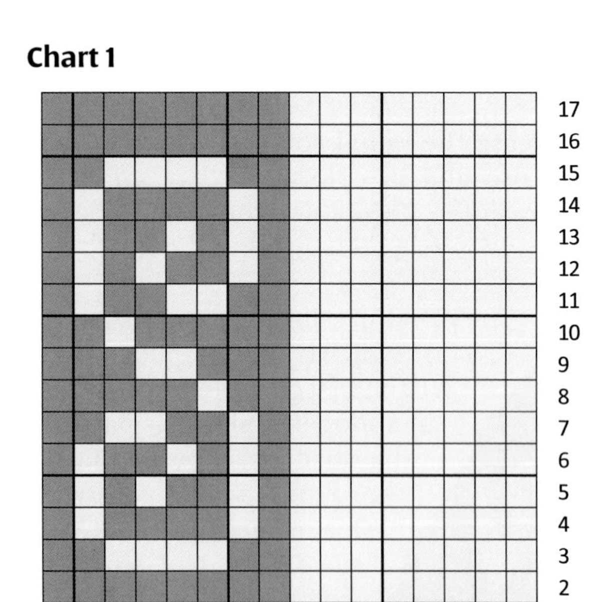

Chart 2a

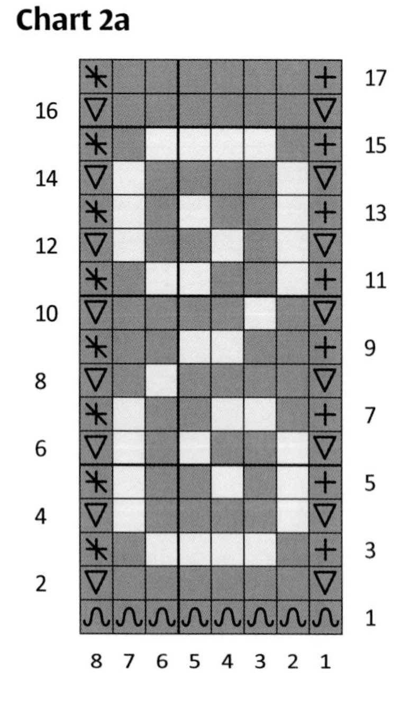

Chart 2b

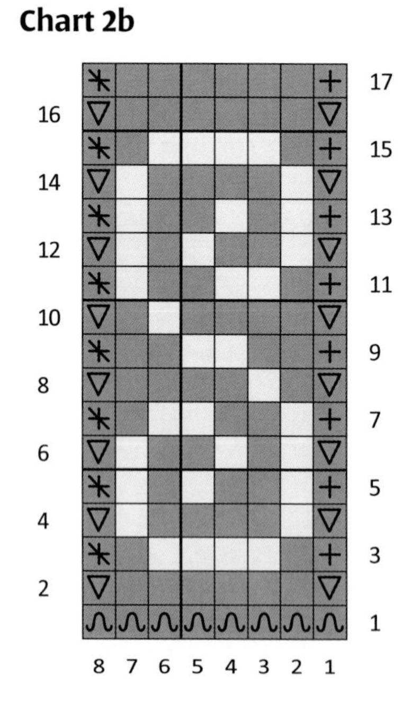

Chart 2c

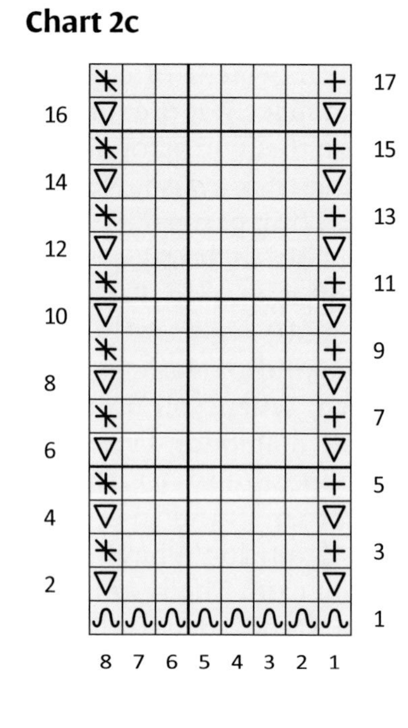

Chart 2d

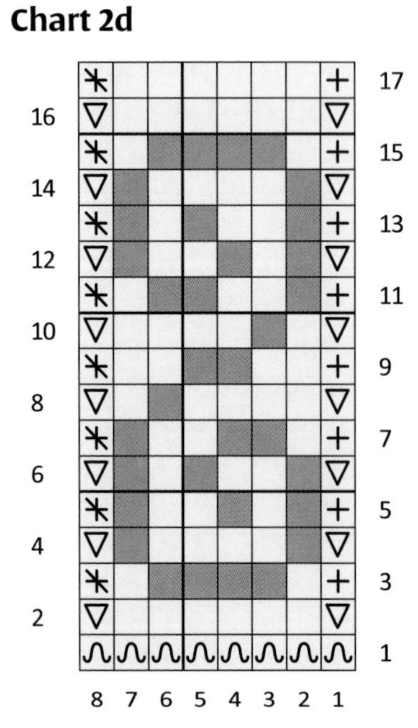

Chart 2e

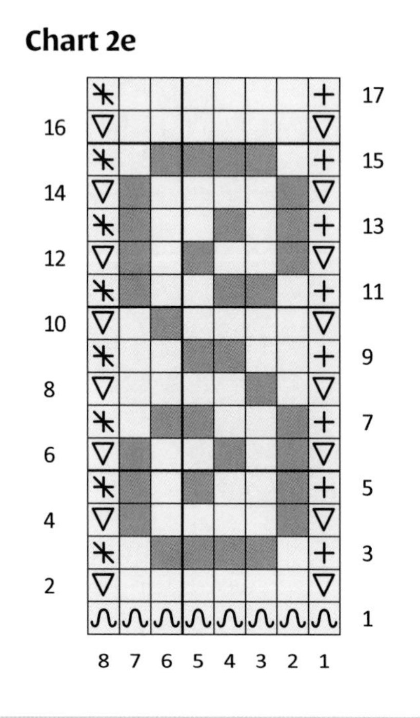

Chart 2f

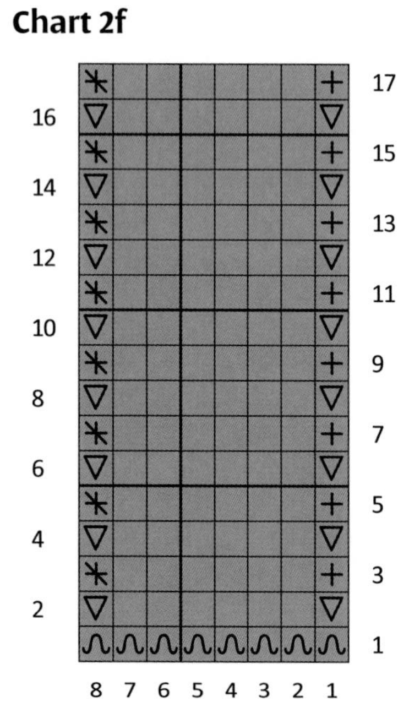

Chart 3a

Chart 3b

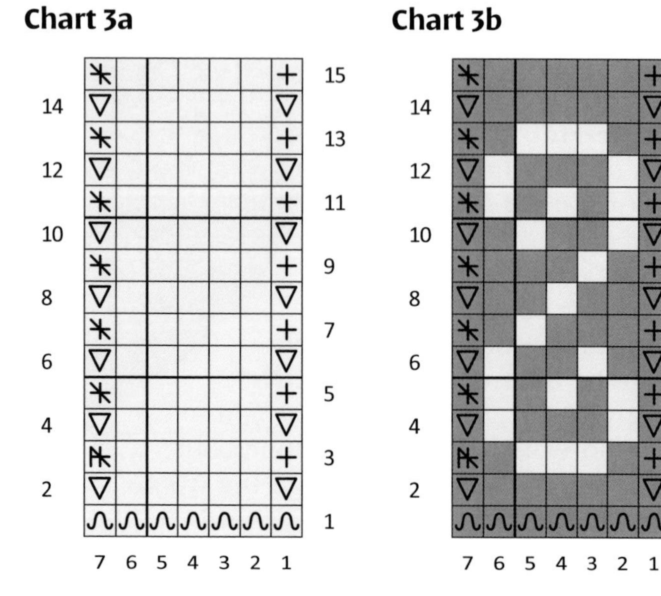

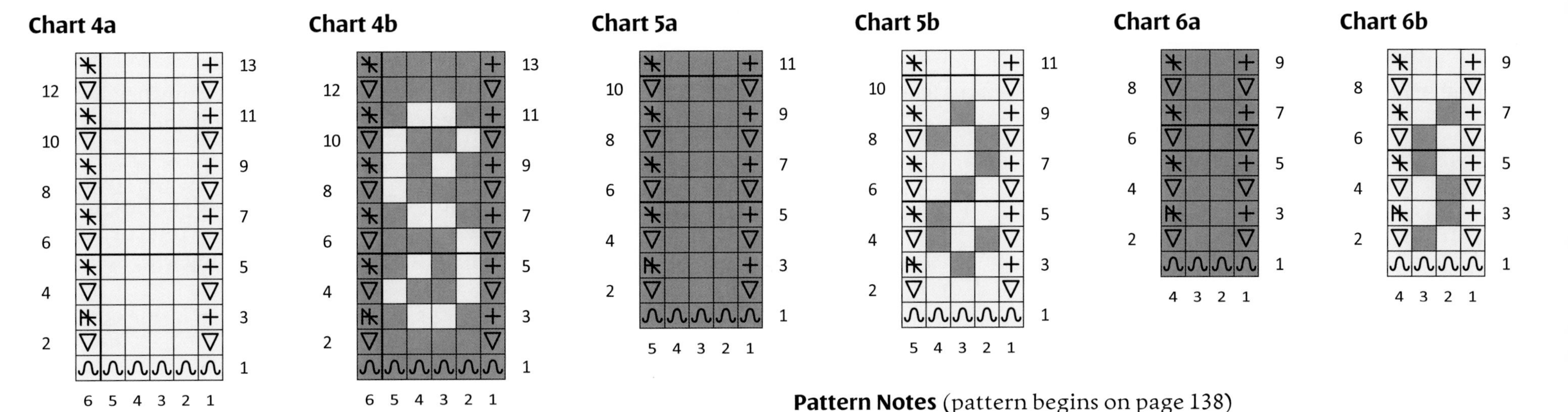

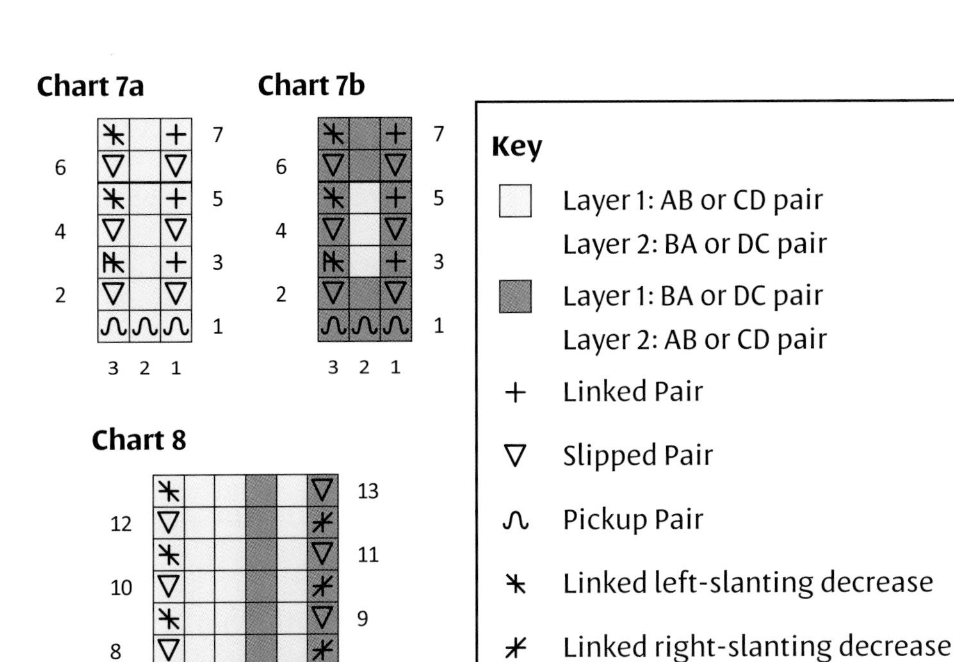

Pattern Notes (pattern begins on page 138)

In Charts 2a-7b, the edges are treated differently than in standard flat double-knitting. The linked and slipped pairs still alternate, but instead of being offset, the slipped pairs are worked at both ends of the Layer 2 rows, and the linked pairs are worked at both ends of the Layer 1 rows. In Chart 8, the edges are also different from standard double-knitting: the first pair in each row is slipped and the last one is a linked decrease.

In Charts 2a-7b, the first linked pair should be worked with a standard knit rather than a KTBL. This is because the pair into which you are working is not a slipped pair but a picked-up pair, and is not twisted in the same way as the others will be. Unlike other flat double-knitting, the first linked pair must be worked because you're going to have to use it to pick up into later.

In Charts 2a-8, the first row of each chart shows the color order of the picked up pairs. At least until the decrease rounds begin, you can follow the charts easily enough without any further glances at the pattern, as long as you understand how entrelac works. Once you get into the decrease rounds, the pattern will tell you where best to pick up a pair from two links.

This is a "tam o'shanter" hat, which is a traditional Scottish shape like a wide beret. The best way to block this is to wet it and put a dinner plate inside the body, making sure not to stretch the brim. Depending on the size of hat you choose, you may find that you'll need a larger dinner plate.

Pattern

For a hat band 17.5 (20, 22.5)" around, CO 112 (128, 144) AB pairs.

Brim

Work 7 (8, 9) repeats of Chart 1.

Body

Switch to 32" circular needle, work 14 (16, 18) entrelac triangles around in alternating color order as described below:

Using color order BA on odd rows and AB on even rows:

1. Work linked pair, wrap & turn.
2. Work slipped pair, turn
3. Work linked pair, work wraps & next pair together, wrap & turn.
4. Work 1 pair, work slipped pair, turn.
5. Work linked pair, work 1 pair, work wraps & next pair together, wrap & turn.
6. Work 2 pairs, work slipped pair, turn
7. Work linked pair, work 2 pairs, work wraps & next pair together, wrap & turn.
8. Work 3 pairs, work slipped pair, turn
9. Work linked pair, work 3 pairs, work wraps & next pair together, wrap & turn.
10. Work 4 pairs, work slipped pair, turn
11. Work linked pair, work 4 pairs, work wraps & next pair together, wrap & turn.
12. Work 5 pairs, work slipped pair, turn
13. Work linked pair, work 5 pairs, work wraps & next pair together, wrap & turn.
14. Work 6 pairs, work slipped pair, turn
15. Work linked pair, work 6 pairs, work wraps & next pair together.

At this point you should be at the end of one 8-pair section and at the beginning of the next 8-pair section. Repeat the same process, now reversing color orders. Alternate these BA and AB triangles until you reach the end of the round. Turn inside out.

Entrelac Rounds

Entrelac Round 1 (Colors C & D):

1. Starting at the tip of the triangle next to the working needle, pick up 7 DC pairs along the edge. Pick up 1 DC pair from between the triangles, similar to a M1L (total of 8 pairs).
2. Turn and keep following Chart 2a (motif), starting with Row 2.
3. On next triangle, pick up 7 CD pairs along the edge. Pick up 1 CD pair from between the triangles, similar to a M1L (total of 8 pairs).
4. Turn and keep following Chart 2c (plain), starting with Row 2.

Work 6 (7, 8) more repeats of Steps 1-4; break yarn. Turn inside out.

Entrelac Round 2 (Colors A & B):

1. Starting at the tip of the diamond next to the working needle, pick up 8 BA pairs along the edge.
2. Turn and keep working Chart 2b (motif), starting with Row 2.
3. Pick up 8 AB pairs along the next edge
4. Turn and keep working Chart 2c (plain), starting with Row 2.

Work 6 (7, 8) more repeats of Steps 1-4; break yarn. Turn inside out.

Entrelac Round 3 (Colors C & D):

1. Starting at the tip of the diamond next to the working needle, pick up 8 DC pairs along edge.
2. Turn and keep working Chart 2f (plain), starting with Row 2.
3. Pick up 8 CD pairs along next edge.
4. Turn and keep working Chart 2d (motif), starting with Row 2.

Work 6 (7, 8) more repeats of Steps 1-4; break yarn. Turn inside out.

Entrelac Round 4 (Colors A & B):

1. Starting at the tip of the diamond next to the working needle, pick up 8 BA pairs along edge.
2. Turn and keep working Chart 2f (plain), starting with Row 2.
3. Pick up 8 AB pairs along next edge.
4. Turn and keep working Chart 2e (motif), starting with Row 2.

Work 6 (7, 8) more repeats of Steps 1-4; break yarn. Turn inside out.

Entrelac Decrease Rounds

Entrelac Decrease Round 1 (Colors C & D):

1. Starting at the tip of the diamond next to the working needle, pick up 3 DC pairs along edge, pick up 1 DC pair from two links, pick up 3 more DC pairs (total of 7 pairs).
2. Turn and keep working Chart 3a (motif), starting with Row 2.
3. Repeat pickups with CD pairs along next edge.
4. Turn and keep working Chart 3b (plain), starting with Row 2.

Work 6 (7, 8) more repeats of Steps 1-2; break yarn. Turn inside out.

Entrelac Decrease Round 2 (Colors A & B):

1. Starting at the tip of the diamond next to the working needle, pick up 2 BA pairs along edge, pick up 1 BA pair from two links, pick up 3 more BA pairs (total of 6 pairs).
2. Turn and keep working Chart 4a (motif), starting with Row 2.
3. Repeat pickups with AB pairs along next edge.
4. Turn and keep working Chart 4b (plain), starting with Row 2.

Work 6 (7, 8) more repeats of Steps 1-4; break yarn. Turn inside out.

Entrelac Decrease Round 3 (Colors C & D):

1. Starting at the tip of the diamond next to the working needle, pick up 2 DC pairs along edge, pick up 1 DC pair from two links, pick up 2 more DC pairs (total of 5 pairs).
2. Turn and keep working Chart 5b (plain), starting with Row 2.
3. Repeat pickups with CD pairs along next edge.
4. Turn and keep working Chart 5a (motif), starting with Row 2.

Work 6 (7, 8) more repeats of Steps 1-4; break yarn. Turn inside out.

Entrelac Decrease Round 4 (Colors A & B):

1. Starting at the tip of the diamond next to the working needle, pick up 1 BA pair along edge, pick up 1 BA pair from 2 links, pick up 2 more BA pairs (total of 4 pairs).
2. Turn and keep working Chart 6b (plain), starting with Row 2.
3. Repeat pickups with AB pairs along next edge.
4. Turn and keep working Chart 6a (motif), starting with Row 2.

Work 6 (7, 8) more repeats of Steps 1-4; break yarn. Turn inside out.

Entrelac Decrease Round 5 (Colors C & D):

1. Starting at the tip of the diamond next to the working needle, pick up 1 DC pair along edge, pick up 1 DC pair from 2 links, pick up 1 more DC pair (total of 3 pairs).
2. Turn and keep working Chart 7a (motif), starting with Row 2.
3. Repeat pickups with CD pairs along next edge.
4. Turn and keep working Chart 7b (plain), starting with Row 2.

Work 6 (7, 8) more repeats of Steps 1-4; break yarn. Turn inside out.

Entrelac Decrease Round 6 (Colors A & B):

1. Starting at the tip of the diamond next to the working needle, pick up 3 BA pairs along edge.
2. Turn and keep working chart 8, starting with Row 2.
3. At row 7, work the first 3 pairs as charted then pick up 3 AB pairs along next edge.
4. Turn and finish working Chart 8, continuing with Row 8.

Work 6 (7, 8) more repeats of Steps 1-4; break yarn. Don't turn inside out.

Break yarns with 8-12" tails. Slide to other end of needle and work slipped BO. Pass end of Color B to inside. With end of Color A, use a tapestry needle to seam the BO edge to the links in the edge of the first Chart 8 repeat. When you've finished with Layer 1, turn work inside out and repeat with Color B end on Layer 2.

Now with both colors together, thread a tapestry needle. Run it behind the 7 (8, 9) links presented on the inside of the inner ring and cinch closed. Weave in ends. Block on a dinner plate (see pattern notes) and enjoy!

CHAPTER 8

Double-knitting Cables

If you've had a chance to check out *Extreme Double-Knitting*, you've probably seen some double-knit cables already. There's a hat named Vasily in that book which uses an all-over three-color cable technique. In that piece, you'll notice that there is no negative space (no background over which the cables might travel). This is due to a limitation I was convinced of in double-knit cables at the time: that double-knit cables could not travel across a background, whether of purls or of a different color or both.

Now, in all the world of knitted cables, there are only two types: crossed cables and traveling cables. A crossed cable occurs when two sections of the same color and stitch are cabled with each other (in double-knitting, this would be the same color order and stitch order). A traveling cable occurs when the two sections are of differing color and/or stitch. All the variations beyond that are just a matter of different shapes and sizes, along with a few special techniques.

When I originally developed double-knit cables back in 2006, I was basing my development on the structural/technique similarities between double-knitting and 1x1 ribbing. Because double-knitting uses a similar knit/purl alternating technique, and reversible cables can be made in 1x1 ribbing, it would be possible to take the whole double-knit fabric, without separating pairs, and cable it. I was right — it was possible — but with that method came the same limitations imposed on reversible cables in ribbing. A cable will not be a mirror image on the other layer, it will be identical. If the cable crosses right to left on one layer, it will cross right to left on the other layer, like turning over a piece of rope. This may be well and good if you're using crossed cables. If the cable is anything more complicated than a simple twisted cable (such as a braid, for example), the other layer will look different but will still be fundamentally a cable. The problem happens when you try to cross part of that cable with the background, making a traveling cable. On one layer, the cable is traveling nicely on top of the background; but on the other layer, the background is traveling over the top, and in the opposite direction. It doesn't look nice, or really anything like a cable.

For a long time, I assumed that there was no elegant solution to this issue. The only thing I could figure out was that each layer could be separately cabled — you'd have to separate the two layers, cable them independently and reintegrate them. To me, this departed so radically from double-knitting that it didn't even deserve the same name. I went to press in late 2011 with *Extreme Double-Knitting* and a cable pattern that had no negative space, because I couldn't figure out how to do anything better.

And of course, because life is learning, in early 2012 I figured it out. Not only can true double-knit cables be done across a background, but they can also be done with or without a cable needle. I know other people have begun working in double-knit cables as well, due to the memetic nature of innovation, but where their techniques often require two cable needles to achieve, mine requires either one or none. And the solutions for both are not only elegant, they're downright beautiful.

Double-knitting Cables The Old Way

About this method, the less said, the better. But I owe it to my technical progression to mention the old way of double-knitting cables if only so you can understand how far we've come in just a few short years.

If you've done cables before (and I hope you have before trying them in double-knitting), this technique will be very familiar to you. The two layers of the work are not separated at any point — you just take a group of pairs and cable them with another group of pairs. A 2x2 cable, for example, will involve two pairs held together at the back or front of the work (depending on the direction needed); two pairs are worked from the needle and then the two held pairs are worked. This set of instructions would be the same for a single-layer cable, if you replaced the word "pair" with "stitch."

The result is, as mentioned earlier, a cable that is only reversible if it's crossed with another cable of the same stitch order (the color order isn't important — you'll still have a reversible cable if the two pair groups are different color orders) and if the crossings are stacked vertically from row to row. If they're stacked diagonally, you're getting into the territory of traveling cables and the other layer of the work won't look identical (or even necessarily similar). The completed cable may also show a little bit of color from the other layer at the crossing (since the layers are arranged front-back-front-back) and will seem a little bulky. There are few legitimate reasons to use this type of cable anymore. Any cable move, crossed or traveling, can be done using the new methods.

Double-knitting Cables the New Way

Both of these processes will generate the same product. Before I show you how to achieve them, it's important that you understand what you're trying to create.

In single-layer cables, you have two groups of stitches involved in a cable technique. One of these groups goes to the back, and the other goes to the front. One way to look at this technique is in terms of product: if the leftmost group goes to the front, it's generally assumed that the cable is traveling or crossing right; if the rightmost group goes to the front, the cable is traveling or crossing left. The other common way to look at cables is in terms of process: the first group of stitches encountered (the rightmost group) is either cabled to the back or cabled to the front. If it's to the back, the leftmost group is at the front, and the cable is crossing right; if it's to the front, the cable is crossing left.

In double-knit cables, you also have two groups of stitches — except that they're actually two groups of pairs. A cable in double-knitting is achieved by separating one of those groups of pairs, moving them in the same direction along the outside of the work on both layers, and reintegrating them before or after the other group on the needle. The other group does not need to be separated, so any double-knit cable technique will focus on keeping those pairs intact throughout the preparation. The pairs that can always be kept intact are those that would, in single-layer knitting, be traveling along the back of the work. In double-knitting, however, they travel inside the work, because the backs of both layers are facing each other inside the work.

Because I'm not trying to express these techniques in text instructions (they're just symbols in charts), I have no need to abbreviate them with a shortened form like C2F or T2R or anything like that. The key gives instructions on working each technique, but the chart symbols are also meant to be as visually descriptive as possible.

For the examples, I'm going to use a 2x2 cable. In a real chart, however, you'll need to look at the symbol and see a few things. First, how many pixels in the chart does it span? Second, is the first or second group the one that will be traveling to the outside of the work? Third, how many pairs will be traveling? Fourth, how far will they be traveling? For example, a 2x2 right-crossing cable spans 4 pairs: two pairs will be traveling left to right by two spaces. There's more to it, of course — you'll also need to look at color order and stitch order. However, those will most often match the row below, so they're less important to deal with right now.

Double-knitting cables with a cable needle

I'm presenting this first, even though this is the second method I developed for double-knit cables. It's partially a necessity (as any time either half of a cable is larger than two pairs, it becomes easier to use a cable needle than not), and partially a comfort to those who want to double-knit cables, but aren't yet familiar with cabling without a cable needle.

The key to this type of cable is to use a U-shaped cable needle. I recommend the little metal ones both for the ease of insertion and their durability. But if you have one of the larger plastic ones, just make sure it's the same size as (or smaller than) your needle size. The U-shaped cable needle can easily pass between the needles without dropping its payload, whereas a straight (or even mostly-straight) cable needle will struggle with the same movement and run the risk of dropping stitches.

The cable needle is used to hold the group of pairs that are traveling inside the work — the background pairs, or simply the ones which are not on the front/outside of the work. The group of pairs that are not held are either worked or slipped (depending on the cable direction) stitch-by-stitch to reassemble their pairs at the far side of the held group.

Each of these techniques will take a whole page spread to explain fully, so they'll start on the next page.

This cable technique will take up the next 4 pairs pictured here. When it's done, the column of KP pairs will have moved 2 pairs to the right, essentially switching places with the 2 PK pairs to its right.

To work a **2x2 right-slanting cable** (2 pairs cabled 2 spaces left-to-right):

Slip 2 pairs onto your cable needle.

Holding the cable needle at the back and the ends in front of the cable needle, work 1 stitch as charted.

Holding the cable needle at the front and the ends in back of the cable needle . . .

. . . work the other stitch in the pair.

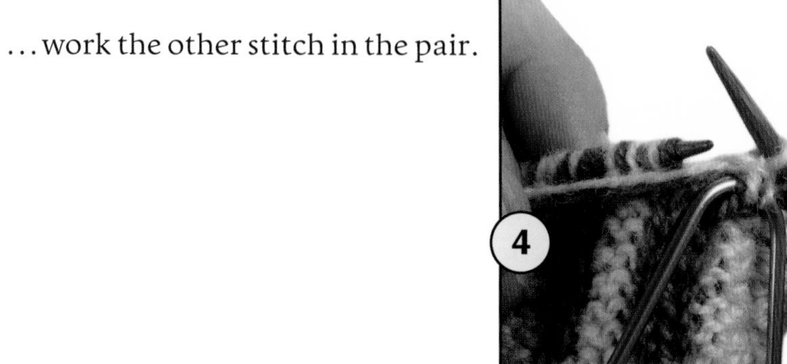

Bring the cable needle to the back again, keeping the ends in between the source needle and the cable needle.

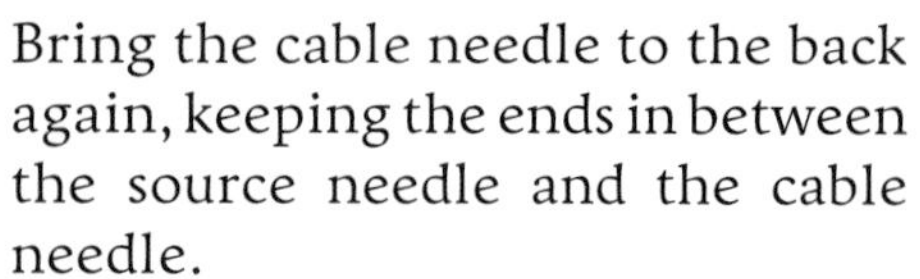

Work the next knit stitch.

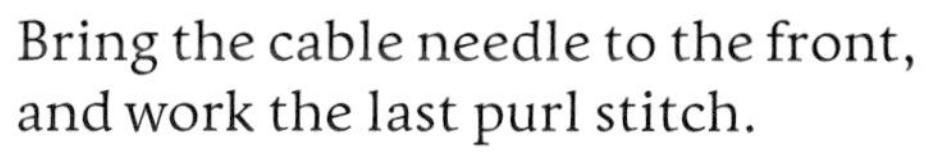

Bring the cable needle to the front, and work the last purl stitch.

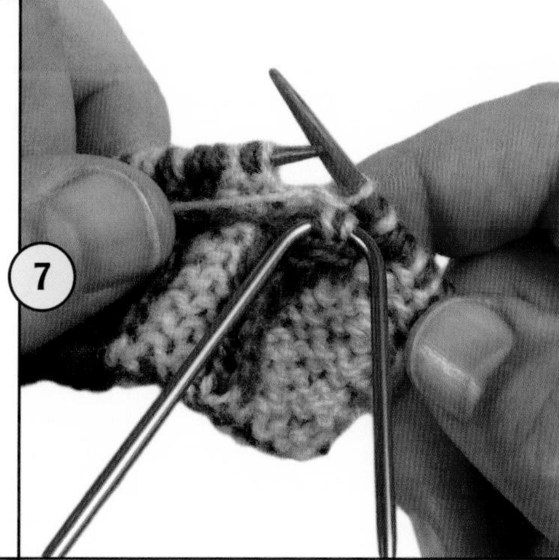

8

The pairs held on the cable needle are likely quite tight by now. Give the pairs a good tug with the cable needle to loosen them a bit, and then slip the held pairs back onto the source needle.

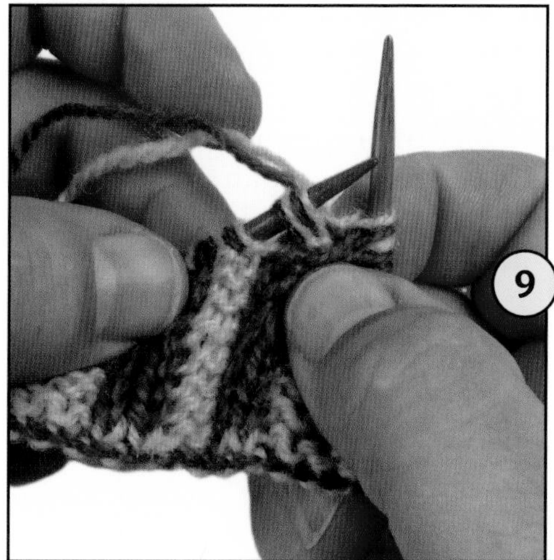

Work 2 pairs as charted

Here's the completed cable move, as viewed from Layer 1 . . .

. . . and here it is again, as viewed from Layer 2.

This cable technique will take up the next 4 pairs; when it's done, the column of KP pairs will have moved 2 pairs to the left, essentially switching places with the 2 PK pairs to its left.

To work a **2x2 left-slanting cable** (2 pairs cabled 2 spaces right-to-left):

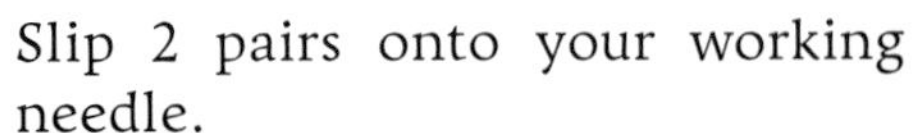

Slip 2 pairs onto your working needle.

Slip the other 2 pairs onto your cable needle.

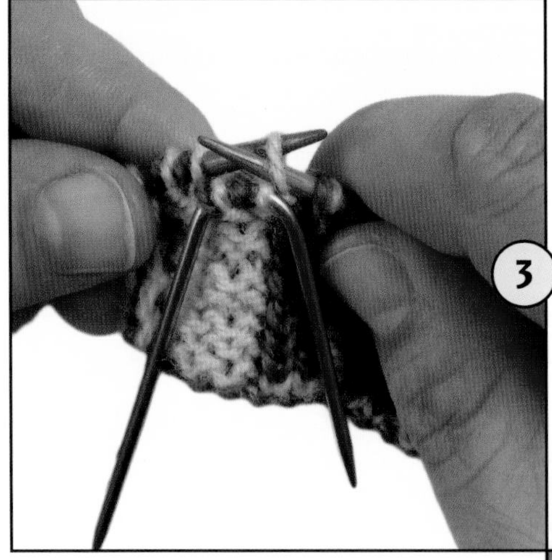

Holding the cable needle at the front, slip 1 stitch back to the source needle.

Holding the cable needle at the back, slip 1 stitch back to the source needle.

Holding the cable needle at the front, slip 1 stitch back to the source needle.

Holding the cable needle at the back, slip 1 stitch back to the source needle.

Here's the completed cable move, as viewed from Layer 1 . . .

The pairs which are held on the cable needle are likely quite tight by now. Give the pairs a good tug with the cable needle to loosen them a bit, and then slip the held pairs back onto the source needle.

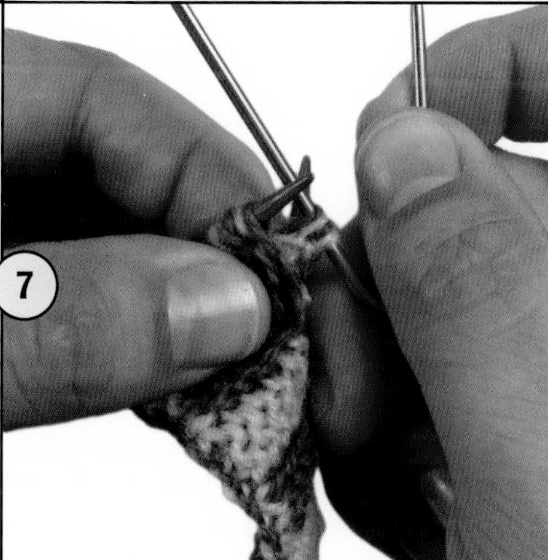

. . . and here it is again, as viewed from Layer 2.

Work all 4 pairs as charted.

When you are transferring the held stitches from the cable needle to the source needle again, you'll probably find that the cable twist makes them quite a bit tighter than normal. Just give them a good tug to loosen them as much as is practical, then carefully — stitch by stitch — slip them onto the needle. Once you've worked them, they'll relax a bit. This is only an issue in the method that uses a cable needle, and this is another reason why I suggested the metal needle, as it's more likely to hold up under the pressure of the tugging you have to do.

Now, to make this more useful for any cable, let's replace the numbers with some variables. Algebraphobes, don't worry — you don't need to solve for X here. X will be the number of pairs cabled along the outside of the work, and Y will be the distance they travel.

To work X pairs cabled Y spaces left-to-right:

1. Slip Y pairs onto your cable needle.
2. Holding the cable needle at the back and the ends in front of the cable needle, work 1 stitch as charted.
3. Holding the cable needle at the front and the ends in back of the cable needle, work the other stitch in the pair.
4. If necessary, repeat Steps 2 and 3 until all X pairs have been worked.
5. Slip the held pairs back onto the source needle.
6. Work Y pairs as charted.

To work X pairs cabled Y spaces right-to-left:

1. Slip X pairs to your working needle.
2. Slip Y pairs to your cable needle.
3. Holding the cable needle at the front, slip 1 stitch back to the source needle.
4. Holding the cable needle at the back, slip 1 stitch back to the source needle.
5. If necessary, repeat Steps 3 and 4 until all X pairs have been slipped back.
6. Slip the held pairs back onto the source needle and work X+Y pairs as charted.

Double-knitting cables without a cable needle

This is the method I prefer. It's fun to do, and it's always nice not to have to break your rhythm by picking up another tool. All three double-knit cabled patterns in this book are done with this method. Of course, the largest cable in any pattern here is 2x2, which is still doable this way.

Before I explain how to double-knit cables without a cable needle, it's important that you understand how to do it in single-layer knitting. I'm not going to go through this in exhaustive detail, as there are plenty of resources both in books and online that can help you learn this technique fully. But the general premise is that you'll use your working needle to hold one group of stitches, then pull the source needle out of all stitches involved in the cable technique. A certain number of stitches will come loose to the front or back of the work. Catch these stitches with the source needle again, and slip the held stitches back as well. Then work all stitches as charted. The important thing is that at some point, some number of stitches will come loose from the needle and need to be picked up again. A pinch at the base of those stitches may help keep them from coming undone. However, their state is tenuous, and I recommend you focus on getting them back on the needle at all (rather than worrying about whether they're seated properly — they can always be fixed on the fly as you work them).

In double-knitting, the terms "back" and "front" often have to become "inside" and "outside," which complicates this move. What you want to do is to let the stitches of one group fall loose on both the front and the back of the work simultaneously, while holding the other group with the needle. You'll then have to rebuild the pairs on the other side of the held group. The difficulty here is that in order to get your needle through the pairs on the far side of the cable technique, you're going to need to pass the needle inside the work.

The method I use to do this is something I call "needle-weaving" — the reason will become obvious when you try it. The idea is that in order to put a needle inside your work, you need to put it in back of your knits and in front of your purls. Pair by pair, you can "weave" your needle through your work until you can access the pairs you need to hold. Then, pulling the other needle out of all of the pairs involved, the stitches you wove past will become loose on their respective layers of the work. A pinch at their bases is useful to keep them from coming undone, since the technique you will need to execute in order to rebuild the pairs on the other side of the held stitches will put some stress on the loose stitches.

Craftstory, continued from page 133

Four years into my stay in Maine, my girlfriend and I broke up; I decided I'd return to school while my credits had not yet expired. I re-entered the art department, and much to my chagrin, the chair of the department who had made the crack about basket weaving was still there (and the department had not changed significantly). I reinserted myself into the sculpture department, and it was that fall when I went to that fateful craft-sharing event where I learned to knit. Just to rub it in the department chair's face, I also taught myself to basket weave and I did a series of pieces that used craft techniques in unusual materials – weaving and basket weaving in salvaged computer cables, and sewing and knitting in rubber tubing. With these pieces and others, I won an award for "most promising sculptor" along with my diploma.

Backing up a bit so we can get back on track: it was fall of 2003 when I learned how to do the knit stitch from someone whose name and face I can't even remember. I made a tiny red garter-stitch square from unremarkable yarn while sitting on a couch in a university common room, and the next day I sought out more yarn and cast on for the requisite garter-stitch scarf. It was charcoal-colored Lion Brand Thick & Quick, worked on US13 needles. When I'd finished that, I found a video online (probably on RealPlayer since this was before the days of YouTube) on the purl stitch and began to experiment.

In the couple of months that followed, I was still knitting in a vacuum. The only knitter I knew in college was the one who taught me how to knit, and I hadn't found any other resources yet. Not knowing about any "real" yarn stores, I bought yarn in the basement of Pearl Art Supply, as well as Ben Franklin when visiting home. Instead of using pattern books, I began experimenting by making graph-paper sketches of knit-purl patterns and working them into swatches and, occasionally, Möbius scarves. I don't know why I gravitated toward Möbius scarves at first – perhaps it was the math geek in me – but I found that, at a certain width, a single ball of Thick & Quick would make a short scarf that would be the ideal length to be stitched end-to-end with a twist. The resulting garment could be worn in multiple ways, but the thing that captivated me about it was its reversibility. A Möbius strip, you see, has only one side – so the fabric must be reversible if the seam is to be as invisible as possible.

Those early Möbius scarves were the source of my fascination with reversibility. I played with reversible knit and purl patterns and made one scarf for each of my immediate family members by Christmas that year, with a few left over for close friends and one or two to keep and use. After that winter break, I vowed to escape the vacuum I had been knitting in and seek out fellow fiber voyagers. The first thing I found was that a yarn shop had recently sprung up on one of the main streets in the town where I was attending college. They had yarns I'd never seen before (they were the first in the Boston area to begin stocking Malabrigo), as well as a knitting group that met on an evening I had free. I was in heaven.

At the same time, I began gathering knitters at the university. We created a knitting group that met in the university coffeehouse. Someone at the university newspaper ran an article on us that specifically focused on me, as the most interesting character to be involved in the knitting resurgence on campus. I was a large guy with long (dyed) black hair, a long black Russian wool coat, and a penchant for goth culture in general. The last person, as they said, they'd expect to pull out knitting needles. Whatever they thought, the article spurred new interest; I was soon part of a burgeoning community of crafters on campus as well as off.

Craftstory, continued on page 165

To work a **2x2 right-slanting cable** (2 pairs cabled 2 spaces left-to-right) **with no cable needle**:

Slip all 4 pairs (8 stitches) to the working needle.

Insert your source needle in between the previous two stitches on the working needle from front to back (in front of the purl, in back of the knit).

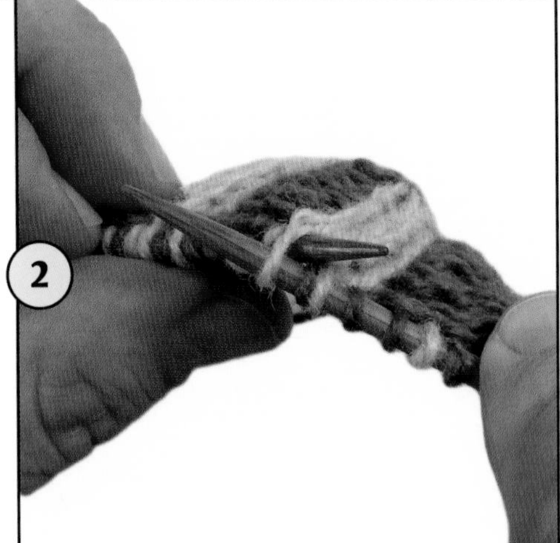

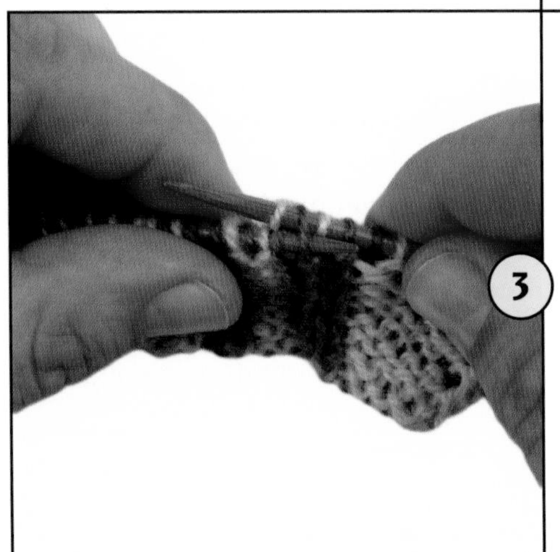

Bring the source needle to the front again, in between the next two stitches.

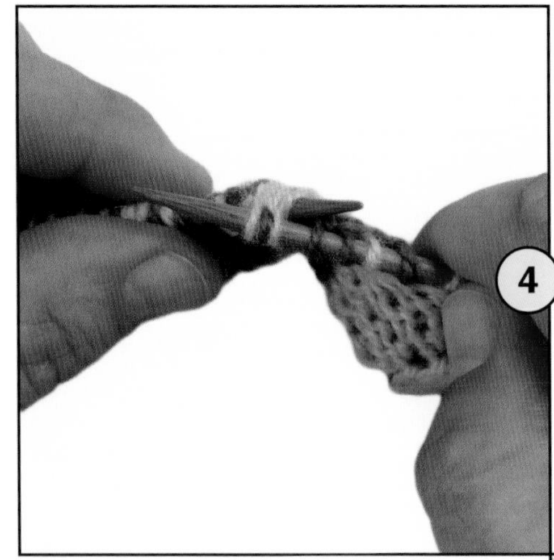

Bring the source needle to the back again, in between the next two stitches.

From the back, skip over the 4th stitch, and insert the needle into the next two pairs (this can be fiddly).

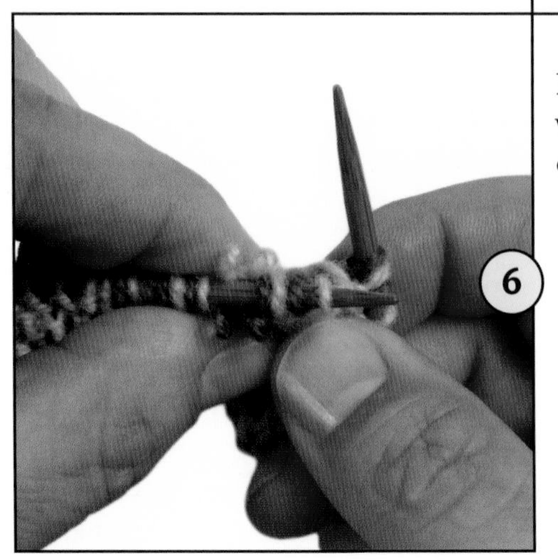

Holding the base of the 2 pairs you wove past, pull the working needle out of all 4 pairs.

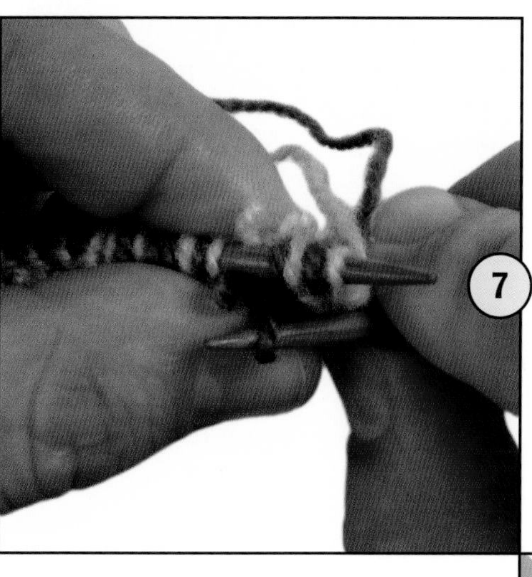

Catch the first loose front stitch on the working needle.

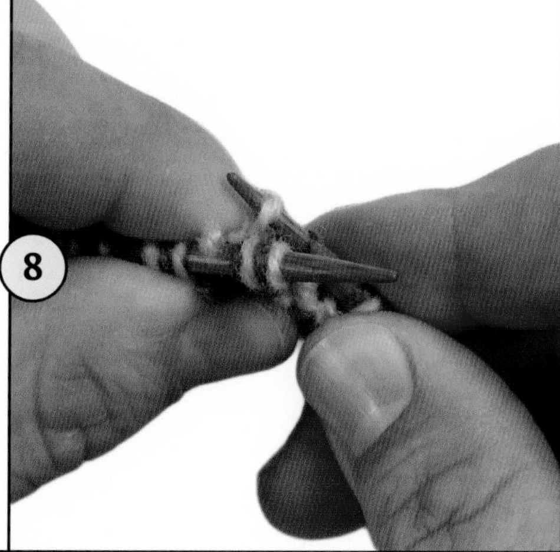

Bring the needle to the back, and catch the first loose back stitch on the working needle.

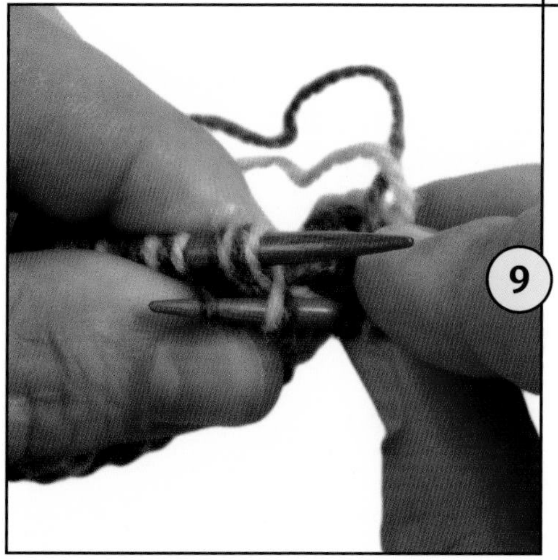

Bring the needle to the front, and catch the second loose front stitch on the working needle.

Finally, bring the needle to the back, and catch the last loose back stitch on the working needle.

Pass 2 pairs back to the source needle, and work all 4 pairs as charted.

Here's the finished cable, done without a cable needle (the back looks the same as Step 11 in the cable needle method, page 143).

To work a **2x2 left-slanting cable** (2 pairs cabled 2 spaces right-to-left) **with no cable needle**:

Everything will be in mirror image from the previous technique. There's no need to slip any stitches to begin with, since we'll be using the working needle and moving right to left.

Insert your working needle in between the next two stitches on the source needle from back to front (in back of the knit and in front of the purl).

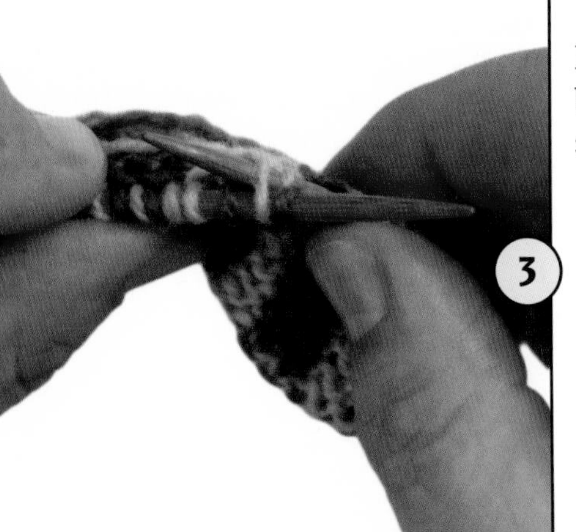

Bring the working needle to the back, in between the next two stitches.

Bring the working needle to the front again, in between the next two stitches.

From the front, skip over the 4th stitch, and insert the needle into the next two pairs.

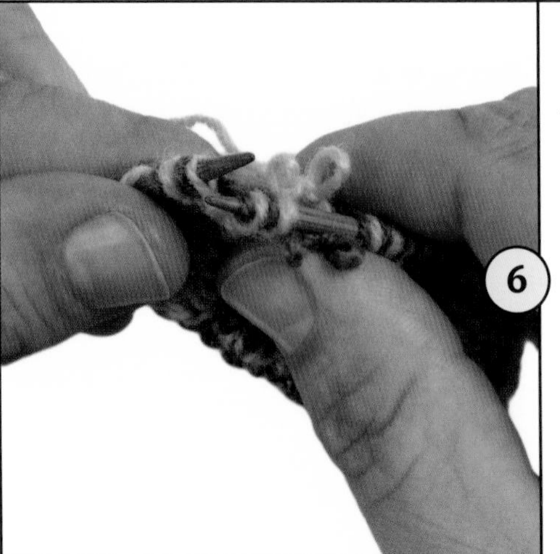

Holding the base of the 2 pairs you wove past, pull the source needle out of all 4 pairs.

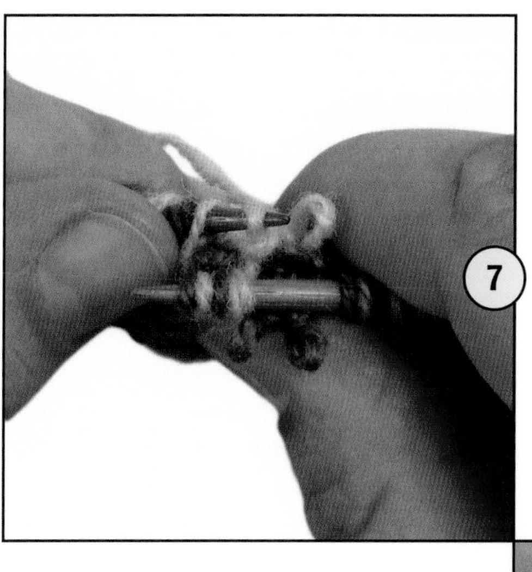

Catch the first loose back stitch on the source needle.

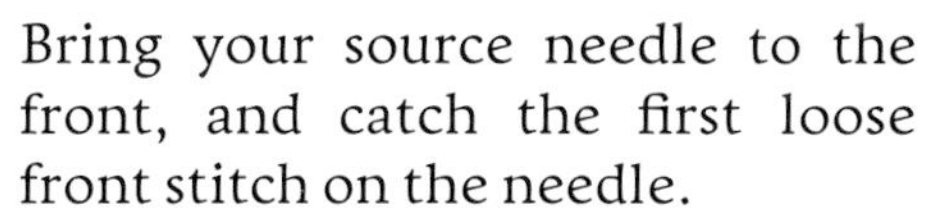
Bring your source needle to the front, and catch the first loose front stitch on the needle.

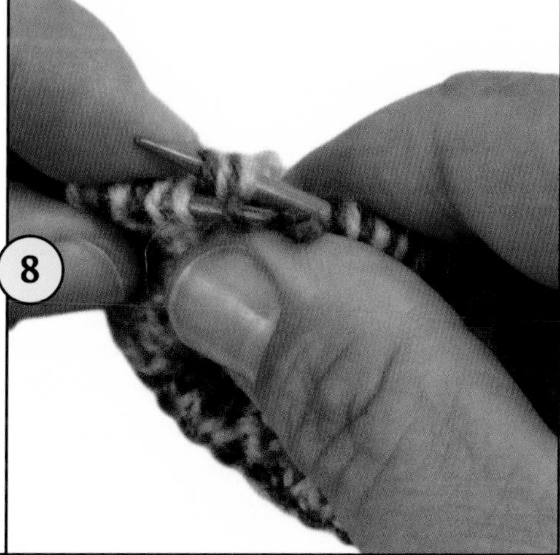

9

Bring your source needle to the back, and catch the second loose back stitch.

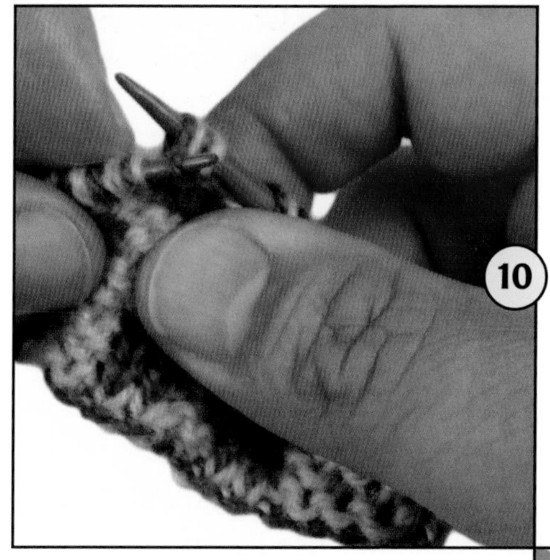

Bring your source needle to the front, and catch the last loose front stitch.

Pass all pairs back to the source needle, and work all 4 pairs as charted.

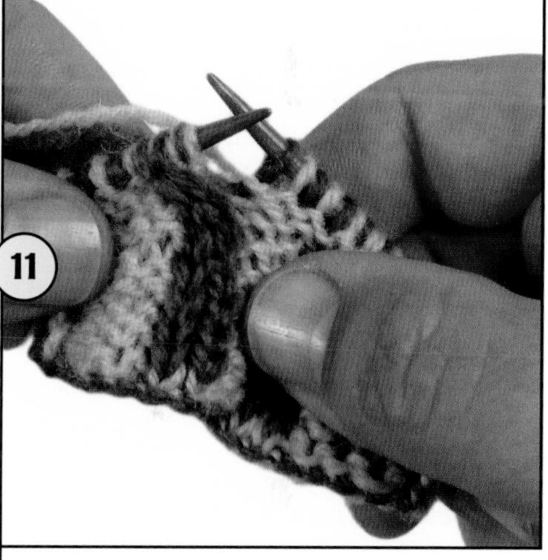

Here's the finished cable. The other layer looks the same as Step 10 in the cable-needle method, page 145.

To help you remember which one to do when, if you want your cable to travel or cross from right to left, you'll also want your needle-weaving to travel from right to left, and vice versa.

As before, here's the formula to work any double-knit cable without a cable needle, at least in theory. In practice, if either X (the number of pairs traveling) or Y (the distance they travel) is greater than 2, it's probably better to use a cable needle.

To work **X pairs cabled Y spaces left-to-right**:

1. Slip all X+Y pairs to the working needle.
2. Weave past all X pairs with your source needle in front of the purls and in back of the knits, ending with your needle on the back of the work and behind the last knit stitch.
3. From the back, insert the needle into the next Y pairs.
4. Holding the base of the X pairs you wove past, pull the working needle out of all X+Y pairs.
5. Catch the first loose back stitch on the working needle.
6. Catch the first loose front stitch on the working needle.
7. If necessary, repeat Steps 5 and 6 until all X pairs have been rebuilt.
8. Pass X pairs back to the source needle, and work all X+Y pairs as charted.

To work **X pairs cabled Y spaces left-to-right**:

1. Weave past all X pairs with your working needle in back of the knits and in front of the purls, ending with your needle on the front of the work.
2. From the front, skip over the last pair of the group of X, and insert the needle into the next Y pairs.
3. Holding the base of the X pairs you wove past, pull the source needle out of all X+Y pairs.
4. Catch the first loose front stitch on the working needle.
5. Catch the first loose back stitch on the working needle.
6. If necessary, repeat Steps 4 and 5 until all X pairs have been rebuilt.
7. Pass all X+Y pairs back to the source needle, and work them as charted.

Changing color/stitch order within a cable

Most of the time, a cable will simply match the stitch and color order of the pairs in the row below, propagating the background and cable colors on each layer, while simply moving the cables around using the cable techniques outlined earlier. However, for various reasons, you may need to change your stitch order, color order, or both within the cable technique.

The most common change is at the top/end of a cable, where it's supposed to close off or just end in a field of the background color/stitch order. Most often, the background is in purls (PK pairs), and the cable itself is in knits (KP pairs). If you refer back to the section on textured double-knitting (page 108), there's a reference to vertical color/stitch transitions. Regardless of the cable movement, the guidelines for textured double-knitting apply here too — a cable that ends by changing both its stitch and color order in the same row will end up with these little blips of color floating above its supposed terminus. However, if you change the color order in one row and then the stitch order in the following row, the cable will appear to melt smoothly into the background.

The other change that is commonly used is a stitch order change in the background. This might be done if the inside and outside of a cable technique are in different textures — or as the second half of the color and stitch order change above. The symbol used for the cable will show a purl dot (or two, or more, depending on the shape of the cable) where you are meant to work a purl, whether or not the stitch you're working into is a knit. Likewise, a cable symbol without a purl where the previous stitch was a purl will be worked as a knit instead. In my own patterns, I have been careful to keep this kind of thing to a minimum, preferring to hide the transitions as much as possible.

Cables and colorwork

Cables are most often worked against a negative-space background — but that negative space need not be negative in both orders. The cables will "pop" more when the cable and the background are different in both stitch and color order, but you can absolutely use KP pairs for both cable and background and only change the color order in the background. One of the options opened up by doing this is the possibility of colorwork in the non-cabled sections. This could mean an all-over pattern over which the cables travel, or it could mean colorwork motifs that are interspersed with the cables. In either case, the row-below phenomenon (see page 37) must be taken into account.

Because cables appear one row below the location where they are worked in the chart, a chart that integrates cables and colorwork will not look the same as the knitting it generates. This may or may not be noticeable, depending on the colorwork — but if the colorwork's position relative to the cables is important, you must shift all of the colorwork one row down.

EXERCISE: Cables & Colorwork

This is a hard thing to visualize, so this exercise will make it more concrete. Essentially, I want you to notice the difference between the charted pattern and the finished piece. As you can see, the eye on the left in the chart is centered, whereas the one on the right is looking down (or to the right, depending on how you turn the work). In the finished piece, the one on the right is (more or less) centered, whereas the one on the left is clearly looking up (or to the left). Don't believe me that this finished piece is generated from the same chart? Give it a try yourself.

Cast on 20 BA pairs and follow Chart 1. Bind off after the last charted row.

Any symbols you're unfamiliar with can be found in the Global Key (page 10). Don't forget to make slipped pairs in the indicated places (not merely at the end of each row). This makes for cleaner cables, and also helps distinguish the outline of the eye from the charted part inside.

Exercise Chart 1

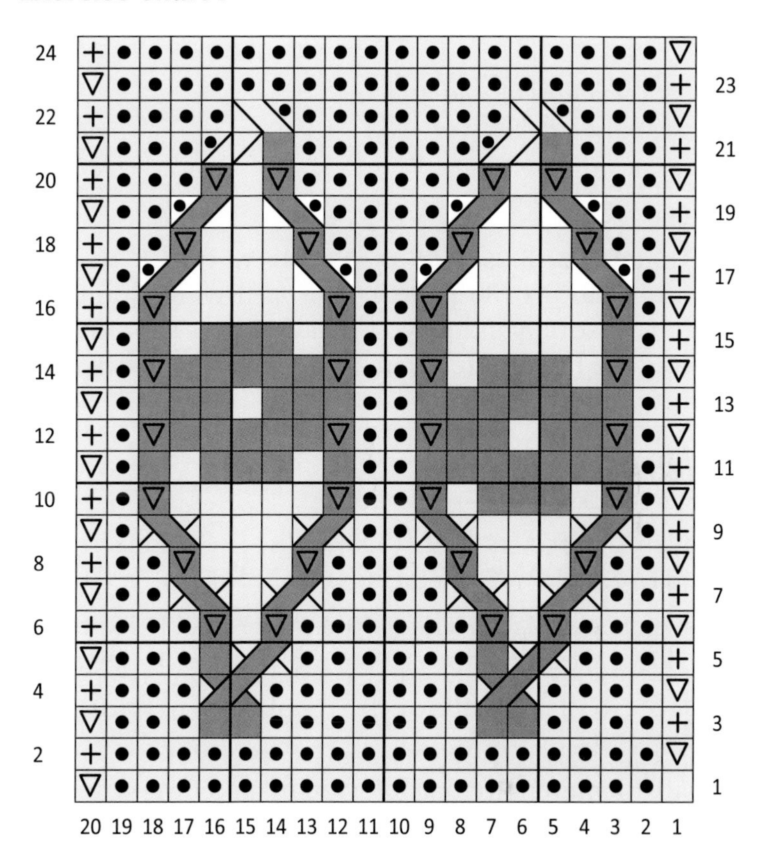

ATYRIA II

a double-knit hat combining off-the-grid colorwork and traveling stitches

Finished size & weight

A 19 (21, 23)" hat will be 8.25 (8.25, 8.5)" tall. For the 21" size, the finished piece uses a total of 80 g (268 yds) of yarn, which translates to about 35% of the total yardage you'll have. There should be no problem making the larger size, even if you wanted to work some extra height into the pattern.

Materials & tools

[Color A]: Seven Sisters Arts Helix (100% Blue Faced Leicester wool; 378 yd/113 g skein); Aquamarine (blue); 1 skein.

[Color B]: Seven Sisters Arts Helix (100% Blue Faced Leicester wool; 378 yd/113 g skein); Branwen (purple); 1 skein.

US 4/3.5 mm 16" circular needle, or size required to obtain desired gauge.

Preferred small-diameter circular solution in matching size.

Gauge in pattern

21 sts/32 rows = 4" in double-stockinette.

Atyria, the second project in my Craftsy class, used my off-the-grid style of decorative increases and decreases, combined with some basic 1x1 double-knit cables. This was the first place my new double-knit cable techniques were taught on a grand scale. However, the pattern was a bit of a rush job, and I knew it. It was a great way to teach the techniques but a poor execution of a pattern. It relied on an obscure technique I called "ghost pairs," which greatly confused some people. Also, the hat was too short and there was no good way to lengthen it.

When I realized that the Craftsy class was now past its third birthday, I checked my contract and I realized that the patterns were my property again, so I redesigned Atyria by lengthening the pattern and removing the ghost pairs. The lengthened version shows a more complete "lifecycle" of whatever fantastical plant is blooming in the motif.

I also took the opportunity to change the yarn I was working with. While I enjoyed working in Lorna's Laces Shepherd Sport for Craftsy, it was a superwash yarn, and I wanted to steer away from that when possible due to the toxicity of the process and the overabundance of this fiber on the market.

I ended up finding Seven Sisters Arts, a company from Maine, at Stitches West of all places. They not only had a heavy fingering BFL, but they also had it in almost exactly the same colors I originally used for Atyria. It turns out the owner is a big fan and was flattered that I'd be working with her yarn. I finished the hat in record time and was able to show her the final version at another show later that same year.

Atyria is a genus of moth. While that's a dirty word to knitters, the vast majority of moths are not likely to eat your yarn stash — and many of them are quite pretty. The spiral motifs in this hat, while clearly meant to represent a fern-like plant, reminded me of moth antennae or proboscises, so I looked for a moth-related name. Atyria is a pretty name and more easily pronounceable than something that ends in -ae, even if moths in that genus don't have any particular relationship to the spiral shape.

Chart 1a

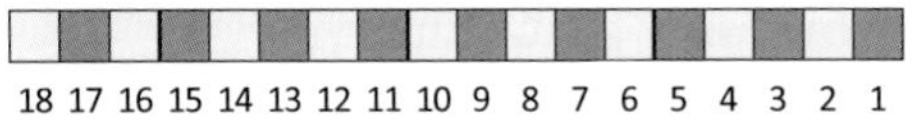

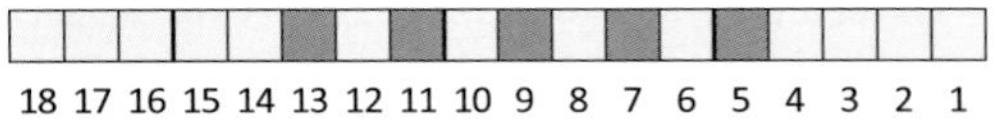

18 17 16 15 14 13 12 11 10 9 8 7 6 5 4 3 2 1

Chart 1b

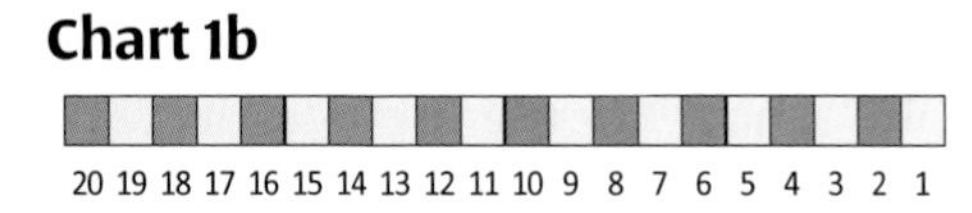

Chart 2a

18 17 16 15 14 13 12 11 10 9 8 7 6 5 4 3 2 1

Chart 2b

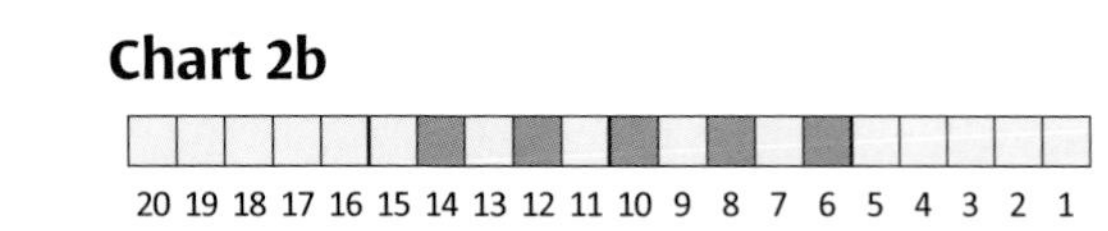

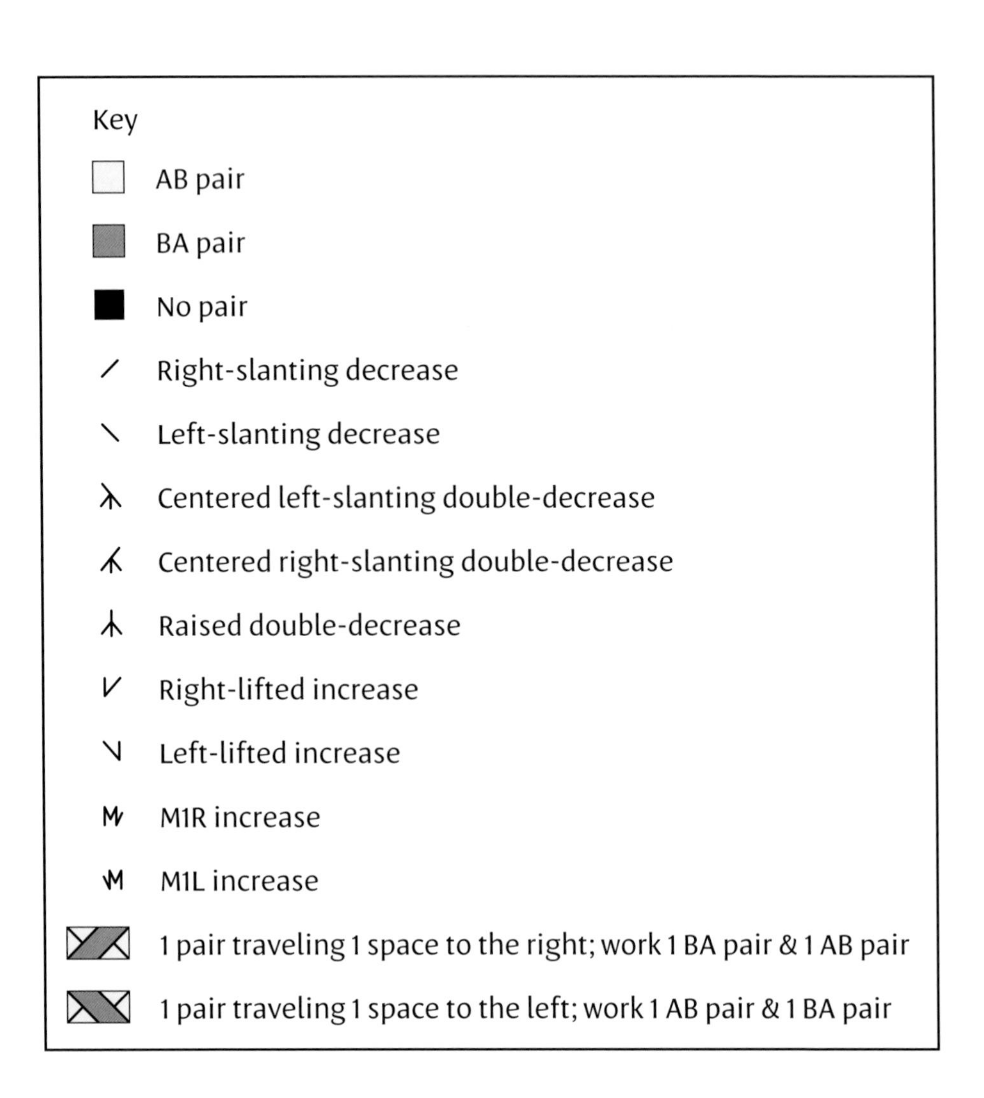

Chart 3a

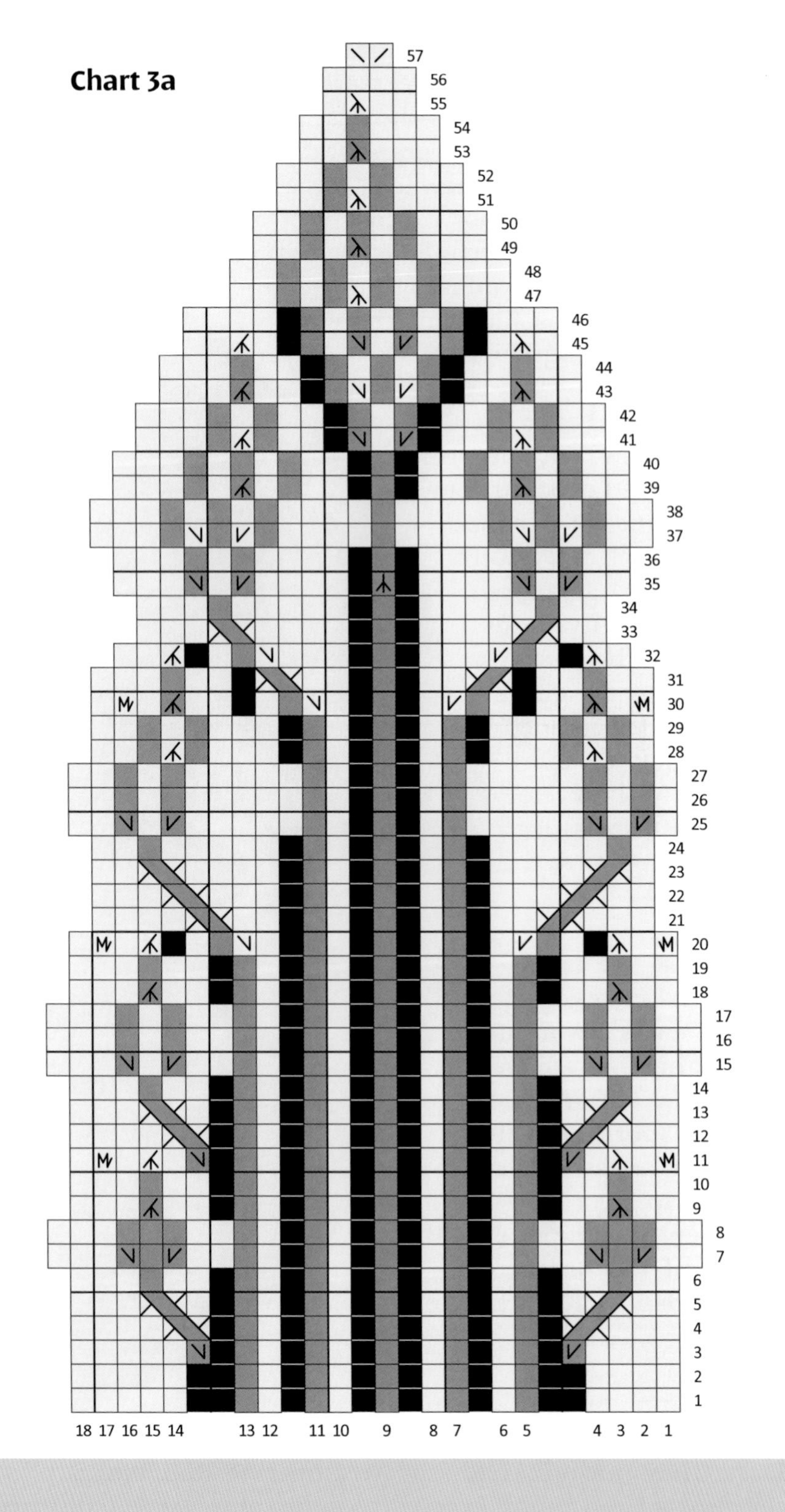

Chart 3b

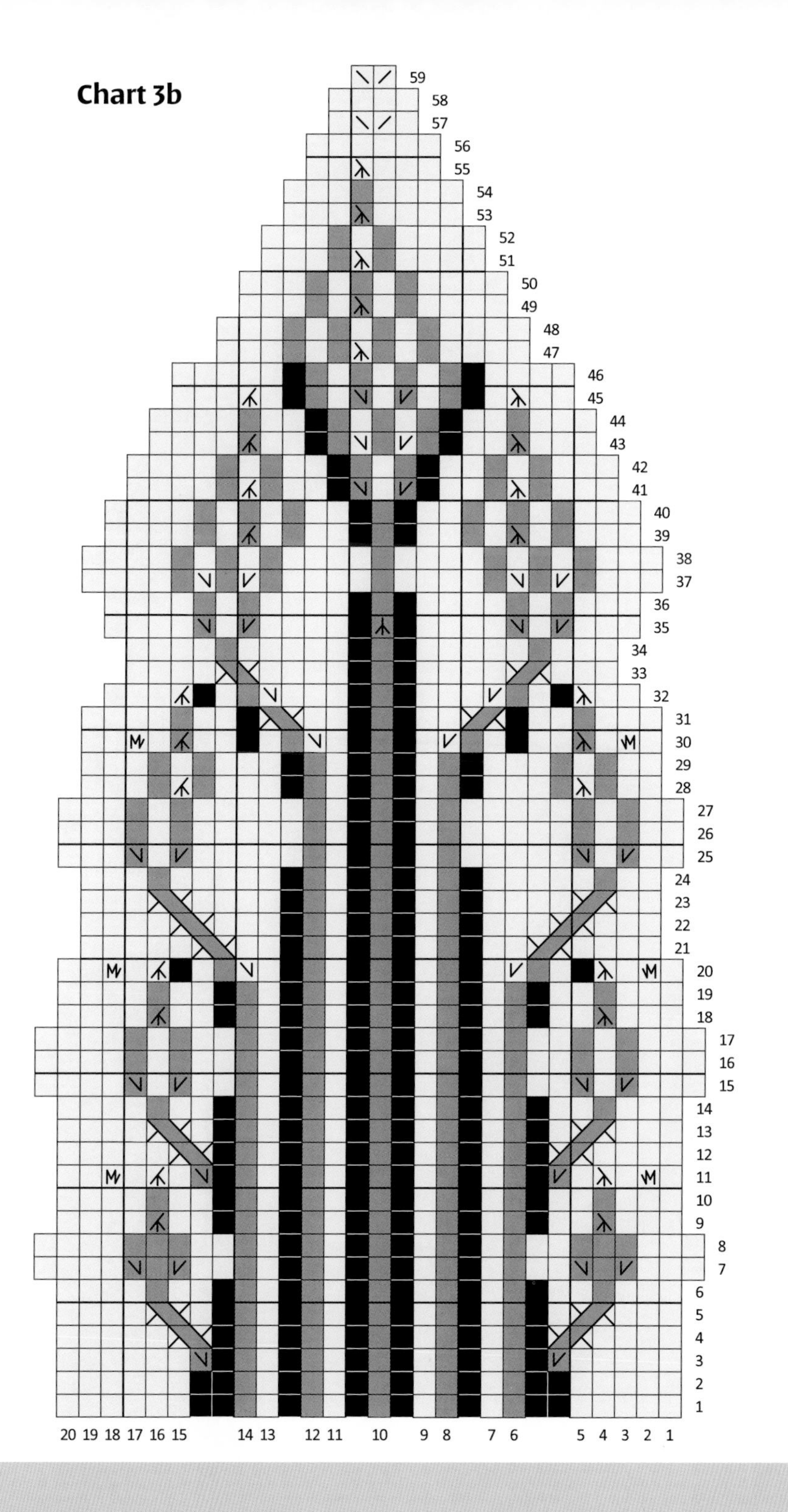

Pattern Notes

If you want the hat shorter than 8.25", you can omit a few rounds of Chart 1a or 2a. The shortest it can get is around 6.5". On the other hand, if you want it longer so you can fold up the brim, you can add rounds in Chart 1a, 2a, 1b or 2b — 1a or 2a will add to the mock-ribbing section; 1b or 2b will add to the "stalks" that rise between the mock-ribbing and the first set of branches.

Pattern

CO 100 (108, 120) BA pairs.

Work 5 (6, 6) repeats of Chart 1b (1a, 1b) around for 14 rounds (approximately 1.5" tall).

Work 5 (6, 6) repeats of Chart 2b (2a, 2b) around for 2 rounds.

Work 5 (6, 6) repeats of Chart 3b (3a, 3b) around.

Cinch the last 10 (12, 12) pairs; weave in ends, block if necessary and enjoy!

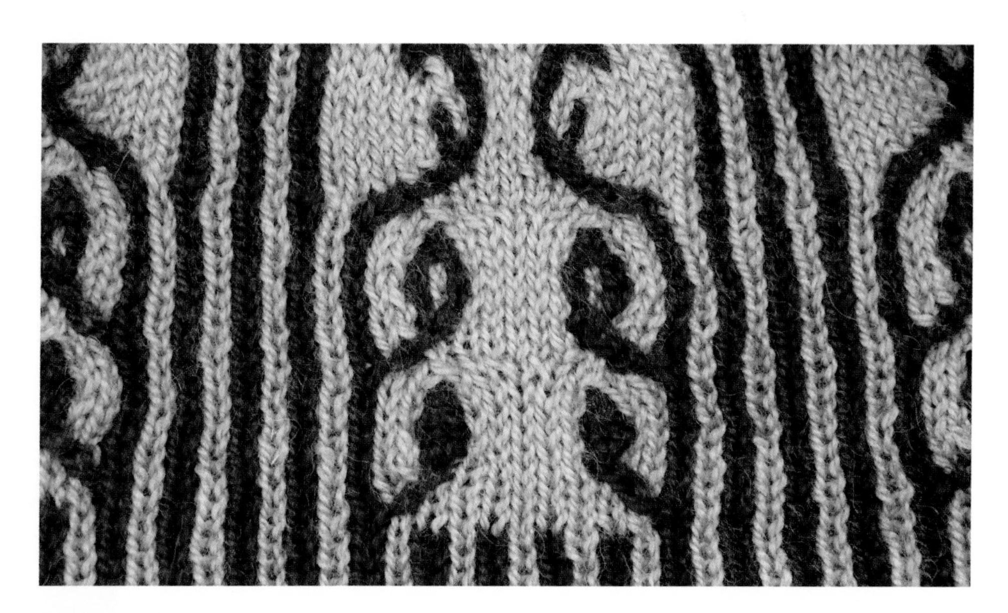

TWICE AS SEXY

an elegant necktie with double-knit traveling stitches

Finished size & weight

A 60.5" long tie will be a good length for a standard knot; a 66.5" long tie will be good for a double Windsor or other more complex knot. The longest size requires merely 28 g (224 yds) of yarn or 14 g (112 yds) of each color. In other words, you would not only have no problem making either tie out of two skeins, you could make 3 of them and still have plenty of yarn left over.

Materials & tools

[Color A]: The Buffalo Wool Co. Sexy (50% bison down, 50% mulberry silk; 400 yd/50 g skein); Natural (tan); 1 skein.

[Color B]: The Buffalo Wool Co. Sexy (50% bison down, 50% mulberry silk; 400 yd/50 g skein); Allure (blue); 1 skein.

US 1/2.25 mm straight or circular needle or needle size required to achieve gauge.

Gauge in pattern

34 sts/48 rows = 4" in pattern, unblocked.

36 sts/44 rows = 4" in pattern, blocked.

Ever since I designed my first two ties for *Extreme Double-Knitting*, I've had people thanking me for breaking the stereotype of the ugly knit tie. Let's face it: a lot of knitted ties are pretty awful-looking. To keep them from curling, you have to work them in garter or seed stitch, sew on some backing, or something. Most of them stop looking like neckties after they've passed below the suit-button area, which means that wearing one without a suit looks terrible. I mean no serious offense to anyone else who has designed one, but I thought I could do better.

For one thing, double-knitting doesn't curl. The two layers cancel that effect out in both directions. For another, shaping is totally worth the trouble. You can make a nice point at the beginning and end, as well as slowly tapering the middle. You just have to do some basic math at the beginning to match your gauge to the size and shape, and you can fill in the inside with almost anything. Where I went a little off the rails with my first two ties was when I decided how to fill them. Those are power ties — complex, bold, and exciting. But what if you want something more subdued, genteel, or dignified? A classic double diagonal stripe is a good bet. But no simple colorwork stripes for me — these are true double-knit cabled traveling stitches. There are no rest rows. By the time you're done with this tie, you'll be an expert at these 1x1 cables.

This is another case of working with a yarn partially because the company has done me a favor. In this case, as with the others, the Buffalo Wool Company has regularly hosted my books and patterns at their booths at various shows where I've been teaching. I wanted to thank them for their help by designing a pattern in their yarn. Fortunately, I don't work with vendors whose yarn I don't already love, so it's a win-win situation. A couple of years before I ever cast on for this pattern, I got the yarn. Every time I saw them after that I had to apologize that I hadn't gotten to the pattern yet. Finally, with the book on the horizon, I decided it was time to redouble (pun intended) my efforts and make sure the pattern came out.

As you can probably tell from the company's name,The Buffalo Wool Company sells buffalo/bison yarn (it's the same animal, just a different name). It's not quite qiviut, but it's up there in luxury and, of course, price. This yarn, called Sexy, is 50/50 bison and mulberry silk, so I thought it'd be a great pick for a tie. It is, however, a lace weight, which means it's going to take some time to do the pattern (not to mention tinier needles than I normally work with). Fortunately, it's a tie, which means it's not all that many stitches to begin with — 30 pairs at its widest.

The name is no big mystery here. The yarn's name is "Sexy," and it's double-knitted, so "Twice as Sexy." Voila!

Pattern

CO 2 BA pairs.

Follow Charts 1-10 in sequence.
Work 16 (19) repeats of Chart 11.
Follow Chart 12.

BO, weave in ends, block if necessary and enjoy!

Pattern Notes

Something I found out while researching ties: evidently, the traditional diagonal double-stripe is not universal. In Europe, the stripes travel upward from left to right, and in America, they travel upward from right to left. By default, this tie will be European on Layer 1 and American on Layer 2. If you have a color preference and want them reversed, just switch Colors A and B as you work the tie.

To lengthen or shorten the tie, add or subtract repeats of Chart 11. Each repeat of that chart is about 2" tall after blocking.

Key

- (light square) Layer 1: AB pair / Layer 2: BA pair
- (dark square) Layer 1: BA pair / Layer 2: AB pair
- + Linked pair
- ▽ Slipped pair
- Right-lifted increase
- Left-lifted increase
- M1R increase
- M1L increase
- / Right-slanting decrease
- \ Left-slanting decrease
- Linked right-slanting decrease
- Linked left-slanting decrease
- Layer 1: 1 pair traveling 1 space to the right; work 1 BA pair & 1 AB pair / Layer 2: 1 pair traveling 1 space to the left; work 1 AB pair & 1 BA pair
- Layer 1: 1 pair traveling 1 space to the right; work 2 AB pairs / Layer 2: 1 pair traveling 1 space to the left; work 2 BA pairs

Chart 1

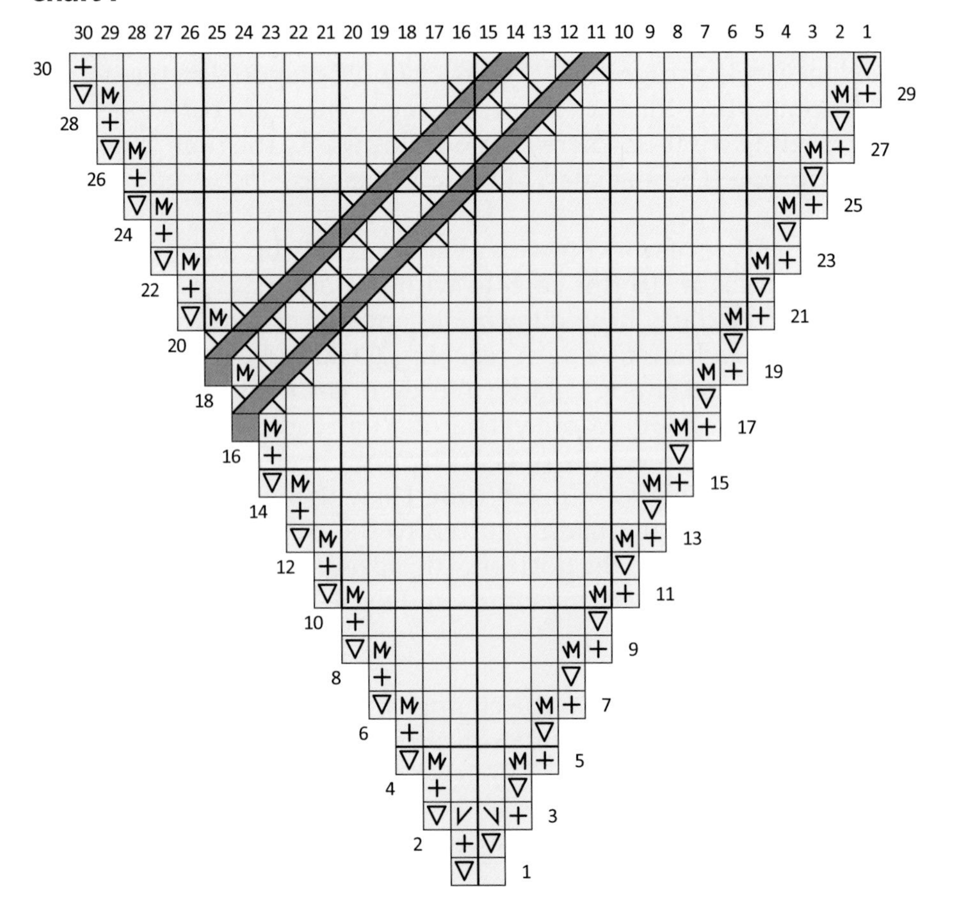

Chart 2

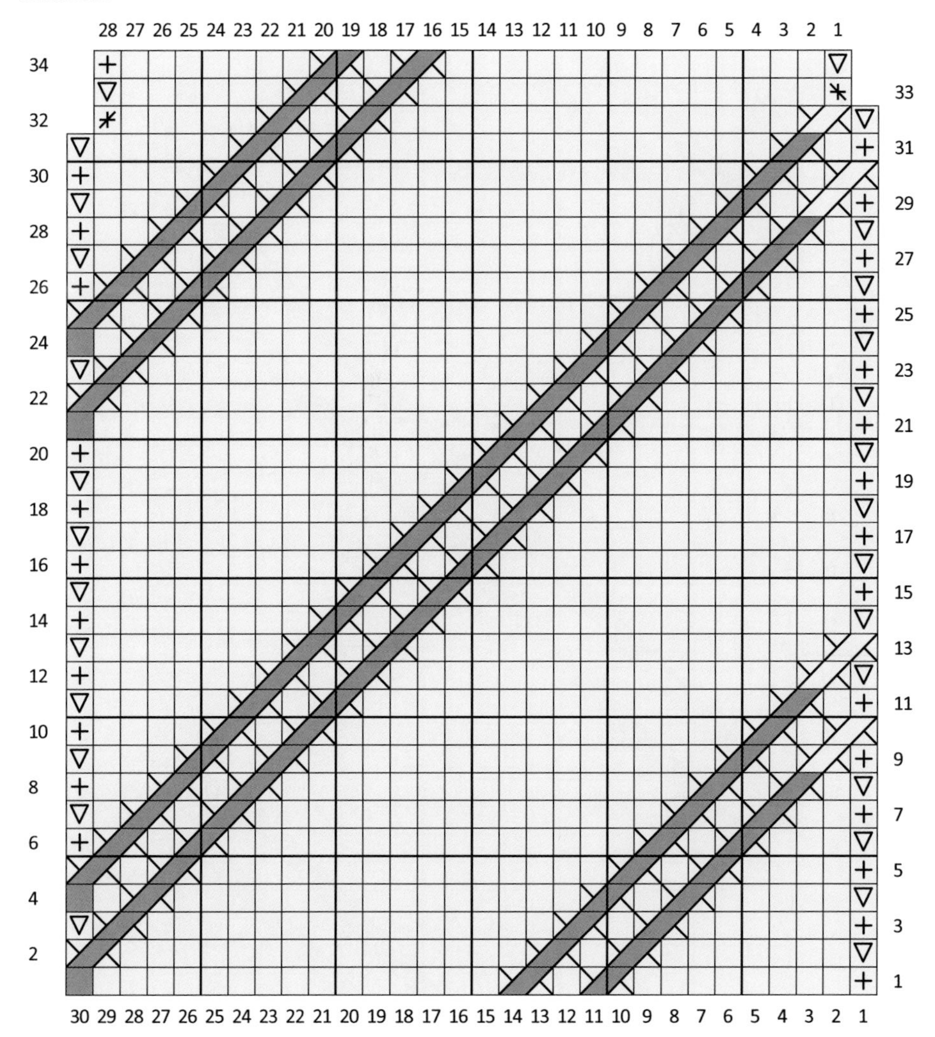

Chart 3

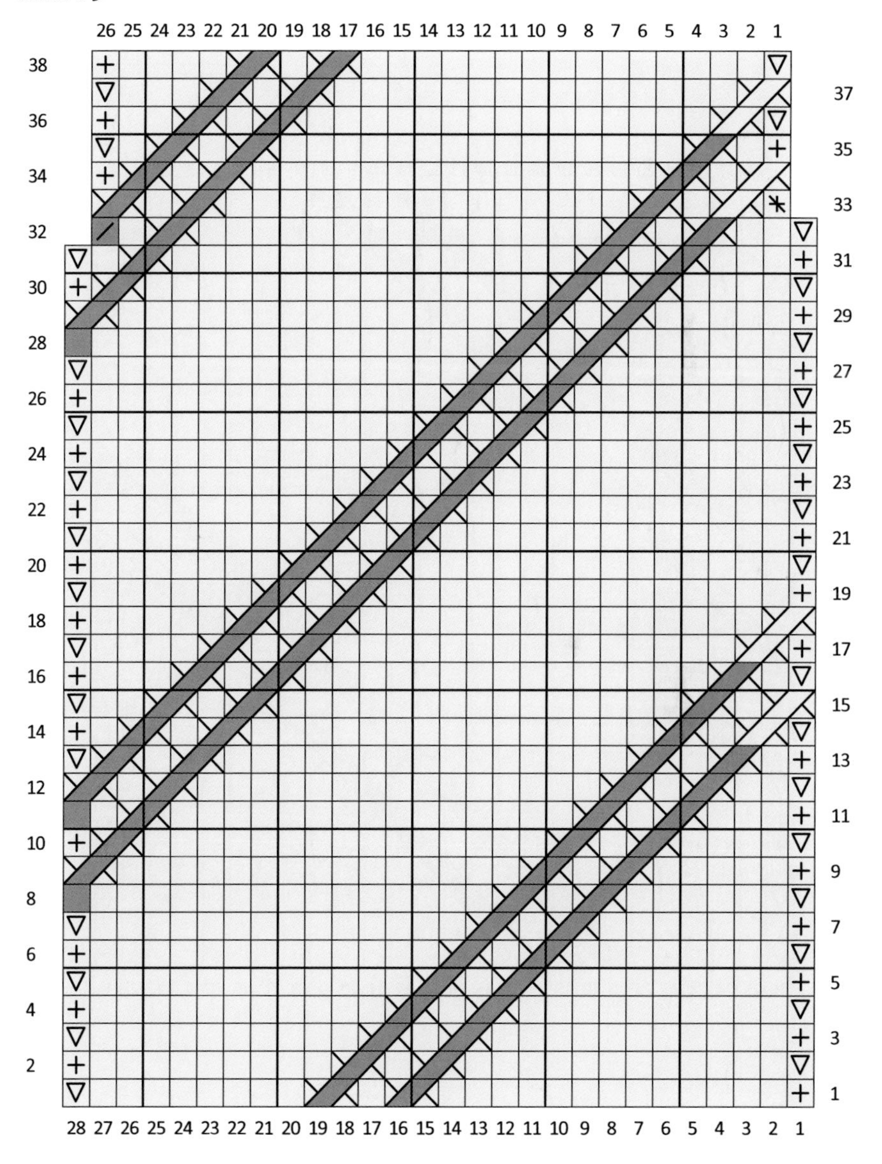

Chart 4

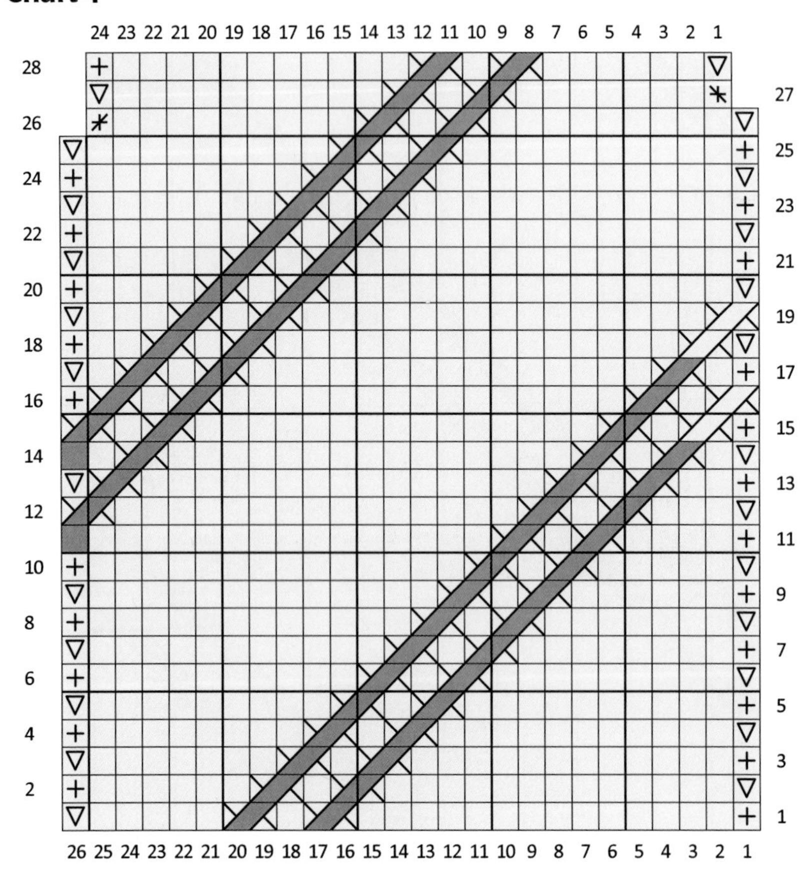

Chart 5

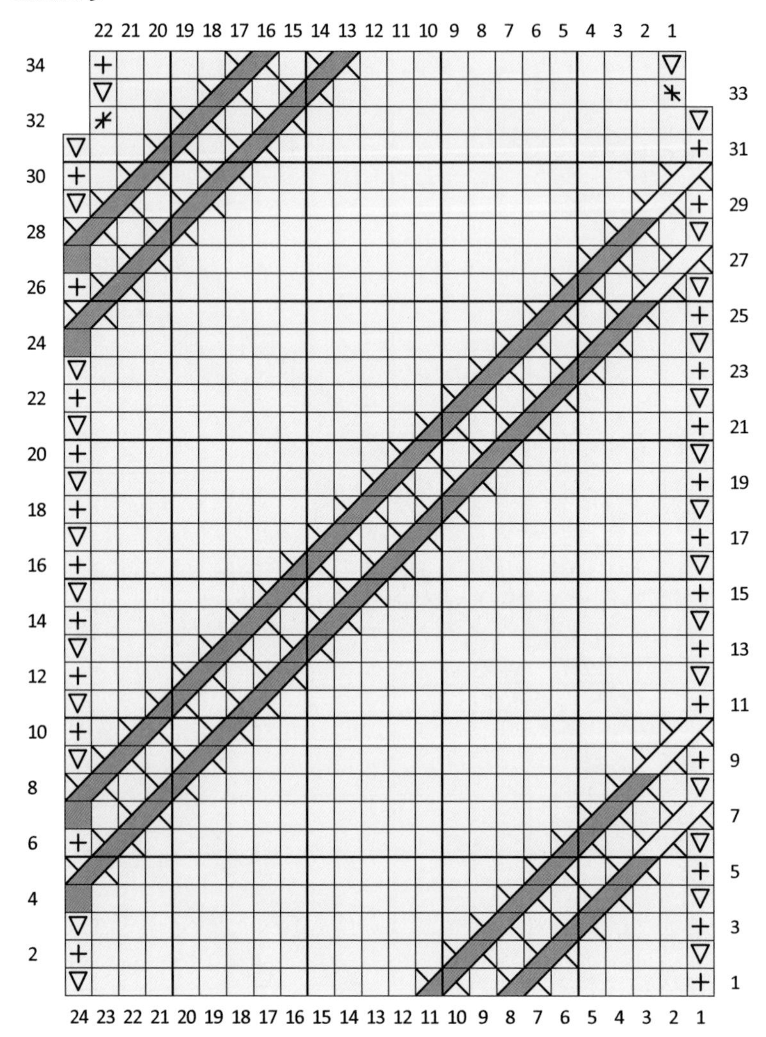

Chart 6

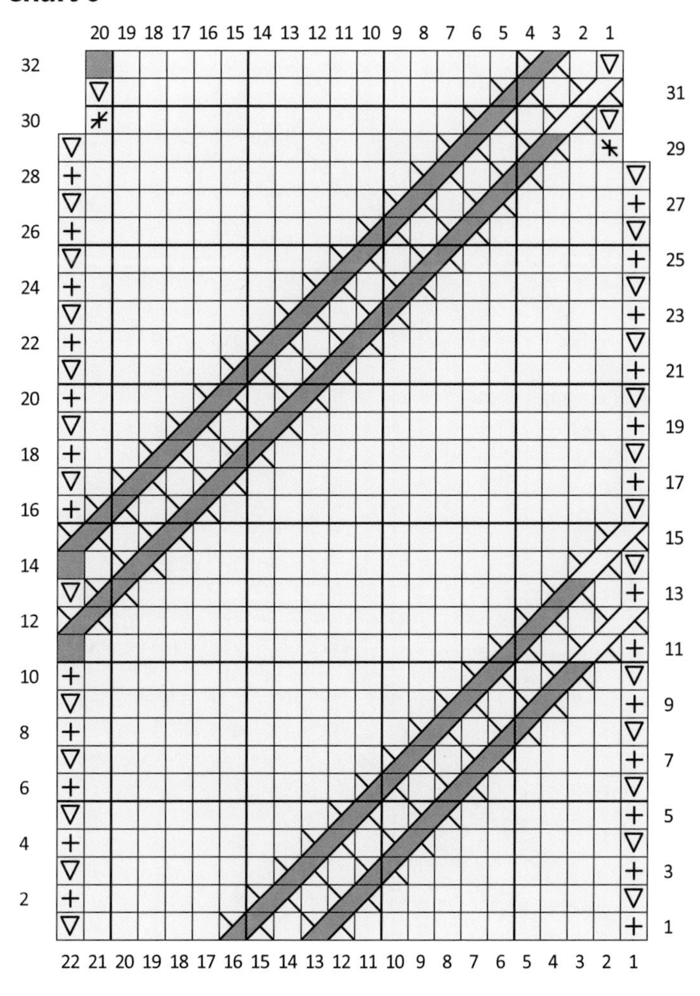

Chart 7

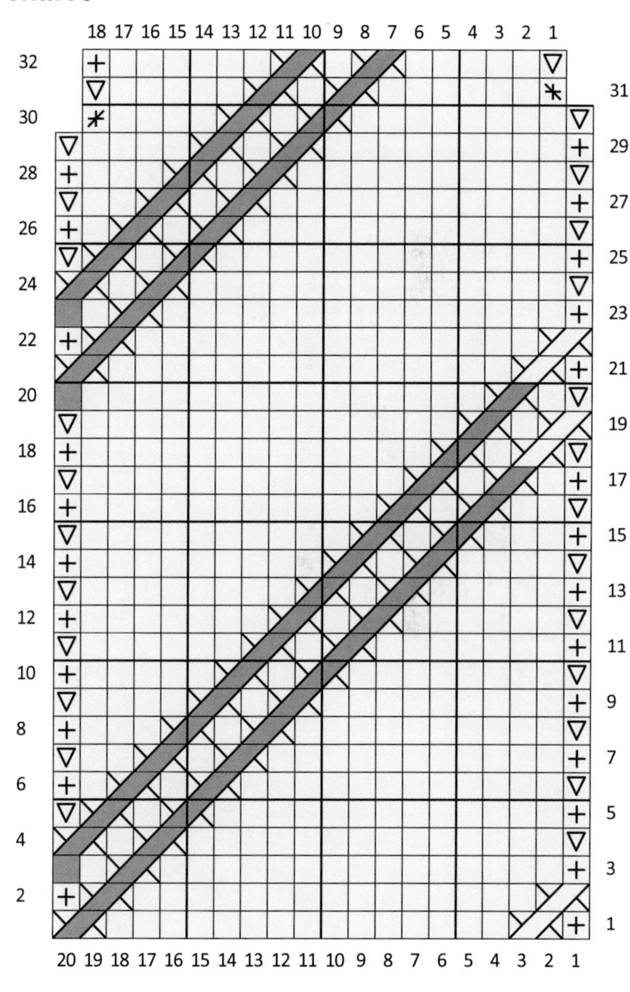

Chart 8

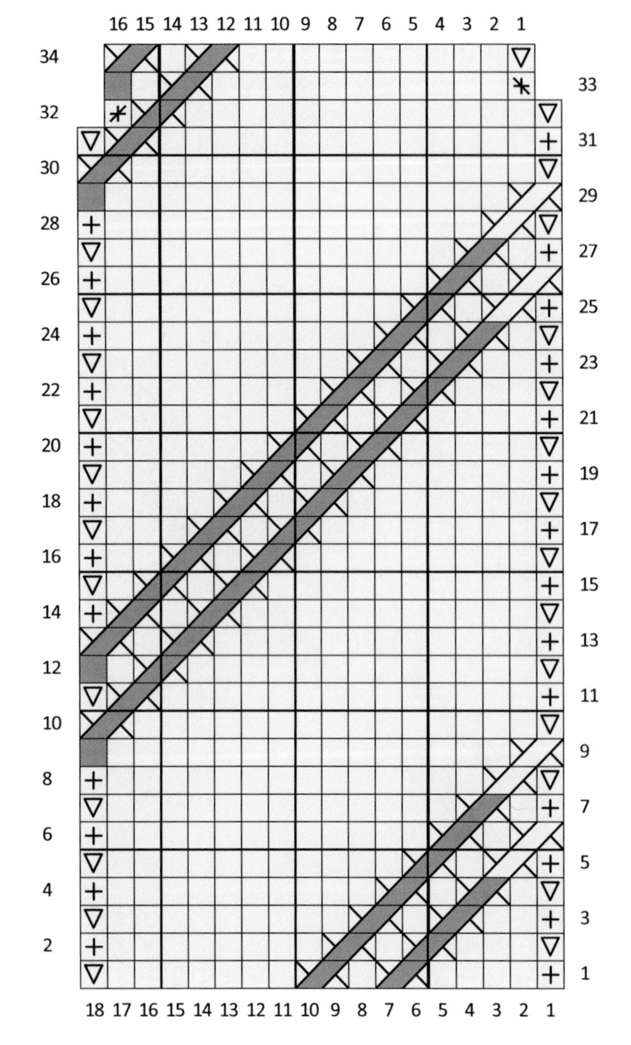

Chart 9

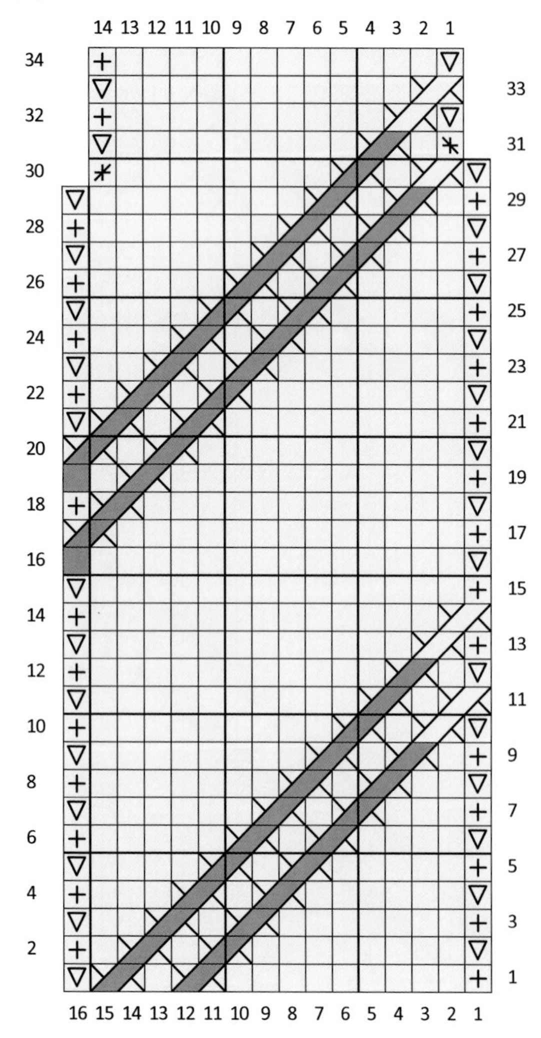

Chart 10

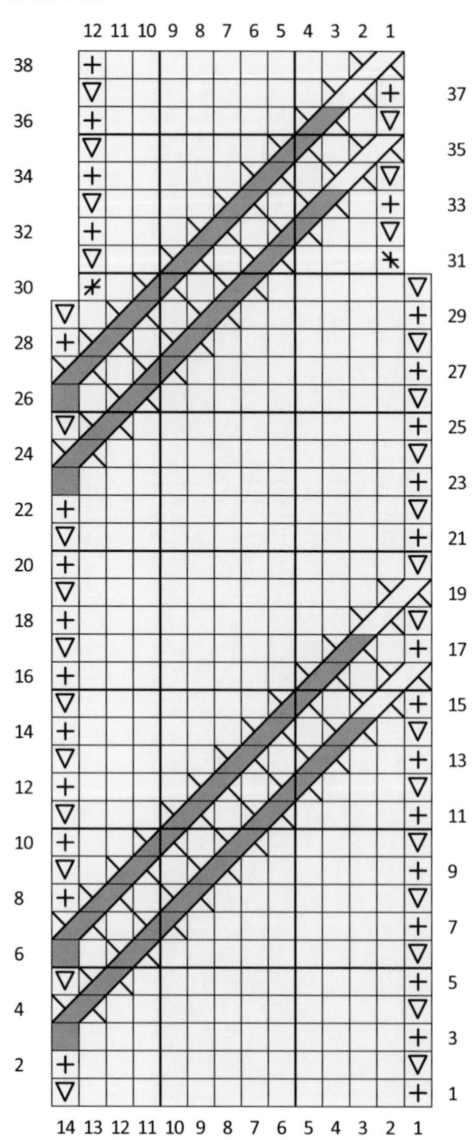

Chart 12

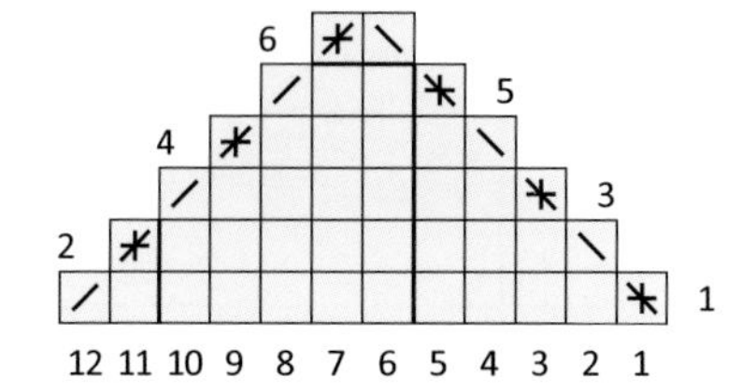

Chart 11

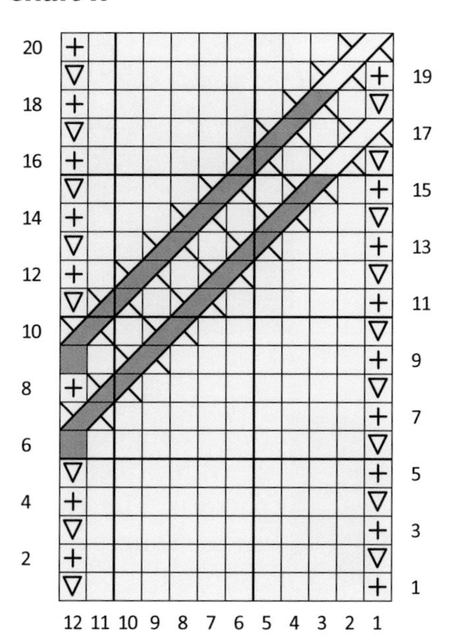

Craftstory, continued from page 147

Alasdair's Fine MATHWEAR

Warm Topological Knitwear for Cool People

When I began designing patterns, I didn't have any concept of how to release them. After all, there were many years between my last published origami model and my first self-designed knitting pattern – and that was the only context I had. I used to go to craft shows with my origami models and sell them (whether or not they were my designs), similar to the way people sell knitted hats and scarves at such events. So this was the context in which I understood knitting. The finished objects were to be gifted or sold; if I had made up the pattern, I just took notes so I could do it again. I never gave any thought to taking notes so that anyone else could knit it. I did a couple of odd pieces on commission, and I knitted a lot of gifts for my family and friends. As I began to play with other mathematical concepts aside from the Möbius scarves (Klein bottles and hyperbolic surfaces were also interesting), I started a "company" and website called "Alasdair's Fine Mathwear" to try to sell the finished pieces. I posted photos and prices and even made a couple of sales to friends. This was well before Etsy, so I had no other real concept of how to do this.

That venture came to an untimely end when the partner of an old friend in the origami-math scene, who was herself a knitting mathematician, took me to task for calling my work "mathwear" since I wasn't a mathematician and didn't have a deep enough understanding of the mathematical concepts behind them. I think she thought I was diluting the relatively small pool of knitting mathematicians, and that I should stop it. At the time, I was a tender newbie trying to find my way in the larger knitting world. I was mortified that I had stepped so hard on someone's feet and I abandoned my "brand." But I didn't abandon knitting – far from it. Instead, I directed my energies in a different direction.

Craftstory, continued on page 169

Double-knit I-cord Cast-on

This is a special cast-on that I developed for the next pattern; if you like it, it works for any pattern with an RDK background. The standard double-knit cast-on just doesn't look very good going straight into PK pairs.

Due to the color changes in the increases, this i-cord cast-on also includes a linked edge along the border between the cast-on and the main body of the work. This makes the i-cord less rounded, since it's held closed on both edges. Also, this cast-on is fairly inflexible. If you find it's not quite stretchy enough for your liking, I'd recommend working it on a needle one size larger than called for in the body. Remember that this will also create cast-on pairs that will be a little larger than needed.

To get AB pairs on the needle, begin by casting on 2 BA pairs. Turn and work 1 AB pair and a slipped pair. Then remove the slipknot.
Turn and work a linked BA pair and a slipped pair.
Turn and work a linked AB pair and a slipped pair.

You are now prepared to begin the cast-on.

1

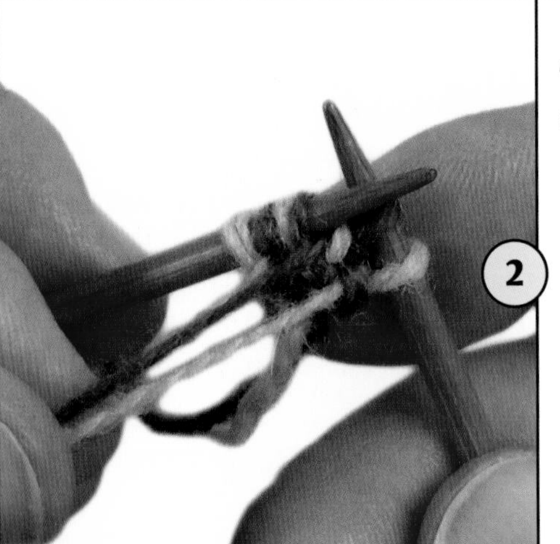

Turn and work a lifted AB right-side increase ...

...then work a linked BA pair and a slipped pair.

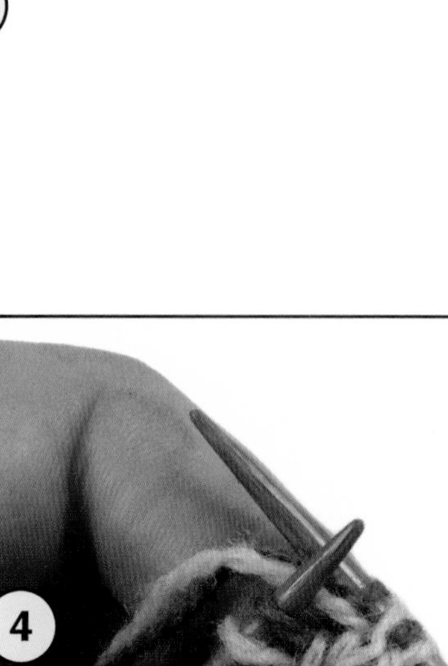

Turn, work a linked AB pair and a slipped pair.

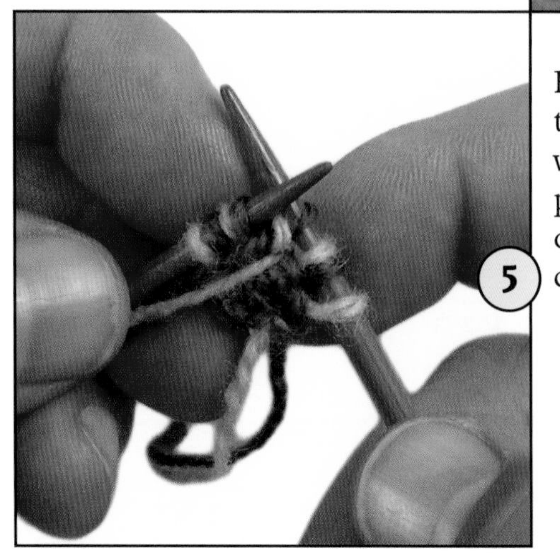

Repeat Steps 2-4 until you have the number of pairs on your working needle called for in the pattern. The two remaining pairs on the source needle should not be counted!

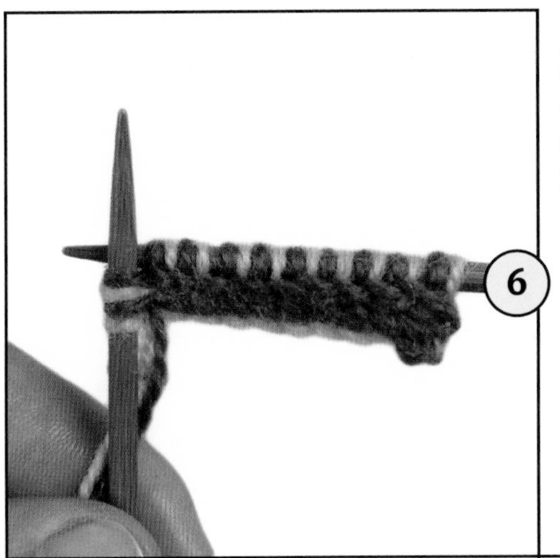

Here's a view of several pairs completed, with a fully-formed i-cord edge. This is as viewed from Layer 1.

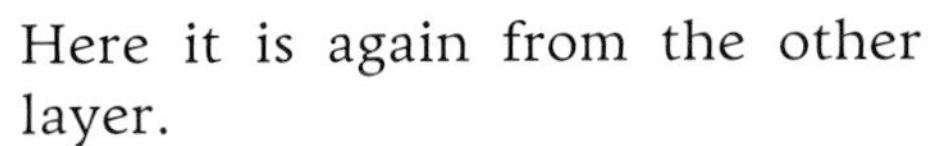

Here it is again from the other layer.

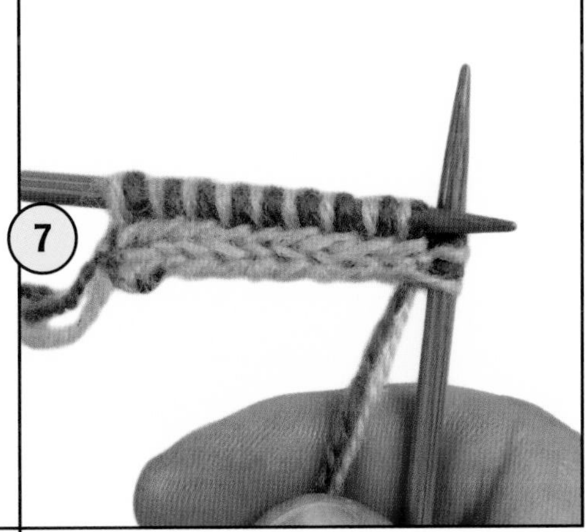

To finish the cast-on, turn, work a linked pair, and then work a standard (not slipped) pair.
Slip 2 pairs back, and work a slipped bind-off on those pairs. Open the last 2 loops very wide and pass both ends (including the yarn balls!) through the loops and tighten.

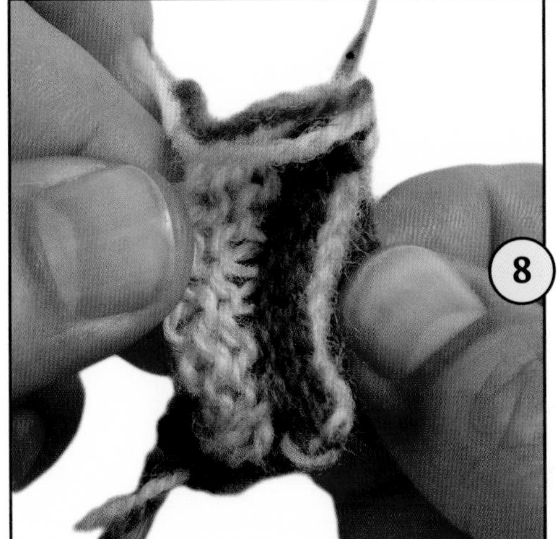

The active ends should now be in position to continue the next row or round.

If working in the round, use the tails to seam the cast-on and bind-off edges together with the No-Brain Kitchener technique.

This photo shows how the edge between the i-cord and the body of the work is nicely linked together.

Heartbound Again, page 170

Double-knit I-cord Bind-off

What's a cast-on without a corresponding bind-off?

No matter what I try, I have not been able to get the edge between the main body of the work and the lower edge of this bind-off to link together. I would have thought that linking the decreases would work as it does in double-knit entrelac, but for some reason, the result is still two separate layers up until the top edge. The benefit to this is that this bind-off, unlike its corresponding cast-on, is puffy and round like a normal i-cord. It's also significantly stretchier — this may be related to the lack of links or just the fact that every stitch is not also sprouting an increase.

At the end of a row, cast on 2 pairs in the opposite color order from the rest of the row. For the rest of this technique, match your color order to these pairs, not the body of the work.

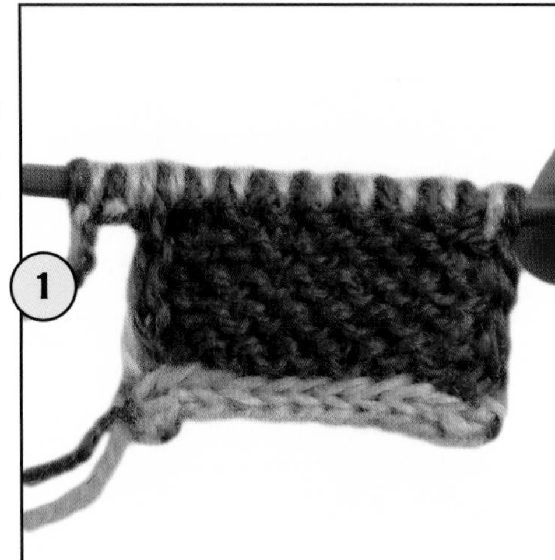

Turn, work a slipped pair, and then reorder the next 2 pairs (one from the bind-off and one from the main body) to prepare for a single decrease.

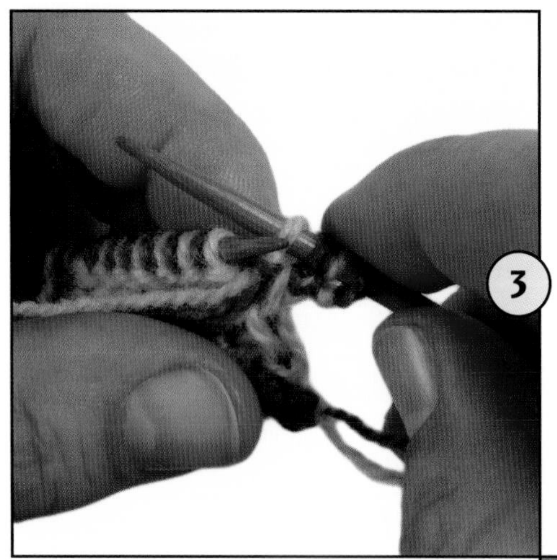

Now, work a left-slanting decrease with the two reordered pairs, matching the color order of the previous pair on your working needle.

Turn and work both a slipped pair and a linked pair (it's totally OK to not turn and do this backward at this point, as you can see I'm doing in this photo).

Turn and repeat Steps 2-4 until you reach the end of the row. For best results, in all subsequent instances of Step 2, slip the first stitch knitwise.

Break the ends, slip 2 pairs back, and work a slipped bind-off on those pairs.

If working in the round, use the tails to seam the cast-on and bind-off edges together with the No-Brain Kitchener technique.

Here's a shot of the completed double-knit i-cord bind-off, as viewed from Layer 1.

And here it is again, viewed from the other layer.

8

Here's what happens if you pull the two layers apart. Note that the edge between the main body and the bind-off is not linked together, as it is in the cast-on. Even if you work linked decreases, the same will occur. For now, it'll have to remain one of life's little mysteries.

Craftstory, continued from page 165

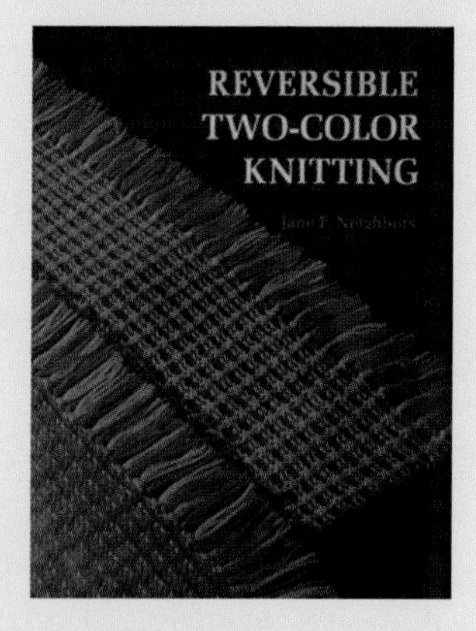

No longer knitting in a vacuum, I got recommendations from some of my new friends on what books and resources to seek out – which led me to the public library on that fateful day when, unknowingly, I pulled my destiny from the shelf. The book was called *Reversible Two-Color Knitting* by Jane Neighbors, and it caught my eye because, as you'll remember, I was fixated on Möbius scarves. I had not done any colorwork at that point, so I saw this as an interesting way to continue my Möbius scarves, but also to play with two-color options. The bulk of this long-out-of-print book involved two-color slip-stitch techniques that created fabric that was reversible, if not actually the same on both sides (so it wasn't actually that useful for the intended purpose). However, there were some patterns that I thought had potential. I made swatches of a few of those, but what really clicked for me lay in the appendix: slip-stitch double-knitting.

Even with my limited colorwork experience, I immediately saw the potential: any two-color chart could be applied to the fabric, without worry about strand length or number of ends. The only issue was that each row would have to be worked twice, which would slow down the work – and of course, that the result would be two (mostly) distinct layers of fabric. I swatched for this too, and I was immediately hooked. The irony is that, to this day, I have yet to design a double-knit Möbius scarf.

From that point on, the story gets more predictable and less interesting. The next several years involved my development of techniques that were not documented in *Reversible Two-Color Knitting*, eventually leaving the archaic slip-stitch method behind for the modern method I've been documenting for the past decade.

Craftstory, continued on page 175

HEARTBOUND AGAIN

a double-knit cabled hat with an i-cord cast-on and a headband option

2 FINE

Finished size & weight

The hat is 8.5" tall from brim to crown and a hat with a 19 (22, 24)" circumference uses about 53 (60, 68) g (a maximum of 226 yds) of each color; the headband is approximately 4.4" tall and a headband with a 19 (22, 24)" circumference uses about 31 (36, 40) g (a maximum of 133 yds) of each color.

Materials & tools: Hat

[Color A]: Jagger Spun Green Line 3/8 (100% organic wool; 332 yd/100 g skein); Lagoon (blue); 1 skein.
[Color B]: Jagger Spun Green Line 3/8 (100% organic wool; 332 yd/100 g skein); Bordeaux (red); 1 skein.

US 4/3.5 mm 16" circular needle or size required to obtain desired gauge.
Preferred small-diameter circular solution in matching size.

Materials & tools: Headband

[Color A]: Jagger Spun Maine Line 3/8 (100% wool; 332 yd/100 g skein); French Blue; 1 skein.
[Color B]: Jagger Spun Maine Line 3/8 (100% wool; 332 yd/100 g skein); Claret (red); 1 skein.

US 4/3.5 mm 16" circular needle or size required to obtain desired gauge.

Gauge in pattern

30 sts/32 rows = 4" in pattern.
25 rows = 4" in double-knit i-cord cast-on.

For quite some time after I began teaching classes in double-knit cables, I didn't have a standalone pattern that incorporated the technique. After I had reworked my class, I took the opportunity to release a pattern called Heartbound, a cabled headband using a reversed-color and reversed-texture background. It was a work in progress, and I informed people of that.

The name "Heartbound" just came to me as I was looking at the cable pattern, thinking it looked a little like hearts all linked together. The word has two meanings, one more archaic than the other; I'll choose the positive and more poetic meaning of "having the heart entirely devoted to someone or something."

Now it's time to pull back the curtain for the full version: Heartbound Again. There is a headband version as well as a full hat version. The cables are seamless due to some slip-stitch trickery, and the cast-on (and bind-off for the headband) is adapted from an i-cord cast-on, so that it mimics the cables. There's also some interesting cable/color/stitch manipulation borrowed from textured double-knitting (see the Eureka hat on page 122) to keep the beginning and end of the cable techniques clean.

Jagger Spun has been around for quite a while, but has recently changed their marketing and packaging efforts to appeal more to hand knitters (they had been selling yarn on the cone primarily for weavers and machine knitters). One of their reps got in touch with me, asking if I'd like to try out some of their yarn. Never being one to pass up a new fiber-related experience, I agreed.

The yarn they sent me was a perfect fit — lots of colors, my favorite weights, and great stitch definition. And, in the sport weight, they even have a 100% organic wool line.

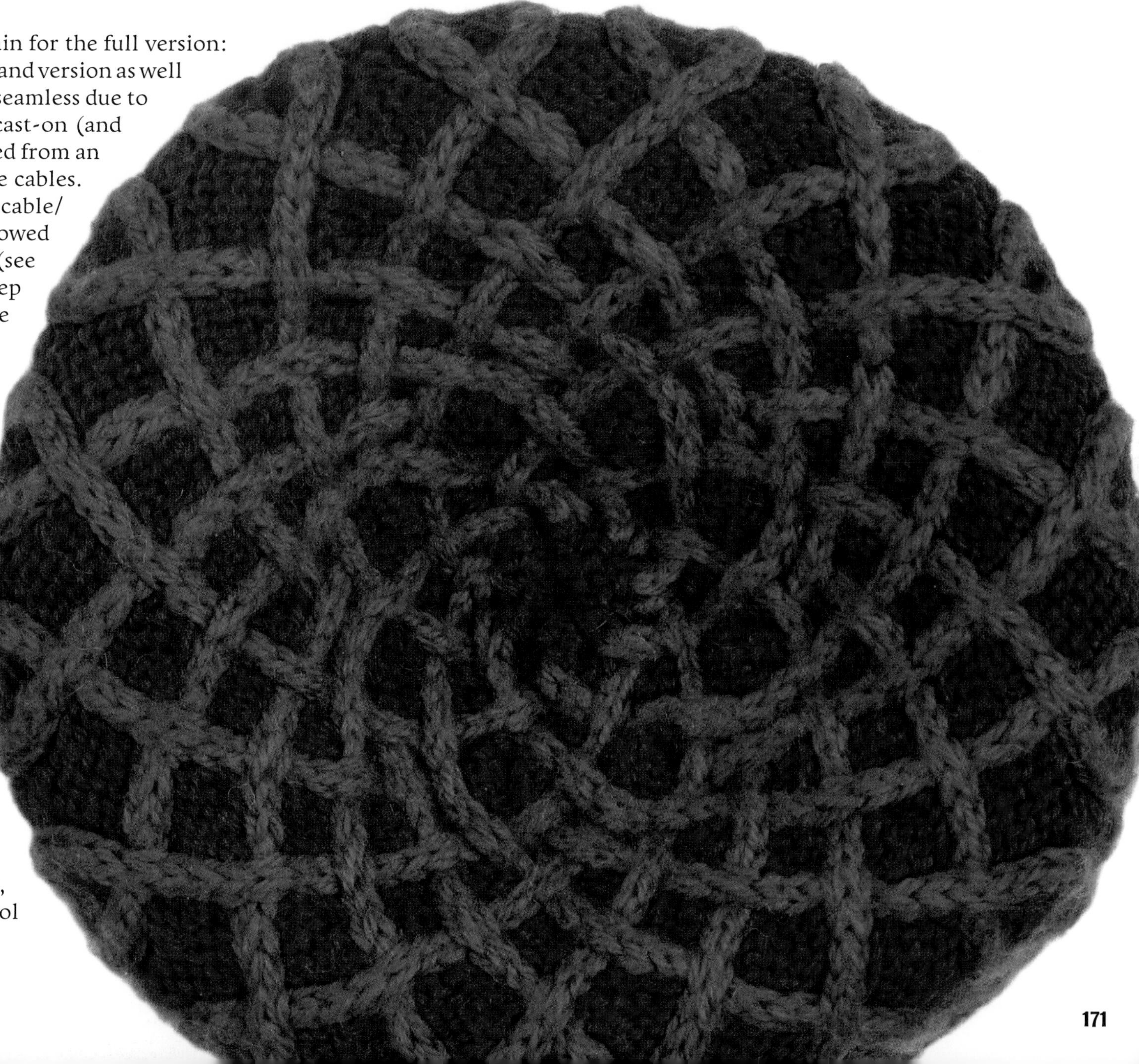

Hat Charts

Chart 1

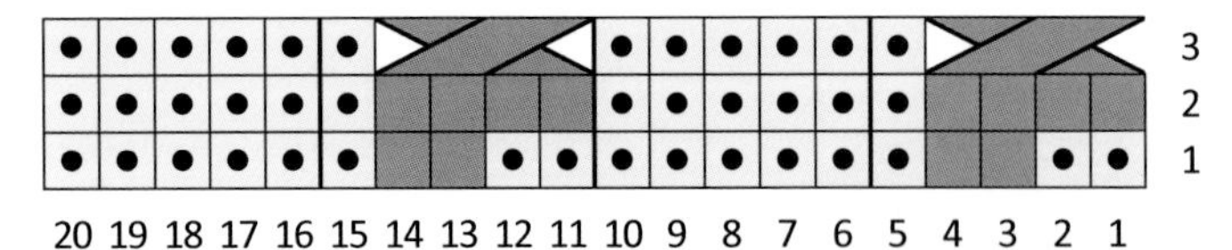

Chart 2

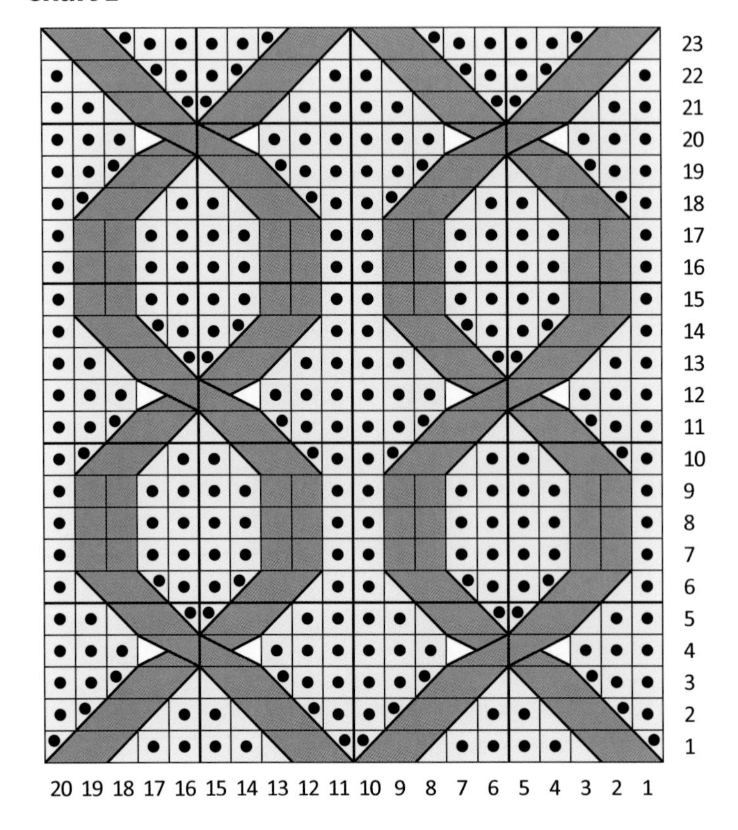

Chart 3

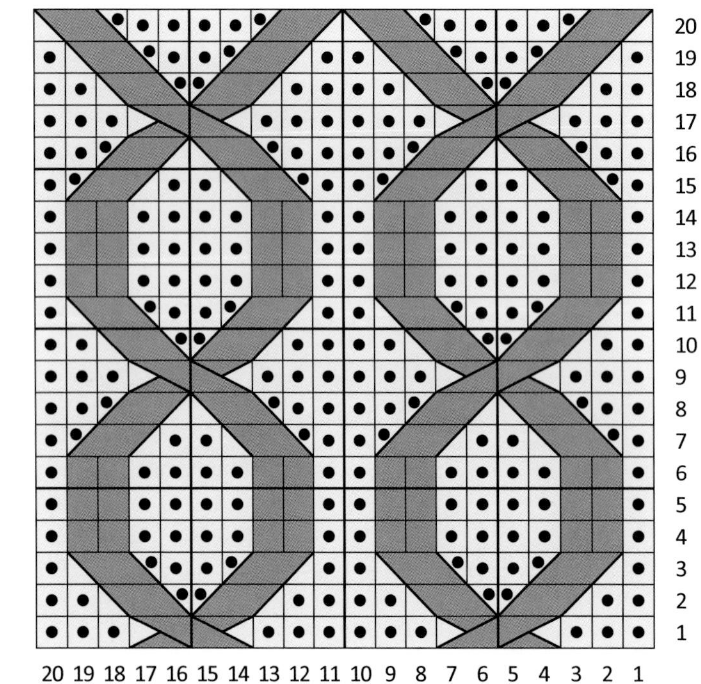

Chart 4

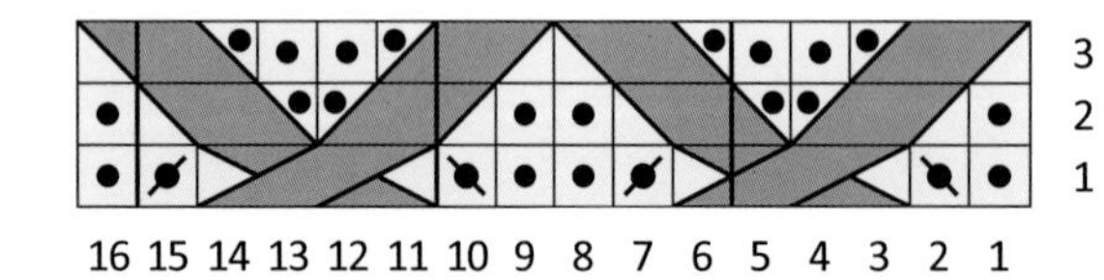

Chart 5

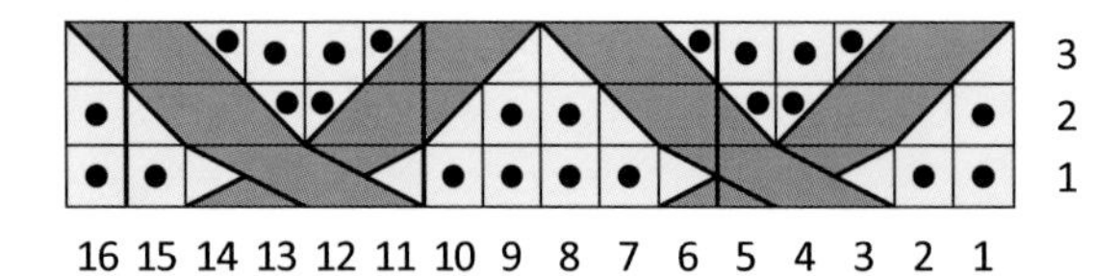

Chart 6

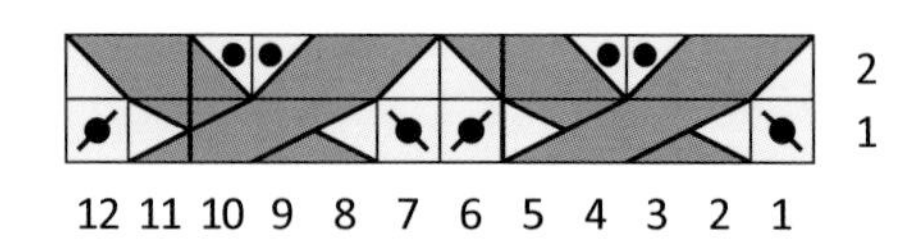

Chart 7

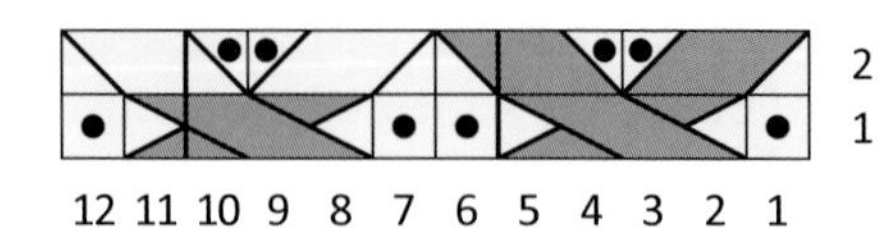

Chart 8

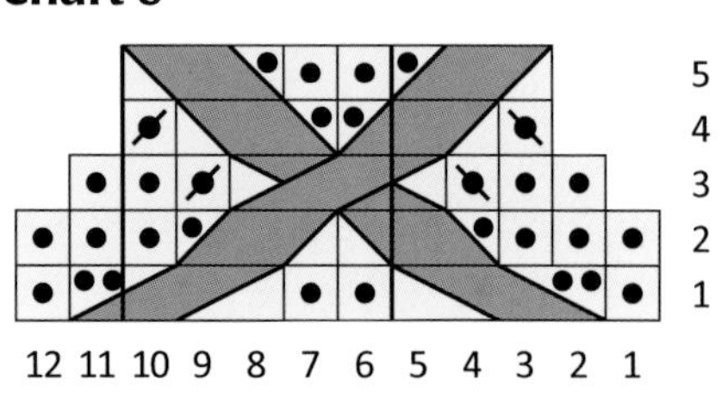

Chart 9

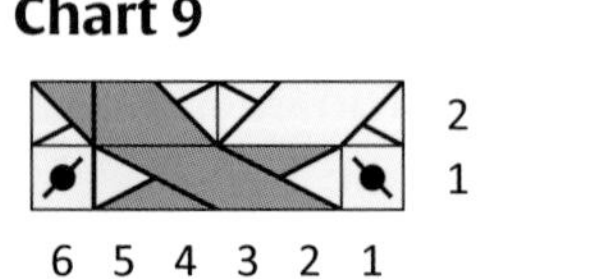

Chart 10

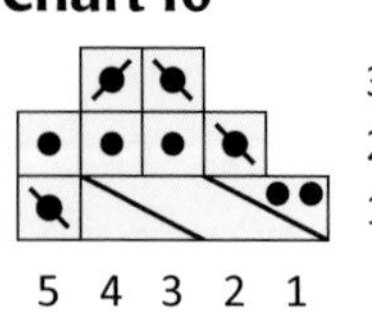

Headband Charts

Chart 3a

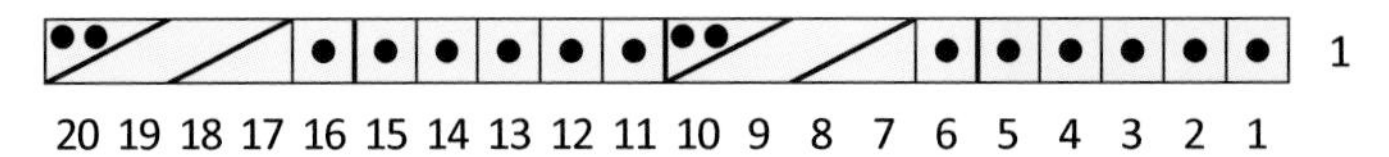

Chart 2a

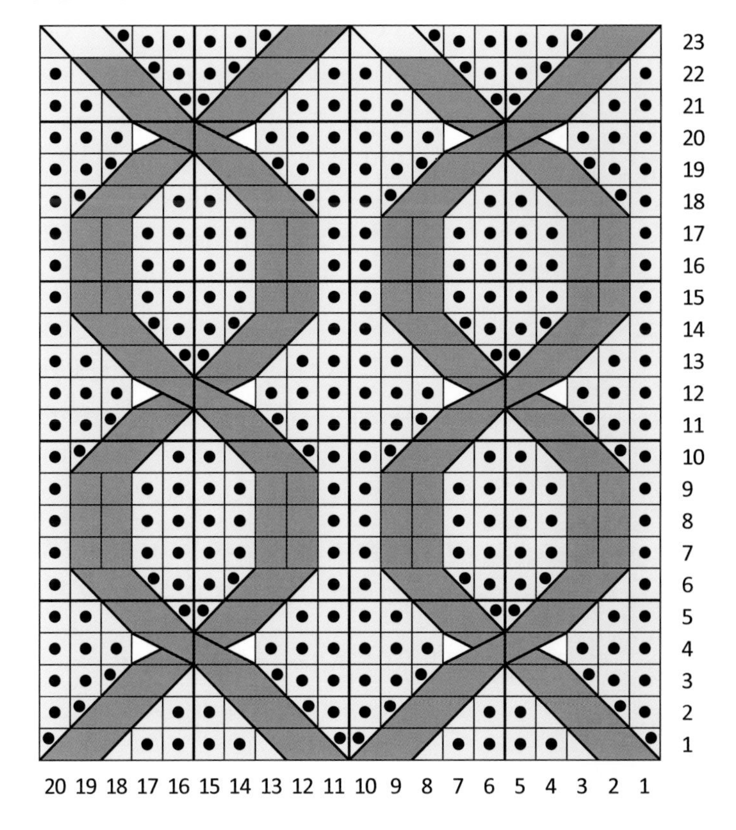

Chart 3

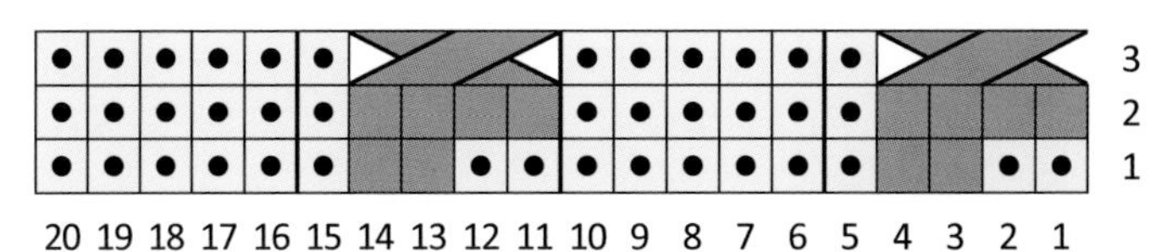

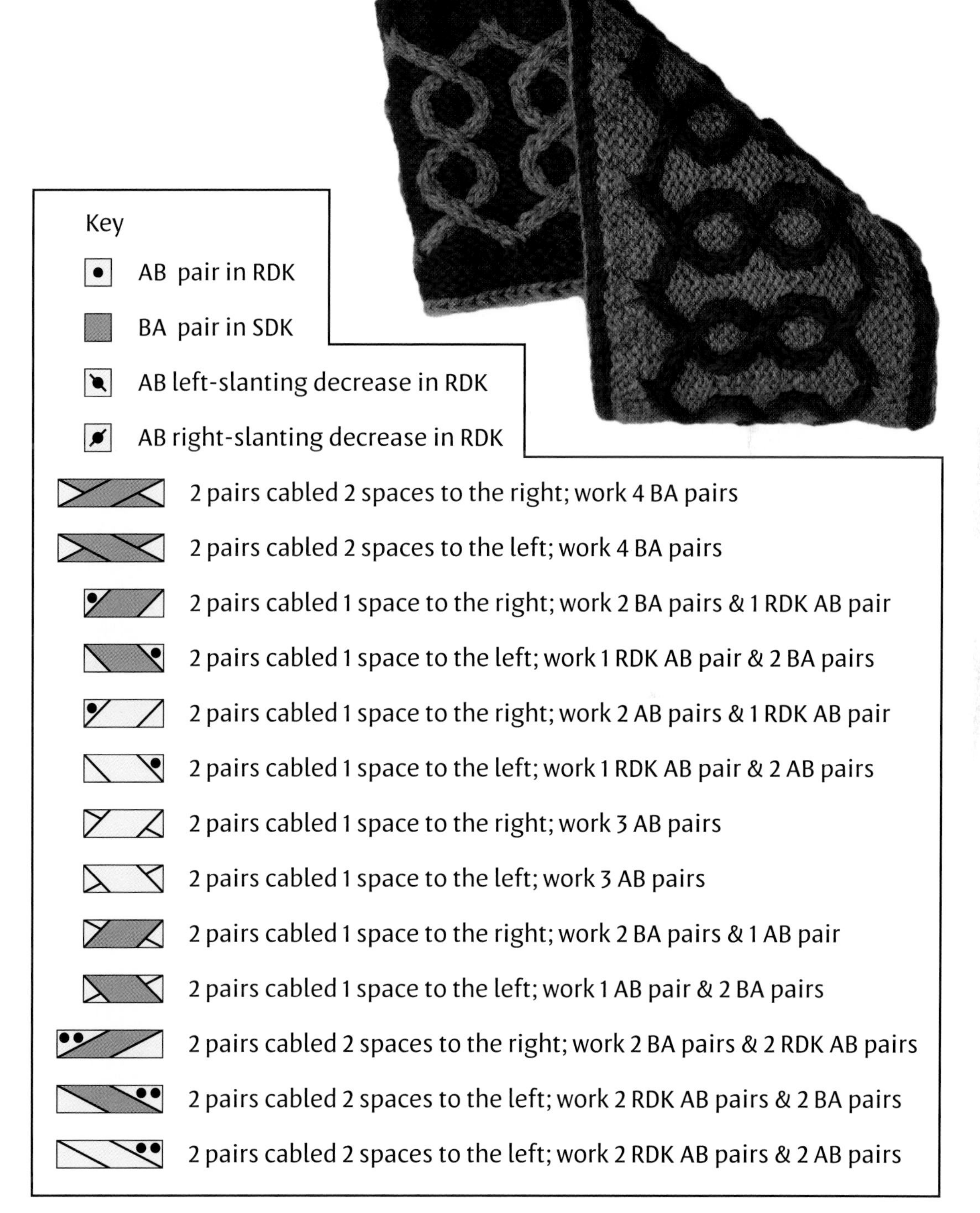

Hat Pattern

Using double-knit i-cord cast-on, CO 105 (120, 135) AB pairs, PM every 15 pairs. Join, being careful not to twist; PM at beginning/end.

Body:

1. RDK AB all pairs to end.
2. Repeat [work 3 pairs, inc 1 pair] to end, slipping markers as you pass them, ending with 140 (160, 180) pairs (20 pairs between markers).
3. RDK AB all pairs to end.
4. Work 7 (8, 9) repeats of Chart 1 around. When working last chart round, RM all except first/last marker.
5. RM, work 2 slipped pairs, PM.
6. Work 7 (8, 9) repeats of Chart 2 around.
7. RM, work 5 slipped pairs, PM.
8. Work 7 (8, 9) repeats of Chart 3 around.

Crown:

Change to your small-diameter needle solution when necessary.

1. RM, work 5 slipped pairs, PM.
2. Work 7 (8, 9) repeats of Chart 4 around, ending with 112 (128, 144) pairs (16 pairs per repeat).
3. RM, work 4 slipped pairs, PM.
4. Work 7 (8, 9) repeats of Chart 5 around.
5. RM, work 4 slipped pairs, PM.
6. Work 7 (8, 9) repeats of Chart 6 around, ending with 84 (96, 108) pairs (12 pairs per repeat).
7. RM, work 3 slipped pairs, PM.
8. Work 7 (8, 9) repeats of Chart 7 around.
9. RM, work 3 slipped pairs, PM.
10. Work 7 (8, 9) repeats of Chart 8 around, ending with 56 (64, 72) pairs (8 pairs per repeat).
11. RM, work 4 slipped pairs, PM.
12. Work 7 (8, 9) repeats of Chart 9 around, ending with 42 (48, 54) pairs (6 pairs per repeat).
13. RM, work 4 slipped pairs, PM.
14. Work 7 (8, 9) repeats of Chart 10 around, ending with 14 (16, 18) pairs (2 pairs per repeat).

Cinch crown, weave in ends, block if necessary and enjoy!

Headband Pattern

Using double-knit i-cord cast-on, CO 105 (120, 135) AB pairs, PM every 15 pairs.

1. RDK AB all pairs to end.
2. Repeat [work 3 pairs, inc 1 pair] to end, slipping markers as you pass them, ending with. 140 (160, 180) pairs (20 pairs between markers).
3. RDK AB all pairs to end.
4. Work 7 (8, 9) repeats of Chart 1 around. When working last chart round, RM all except first/last marker.
5. RM, work 2 slipped pairs, PM.
6. Work 7 (8, 9) repeats of Chart 2a around.
7. RM, work 2 slipped pairs, PM.
8. Work 7 (8, 9) repeats of Chart 3a around.
9. RDK AB all pairs to end.
10. Repeat [dec 1 RDK AB pair, RDK 2 AB pairs] to end, ending with 105 (120, 135) pairs.
11. RDK AB all pairs to end.
12. Work double-knit i-cord BO.

Weave in ends, block if necessary and enjoy!

Craftstory, continued from page 169

I began teaching double-knitting only a couple years after learning it (which may have been a mistake), but I got better and better at teaching it as I learned more and more about the technique. Even after I adopted the modern method, I continued teaching the slip-stitch method, because I was under the (probably mistaken) impression that it was better if other people began learning in the same place that I had learned. Eventually, I left the world of slip-stitch double-knitting behind altogether, as I began to understand where its limits truly were. There were things I simply could not do until I adopted the modern method completely, so I also reformulated my workshops for that method. I continued to develop techniques, all the while scouring every text I could find for any prior art.

In those early days, still years before *Extreme Double-Knitting* took shape, I began to realize that much of what I was doing was not documented. I'd consulted with knitters far more experienced than I, and read reference books and pattern books, trying to find anything but the most basic of double-knitting technique documentation. Even the holy grail of knitting techniques, *Principles of Knitting* by June Hemmons Hiatt, at that point only dealt with the archaic slip-stitch method. I had high hopes for the out-of-print book *Notes on Double Knitting* by Beverly Royce, but when I finally found a copy, dealt overwhelmingly with tubular double-knitting and, again, the slip-stitch method.

Eventually, I began to come to the conclusion that, if so little of what I was doing was documented, it might fall to me to document it. This was not a job I wanted, nor was it one I was suited for at that early date. Thankfully, I didn't pursue it; but it stayed at the back of my head like a candle in a distant window, appearing occasionally through the forest of other ideas and plans for the future. To be honest, when the opportunity finally came, I felt barely more qualified, but I took it.

In 2004, around the time I started to branch out to find the wider knitting community in the Boston area, I had begun to attend a number of knitting groups. Knitting was beginning to explode again, and these groups were popping up everywhere. I attended a group that met at a coffee shop in Cambridge, one that met at a Panera in the suburbs closer to where I was living, and one that met at another coffee shop in Somerville. The common denominators seemed to be me and one girl, a young massage-therapist-in-training who worked at Woolcott & Co in Harvard Square (now sadly closed). Since she lived along the way from my home into the city, she and I would often meet up on the bus, and we struck up conversations en route to the knitting groups. At the risk of simplifying things greatly (but to save both of us the indignity of airing our awkward romance) we eventually became a couple, and she moved out of her parents' place and in with me. Yes, that's right – I picked up Amanda, my wife-to-be, at a knitting group. It wasn't my intention; but it happened, and I think we both feel very lucky that it did.

One night, I was heading to my Harvard Square group. Sitting near the front of the bus was a guy I'd never met who was knitting as well! I sidled up to him, pulled out my knitting, grinned, and invited him to the knitting group. Then, as an afterthought, I introduced myself. This turned out to be Guido, who went on to podcast "It's A Purl, Man"; but more importantly, who joined me and his friend Alanna to found the Common Cod Fiber Guild. For the first few years, he was the president, I was the treasurer, and Alanna was the secretary. The Guild has a larger board now and is flourishing without us, but we gave it the jumpstart it needed. Boston already has one knitting guild, plus at least one more on the outskirts of the city – but we felt it could do with one more. The established guild in Boston meets at mid-day on a weekday, which works for some – but the young urban professional crowd (which was getting heavily into knitting at that time) often couldn't swing it. We decided to have our guild meetings on Friday nights, and they were often followed by a trip to a bar by quite a number of members. We attracted some of the members of the guild in Boston eventually, but our membership was largely younger and geekier. It didn't hurt that we held (and still hold) our meetings at MIT.

Craftstory, continued on page 181

CHAPTER 9

Double-knitting Lace

I am no longer the only person designing in double-knit lace. As a matter of fact, since my passing mention of it in the appendix of *Extreme Double-Knitting*, several other people independently began developing their approaches to the technique. I've been following them with interest, but it's only relatively recently that I've been ready to release my contributions to the genre.

I wanted to make sure I had a deep understanding of double-knit lace, which meant I had to have a better understanding of lace itself. I've done lace (even very complicated lace) but I just followed the chart and the instructions — and even then I didn't totally understand everything I was doing. Through the experiments I did in double-knit lace, I learned more about lace in general, and I am ready to show what I've learned.

It is important to me (and probably a comfort to you) that I use chart symbols that are recognizable and familiar whenever possible, which has helped me generate charts that could just as easily be drained of their colorwork and worked in single-layer knitted lace. The only difference between a single-layer lace chart and a double-knit lace chart is that most of the time there will be some colorwork in the double-knit version — and there may be different symbols for the edging if the piece is worked flat.

Colorwork in lace is not something that is commonly done, because stranded colorwork can't easily be combined with lace due the strands being visible behind the yarn-overs. However, it's almost necessary for double-knitting, and since it's easy to add, we may as well use it. It should be used sparingly — colorwork in lace can be garish if overused. I typically use it not to draw a motif separate from the lace, but to pick out and emphasize patterns that are already within the lace. In some cases, these patterns may not be immediately visible until they're emphasized in colorwork, which adds a level of intrigue to the pattern.

My approach to double-knit lace, like my approach to anything else in double-knitting, is to try to find the most elegant solution. In this case, I have found four different solutions, plus variations. Three of them can be worked from any lace chart, provided you already know how to work the non-yarn-over techniques in double-knitting. The first two are candidates for the most elegant solution, and I think that the second one wins the prize — but you may feel differently. They all have their pros and cons in process and product, and I'll outline those for you as I explain how to do them.

The first three methods are distinguished only in the technique used to follow the yarn-overs. The decreases and other supporting techniques are all the same as they would be in standard double-knitting unless stated otherwise. The fourth method is a little more specialized.

Spring Willow, page 182

Method 1: Linked Double-knit Lace

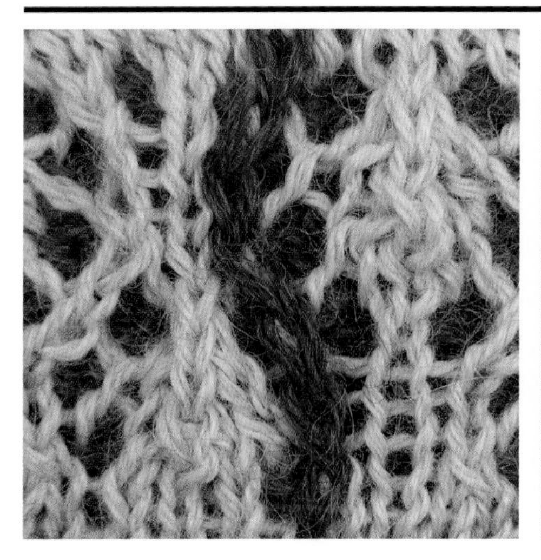

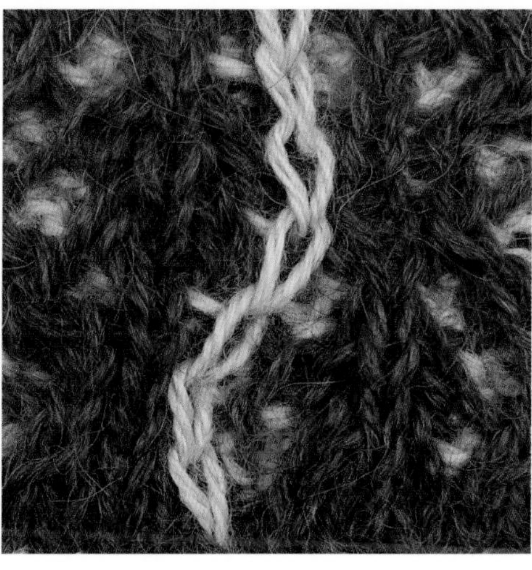

Pros

- Can be worked from a standard lace chart
- Creates a stable fabric, even without color changes
- Both layers of the work have a built-in background
- Offset holes mean garment can be worn in colder weather

Cons

- The yarn ends twist around each other once per yarn-over
- Can conflict with color changes

This method is the most direct translation of lace to double-knitting. In single-layer lace, a yarn-over involves a counterclockwise wrap around the needle. When the resulting yarn-over stitch is worked in the next row, it's knit or purled like a regular stitch, creating a nice open hole. In linked double-knit lace, both ends follow the same path simultaneously, matching the color order called for in the chart. In most cases, a yarn-over pair will match the color order of the pairs on either side of it, but not always. If it's easier, you can do the two yarn-overs separately, making sure to work them in the correct order for your pair.

In this method, the fabric becomes linked together at every yarn-over. A fabric with lots of yarn-over pairs needs no color changes to keep the two layers connected. Also, due to the positioning of the link, the fabric is held together in such a way that the holes don't line up on either layer. This means that you'll be able to see the color from the other layer of the work through every yarn-over hole. A built-in background can be a big plus — the lace is still very prominent, but there's more coverage so a garment made using this method can be worn during colder weather. Also, because no color changing is necessary, this method is the easiest way to adapt an existing single-layer lace chart to double-knitting. However, the link is often visible in the upper left corner of each yarn-over hole, especially when using colorwork. If this is happening a lot, I recommend trying Method 2 instead.

When you work the knit stitch of the pair following the yarn-over, take the yarn from underneath unless there's a color change. This causes the link to occur, and is the most natural way to pick up the yarn. If you pick up the yarn from over the top of the other strand, it will cause the fabric to unlink, but you'll run the risk of having the color order switch on the needle, causing difficulties in the next row or round.

The other thing that the link does is to create a twist in your yarn ends. This doesn't mean anything for the product but does slow down the process. When every yarn-over you do creates one full twist between the ends, you will end up with lots of twists that you will need to get rid of. If you choose not to do colorwork, you will have nowhere to get rid of those twists, and you will periodically have to untwist your ends somehow.

So you can choose to do colorwork alongside your linked yarn-over pairs, and every color change will allow you to untwist one of the twists created by the yarn-overs. However, it's very likely that you will have fewer color changes than yarn-overs in any given row, so you will still accrue twist that you will need to deal with some other way.

Here's a tip for working a decrease (or double-decrease) directly after a yarn-over pair: reorder for the decrease first. When you reorder your pairs for a decrease, there's a lot of slipping back and forth. Doing this while a yarn-over pair is hanging loose on your needle is a sure way to lose your yarn-over pair. Once you've reordered for a decrease, do your yarn-over pair, and then immediately lock it in place with the decrease move that comes right after it.

Method 2: Unlinked Double-knit Lace

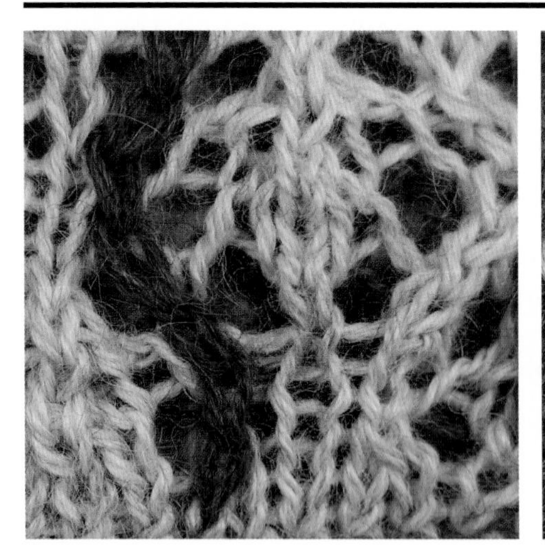

Pros

- Can be worked from a standard lace chart
- Does not cause conflicts with certain color changes
- Does not cause yarn ends to twist up

Cons

- Two layers will be separate
- Requires more attention on the next row

This method is my preferred solution; even though the process is a little unorthodox, the product has the purity the others lack. Done properly, this method will give you two separate layers of lace, just as you would end up with two separate layers of stockinette in double-knitting without color changes. The unlinked layers will tend to line up with each other so that the yarn-over holes will show all the way through the work.

You can get this fabric by following the linked method with the modification of picking up the first stitch of the pair after a yarn-over from over the top rather than underneath. However, that solution lacks elegance because it lacks repeatability — the pair doesn't "want" to stay in the right order and will sometimes switch on you.

To keep both process and product clean, use reverse yarn-overs instead. Rather than wrapping the yarn counterclockwise, as with normal yarnovers, wrap clockwise (as before, being careful to match the color order called for in the chart). This is a slightly larger movement since it takes nearly a full turn around the needle, and it's a little awkward to do since the yarns may not "want" to sit in the right order — but once the technique is done, it's totally stable. You can get around this temporarily by wrapping the yarns separately in the right color order, but the more you do the reverse yarn-over, the more natural it feels.

However you do it, since the yarn-over pair is now seated backward on the needle, you'll have to treat it differently on the next row or round. While following unlinked double-knit lace, all yarn-over pairs must be knit and purled through the backs of their loops. If you knit and purl normally, you'll twist the holes closed (or at least smaller). However, this is helped along by the process — it feels awkward and unnatural to knit or purl normally into a stitch which is seated backwards, and even more so for a yarn-over. It's something you have to do intentionally, so it's harder to do by mistake. By contrast, knitting or purling into the back of the loop feels natural and preserves the openness of the yarn-over.

While using this method, you pretty much have to integrate colorwork, since nothing else will as effectively keep the fabric linked together. Since this yarn-over method doesn't twist the ends around each other, there's no need to make your color change in one direction or the other. You will, however, end up with twisted ends from the color changes as you usually would. The issue with yarn-over pairs next to colorwork also doesn't matter as much here — there's no more conflict here than in standard double-knitting. However, if you have a yarn-over next to a color change, you may see a little bit of the crossover where the colors switch layers.

The same tip I gave in the linked double-knit lace section (page 177) for doing a decrease directly after a yarn-over pair holds true here as well.

Method 3: Single-layer Double-knit Lace

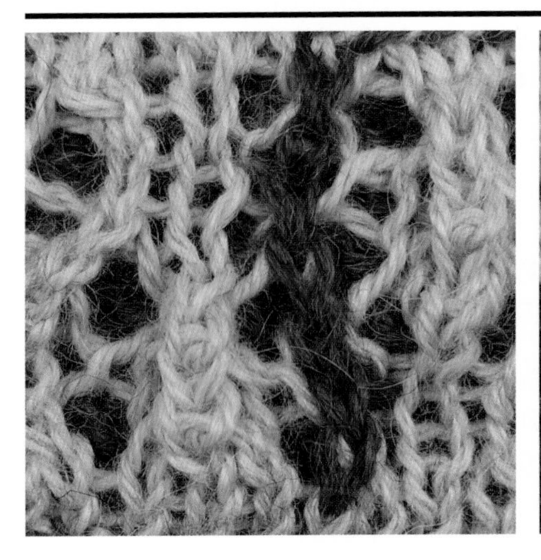

Pros

- Can be worked from a standard lace chart
- Can be worn in coldest weather
- Built-in background for lace layer

Cons

- Layers are unlinked without colorwork
- Not necessarily reversible
- Requires more planning

This method is misleadingly named; there are actually two layers but only one of them is lace.

Single-layer double-knit lace has limited usability, but if you want to wear lace in the winter, this may be the one for you. The fabric is nominally reversible, with solid knitting on one layer and lace on the other. The non-lace layer is not plain knitting, as it still has a sort of "echo" of the lace pattern on it. Depending on your pattern, this may or may not be attractive, and depending on the garment you may or may not ever see it. Most of the time, you're going to want to show off the layer of lace.

The key to this effect is that yarn-overs are a type of increase. If you want holes on both layers of the work, you're going to want to make sure a yarn-over has a corresponding yarn-over on the other layer. But it isn't necessary. To keep the pair count consistent, you just need to have a corresponding increase on Layer 2 when you make one on Layer 1; they need not be the same type.

The most effective way to do this is to use a purl-side M1 increase for Layer 2 (see page 56). An M1 is related to a yarn-over — it's just a smaller loop (without the slack provided by a yarn-over) that is twisted closed. All you need to do is to bring both yarns to the front, do a regular (not reverse) yarn-over with the first color (as charted), bringing it all the way around to the front again. With the second color, make an M1 increase (L or R, depending on your preference) on the purl layer. This will also serve to anchor the yarn-over in place so that you need not reorder your pairs before the yarn-over if it's followed by a decrease.

If you want to make the non-lace layer even cleaner, you can opt to do M1L and M1R, or even purl-side lifted increases. However, this would require an entirely new notation system, and I find that doing generic M1s where needed is usually perfectly fine.

The single-layer double-knit lace method, like the unlinked method above, has its layers disconnected. For this reason, I recommend you use colorwork to keep the layers together. On the non-lace layer, there will also be colorwork but no holes, which can make an intriguing fabric.

When planning a piece using this technique, you will have to give careful consideration to the outcome. Since the two layers look significantly different, you'll need to decide which color you want to be the lace and which the background on the lace layer of the work. You won't simply be able to turn it inside out and have the same pattern in reversed colors on the other layer.

Method 4: Stockinette-Backed Double-knit Lace

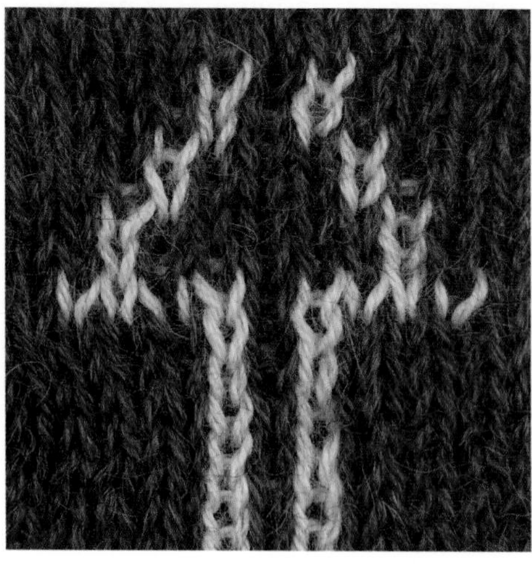

Pros

- Layer 2 looks like stockinette
- Can be worn in coldest weather
- Built-in background for lace layer

Cons

- Can only be worked in specific circumstances
- Layers are unlinked without colorwork

This method only works when the yarn-over and decrease are right next to each other. If a pattern consists entirely of this type of yarn-over/decrease (or decrease/yarn-over, or yarn-over/double decrease/yarn-over) combination, it will be possible to work one layer in stockinette. As with single-layer double-knit lace, the two layers are unlinked, so colorwork will need to be employed to keep the two layers together. In cases where the colorwork is integrated into the decreases, the stockinette layer will not look the same, as there are no decreases. At best, you will end up with a pixelated translation of the same pattern; and at worst it will be unintelligible.

Your other option is to leave the colorwork off the stockinette layer, and when you do colorwork on one layer, do the same color on the other layer, matching the background and creating the illusion of plain stockinette with no color changes. This uses two-pattern techniques to create a direct link between the knit and the purl in a pair. As long as the colorwork on the lace layer is used sparingly, there should be no issue doing this.

Like other double-knit lace, this technique requires reordering of stitches to accommodate the decreases. However, unlike other double-knit lace, the chart cannot be followed precisely stitch by stitch or pair by pair. Instead, you have to work the yarn-over and decrease as a single integrated technique.

YO-Dec

Reorder your next two pairs from KPKP to PKKP thus:

1. Insert the working needle into the second stitch on the source needle from behind.
2. Pull the source needle out of two stitches.
3. Catch the loose stitch at the front with the source needle.
4. Slip one stitch back to the source needle.

Then:

1. Wyif, YO with color indicated by chart; P1 in opposite color.
2. Wyib, decrease next 2 stitches (k2tog or SSK depending on the chart) in color indicated by chart. Wyif, P1 in opposite color.

Dec-YO

1. Reorder your next two pairs to KKPP as usual (see page 50).
2. Wyib, decrease next 2 stitches (k2tog or SSK depending on the chart) in color indicated. Wyif, P1 in opposite color.
3. Wyif, YO with color indicated by chart, P1 in opposite color.

YO-DDec-YO

Reorder your next 3 pairs from KPKPKP to PKKKPP as follows:

1. With working needle, hold second stitch on source needle in place from back.
2. Pull source needle out of 2 stitches, catch loose stitch at front.
3. Slip 4 pairs.
4. With source needle, hold second stitch on working needle in place from back.
5. Pull working needle out of 2 stitches, catch loose stitch at front.
6. Slip 4 stitches back to source needle.

Then work the reordered stitches as follows:

1. Wyif, YO with color indicated by chart, P1 in opposite color.
2. Wyib, work double-decrease as charted in color indicated. Wyif, P1 in opposite color.
3. Wyif, YO with color indicated by chart; P1 in opposite color.

Craftstory, continued from page 175

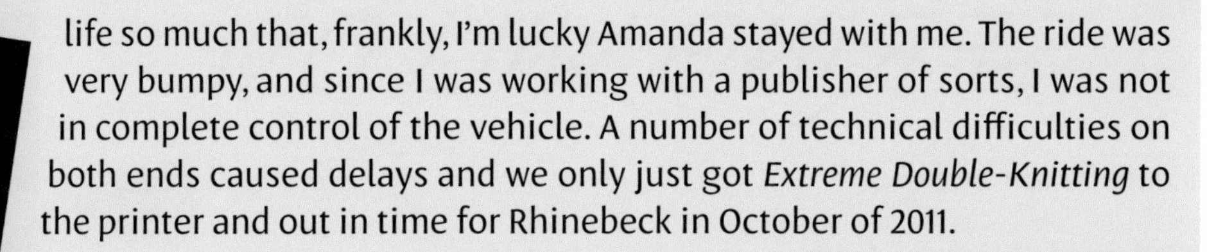

Over the next several years, I continued to develop techniques, honing two-pattern and multicolor double-knitting and beginning to work on my off-the-grid style. Mostly, however, I was teaching. I taught my first workshop in May of 2006, and my first one out of state (in NYC) in January of 2007. By 2009, I had given up on the slip-stitch technique entirely and began teaching more and more workshops in the "modern" style. Finally, in November of 2009, I was simply in the right place at the right time to get the ultimate teaching opportunity. The Guild speaker that month was Shannon Okey, who was expanding her indie publishing house Cooperative Press. At the bar after the event, some of us were knitting; I was working on the prototype for the Victorian Raffia scarf, and it caught Shannon's eye — she said I had to write a book for her. So there it was: a month after I got married to a girl I met at a knitting group, I was going to begin writing that book I had imagined four years past.

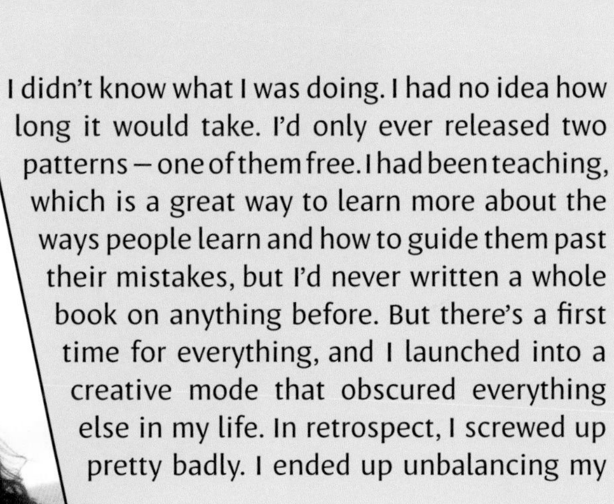

I didn't know what I was doing. I had no idea how long it would take. I'd only ever released two patterns — one of them free. I had been teaching, which is a great way to learn more about the ways people learn and how to guide them past their mistakes, but I'd never written a whole book on anything before. But there's a first time for everything, and I launched into a creative mode that obscured everything else in my life. In retrospect, I screwed up pretty badly. I ended up unbalancing my life so much that, frankly, I'm lucky Amanda stayed with me. The ride was very bumpy, and since I was working with a publisher of sorts, I was not in complete control of the vehicle. A number of technical difficulties on both ends caused delays and we only just got *Extreme Double-Knitting* to the printer and out in time for Rhinebeck in October of 2011.

One of the big catalysts that allowed me to make fast progress on the book came in the form of a surprise invitation to Cat Bordhi's first and only Visionary Retreat for men. If you're not familiar, the Visionary Retreats were gatherings of established and aspiring self-publishing knitting authors. As you can probably imagine, most attendees of these retreats are women, but I guess at one point there were enough men that Cat decided to do one just for us. My timing was a little off, as I already had my book deal; but seeing as I was working with an unconventional publisher, much of the conversation was still applicable to me. I tried my best to be of use to the other guys as well. Many of the guys at this retreat have gone on to do amazing things, and they are even more well-known than I am — Stephen West, Franklin Habit, Charles Gandy, to name a few. But after my presentation to the group, Cat said something to the effect of "There are four true geniuses in the knitting world, and I've just met the fifth." I don't know if I agree, but I'll take the compliment.

Craftstory, continued on page 185

SPRING WILLOW

a double-knit lace cowl

Finished size & weight

For a blocked cowl 29 (35, 41, 47)" around by 11.5" tall, you will be using a maximum of 3.23 oz (311 yds) of each color, so you should have enough in one pair of skeins to do whichever size you prefer.

Put another way, each Chart 2 repeat is approximately 5.8" wide by 1.6" tall after blocking, and approximately 64 of these repeats can be made from a single pair of skeins. As worked for the sample, there are 42 (6x7) repeats and the piece is about 35" around by 11.5" tall. You can change the circular and vertical repeats; as long as the total number of repeats is 64 or less you'll be okay.

Materials & tools

[Color A]: Anzula Squishy (80% superwash merino, 10% cashmere, 10% nylon; 385 yd/4 oz skein); Avocado (green); 1 skein.

[Color B]: Anzula Squishy (80% superwash merino, 10% cashmere, 10% nylon; 385 yd/4 oz skein); Rootbeer (tan); 1 skein.

US 6/4 mm 24" circular needle or size needed to achieve gauge.

US7/4.5 mm 24" circular needle (or one size up from main needle).

Gauge in pattern

20.5 sts/39.5 rows = 4" in pattern using smaller needle, unblocked.

16.5 sts/29 rows = 4" in pattern using smaller needle, blocked.

This pattern came from a similar situation to Heartbound. I needed a pattern to illustrate techniques I was beginning to offer in workshops so that people would have a chance to try some double-knit lace in an actual pattern. To be honest, it had not gone unnoticed that there were some other innovators who had, whether with the help of *Extreme Double-Knitting's* appendix or not, begun to play with double-knit lace and publish patterns using it. I was excited to see this but also galvanized to release a pattern to capitalize on the knitting community's apparent interest in the technique. Besides, my design sense and style are uniquely my own and often recognizable to others — and the same goes for my double-knit lace when compared to others' designs. Not only do I have a method to do it, but I also have multiple variations, each with unique properties. Of course, I do have a preferred method, which is the one I'm using here. The lace pattern is subtly modified from something in a Barbara Walker treasury, then further modified for working in the round.

Superwash merino, cashmere, and silk — it's become such a common luxury blend that it even has its own acronym: MCS. I met the folks behind Anzula, a luxury yarn company from California, at a trade show where direct sales aren't allowed, but where yarn companies and designers network on the side. Anzula came to the show with suitcases full of yarn to entice designers, and I got to sit and fondle the skeins for quite some time before I settled on the MCS base they called "Dreamy" in a particularly unlikely pairing of colors. This was well before I had a plan on what to do with them.

When I began casting about for yarn for this pattern, I selected these colors from my stash. Because the pattern takes advantage of larger color areas and single columns of stitches, I was able to get away with a slightly lower-contrast color combination. When I showed Anzula this pattern, they decided they wanted one for their trunk show but were out of Dreamy. Instead, they asked me to substitute "Squishy," which replaces the silk with nylon (but otherwise keeps a similar blend). I'd be hard-pressed to tell the difference. I'm not even sure which one I have and which one travels with Anzula now.

Normally, I shy away from naming my pieces after the colors I choose. I want people to feel free to experiment with colorways, and referring to a pattern as "Red Sweater #45" is going to unfairly bias people against knitting the pattern in blue yarn. But in this case, the temptation was too great; I thought of the pattern as "Spring Willow" due to the new-growth tan and green colors it's done in, and the name stuck. It fits because of the hanging, ripply columns and the openwork between; the colorways just sort of help the image if you want them to.

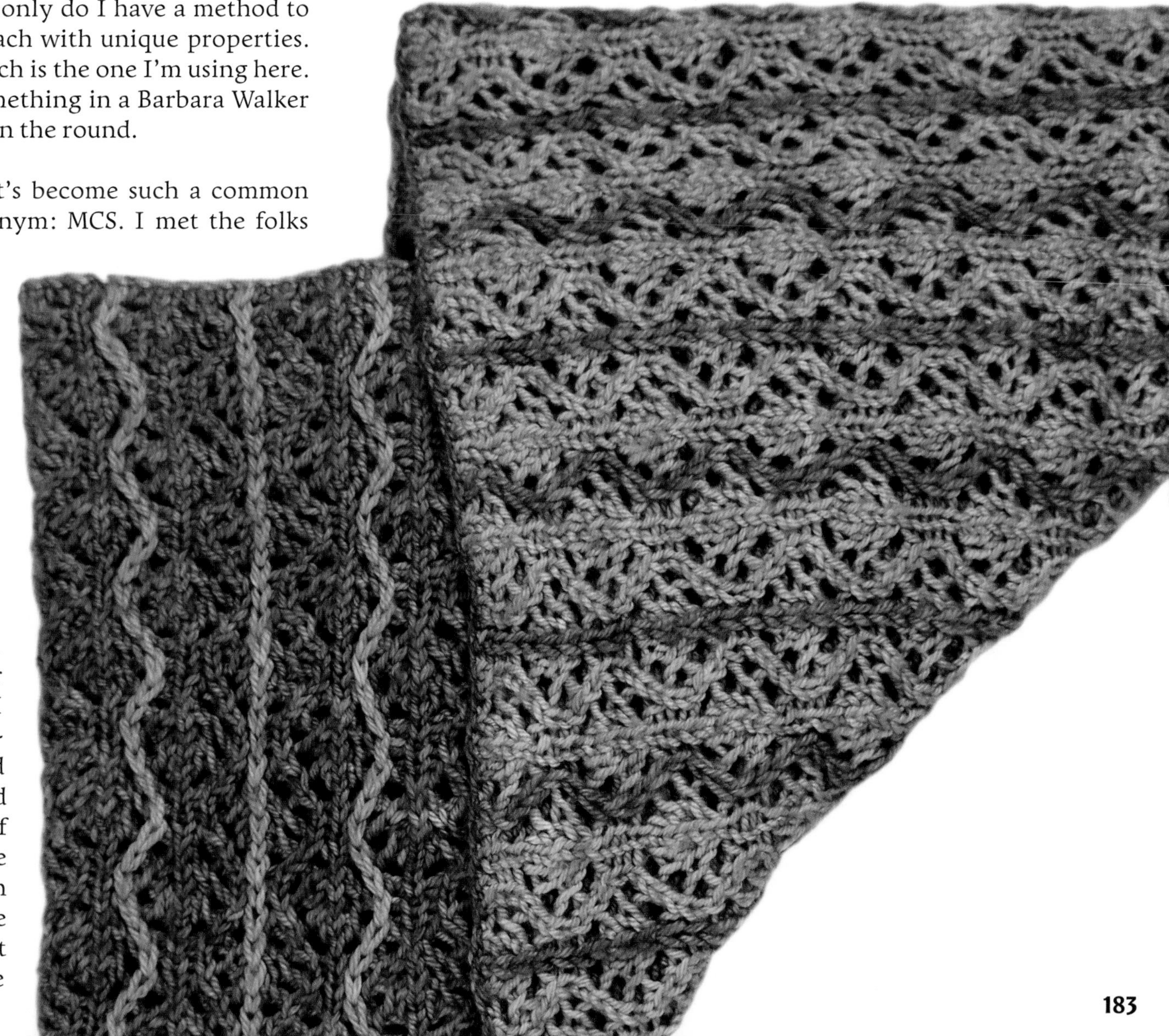

Chart 1

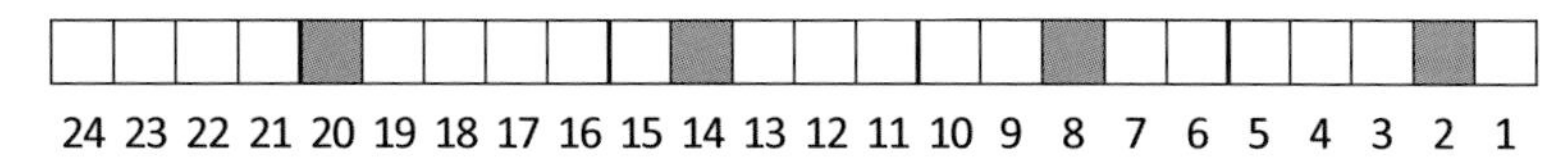

Chart 2

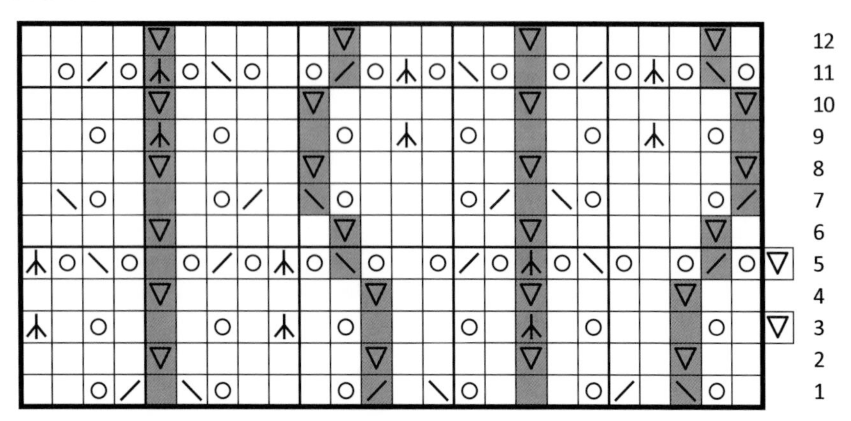

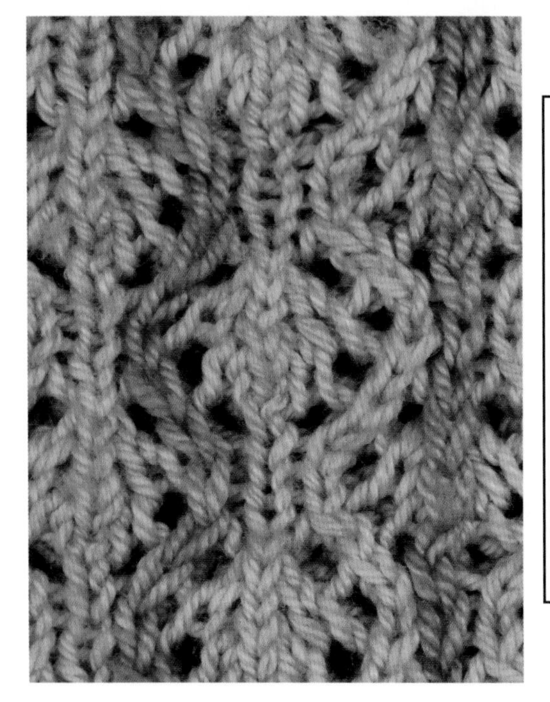

Key

- □ AB pair
- ■ BA pair
- ○ Yarnover pair
- / Right-leaning decrease
- \ Left-leaning decrease
- ⅄ Raised double-decrease
- ▽ Slipped pair

Pattern

Use your smaller needle to CO 120 (144, 168, 192) AB pairs.

Remove slip knot. Join in the round, being careful not to twist. Optionally, place a marker. Work 5 (6, 7, 8) repeats of Chart 1 around.

Using the unlinked double-knit lace method, work 5 (6, 7, 8) repeats of Chart 2 around, repeating Rows 1-12 seven times or until desired height is reached.

In Rounds 3 and 5, work 1 slipped pair before beginning round. In all subsequent repeats within those rounds, work only the portion of the chart inside the bold outline (See section on Ghost Pairs below). All other rounds are simply worked as charted.

Using your larger needle, BO in AB pairs, weave in ends, block and enjoy!

Ghost Pairs

This is a technique I have tried to shy away from because it's hard to explain — but intriguing. When working with increases and decreases in the round it is sometimes necessary. I haven't found another name for this technique so I've given it my own — if there is another name for it, I feel sure someone will tell me.

A **ghost pair** occurs at the beginning of a round when there is a decrease at the end of the repeat that incorporates the first pair of the next repeat. At the end of the round, there must be a pair which can be incorporated into that decrease. The way the repeat lines up, there is an extra pair that must be processed before anything else can be done. The ghost pair is that pair — it appears at the beginning out of nowhere, and disappears at the end of the round.

I notate these pairs with a pixel that occurs outside the repeat. I put a heavy line around the repeat so it's clear that these ghost pairs are outside. Whenever possible, ghost pairs are slipped rather than worked.

Craftstory, continued from page 181

Extreme Double-Knitting was the real beginning of my knitting career – not merely a hobby anymore. With a book on the market being touted as an indispensable reference to all things double-knitting, I got invitations to teach at progressively larger and more distant venues. I got requests to design patterns for yarn lines and magazines. I was invited to speak to knitting guilds. I was even courted by Craftsy and I got in near the ground floor when they were still around a year old. And of course, after the first book was done, I went back to developing and designing new techniques and patterns. With all of this body of work, I felt it was past time to revisit the idea of a business name. The choice was simple: Fallingblox Designs.

Which brings me to another question that I get asked a lot: What's in the name "Fallingblox"? What does it have to do with knitting? The answer: Nothing whatsoever. If you look at my logo, you'll notice there's a blue L-shaped block under the lettering. This is a tetromino, also known as one of 7 Tetris blocks. As a budding computer geek during the 1990s, thanks in part to my stepfather, I embraced a certain subset of computer games which involved a puzzle or problem-solving component. One of these I particularly gravitated toward was Tetris. In the days before the Tetris Company, this type of falling blocks game was regularly assigned as a project for programming students, so there was a glut of "Tetris clones" out on the bulletin boards and FTP servers (this was before the modern Web). I began collecting them, and I continued doing so as the Web made it easier – and I amassed what was, at the time, the world's largest collection of Tetris clones. There are over 800 of them in my collection, most written for DOS and early versions of Windows. Many are no longer playable without an emulator. The entire collection fits on a burned CD with space to spare. I took the internet handle "Fallingblox" back then and created a website called "Tetris Overload," where I reviewed and provided download links for the collection. I shut down the site before it even really got off the ground, after receiving a cease-and-desist letter from the newly-minted Tetris Company – but I kept the name.

Fallingblox Designs was in its infancy, so to speak, as I transitioned from tenuously math-related single-layer knitting to the beginnings of double-knitting in 2005, but it didn't grow beyond a concept until much later. I released my first pattern in 2006 as a free download on my website, before Ravelry was even a thing (they appeared on the scene in May of 2007). Later in 2007, I joined Ravelry, but I didn't release Falling Blocks, my first paid Ravelry pattern, until early 2010. I did have a pattern released with Twist Collective in late 2009, and it was probably that experience that got me thinking about releasing more. But by 2010, I already had my book deal with Cooperative Press, and in a way I think the release of Falling Blocks was a bit of a teaser for what eventually became *Extreme Double-Knitting*. But when those early patterns were released, I had no need of a business name. It was good enough to simply release them under my own name. However, as the book release date loomed closer, I thought it would be a good idea to incorporate, even if only as a sole proprietor – and Fallingblox Designs became not only a concept but a real side-business that was making real money.

It still didn't make enough money to consider quitting my day job – and to this day I've still never been willing to make that leap. Unlike many other professional knitting designers, I have a day job doing computer repair for a university (the same one I graduated from), which I have held for over a decade. However, in recent years, my boss (who is also a knitter) has allowed me to shuffle my hours in various ways to make it easier for me to pursue my knitting career. As I travel all over the country to teach, it's helpful to have flexible hours that allow me to take time to travel. And as I spent time writing this book, it was helpful to have the freedom to take time to do so. In fact, I've been allowed to go part-time at work until the book is done, just to make things even simpler. Without that time, I'm not sure I would have survived the book-writing process with as much of my mind intact.

It remains my dream to someday go full-time with my knitting career, but I worry that it would irrevocably change the nature of the work I do. If I relied on the income from my knitting career, I'd be forced to take many more contracts and do much more work that I don't get to choose. I wouldn't have as much creative freedom, and I'm not sure I'd enjoy it as much. But maybe I would, and I don't doubt that at some point I'll find a way to make that final leap out of the IT world and into the knitting world full-time.

Alasdair Post-Quinn

Special Techniques: N and Reverse-N

I don't even know how to name this technique, so I'm naming it "N" after the shape of the symbol — which is, in turn, fashioned roughly after the shape of the resulting stitches. It's a combination lifted increase and single decrease, but not the same combination or use as the "shift 1" technique used in *Extreme Double-Knitting*. Instead, you're lifting the leg of a stitch in a row below and decreasing it with the next or previous stitch, depending on the direction. The reason it's necessary is that there are places where I needed the look and structure of an increase, but didn't want or need the extra pair. If there's space, you can just do an increase and a decrease next to each other. But in cases where there's not room to do that (as is the case in the next pattern), this pair of techniques is useful.

To work an **N**:

Bring yarns to the back. With the source needle, pick up the left leg of the stitch two rows below the previous front-side stitch on the working needle, from inside to outside.

2

Use the picked-up stitch and the next stitch on your needle to work an SSK in the color indicated by the chart.

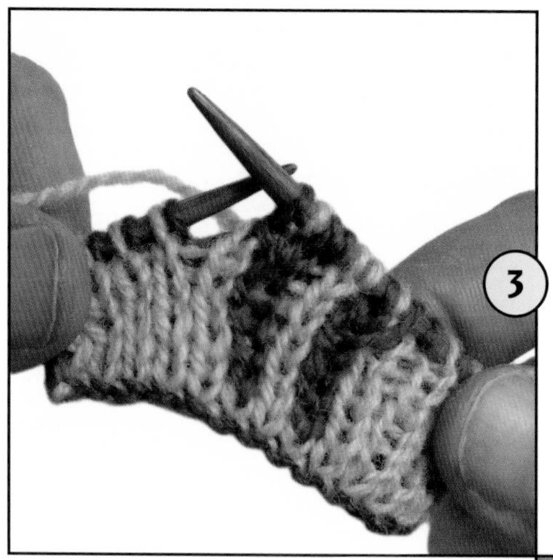

Here's the completed N stitch on Layer 1.

Bring yarns to the front. Flip the work up a bit so you can see the back. With the source needle, pick up the left leg of the stitch two rows below the previous back-side stitch on the working needle, from inside to outside.

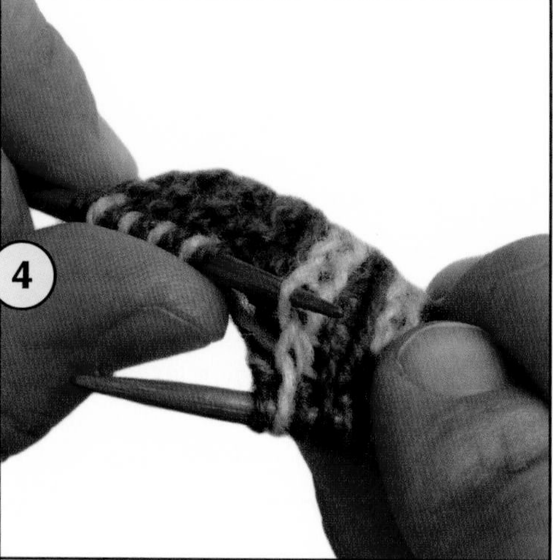

Bring the work back to a more natural position. Slip 1 PTBLwise, and slip 1 back.

P2tog in the opposite color from that used for the knit stitch.

Here's the completed N stitch on Layer 2.

There are three N stitches in the photo to the left. See if you can figure out where! If you give up, check Chart 1c on page 193.

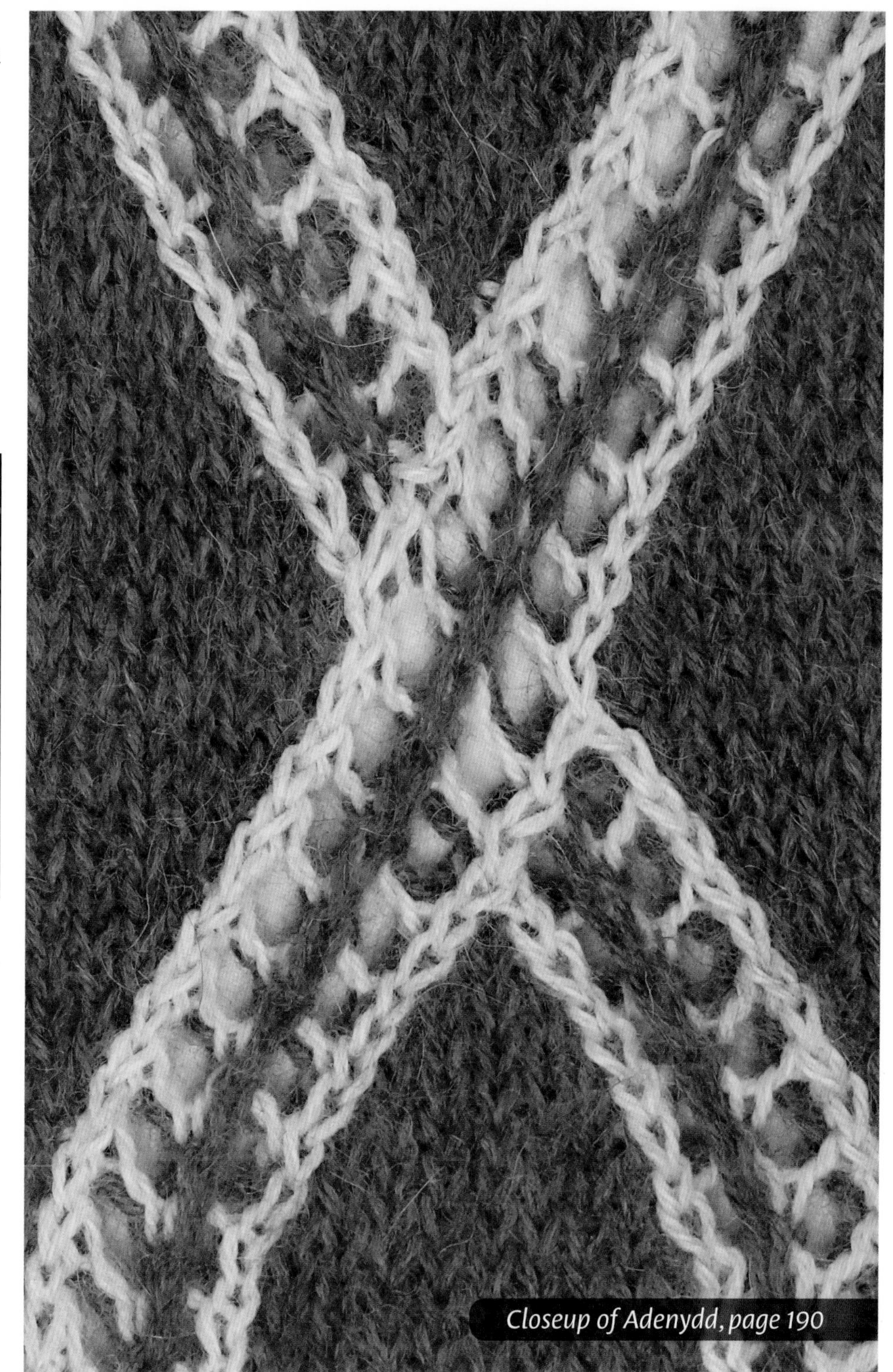

Closeup of Adenydd, page 190

To work a **Reverse-N**:

Wyib, slip 1 stitch purlwise.

Use the working needle to pick up the right leg of the stitch below the next front-side stitch on the source needle from inside to outside . . .

. . . and place on source needle.

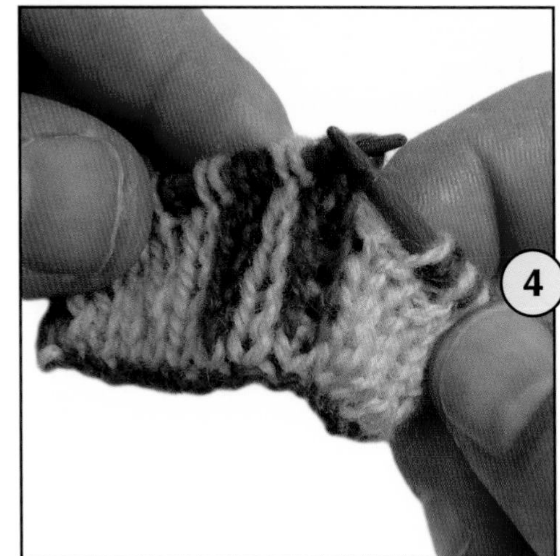

Slip 1 stitch as if to PTBL . . .

. . . and slip 2 stitches back to the source needle.

K2tog in the color indicated by the chart.

Here's the finished Reverse-N stitch as viewed from Layer 1.

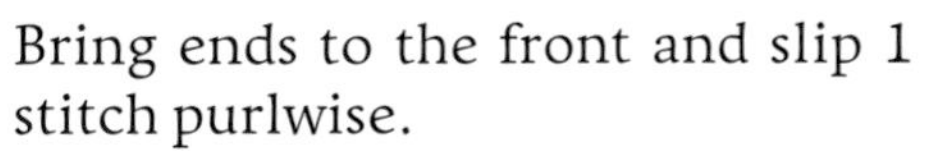

Bring ends to the front and slip 1 stitch purlwise.

Flip your work up a bit so you can see the back. Use the working needle to pick up the right leg of the stitch below the next back-side stitch on the source needle from inside to outside . . .

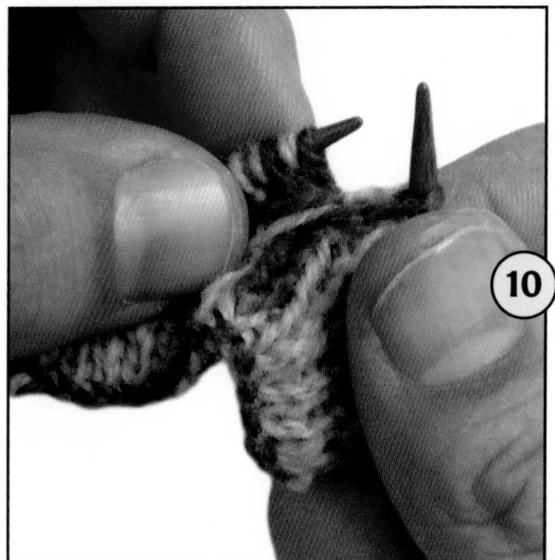

. . . and place the picked-up stitch onto the source needle. Slip 1 stitch back to the source needle.

SSP in the opposite color from the previous knit stitch.

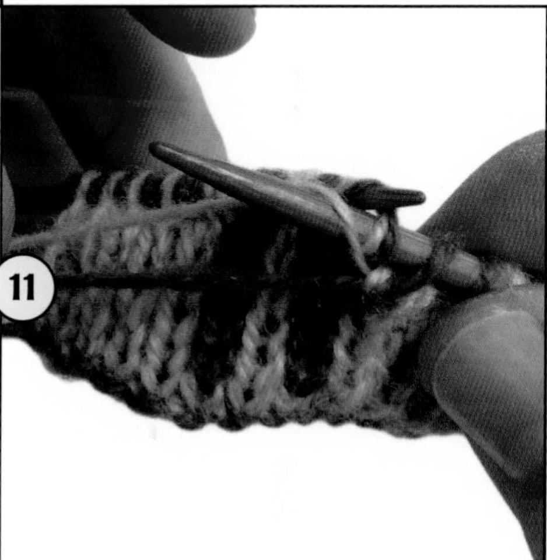

Here's the finished Reverse-N stitch as viewed from Layer 2.

ADENYDD

a double-knit lace shawl with modified Faroese construction

Finished size & weight

After blocking, this shawl is approximately 7.5' wide by 3.75' tall and uses about 11.25 oz (929 yds) of each color; since you'll have 16 oz of each you'll be fine.

Materials & tools

[Color A]: Galler Yarn Prime Alpaca Heathers (100% superfine alpaca; 660 yd/8 oz skein); Ice Blue 211; 2 skeins.

[Color B]: Galler Yarn Prime Alpaca Heathers (100% superfine alpaca; 660 yd/8 oz skein); Dark Turquoise 223; 2 skeins.

US 8/5 mm 60" circular needle or size required to obtain gauge.

Gauge in pattern

16 sts/26 rows = 4" in pattern, unblocked.

18 sts/22 rows = 4" in pattern, blocked.

As I did in *Extreme Double-Knitting*, I'm ending this book with a "magnum opus" — a large, complicated, and gorgeous pattern that will really get people's hearts racing and minds expanding.

It had been more than a year since Spring Willow came out as a pattern, and I hadn't done any other double-knit lace. Not one to rest on my laurels, I felt I had to do at least one more thing for the book in double-knit lace to really show off the possibilities. And what better than a shawl? There are so many shawls out there; it's a popular garment to really show off a pattern or a yarn. I had designed one before, but it was a simple triangle worked from the point up. I wanted to branch out, so I took advantage of my local guild's speaker series and attended a workshop by Anna Dalvi. I learned about various shawl shapes and how to break them down into manageable chunks. I had chosen a lace pattern (again, from one of the Walker treasuries), but then I decided I wanted to use Faroese construction — from the center of the longest side of the triangle outward, ending with the two other sides of the triangle. In this direction, the lace pattern I had chosen would have ended up upside down, and since it was supposed to evoke the image of feathers (or perhaps scales) on wings, the orientation was important. I began playing with the chart, first by just flipping it upside down, and then by tweaking what didn't work. Eventually, I asked for help from more experienced lace designer, "MMario," while at the Men's Spring Knitting Retreat; he made some suggestions that pointed me in a different direction. I ended up scrapping the original pattern altogether and building a new one from scratch, which finally gave me a more significant understanding of lace design than I had previously.

For years, I have been going to local sheep and wool festivals; here in New England there are plenty. Years ago I came across a few vendors that sold giant hanks of sport weight alpaca for very reasonable prices. They had different names, but all seemed to be more or less interchangeable. I assume that this was because the fiber was all processed at the same mill. These hanks were all in natural alpaca colors — any color you like, as long as it's white, cream, brown, charcoal, or black. Much later, in a yarn shop in Brooklyn, I found a dyed version of the same yarn: same giant hanks at a good price, but in an added variety of amazing colors that I hadn't seen before in this context. I was excited to try it, and bought a couple of colors that, in retrospect, were perhaps not the best choices. But I loved working with the yarn. In lieu of any shops carrying it in the Boston area, I contacted the company, Galler Yarn, for more in different colors.

As I mentioned earlier, this shawl is meant to evoke the image of wings. Whether bird wings or dragon wings, I'm not sure. Perhaps it depends on the colors you pick. Anyway, given the Celtic knotwork motif around the wings, I figured a Gaelic word would be ideal. However, the word for wing (sgiath) in Gaelic isn't terribly friendly to the English palate, so I looked into surrounding cultures. In Welsh, the word for wing is "adain" and the word for wings is "adenydd." I know a little Welsh pronunciation so I amended that to "Adenyth" to make it easier to say. My Welsh step-stepmother (long story) told me that's not right — evidently I don't know enough Welsh pronunciation after all. The -dd is pronounced as a voiced -th, as in "the" or "there," and replacing it with a hard -th could make it a different word. In fact, it's not; Adenyth is just a proper name and has no other meaning that I could find. However, I decided it would be better to have a unique name for this pattern and a teaching moment, and save Adenyth for a derivative pattern I have in mind for later.

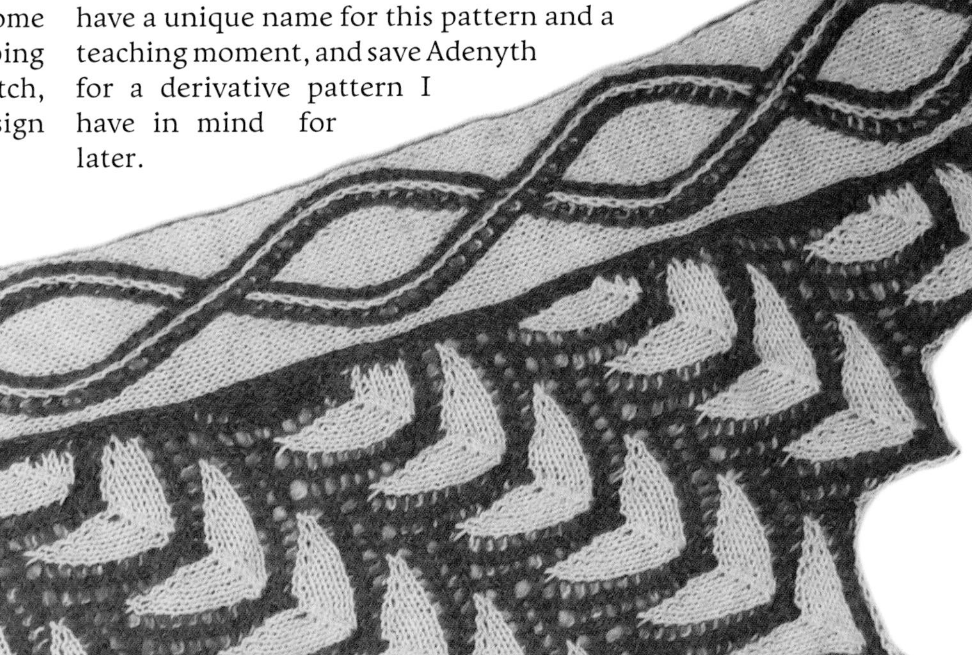

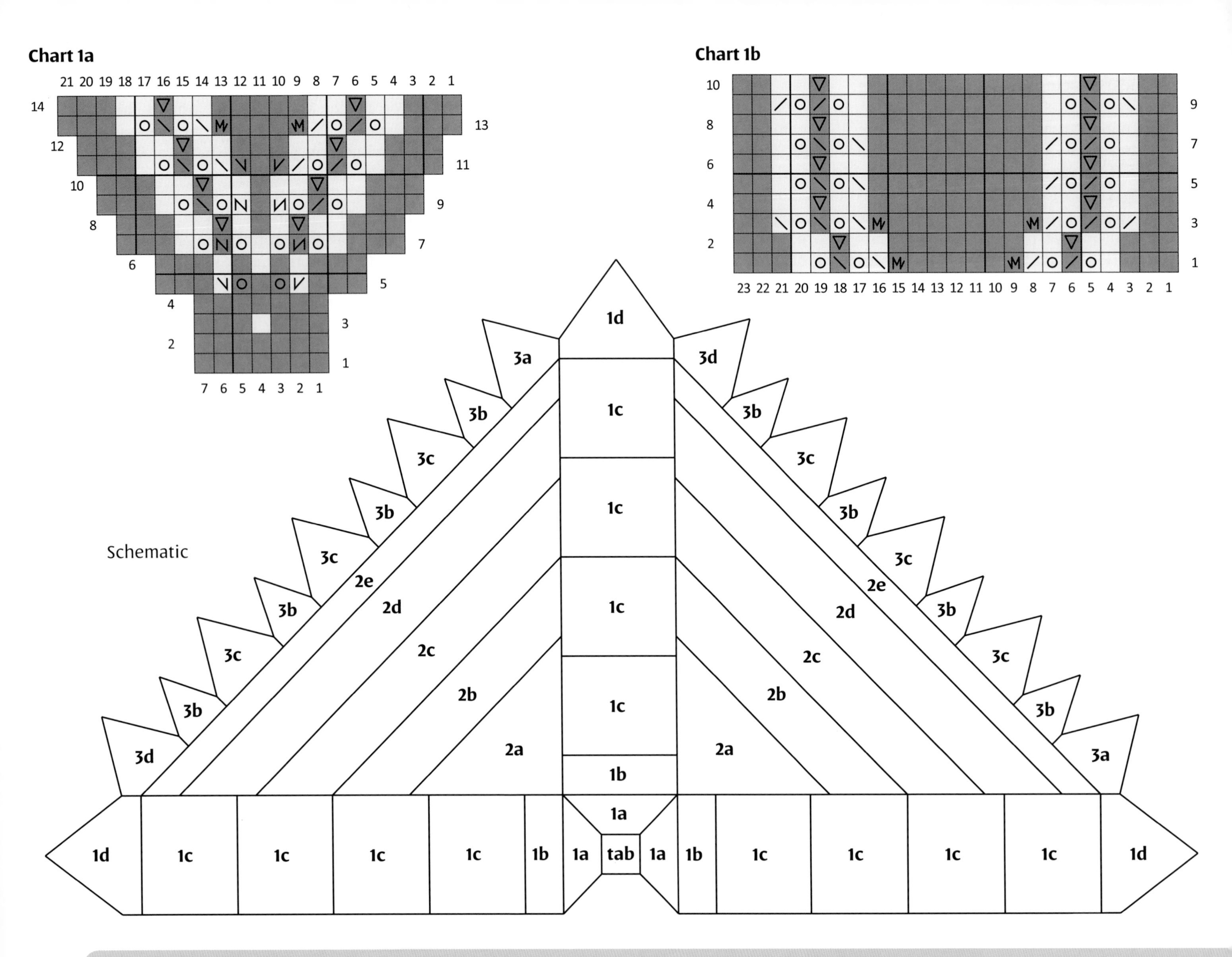
Chart 1a
Chart 1b
Schematic
1d
3a
3d
1c
3b
3c
2e
2d
2c
2b
2a
1b
1a
tab

Chart 1c

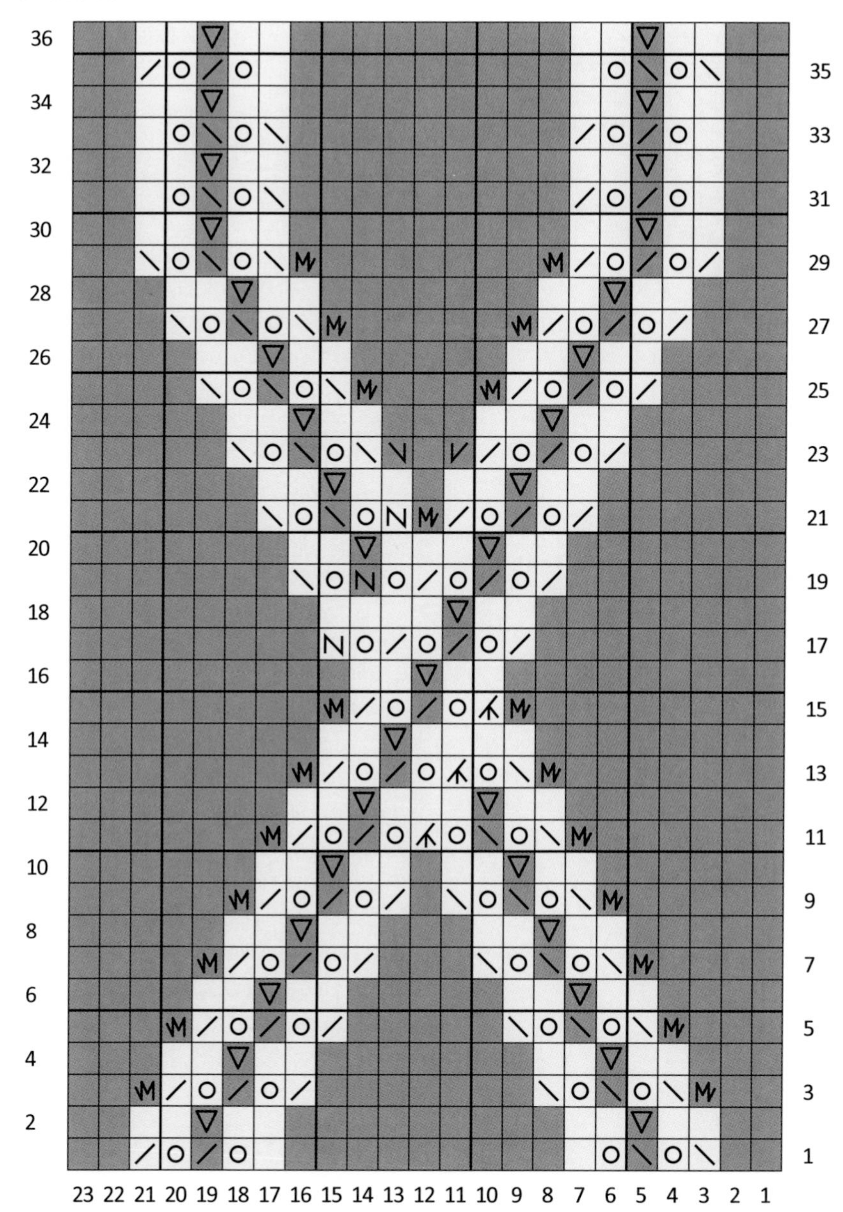

Chart 1d

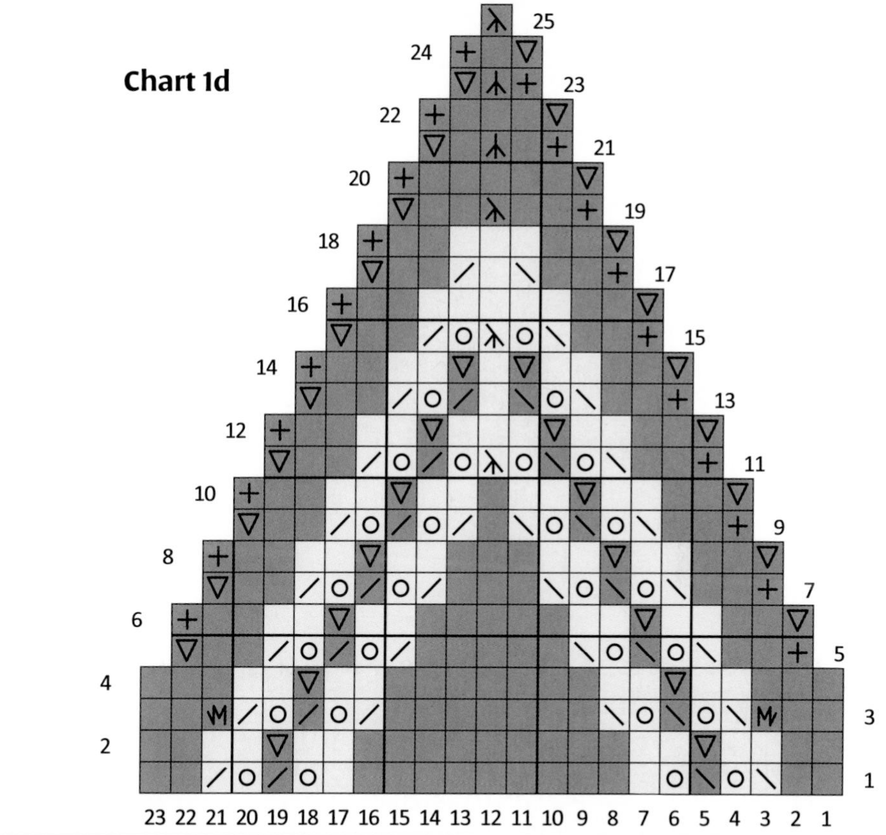

Key

- Layer 1: AB pair / Layer 2: BA pair
- Layer 1: BA pair / Layer 2: AB pair
- + Linked Pair
- ▽ Slipped Pair
- ○ Yarnover Pair
- / Right-leaning Decrease
- \ Left-leaning Decrease
- Raised Double Decrease
- Right-leaning Double Decrease
- Left-leaning Double Decrease
- Right-lifted Increase
- Left-lifted Increase
- M1R Increase
- M1L Increase
- N N
- Reverse-N

Chart A

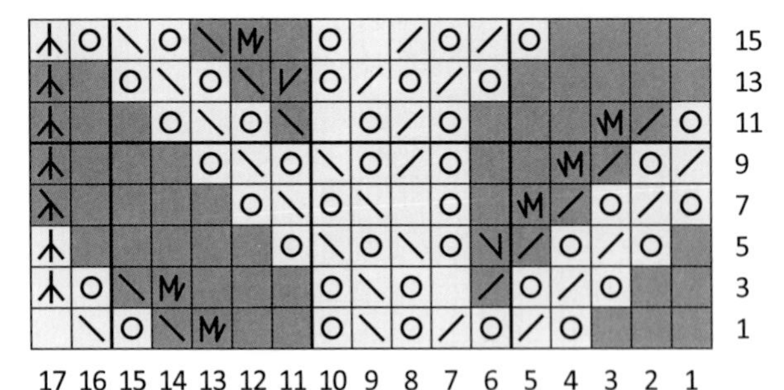

Chart B

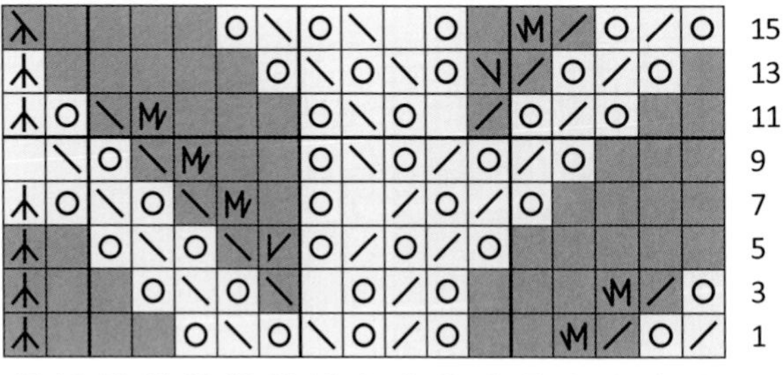

Chart 2a

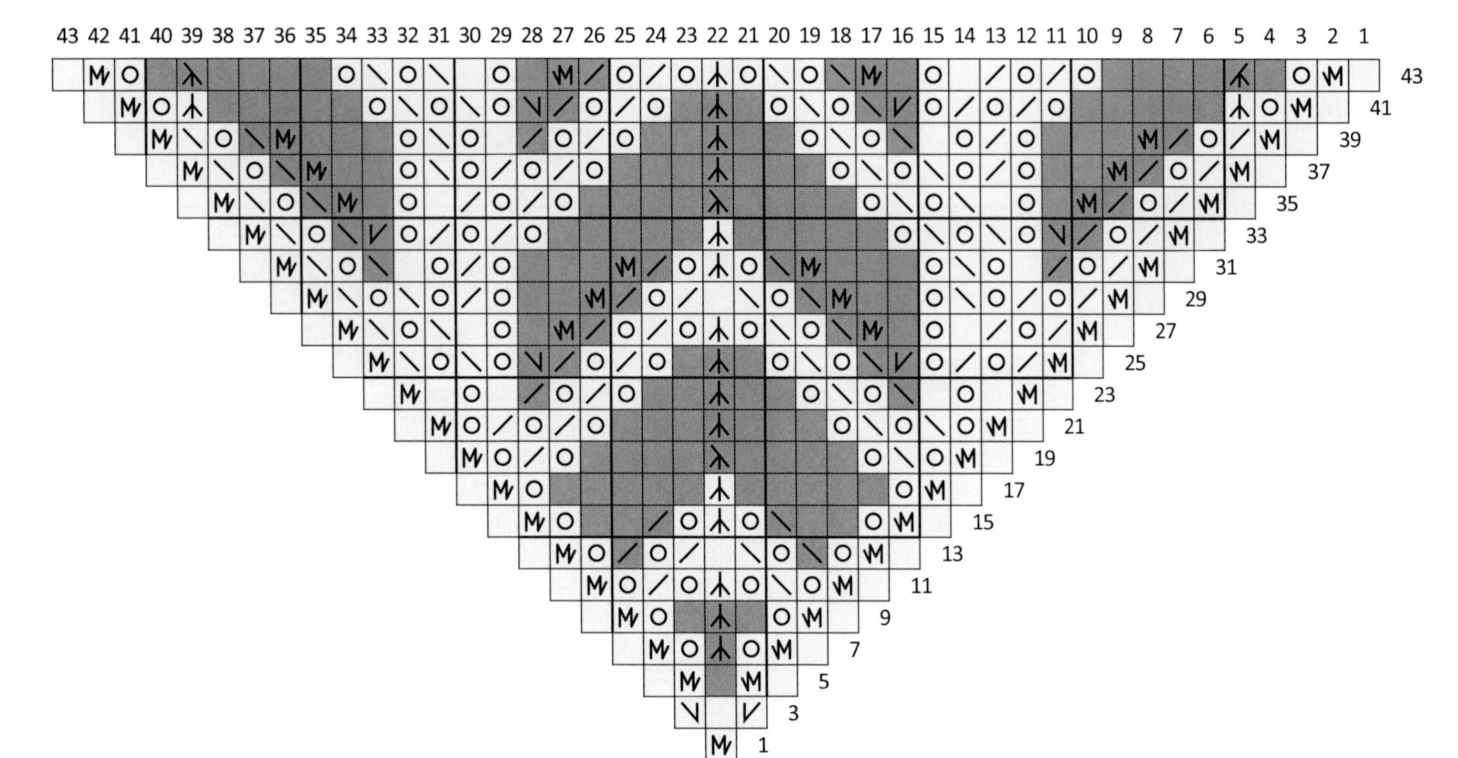

Pattern Notes

Whenever you have the opportunity to make a color change between two standard double-knit pairs (not YO and pair or vice versa), make your color change counter-clockwise. This will untwist the yarn from all the places you were forced to color change clockwise in the Layer 1 (YO) rows.

In Charts 2d and 2e (Rows 1 and 3 respectively), where the final A or B block in a row has a symbol inside it, this is the move you should work in place of the symbol in the final pixel in that block. It's meant to keep the decreases closest to the edge clean by mirroring them with the ones that preceded the A/B blocks on the other side.

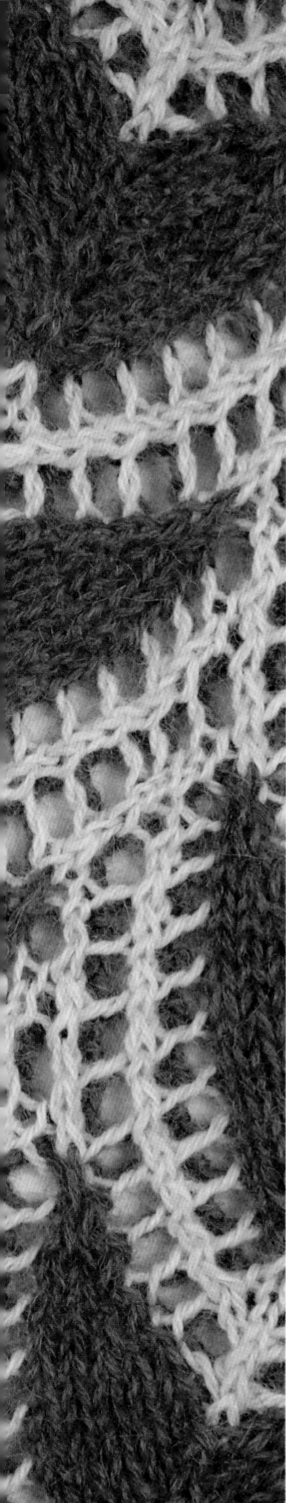

Chart 2b

75 74 73 72 71 70 69 68 67 66 65 64 63 62 61 60 59 58 57 56 21 20 19 18 17 16 15 14 13 12 11 10 9 8 7 6 5 4 3 2 1

B A

B A

31 29 27 25 23 21 19 17 15 13 11 9 7 5 3 1

45 44 43 42 41 6 5 4 3 2 1

Chart 2c

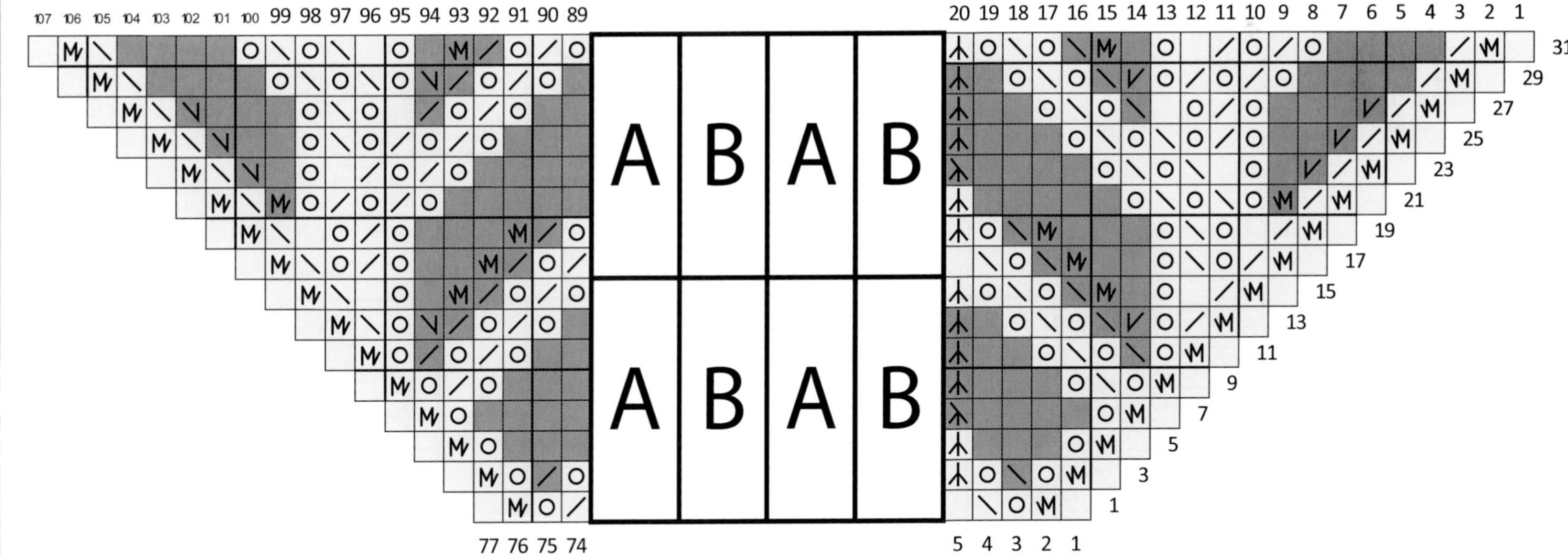

Chart A

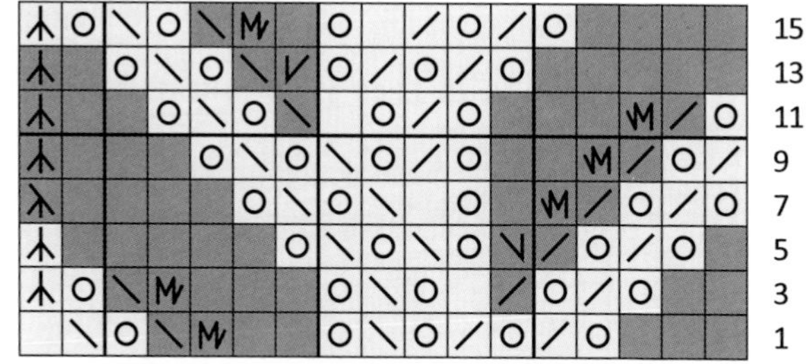

Chart B

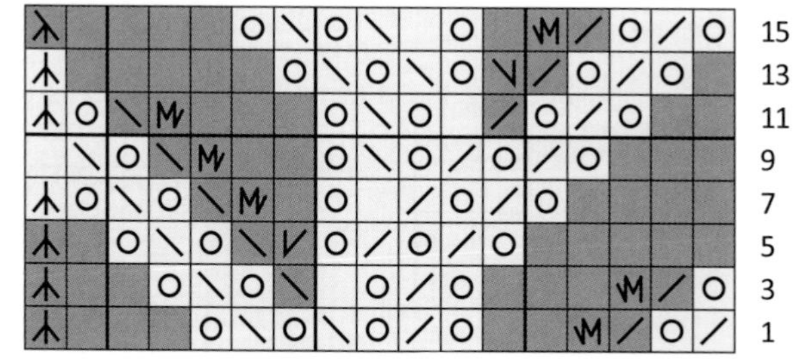

Chart 2d

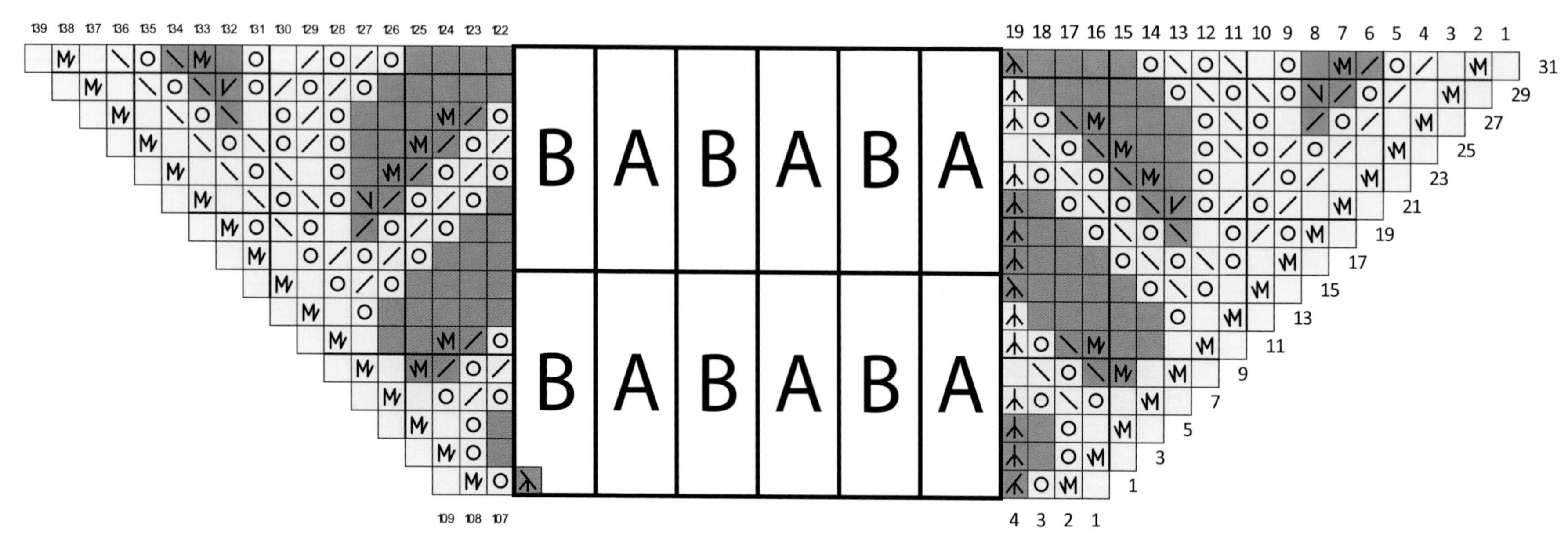

Chart 2e

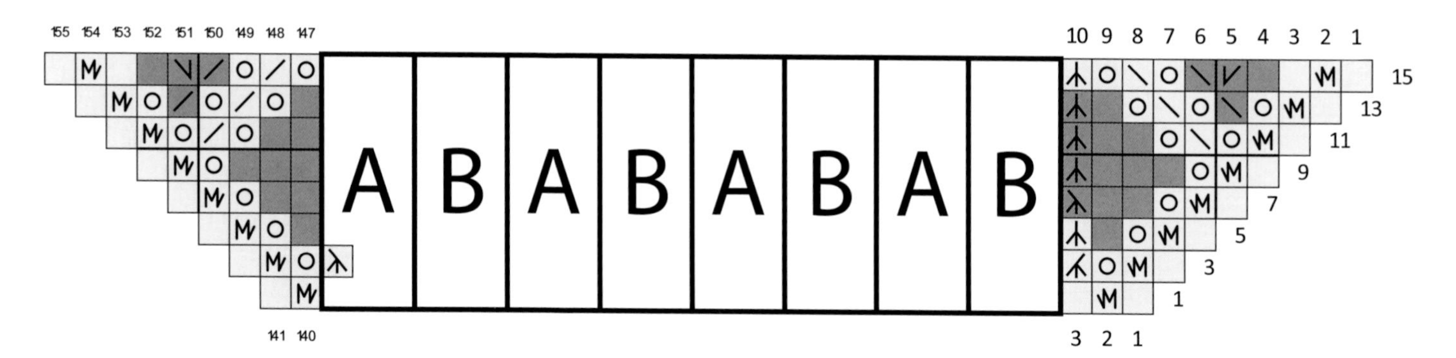

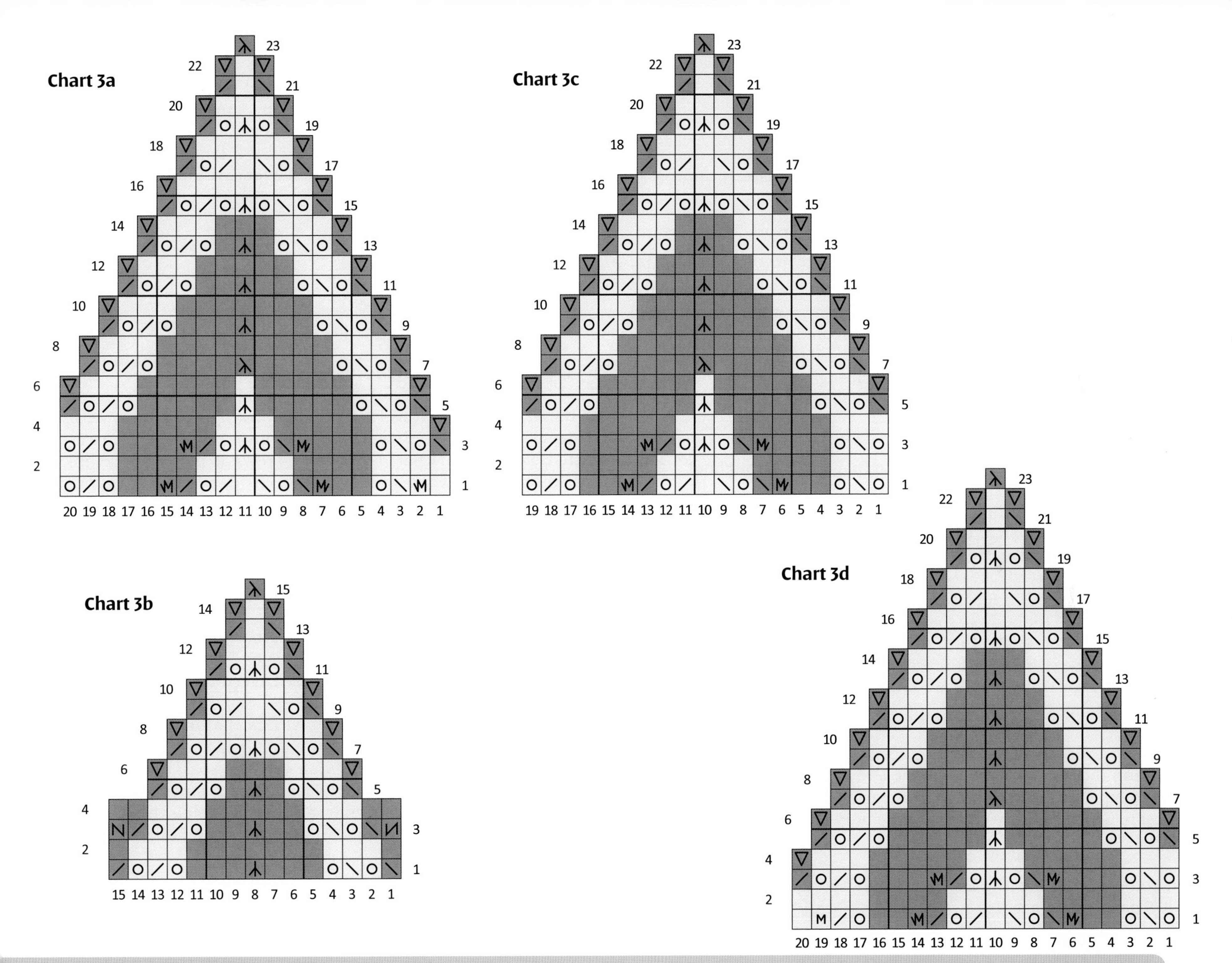
Chart 3a
Chart 3c
Chart 3b
Chart 3d

Pattern

CO 7 AB pairs.

Double-knit tab

1. Work a normal double-knit row in BA pairs with no linked or slipped pairs on either end. Remove slip knot. Turn.
2. Right-lifted increase one AB pair along edge; work 7 pairs & turn.
3. Right-lifted increase one BA pair along edge; work 7 pairs & turn.
4. Work 6 more repeats of steps 2 and 3, ending with 21 pairs on the needle. Since you're working on a circular needle, you can push all the pairs onto the cord and pull the middle 7 pairs up — the two side groups of 7 pairs each should relax until you can see a 3-sided rectangle with 7 pairs on each edge.

Body

Use the unlinked double-knit lace method (page 178) throughout.

Work 3 repeats of Chart 1a across, making sure to work a linked pair at the beginning and slipped pair at the end of each row. This is not charted but should be done to keep the edge clean and closed. There are now 63 pairs.

Work Chart 1 progression for beginning, center back, and end axes and Chart 2 progression for body of shawl in between the axes. As you begin, it will be Chart 1b, 2a, 1b, 2a, 1b. Since 2a has 44 rows and 1b has a 10-row repeat, you will be switching to 1c well before you leave 2a. 1c will keep repeating until you run out of Chart 2 rows in 2e. See the schematic (page 192) for a reference.

Chart 2 rows follow a simple Layer 2 formula — match everything you see, keeping the YO holes open. Chart 1 rows are mostly the same but there is a slipped pair that happens in a specific place on Layer 2 rows; for this reason, Chart 1 is fully charted while only Layer 1 rows are charted in Chart 2.

When you have finished the last repeat of Chart 2e and 1c, you should have 379 pairs on the needle.

Edging

The key to getting this to look right is to follow a sequence of charts in order. This is fairly simple: above the Chart 1 sections (you should have just finished Chart 1c), work Chart 1d. Above the Chart 2 sections, work Chart 3a on the right edge and Chart 3d on the left edge, alternating Charts 3b and 3c between them. So the sequence of charts to follow would be:

[1d, 3a, [3b, 3c]x3, 3b, 3d]x2, 1d

Or, if you don't like algebra:

1d, 3a, 3b, 3c, 3b, 3c, 3b, 3c, 3b, 3d, 1d, 3a, 3b, 3c, 3b, 3c, 3b, 3c, 3b, 3d, 1d.

This is also, thankfully, visible in the schematic.

For the first 4 rows of this, you will be working all the way across the garment. Starting with Row 5, you will finish each point separately as charted. Note that in Chart 1d, the first 4 rows do not show the links and slips, since those will appear only on the outside edges of the garment, as you have been doing for the rest of the work. Once we are into the points, the links and slips are now charted. However, you will also notice that there are no links on the edges of Charts 3a through 3d. This is because these points use a version of the color-changed double-knit selvedge technique.

You will also notice that, due to the unusual placement of the slipped pairs (at the beginning AND end of all Layer 2 rows), Charts 3a through 3d are fully charted rather than only the Layer 1 rows.

For ALL of the points, the last row will be the final double-decrease. After working that, you will have one pair left on the needle. Instead of a traditional bind-off, simply break your yarns and pass both ends through both loops of the remaining pair. Then, begin the next point. This will create a prodigious number of ends to weave in but it is the only practical way to have the pattern continue into the points as it does.

Block, weave in ends (it is best for this pattern to weave in your ends after blocking), and enjoy!

CHAPTER 10

Appendix

In *Extreme Double-Knitting*, I had an appendix that was full of tidbits of techniques that I just didn't have time to work into a pattern for the book or hadn't explored as fully as I might have liked. The reasoning for this was twofold: first, to make sure that techniques that were important to understand were covered, whether or not they were used in the patterns (e.g., slip-stitch double-knitting). Second, to remind me to try to flesh out some of these techniques later (for example, textured double-knitting and double-knit lace).

The appendix in this book is, understandably, a bit smaller. I have explored much further, documented more, and used more of my findings in patterns than I had at the time of the previous book's publishing. I am not under the illusion that I have reached the end, but I also have not explored that far beyond the scope of this book — so there's less I can include here. Also, the techniques I am including seem much more strange and alien than many of those I showed before. On the other hand, perhaps 5 or 10 years down the road these techniques will seem commonplace, and there will be even stranger things to show in the appendix of my next book.

If you are interested in an in-depth exploration of slip-stitch double-knitting and its very weird cousin quadruple-knitting, please consider searching out a copy of *Extreme Double-Knitting*. If you are interested in tubular double-knitting, search out Kelly Klem, whom I believe will have a book out on the subject soon if she doesn't already. The other techniques I dealt with in my previous book's appendix are much more thoroughly documented in this book.

Japanese Double-knitting

I wish I could give a better justification for the name of this technique, or provide references. The only explanation I can give is that I once saw this technique used in a Japanese pattern. I have never seen it again in any other pattern and I can't find the original one. However, since it symbolized a different perspective on double-knitting, it intrigued me.

In standard double-knitting, color changes are achieved by changing the color order — bringing the color that was previously used on the back to the front (and vice versa). This is a current-row technique, meaning that the row below is unchanged, and the color changes happen in the current row. A color-changed row will consist of KP pairs in AB and BA color orders.

A color-changed row in Japanese double-knitting will instead consist of KP and PK pairs in AB (or BA) color order throughout. It is possible to create standard double-knitting entirely consisting of PK pairs by simply purling the first stitch in the pair with yarns in front and knitting the second stitch with yarns in back. If you do this consistently, you will end up with double-knitting; but if you combine this type of PK pair with standard KP pairs, you will pull the layer that was previously a purl through the fabric in the row below and make it a knit (and vice versa). The result is a sort of crenellated pattern at the horizontal color changes, with pairs that do not change color order throughout the row. This is a row-below technique; although there's no explicit preparation, the technique visibly affects the row below. In a way, this is very much like quilted double-knitting, except that instead of pulling one stitch through the other, they rotate around each other — the new stitches appear between the columns of the previous row, not aligned.

To my eyes, this is not an attractive look, but you may feel differently. One benefit is that the layers end up linked together vertically as well as in the color changes within the row. It works better for large color blocks rather than intricate motifs, which tend to get lost.

Filled Double-knitting

I used to call this quilted double-knitting, but with the new technique Lucy Neatby and I have been putting into practice (see page 120), I think a new name for this technique is in order.

Double-knitting, as you will have noticed, is hollow. When you have a large area of one color order, you can pull the two layers apart. If you can fully enclose this area, you can temporarily separate the layers and fill the space with batting.

One way to enclose the area is to use MKs and MPs (see page 110). Instead of using them to cover an area, you can work a single one (or a line of them) in the midst of a field of standard double-knitting. This creates a connection between the layers that is also visible on both layers, as if the layers were stitched together after the fact. If a simple pattern is "drawn" with these marled pairs, the area they encompass will be hollow and enclosed by the outline of those pairs.

The other way is perhaps less elegant, since it's not universal — but it's worth including as an option, especially if you don't like the look of the marled pairs. An area can be enclosed by using a combination of standard double-knit colorwork and, if needed, quilted pairs. The area to be filled will end up color-changed from the background. It is best to keep this motif simple because if it's too intricate, it will be difficult to fill it. The vertical color changes will not be linked together unless you do quilted double-knit pairs, which will necessarily change the color order of the pair.

However you choose to do this, as you reach the top of the enclosed area but before you fully finish enclosing it, you need to open the fabric a bit to fill the space between the layers.

I generally find that a gap of 3 pairs is enough, but if you're working in very fine yarn, you may need a larger gap. All you need to do is to reorder your pairs as if you were working a double-decrease, stopping before slipping the pairs on your working needle back to your source needle. With the two groups of stitches on either needle, you can pull the layers apart and poke a finger (or something) into the hole. Take a bit of batting and push it inside; add more batting bit by bit until it's as filled as much as you want it, or perhaps a tiny bit more depending on how much more area you're going to be making before it's fully enclosed. Then, return the pairs to their normal interlaced order and continue with your pattern.

Here's one way to re-interlace a separated group of 3 pairs; if you find another way that works better for you, by all means use it:

1. Drop the first 2 knits on the working needle and hold them carefully with your thumb and forefinger.
2. Slip 1 stitch from the source needle; pick up one held stitch.
3. Repeat Step 2.
4. Slip 5 stitches back to the source needle.

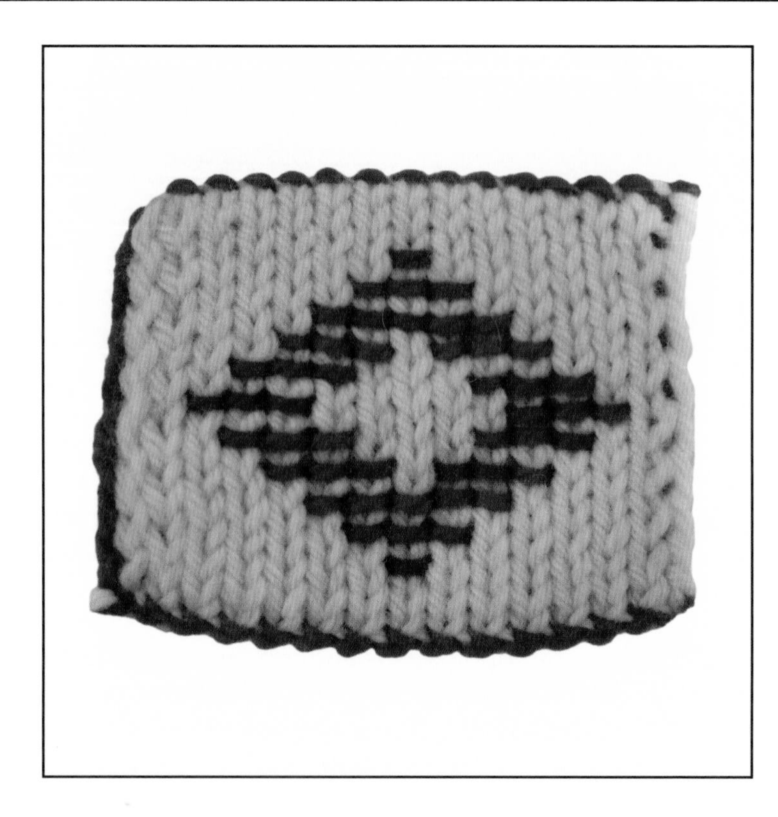

This is another example of a bug becoming a feature. It's a prominent mistake — even addressed as such in the section on troubleshooting (page 40) — that I've seen made by my one or more students in almost every class: namely, the bar.

The effect of this method is to create a bar on the outside of the work. On the opposite layer, a less-defined vertical line will form. The more bars done one above the other, the more pronounced the vertical line will become. Bars done one after the other within a row will create a clean horizontal line that will look "stitched" on. On the other layer of the work, there will be a small vertical line in the same color for each horizontal "stitch."

There are two different techniques — one for creating a bar at the front of your work (and a vertical line at the back), and one for creating a bar at the back of your work (and a vertical line at the front). The two techniques can conceivably be combined within the same fabric; I have theorized that something very much like a maze could be "drawn" this way. The planning for such an endeavor would be daunting, to say the least. The examples below assume that the fabric is all one color order throughout, and the only "colorwork" is from the barred sections. I will leave further developments in this technique for later.

To make a bar at the front (assuming AB pairs; reverse colors for BA pairs)

1. Bring Color A to the back from underneath the Color B end.
2. K1 in Color A.
3. Bring end of Color A forward.
4. P1 in Color B from over the top of the Color A end.

To make a bar at the back (assuming AB pairs as above)

1. With both yarns in back, K1 in Color A.
2. Bring Color B to the front from underneath the Color A end.
3. P1 in Color B.
4. Bring end of Color B to the back.
5. When beginning the next pair, K1 in Color A from over the top of the Color B end.

Massively Multicolor Double-knitting

In multicolor double-knitting, the more colors you use, the more rigid and unmanageable your fabric becomes. One way to get around the limitations of higher numbers of colors is to mix the colors on the fly, using carefully chosen colors. Using a technique similar to marled knitting, you can have a comparatively large number of finer-gauge yarns, and instead of choosing one for each stitch, you'd choose two. If you consider each mixture of colors to be one simulated color, four colors could simulate 6 colors; or five colors could simulate 10 colors. The rule seems to be that for X colors of yarn, you can make X*(X-1)/2 two-color mixtures.

Regardless of the number of colors you're using, cast on with four colors held together in two groups of two. This will anchor most or all of the yarns in the first row, and it will also set up the stitches as groups of two (so that each pair is made up of 4 yarns). If you're working in five or more colors, add in the other yarn(s) as you begin the first row.

Because you're doubling up the yarns, your gauge will be (roughly) cut in half. This means that you should figure your needle size based on the combination of two yarns held together. If you're working in lace weight, use a needle suited to fingering or sock weight yarn. If you're working in fingering weight, use a needle of the correct size for sport weight or light DK weight. And so on — but I don't recommend going much heavier than that if you want the resulting fabric to be wearable.

To test this technique, I used five colors of lace weight yarn. Since there's no simple logical relationship between the knit layer and the purl layer when working in this many colors, it made most sense to chart a two-pattern piece. To chart this, I also had to create a new notation that shows the color mixture in each knit or purl stitch.

The resulting chart, like most two-pattern charts, doesn't include the selvedges. If working in four colors, you can cast on two extra pairs to act as the linked and slipped pairs. When you work them, just match the color mixture you used in the cast-on. If you are working in five colors, cast on four extra pairs and do a multicolor linked pair with the fifth color as well.

One of the reasons this swatch is so small is that end management in this type of knitting is nearly impossible, and a braid with 5 or more strands is ridiculously hard to undo. Good luck!

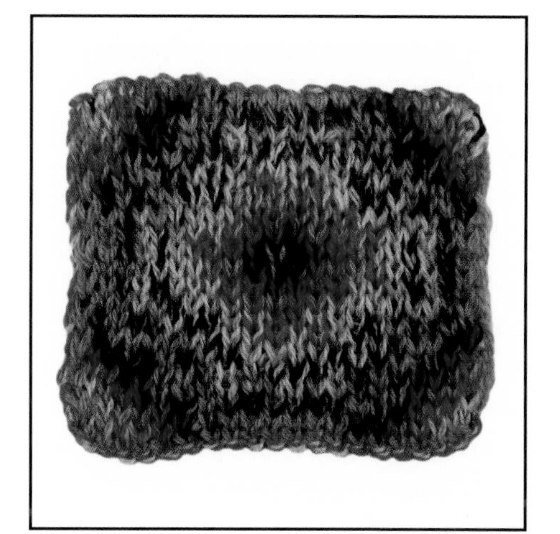

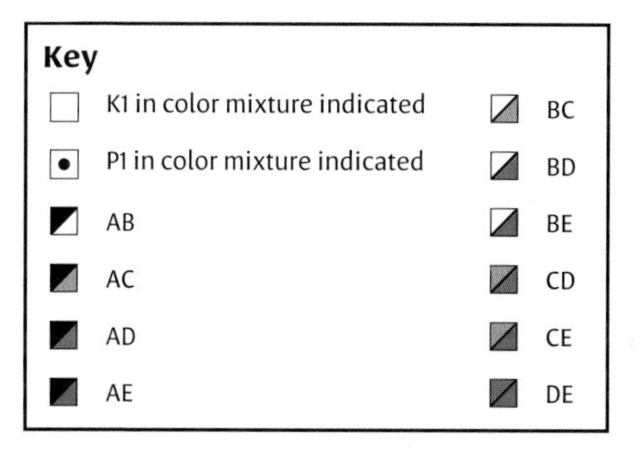

Chart

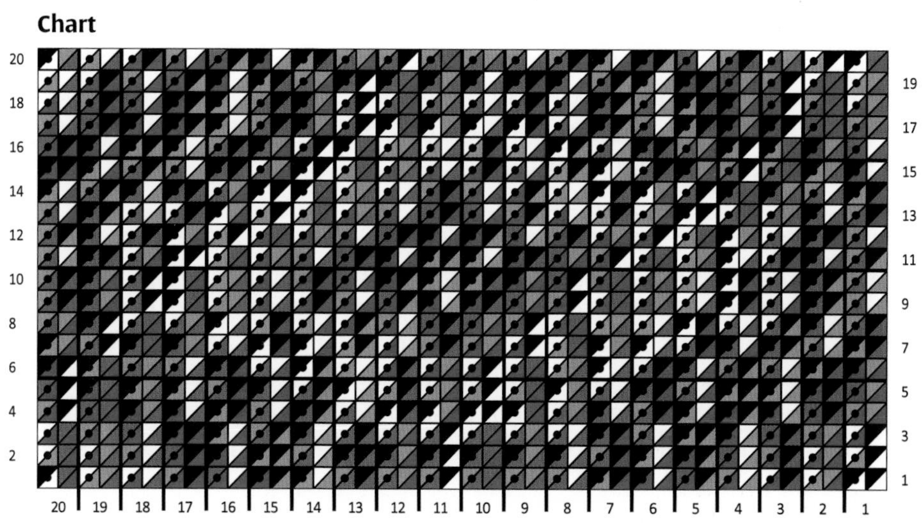

AFTERWORD

At the end of writing a book or pattern, I'm always a little torn: when do I stop? How much is too much? Have I written enough? Is it clear enough? Will people love this thing I made as much as I do? What can I do to make sure they do?

I have to step back, breathe, and let it go. Because, of course, I can't make everyone happy. There will be people who love the simple fact that this book exists so much that they'll overlook any little things I may have missed or mistakes I may have made. And then, there will be people who expect perfection and will be disappointed with anything that doesn't meet that expectation. And of course, dear reader, you probably fall somewhere in between.

What I hope you realize is that I am an expert in a field that dwells in a niche within a niche within a niche. This book will never be a best-seller, because the people to whom it might appeal are just too few in number. For that reason, no major publisher would touch it. As a self-publishing author, I am in complete control of my product — which sounds glamorous until you realize that I don't have anyone to give me an advance payment. I also don't have an editorial board, a professional photographer, a professional designer, or any of the personnel at the disposal of your average published author.

I have contracted several people to help with various things I can't do on my own, but by and large this book is the realized vision of one person, and as such, may have that person's flaws baked into it. If you find one of those, it's my hope that you'll take it for what it is: evidence that this book was written by a human being, minimally filtered through editors, and all the more authentic for that.

Whether you came to this book with no double-knitting knowledge or an abundance of it, I hope you've learned enough to have made the purchase worth it. What I really consider my mission in knitting is to get these techniques out into the world, where they can gain a life of their own in people's knitting and, hopefully, in other people's designs. And just perhaps, now that your mind is absorbing this new knowledge, you'll begin coming up with new developments in double-knitting yourself!

I hope you've found this book to be helpful or at least interesting. If you feel like giving back in some small way, here's how you can help me:

- Small-time designers, like myself, live on referrals. If you love my work, share the love: tell your friends, give this book as a gift, or otherwise get the word out. But if you've got the eBook version, please don't share that (and if you got this from a friend and didn't pay for it, do the right thing and buy your own copy).
- If you want to tell the world, I'd love a review on Goodreads, Amazon, my own website, your blog, or on a podcast. If you blog or podcast about it, send me a link, and I'll add it to the collection on my website!
- On the other hand, if you didn't like the book, or want to give me some constructive feedback, I'd be happy to receive that through the contact form on my website. Just be gentle; I'm a human with feelings and this is just a knitting book.
- If you aspire to use a technique you learned from me in your own pattern, I'd really appreciate it if you gave me a little credit. I can't (and wouldn't want to) copyright my techniques, but it has been a large part of my life's work to develop them. One of the ways I can afford to keep doing this is if people let others know how they learned their skills.
- If you want to take a hands-on class from me, tell your local yarn shop or guild to get in touch with me. I do travel to teach, and I am always happy to meet people who are excited to learn new things.

Thank you so much for your support; if you want to keep tabs on me and find out what other interesting things I'm up to, visit my blog or website; follow me on Facebook , Twitter, Pinterest, or Instagram; join the Fallingblox Designs group or the Double Knitting group on Ravelry; or sign up for my email list.

Alasdair Post-Quinn
Softwear Engineer, Fallingblox Designs
www.double-knitting.com

ACKNOWLEDGMENTS

This book has been a self-published project spanning the better part of 2 years — but it hasn't been a solo endeavor. I'd like to thank the people who helped me get this far.

Shannon Okey and the good folks at Cooperative Press, for picking up my first book and getting me on the road to professional designership.

The awesome folks behind all the yarns I used in this book, whether or not they provided yarn support: **Stephanie Griego** at Dirty Water Dyeworks, **Sarah Dimond** at Plucky Knitter, **Jeffrey Wall** and **Dennis Rinkenberger** at Wall of Yarn, **Ana Clerc** at Yarn Carnival, **Babs Ausherman** at Miss Babs, **Carl Koop** at Bijou Basin Ranch, **Kate Bachus** at A Hundred Ravens, **Pam Allen** at Quince & Co, **Karen Grover** at Seven Sisters Arts, **Ron & Theresa Miskin** at The Buffalo Wool Co, **Sabrina Famellos** at Anzula, **Star Galler** at Galler Yarns, and the good folks at Jagger Spun.

My patient and photogenic models, without whom my garments would be far less exciting to look at: **Allison Warmuth**, **Patricia Grahmann**, **Grace Zimmerly** and **Stan Monfront**.

My editorial team, without whom this book might be nearly unreadable: **Daniela Nii**, **Shelly Bouchat**, and **Melissa Curran**.

My sample knitters, who worked some big projects, so I could save my energy for the heavier lifting: **Annie Webber**, **Charles Parker,** and **Mari Weideman**.

Roger Mohn at Versa Press, the Illinois-based company who printed this book, for putting up with my hypothetical questions and borderline inexperience.

My publicist, **Jocelyn Grayson**, for taking some of the burden of publicity off my shoulders.

And, last but not least, my *Double or Nothing* focus group, for fielding all kinds of weird questions as I endeavored to make this book as accessible and useful of a resource as possible.

BIBLIOGRAPHY

These resources deal primarily with double-knitting — not all are in print, but I have listed them in chronological order by their most recent date:

- Belle, Anja. *Knitting Double*. Pomfret, VT: Trafalgar Square Books, 2014. Print.
- Post-Quinn, Alasdair. *Extreme Double-Knitting: New Adventures in Reversible Colorwork*. Cleveland: Cooperative Press, 2011. Print.
- Baber, M'Lou. *Double Knitting: Reversible Two-Color Designs*. Pittsville, WI: Schoolhouse, 2008. Print.
- Neatby, Lucy. *Double Knitting Delight 1*. Nova Scotia: Tradewind Knitwear Designs, 2007. DVD.
- Royce, Beverly. *Notes on Double Knitting*. Pittsville, WI: Schoolhouse, 1994. Print.

These books have some content that would be useful to those pursuing greater knowledge of double-knitting:

- Hemmons Hiatt, June. *Principles of Knitting, The*. New York: Touchstone, 2012. Print.
- Bortner, Gwen. *Entrée to Entrelac*. Sioux Falls, SD: XRX Books, 2010. Print.
- Neighbors, Jane F. *Reversible Two-Color Knitting*. New York: Scribner, 1974. Print.

These books focus on other reversible colorwork techniques that may also be of interest:

- Marchant, Nancy. *Knitting Fresh Brioche: Creating Two-Color Twists & Turns*. New York: Sixth And Spring Books, 2014. Print.
- Twigg, Vicki. *Twigg Stitch: A New Twist on Reversible Knitting*. Loveland, CO: Interweave, 2014. Print.
- Schreier, Iris. *Iris Schreier's Reversible Knits: Creative Techniques for Knitting Both Sides Right*. New York, NY: Lark, 2009. Print.
- Barr, Lynne. *Reversible Knitting: 50 Brand-new, Groundbreaking Stitch Patterns*. New York: Stewart, Tabori & Chang, 2009. Print.
- Marchant, Nancy. *Knitting Brioche: The Essential Guide to the Brioche Stitch*. Cincinnati: North Light Books, 2009. Print.

ABOUT THE AUTHOR

Alasdair Post-Quinn is the author of *Extreme Double-Knitting*, the Parallax series, and various standalone knitting patterns. He lives in a small apartment in the Boston area with his loving wife and indifferent cat, and he has a part-time computer repair business on a university campus. He can sometimes be found in Boston-area knitting groups, Indian restaurants, nightclubs, or bike paths.

He teaches multiple levels of double-knitting all over the US and his teaching reaches worldwide with his Craftsy class.

For more information about how Alasdair became a knitting designer of note, if not fame, turn back to page 17 and begin reading the **Craftstory**.

Find Alasdair online:
Website & Online Store: **www.double-knitting.com**
Blog: **www.fallingblox.com**
Facebook: **www.facebook.com/fallingblox**
Ravelry: **www.ravelry.com/groups/fallingblox-designs**

If you've enjoyed *Double or Nothing* ...

Visit **Fallingblox Designs** online at www.double-knitting.com for more double-knitting adventures by Alasdair Post-Quinn.

This book was laid out in Adobe InDesign CC. The photos were edited with Adobe Photoshop CC, and the charts were created with Adobe Illustrator CC (with numbering assistance from Microsoft Excel).

Model photos were taken on-site in Boston and New York City with a Sony Alpha NEX-6 camera. Standalone sample photos were taken at the Fallingblox Designs studio in Cambridge, MA with the same camera. Technique photos were taken in the same location with a WhistleCam-triggered iPad Mini on a rig built from components by Three Legged Thing, Promaster, and iOgrapher.

Technique photos were made possible by manicures from G2O Spa & Salon in Boston and the spot-healing brush in Photoshop. Yarns used for the technique photos are by Rauma, Swans Island, Quince & Co., and Galler Yarns; and the needles are by Hiya Hiya.

The fonts used for the layout of this book include:

Inconsolata, a monospaced font, used in the table of contents.

Leksa, a humanist serif font, used for the body text.

Leksa Sans, a humanist sans-serif font, used in the Craftstory.

Leksa Sans Bold, a humanist sans-serif font, appearing in the headers and subheaders.

REISLUST, A DECORATIVE FONT, FEATURED IN THE TITLES.